MW00807443

i

The Walking People

A Native American Oral History

OTHER BOOKS BY PAULA UNDERWOOD

Who Speaks for Wolf:
A Native American Learning Story

Three Strands in the Braid:
A Guide for Enablers of Learning

❋ ❋ ❋

BOOKS FORTHCOMING

A Tribe of Two

White Eagle's Songs

The Walking People

A Native American Oral History

Paula Underwood

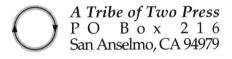

A Tribe of Two Press
P O B o x 2 1 6
San Anselmo, CA 94979

INSTITUTE OF
NOETIC
SCIENCES

THE WALKING PEOPLE:
A Native American Oral History

Copyright© 1993 by Paula Underwood. All rights reserved.

Printed in the United States of America. No part of this book may be used or reproduced in any manner whatsoever without express written permission except in the case of brief quotations embodied in critical articles and reviews. For information address: A Tribe of Two Press, PO Box 216, San Anselmo, CA 94979.

FIRST EDITION

Library of Congress Cataloging-in-Publication Data

Underwood, Paula

The walking people: a native american oral history / Paula Underwood --1st ed.

p.   cm.

Includes annotations and footnotes.

ISBN 1-879678-07-1 (hardback) -- ISBN 1-879678-10-1 (pbk.)

1. Indians of North America -- Legends 2. Indians of North America -- History 3. Oral tradition -- North America. I. Title.

E98.F6U53 1993

398.2' 08997 -- dc20   93-27754

CIP

Dedication

To all those who went before
      Sitting at the edge of any fire at all
      Patiently learning each and every song

To all those who may now follow
      Patiently turning each and every page
      On which these songs are now sung

To all these

But most of all to my Grandfather's Grandmother
      Who walked away from her People
      At a time of Great Change
      So that the children's children's children
      May yet learn

This patient weaving
Of Ancient Tellings
Is most gratefully dedicated.

Edited by Jeanne Lamar Slobod and Barbara McNeill

Design, layout and production by David Johnson

Photo Credits:

Cover (River stones): Margaret Jackson, 45 Apache Lane, Sedona, Arizona

Photograph of Paula Underwood: Sterling Photographers,
Arlington, Virginia 22202

"First Principal Telling" (page 2): David Smith,
6124 Fairway Drive, Cincinnati, Ohio, 45212

"Second Principal Telling" (page 80): David Smith

"Three Mountain Tellings" (page 434): Richard Blair,
Color & Light, 2207 Fourth St., Berkeley, California, 94710

"Grass Ocean" (page 496): David Smith

"First People's Child" (page 536): David Smith

"We Call the River Beautiful" (page 550): David Smith

"Eastern Ocean" (page 670): David Smith

"Beautiful Lake" (page 718): Don Landwerhle,
courtesy of Image Bank West, San Francisco, California

Covers printed by Paris Printing, Novato, California

Text printing and binding by Edwards Brothers, Ann Arbor, Michigan.

Text printed on 50# Glatfelter. Type is set in FFScalla.

Foreword

When I was a child my father sang me endless songs about a People who walked vast distances, struggled against high odds, succeeded, failed, but above all else, continued.

I learned these songs from him. And then one day he asked me what I knew "Why," I said, "I know the vast history of a whole People who continued and continued over thousands of years."

"Do you?" he asked, "And how do you *know* such things?"

We discussed this for a long time, deep in conversation, deep in thought. Each time I told my father I knew such things had happened he reminded me of what 'know' means, until at last I said,

"I *know* my father lifted his head and sang. I *know* I heard him. I *know* these are his songs. I *conclude* they contain much accuracy because I *feel* the reality behind the words and because my father *seems* to me the kind of person to take no such task lightly and because it seems to me his father would have been such an one also.

"Perhaps during my life I, too, will go and look and see for myself the accuracy of these words. But until then, I accept my father's task as he accepted the task from his father. I shall perpetuate these words. I will take upon myself the further task of forming them in English, accurate always, beautiful if possible.

"But beyond this I will make no further claim:

"My father lifted his head and sang.

"I heard him."

—Paula Underwood

Acknowledgements

A grateful heart remembers . .

All those Ancient Ones who, one after the other, never forgot to remember, spilling out into willing ears all these gifts of Wisdom,

Those three of my own family who, generation after patient generation, enabled the learning of One to Follow,

Those many and wondrous beings who have helped along the way:

Ann Schrogie, who encouraged the first writing down;

Marianne Karydes, who came to hear the first reading;

Sonja Elmer, who patiently typed page after page;

Laurie Alison Spencer, who began conversion of these pages to a new and binary language;

Randal McDonald Spencer, who eased the path toward this new technology with his understanding;

Meredith Slobod Crist, who showed me the light of the new vision these Tellings enabled;

Jeanne Lamar Slobod, who added purpose and dedication to a long standing friendship and who has never forgotten to help once more;

Robert Louis Slobod, who never flagged in his patient and willing support;

All these and countless others added support, effort, listening ears, and advice to the sometimes torturous process of evolving an Oral History, sung in the Ancient Way, into viable visual transmission;

First among these is Jeanne Slobod -- it is she who has most carefully evolved a written text into word patterns on pages which retain as much as they can of the visual and auditory impact of an Ancient Telling -- the visual syntax is mainly hers;

Barbara McNeill, who continued this participant editorial process, shaping each page with patient care;

Willis Harman, who understands the potential value of Ancient Wisdom;

Joan Langwell, who translated from one binary language to another;

Dave Johnson, who exhausted his well-being in patient hours of design and production;

And a grateful heart remembers those who enabled in a different way those who paid for paper and pens, printing and publishing --

The initial and generous grant came from the Meredith Slobod Crist Memorial Fund, from Jeanne and Bob Slobod, who have always understood the learning implicit in Ancient Wisdom,

It was augmented with continuing generosity by two grants from Hu and Molly Root, whose interest in Ancient Wisdom continues to this day,

And by a grant from the Manitou Foundation, from Hanne Strong, who also values Ancient Wisdom,

To which was added a generous gift from Sandra Wright Houghton, who hears the echoes of Ancient Wisdom,

All this built upon a grant from the American Association of University Women (AAUW) Educational Foundation to enable transmission of an oral history to computer format,

All these were joined by many others with contributions of all and various sizes, and who are recognized here for their wisdom and for their generosity.

Words cannot say

Nor any Song truly tell

What gratitude is here

In one yearning Heart

So be it . . . .

Introduction

This is an oral history transmitted in the ancient way.

As with many other oral traditions and histories, extensive testing and training are necessary before you are even invited to hear what you may one day have responsibility for.

From my earliest days my father tested and trained my memory. This involved acts as simple as turning me away from where I had been looking and asking me what I had seen. This would be repeated again and again without warning until you did -- or did not -- learn the art of taking mental pictures of anything you looked at and the art of recalling that image as if you looked at it anew.

This was never done as a pass/fail test, nor was any pressure at all put on me to succeed. If I was not appropriate to this task, why would he want to rest it on my shoulders? Yet, neither was it a game. It was a learning -- an opportunity to understand life better.

When he was reasonably sure I had the developable capacity to learn at least much of this history, I began to hear small "snippets and sections" -- much like the teasers you see of "coming attractions" in movie theaters -- enough to whet the appetite. To learn the whole story, certain other things were necessary first -- like showing the ability to listen with absolute attention, like staying awake concentrating on one thing for a day and a night, like memorizing other things . . songs or poems, like demonstrating an ability to understand.

When my father was reasonably sure I had some small skills in each of these areas, I began to hear the full length of the history, one small part at a time, still testing for understanding. As I thought I had learned any section, I was encouraged to "give it back", but never in the same way it was given to me. This taught me two things. First, not to be too hasty in assuming I had already learned it. Second, hearing something -- and understanding it -- are two different steps.

When it finally seemed to me that I might risk "giving back" one whole section to my father, I learned something new. I was asked to give it back to him three times -- in three different ways -- no one of which could be the way in which my father presented it to me.

I should be able, you see, to demonstrate an absolute understanding so sure that I could restate it in any contemporary language, so that it might be more understood than "wondered at". As my father pointed out, language changes! Many people did not even understand the language of Shakespeare which his mother often read out loud. Little value in a history so couched.

Knowing as I do how many patient years are spent in this learning, I have a profound respect for the probable accuracy of all I learned from him. As suggested in the foreword, I have indeed found and seen many of the possibilities described herein. Many things I was told were impossible or non-existant when I was a child -- or as recently as five years ago -- I have now walked through . . or found in some more recent research. I have a profound respect for the probable accuracy of all I learned from my father.

Yet, where did my father learn such things?

Five generations ago, a young woman, growing in wisdom, took up and was given responsibility for all this ancient learning. She was Oneida, one of the Five first Nations of the Iroquois Confederacy. Her Clan was Turtle. She was my grandfather's grandmother. She saw all this Ancient Wisdom disappearing around her and grew determined it should not die, but be perpetuated down the generations, until a new generation learned to listen. It should then be given as a gift, she said, to all Earth's children willing to listen.

She took her learning west to Illinois, where my grandfather learned it from her. It was he who finally taught it to my father on their Nebraska farm. In my turn, in the house my father built in Los Angeles, I took up this responsibility with very willing hands, learning the nature of dedication from all these Ancient Tellings, accepting the further responsibility to write them down in English, the language of this broader Nation.

This lineal transmission into written form was decided on nearly 200 years ago, as between my grandfather's grandmother and the Keeper of the Old Things from whom she learned. This specific responsibility to enable that Ancient Keeper to speak through us to the Seventh Generation hence was accepted at that time and in every generation since.

As it was then agreed, so it has been done.

Whether this ever was the history of the Iroquois -- or of one group who joined them -- I do not know. But I am certain it is the history of my ancestors, who -- in a direct line down uncounted generations -- never forgot to remember.

On behalf of them, and of the five most recent generations, I give it to you now as it was intended, a gift . . for listening ears.

Kind thoughts come . .

Contents

The First Principal Telling

The Land Of So Long
No One Remembers How Long

THEN
    Our People were settled
        with the mountains to our back
            facing to the East and to the South.

    Our Center was a sand beach
        lying at the foot of the mountains
        curving away to the left and right
        ending in sharp cliff faces
            where the rocks broke away
                and fell straight down
                    to become one with Ocean.

IN THAT TIME
    When the world was cold
        the deep, dark places in the mountains
            were valued for their warmth.

    And when the world was warm
        the open beach was of greater value.

TWO TIMES
    had beach disappeared beneath a rising Ocean
        little was left at high tide
            that one could stand on.

TWO TIMES
    had the sand reappeared
        from beneath a shrinking Ocean.

IN EACH SUCH TIME
   Since the world was filled with greater cold
      and the deep, dark places were of greater value
         it was logical to conclude
            that much of Ocean
               went away somewhere to become ice.

And since it was well known
    that to the North and West
        the world was colder at these times
            than it was at Ocean's edge
        it was logical to conclude
            that this great ice lay to the North

For surely
    East and West have no such power.

AND AT THAT TIME
    Our People sent forth a party of Go and See.

And even did they return -- wrapped in fur --
    to speak of great cold and walls of ice
        so high no one could climb them
        nor any survive near them
            save the Great Beasts
               which Our People did not find attractive.

AND DURING THIS TIME
    OUR PEOPLE CAME TO KNOW
        THE NATURE OF THE WORLD AROUND THEM
    SO THAT THEY UNDERSTOOD
        HOW IT WAS FOR OTHERS
            DURING THIS TIME OF GREAT COLD.

AND THE PEOPLE SPOKE TO ONE ANOTHER
    And saw that all Walk Two Legs
        might well be divided from one another
           in two ways.

FIRST FINGER SAYS
    They may be divided
        as to whether they are Place Keepers
           or Followers After

AND THAT PLACE KEEPERS
    maintain themselves in one place
        in a manner which makes that possible
           even as we did by hunting small things
               the greatest of which was Sharp Tusk
           and by planting beans
               as the women had learned to do
           and by gathering
               That Which Grows Below Ground
                  and the fruits of bushes
           and by drying some of these
               for the Long Cold.

BUT THE FOLLOWERS AFTER
    maintained themselves
        among the leavings of the Great Herds
        and by gathering
            That Which Grows Along the Way

    and neither did they plant wherewith to live
        nor dry nourishment against the Long Cold --
           for the Herd was always before them
           and food might be found
               during the Long Cold
                  among the old and dying.

NOW
    It seemed in no way better
        to be a Follower After
           and in some ways worse

    For they lived
        among the dung of the Great Beasts
        and sometimes under their heavy feet

    And this seemed to us health-giving
        in neither case

    Neither was it our wish
        to pick over the dung for seeds as they did.

AND SO
    WE CAME TO VALUE OUR WAY OF LIFE
        ABOVE ALL OTHERS
    AND TO SUSTAIN A GREAT WISH
        TO PRESERVE IT AGAINST ANY AND EVERY EVENT
        FOR IT WAS GREATLY PLEASING TO US.

AND SO
    The men taught themselves
        to hunt Sharp Tusk in a less dangerous manner
           by daring these sharp-pointed-tusks
               to charge at them
                  in a narrow, rocky defile

    So that the food gatherer
        might leap up appropriately
           foot wedged against either side
             -- high enough
               so as to be safe from Sharp Tusks
        and to bring their heavy staves down
           with great energy against Sharp Tusk's spine
             so as to break his back in an instant.

    And once a man had learned this skill
        Sharp Tusk could harm him in no way.

    And the People were greatly glad to see Sharp Tusk
        as this was excellent food
           against the Great Cold.

AND ALSO AT THIS TIME
The men taught themselves another skill

For they saw how it was
with the women and the Great Bears
that liked our deep, dark places as well as we.

For when the men
worked to cause such a Great Bear to leave
they learned to sit
one upon the shoulders of another
so as to match his height
and to strike at where-head-meets-neck
so as to daze our Brother Bear
and to cause him to seek sunlight.

But when the women
defended themselves from Brother Bear
they used their staves
to poke bear in the soft belly
so as to cause him pain
and make Bear wish to find a safer place.

AND THE MEN SAW
That this would be better done
were the stave pointed --
and they learned a way to grind the stave
against rough stone
so as to leave a very sharp point
and the point was so sharp
that the women used it with great care
for they had no wish to harm their Brother, Bear
but only to cause Bear to leave
and find another place.

AND IT CAME TO BE
That Many Women Pointed
was more effective.
than Two Men As One.

AND FROM THIS
THE PEOPLE LEARNED TWO THINGS . .

HOW THE PEOPLE MIGHT LEARN
FROM WATCHING ONE ANOTHER

AND HOW MANY MIGHT DO

WHAT FEW-ALONE COULD NOT

EVEN THOUGH EACH OF THE MANY

HAS LESS STRENGTH.

NOW SECOND FINGER SAYS
    That all Walk Two Legs might also be divided
        between those who knew Ocean
           and those who did not.

For those who knew Ocean
    saw that the world was mainly water
        which was surfaced here and there
           by islands great and small.

But those who did not know Ocean --
    whose People had always lived on a land base --
    saw that the world was a flat land
        surrounded by great rivers.

  AND OUR PEOPLE
    HAVE ALWAYS BEEN AN OCEAN PEOPLE.

NOW IT HAS BEEN SAID
    THAT WE VALUED OUR WAY
        AND WOULD DO MUCH TO MAINTAIN IT.

EVEN SO
    AS THE WORLD WARMED AGAIN
        AND OCEAN ROSE TO COVER SAND
    DID WE FIND IT NECESSARY
        TO REORGANIZE OUR PEOPLE
    SO WE MIGHT FLOURISH DURING THIS NEW TIME
        AS WE HAD DURING THE OLD.

FOR THE OLD TIME
    Required a special agreement
        whereby each deep, dark place
            was divided into two areas.

    That which was most protected from the cold
        was the province of the women

    And among the women
        was always chosen one wisest
            to guide the resolution of disputes.

    And to her were given two Learners
        who would assist her
            in the gathering of wisdom
            and in the managing of Many People Together.

    And one of these
        might become She Who Is
            when That One left us to Return.

AND THESE THREE IT WAS
    who lived among the People
        and watched with compassion
            as they became who-they-were
        and spoke when appropriate
            so that all might live together
                in gladness at the living.

AND THESE THREE IT WAS
    who chose the Special Persons --
        those wise in the ways
            of planting and gathering and drying
        so that the young might learn
            and therefore flourish.

FOR IT WAS THE WILL OF THE PEOPLE
    TO CONTINUE TO BE WHO-THEY-WERE.

NOW
That which was not so protected from the cold
was given over as the Place of Learning

And the women might gather here close to light
to learn the art of weaving nets.

But most of this area
was reserved for the men
and for their Special Persons.

For I tell you now
that even as the women
chose She Who Is and her two Learners

So did the men
choose First Among Us and five Learners
to aid him in teaching the skills
of snaring small creatures
and that most difficult skill of all --
Break the Back of Sharp Tusk.

AND SO IT WAS
That he who was First Among Us sat and wondered
how this might be appropriately accomplished.

And he saw within himself
that if Great Bear
would only stand quiet against the wall
this might be done.

And he laughed
at the image in his mind
of Great-Bear-Standing-Quiet
until others came to ask his focus

But he could not speak for laughing
until he began to see in his mind
a simple image of Bear-Standing-Quiet
and to wonder how this might be done
until it was so great within him
that he could neither hunt nor show
until it was resolved.

AND SO
    All his waking thoughts were spent in seeking
        and sleeping he saw images of Bear and Tusk
           and even dove and hawk
        and how the young might learn in safety

AND HOW IT MIGHT BE
    THAT THE PEOPLE WOULD INDEED FLOURISH
    AND KNOW THE JOY
        OF WISDOM-WITHOUT-PERIL.

AND NOW
    First Among Us
        turned his thoughts to the Earth
           which is our Mother
        for she feeds us and bathes us and protects us
           even as a Mother will --

And he asked our Mother, Earth, for an answer
    and she spoke to him
    and she said --

    "Look at me --
        for I contain the answer."

And he looked and he saw
    that some earth was yellow and some was red.

And he looked at the growing things
    and he saw green and blue and purple.

And he thought

    "WHAT IS IMPOSSIBLE FOR ONE
    MAY BE POSSIBLE FOR MANY."

AND SO
    berry became one with earth
        and chalk was mixed with clay.

AND SOON
    BEAR-STOOD-QUIET-AGAINST-THE-WALL
    FOR ALL TO SEE -- DEVOID OF PERIL.

NOW
    LET US HONOR THIS MAN
        FOR HE BROUGHT US WISDOM.

    LET US HONOR THIS MAN
        FOR HE BROUGHT US JOY.

    LET US HONOR THIS MAN
        FOR HE BROUGHT US CONTENTMENT
        AND MANY WAYS OF LEARNING.

    SO BE IT

NOW -- AS I HAVE SAID --
    The world was growing warm again
        and Ocean rose to meet us sooner every day

So that even as the People
    sought to come out of the deep, dark places
        and live on the sand in the open air . .

Even at that time
    the sand grew less
        as the people grew more.

AND WE SAW
    THAT IT MUST AGAIN BE AGREED
    AMONG THE PEOPLE
        HOW WE MIGHT LIVE TOGETHER.

NOW
    The Great Gift
        that Standing-Bear had brought us
          was still strong in our minds
        and pointed lance and nets and planting beans
        and the skill to soften skins.

WE SAW WERE EACH HIGH IN VALUE
    AND SO WE THOUGHT
        FIRST LET US HONOR SUCH AS THESE.

AND SO
    Those who were chosen as First Among Us
        were given by all the People
          the right to choose
            a soft sand bed and first access to Ocean.

And those who were of frail health among us
    were given by all the People
        the right to a bed
          in the deep, dark places
    and these places
        were still for learning
    so that the practices
        of helping others heal
          were also concentrated in these places.

And as for the others
    they were asked
        to find a way to live among the Mountains.

And for these
    there was always the possibility
        they might teach themselves
            a way so appropriate for living
    that all the People
        might give to them the right
            of a soft sand bed near the Ocean lapping.

And to these Mountain People
    were given
        the managing of the hot spring waters
    which were much sought after by the old
        and those whose body was sore.

And the right to these waters
    was granted by the Mountain People to

      First -- those-who-had-need and

      Second -- the First Among Us and

      Third -- to the Mountain People themselves.

AND IN THIS MANNER
    were the Long Colds made easier
        for those to whom it gave pain.

AND IN THIS MANNER
    was life made easier for those
        whose life was more difficult
            in the Mountains.

AND THIS WAS THE MANNER
IN WHICH THE PEOPLE LIVED
FOR SO LONG
NO ONE ANY LONGER
REMEMBERED HOW LONG.

The First Among Us
at the Water's edge where the food was fresh.

The Ailing Among Us
close to them and tended by them
with the Learning Place between.

And the Mountain People
living beyond

With Ocean food a special pleasure
and warm pools close at hand

And cultivated beans
flourishing in many places

And berries and other food
encouraged here and there.

And bear
slowly disappearing

And Sharp Tusk
living at the edge of the People
so that those who sought this food
must walk farther and farther.

AND SO IT WAS
That the First Among Us
often made short camp
among the Mountain People.

AND WE SAW THAT THIS WAS GOOD

AND THERE WAS MUCH JOY AMONG US
IN THE MANNER OF OUR LIVING.

The Day Of Rocks Like Rain

NOW IT WAS
    That the People
        sent forth parties of Go-and-See
            to learn the manner of the land around them.

And they found
        that they were North and West and North again
            of a lesser water almost enclosed by land
        but at the South and East and again South
            was a semi-circle of islands
                which almost made it possible
                to walk around this water.

And some of the strongest among us
        would sometimes swim from one island to another
            to make this circle.

AND SOME OF THEM WERE NEVER SEEN AGAIN.

But others Went-around-the-World
        and returned to our Center Place
            with many gifts of wisdom and much learning.

AND EVEN THEN
    DID WE VALUE OUR WAY AS GREAT
AND EVEN HAD WE EVERY WISH
    THAT IT SHOULD CONTINUE.

BUT
        many People knew this would not be
            and were restless at our edge
                bringing back new learning
                    that might aid us.

AND THEN IT WAS
    THAT THE WORLD BEGAN TO CHANGE.

FOR SOMETIMES
    People would run from one place to another

    And if you asked their purpose would answer
        that there was too much energy in this place
        and that they longed to be elsewhere.
    And some even went beyond the Mountains
        and lived at the edges of the Great Dry Place
        that lay beyond
            and for which we had no fondness
            and they would not return.

    But the First Among Us
        still lived at the Edge of Waters

    And at this time First Among Us
        was many people of many ages
            and women and men among them
        so that they were almost a people
            unto themselves.

AND WHEREAS
    WISDOM MIGHT COME FROM MANY SOURCES

AND WHEREAS
    THIS WAS WELL UNDERSTOOD

    THIS WAS OUR CENTER PLACE FOR WISDOM
    WITH THE LEARNING PLACE ABOVE

AND FOR US
    IT HAD AN ENDLESS VALUE.

BUT THE WORLD CHANGED
    And that which seemed too much energy for some
        became too much energy for all.

    And Those Who Fly rose in the air
        and would not come down.

    And Sharp Tusk ran among us
        as if he no longer knew
           that we were Back Breakers.

    And all things moved
        and could not help themselves.

    And First Among Us sought the Ocean
        and looked to see what it might bring.

AND THEN ALL THINGS CHANGED.

    And a sound came to us
        like the distant roll of thunder.

    And small rocks rose
        and settled in their place
        and some came falling down the hill.

    And Earth began to roll and heave
        like Sharp Tusk caught in a heavy net.

    And the Earth cracked and broke apart
        as if it were not one whole.

    And the People
        cried out in anguish at too much change
           and could not run for falling
           and some were crushed by rocks falling down
           and none could anywhere stand.

    So that when the Earth stilled
        many lay wounded
           their Spirits running out upon the Earth.

And those who stood were puzzled what to do
some ran toward the safety of Ocean
where there are no rocks falling
and some tried to help the wounded
so that they might walk to a safer place
and the women found the small ones
and called the others to them
and held them close
to protect them from the flying rocks
with their own bodies.

FOR THEY ALL KNEW
THAT IT WOULD COME AGAIN.

AND SURELY IT CAME

As the Earth turns
and allows us once more to look at Sun

IT CAME

And the Earth rolled and heaved
in such great convulsions
that rocks fell from the Mountain
as if they were rain.

And hardly a person could stand
that had not been struck by rock

And many fell screaming
from the side of Mountain.

AND THE EARTH ROLLED

AND THE ROCKS FELL

AND THE PEOPLE CRIED OUT

So that the air
was so filled with thunderous noise
that it seemed
no longer possible to breathe
and it seemed
as if those who were not crushed by rock
would suffocate from too much noise.

AND
    For the First Among Us
        it was little better.

    For although they did not stand on Mountains
        rocks still thundered down among them
            crushing many.

    And when the Earth was still
        they tried
            to bring the Ailing and the Learners
                out of the deep, dark places
            but some of these were already sealed shut
            and the destruction within
                was terrible to see.

    But again they tried
        till all who could be reached
            lay safe upon the sand
                except for the stones
                    which sometimes still crashed among them.

AND THEN
    The Mountain People
        made a great rush to the safety of Ocean.

    And all those who could reach the sand stood upon it
        until the sand seemed to disappear
            beneath too many feet.

    And all those in the Mountains
        tried to find a place safer from rocks
            in the flat valleys.

NOW
  Above the cries of the People
    some began to hear a distant sound
    and others saw that the sands grew wider
      until the Ocean had entirely gone away
    and our bay lay before us devoid of Ocean.

AND SOME CRIED OUT
  that the Earth had split
    and all the waters had run away beneath.

BUT OTHERS KNEW
  that Earth was one whole
    and there was no place in the Center
      for water to go.

AND SO SOME THOUGHT
  perhaps Ocean had gone away again to become ice.

But those coming down from the Mountains
  to fill up the new sand gave a great cry
    and cried DANGER
    and cried RUN AWAY FROM OCEAN
    and cried OCEAN COMING LIKE A GREAT WALL.

AND THERE BEFORE THEM
  was their sheltering Ocean.

THERE BEFORE THEM
  were the kind waters
    which had brought them food
      and the joy of swimming.

THERE BEFORE THEM
WAS THE CENTER OF THEIR WORLD
risen up like an angry Mountain
risen up like an enraged Bear
risen up beyond a Great Storm's fury.

IT CAME LIKE A CRUSHING ROLLING DEATH
And fell upon the First Among Us
fell upon the Ailing
fell upon the Learners
fell upon those who sought safety from the rocks

FELL UPON THEM
AND RETURNED TO OCEAN

So that those high enough on the Earth Mountain
to escape this Water Mountain
watched in horror
AS ALL BELOW THEM WASHED AWAY.

IN AN INSTANT
    They were gone -- these First Among Us.

IN AN INSTANT
    They were gone -- the Ailing.

IN AN INSTANT
    They were gone -- the Learners.

IN AN INSTANT
    ALL OUR WISDOM WASHED AWAY
        AND THE PEOPLE
            STOOD NAKED AGAINST THIS CHANGE.

AND
    The People howled like one wounded
    and they said to one another

        THERE IS NO SAFETY
            IN THE MOUNTAINS

        THERE IS NO SAFETY
            IN THE SEA

        THERE IS NO SAFETY
            IN OUR CENTER PLACE

        SAFETY
            LIES ONLY TOWARD THE GREAT DRYNESS.

And they turned and ran --
    those who could run.

And they turned and walked --
    those who could walk.

And they turned
    and helped the unstable.

THEY TURNED AS ONE PEOPLE
    AND WALKED TOWARD THE GREAT DRYNESS.

AND
    The rocks still fell.

    And sometimes
        the Earth still shook and heaved
            but they walked -- those who could
            and they arrived -- those who could

        AND WERE NO LONGER TROUBLED
        BY FALLING ROCKS LIKE RAIN
        NO LONGER TROUBLED
        BY THIS DANGER.

AND FOR SO LONG
    NO ONE REMEMBERED HOW LONG

        THIS WAS THE FIRST DECISION
        THAT THE PEOPLE MADE
            WITHOUT THE FIRST AMONG US.

The Great Dryness
And How The People Learned A New Way

FOR THREE DAYS
    They stayed at the foot of the Mountain . .
        those who could walk.

FOR THREE DAYS
    Their cries sounded down the valleys.

    Few there were who maintained cohesion
        with those who had been members
            of their close knit group.

    They were scattered or lost beyond retrieval.

FOR THREE DAYS
    NO ONE SPOKE A WORD
        AS TO THAT WHICH FOLLOWS.

FOR THREE DAYS
    THERE WAS NO WISDOM
    ONLY SORROW
        WAS IN THE HEARTS OF THE PEOPLE.

NOW -- AT LAST
    Someone spoke and asked . .
        "Are there any among us
            who were first?"

    And three men arose and said
        they had been hunting in the Mountains
            far away from Oceans Running Fast.

    And to these
        we turned for Wisdom.

BUT THEY SAID . .

"Ask us about hunting
    or about deep Ocean creatures
    or about Walk the World.

"All these can we tell you.

"But Our People are Ocean People
    and have turned away
        from the Great Dry Places
    and about this place we know three things . .

"If you walk straight ahead
    to the West and North and West again
        you come to mountains
    and between here and there is little water.

"If you walk North and East and also North
    you come to Walk by Waters
        and are able in that way
            to walk North of Ocean
            to the Great Island That Lies Beyond --
following this way
    are many herds if Ocean is low
    and only Two-Legs if Ocean is high.

"Now, if you walk to the South and West and South again
    you come to other mountains
        through which there may be valleys enough
            to walk to that which lies beyond --
    and beyond this once lay the Ocean People
        of whom our ancestors told us
        and whom we have no wish to see again.

"SO -- AS FOR US
    WE WOULD CHOOSE NORTH."

BUT THE PEOPLE SAW
   That North was a long path
      and South a dangerous one
      and West a dry one . .
      and were confused.
   And so they sat and talked among themselves.

UNTIL AT LAST
   One rose who was not First and said . .

     "This side of our mountain is dry
       but the other side is wet
       and maybe this is only close-to-Ocean wetness
       but maybe Western Mountains
         are also wet on this side.

     "Then I say let us walk West
       and find these mountains.

     "For surely there is water somewhere
       and surely we can find it
       and surely none of us will return
         to Mountains-by-the-Sea --
           not even for water."

   AND EVERYONE SAID THIS WAS GOOD.

AND AT FIRST LIGHT
   All rose and walked West and somewhat North
      fanned out across the flat land
      so if there were water
       someone would find it.

AND IN THIS MANNER
   Did the Walking People
      cross the Great Dry Place
      and few were lost.

BUT
   There was much Learning in the walking
      as few had seen this dryness
      and none knew
         what might be consumed in safety.

AND THE PEOPLE SAW
    THAT OF ALL THEY HAD LEARNED
      FROM ALL THE GENERATIONS
        OF GO AND SEE
          WHO HAD RETURNED
    IT WAS STILL NOT ENOUGH.

FOR
    Our old way of life --
    Our long-established way
      of focusing thought and learning --

    All had been swept away in an instant
      and the People
        stood naked against this new cold.

    And a Great Resolve swept through them
      and they said this so often to each other
        that it became a Song for Walking . .

    "LET US LEARN
      FROM EVERY WAKING MOMENT.

    "LET US LEARN
      EVEN AS WE SLEEP.

    "LET US LEARN
      AND WATCH OUR BROTHER WALKING

    "EVEN THOUGH
      HE CHOOSE A SHARP AND STONY PATH."

AND
    Through the Great Dryness
      the People at last
        reached the Western Mountains
          and found a small stream
        which was barely enough to sustain them . .
      but here they stayed
        for it was necessary
          for them to gather strength.

NOW IT WAS
   That the People
      asked three among them
         to find a better way . .

One was asked to go South
    along the edge of mountains.

One was asked to go West
    to see if more water lay higher up.

And one was asked
    to learn about the land
        between here and Walk by Waters.

And he who went West
    returned first to tell the People
        that sources for this small stream
            already grew less
    and it seemed to him
        that perhaps the changing of the sun
            had already driven some water away
        and that they must find another source.

In two days he who went North
    returned and said that way lay only dryness
        until you came to an increase in grass
    but that he had found no standing waters.

He who went South
    had not returned
        and no one knew what he had found.

NOW
   The People spoke much among themselves.

They saw that they must leave
    and among them was no will to stay.

Then one man had a strong vision
    and saw grass and flowers
        and waters running down
    and knew these lay to the South
        but could not say how far.

AND MANY SPOKE TO FOLLOW HIM.

But one old woman spoke and said . .

"I have seen no such vision
        but my brother from the North
                has seen grass that he has walked to
        and it is logical to conclude
                that water is more where grass is more.

"And so I turn my own eyes
        to the North
                and ask who will to walk with me.

"For I have a great desire
        to see Walk by Waters
        and to learn
                whether it can now be crossed
        for it would please me greatly
                to see the Great Island That Lies Beyond."

AND MANY SPOKE TO JOIN HER

AND SO IT WAS
        Because South is warm and North is cold
                two out of every three turned South.

But because
        many thought that Walk by Waters
                would be worth the seeing
And because
        beyond lay a Great Island
                that might yet contain a place for them
And because
        they feared the Ocean People to the South
                one in three turned North
                        with Snow on Top
                                and followed her path to Wisdom.

AND FEW OF THEM
        WERE SORRY FOR THEIR CHOOSING

FOR THEIR WAY WAS HARD
        AND THE CROSSING DIFFICULT

BUT THEY FOUND AT LAST
        A NEW WAY.

AND
    WE ARE THE CHILDREN
      OF THOSE WHO WENT NORTH.

    WE ARE THE CHILDREN
      OF THOSE WHO CHOSE
        TO LOOK AT WALK BY WATERS.

    WE ARE THE CHILDREN
      OF THOSE WHO CHOSE
        TO WALK WITH ANCIENT WISDOM
        AND TO HEAR HER TELLINGS.

LET US HONOR THEIR WAY

LET US HONOR THEIR SPIRIT

LET US HONOR THEIR WISDOM

LET US FOLLOW THEIR PATH.

How The People Walked North And Learned To Live With Dryness

NOW THE PEOPLE SANG A NEW SONG

  LET US LEARN ALL WE CAN

  LET US SEE ALL THERE IS

  LET US HEAR EVERY SOUND

  LET THOSE WHO COME AFTER

    RECEIVE THIS GIFT.

AND FIRST
    They learned the wisdom
        of the skin carriers
            some of the women had made
                for they found no water.

    Even though
        some climbed up into the lower mountains
            they found no water.

    And soon it was
        that some came to lie still against the Earth
            for lack of water.

    But Snow on Top walked on
        and many still could follow.

AND AS THE DAYS PASSED
    They learned
        to consume plants that contained moisture
            and learned to tell which were safe
                and which not.

    They learned
        that dew might be found in the early morning
            which could make the difference
                between walking-on and lying still.

They learned
   not to cook lizards and small birds
      before they drank the blood.

And they learned
   that raw food gave more moisture than cooked
      and that the energy saved
         might be used for walking.

AND AT LAST
   They learned the wisdom
      of walking by night
         and finding shade by day.

FOR SNOW ON TOP
   HAD SPOKEN ONLY WISDOM.

AND AT LAST
   The People understood
      and they said to one another . .

PERHAPS AT LAST WE HAVE LEARNED
THAT WISDOM HIDES UNDER SNOW
AND NEEDS ONLY THE WARMTH
   OF OUR LISTENING
      TO MAKE ITSELF APPARENT.

NOW
   LET US ALL REMEMBER THIS LEARNING
      SO THAT MORE MAY CROSS IN SAFETY
         AND FEWER LIE STILL AGAINST THE EARTH
            FOR LACK OF LISTENING.

FOR NOW
   The People saw at last increasing grass
      and fell upon it with a great cry
         and consumed much
            as it contained moisture.

But those who did
   felt pains at night.

AND SNOW ON TOP SAID . .

   "Too much is very little
      when none at all preceded."

But the People were glad of their arrival
for soon it rained
and hands and feet grew soft again
and stomachs full.

For many creatures ran among the grasses
and seeds appeared
that might be crushed and eaten.
And fires were built again for cooking.

AND THE PEOPLE
  REJOICED AT THE ARRIVAL OF ENOUGH.

AND THE YOUNG AGAIN
  BEGAN TO PROSPER.

How The People Crossed The Grassland And How They Found Walk By Waters

THIS IS THE TELLING
OF WALKING ON GRASS
AND HOW THE PEOPLE FOUND OTHERS

FOR
As they walked North and East and also North
they saw something on the horizon
they did not understand.

They thought at first it was a Great Beast
but it did not move
only remaining still at their approach.

They saw that it was hollow
and Two-legs lived inside.

And this was a great wonder to them
for these Two-legs
had used many sticks and many hides
to make a round dwelling like a turtle shell
and in the center of the top
had left a hole.

And the People saw that this was for smoke
for the remains of fire lay beneath.

And the People wondered
why these ones would work so hard
when living among grass was pleasant.

AND SNOW ON TOP SAID . .
  "I can think of two things
    that might explain this --

"First, perhaps Wind blows strong
    from time to time
      and this round place
        gives shelter they are glad of

"Or perhaps
    it grows very cold here during Long Cold
      and perhaps snow lies deep --

"But in either case
    this tells us to hurry on
    or learn to build round houses --

"For surely they do not do this
    only to amuse themselves."

AND SO THE PEOPLE MOVED ON
  Not wanting to meet these Two-legs
    for some people
      are angrier than others
    and there was among Our People little strength.

NOW
  After they crossed many undulations in the land
    there came a noise that was strange to them
    and they called it
      Thunder on the Earth.

And some of the People
    thought of Mountains-Falling-Down
    and threw themselves upon the earth.

But others said . .
    This must be Many Four-leggeds coming
      and rose to run for they had no wish
        to be bent like grass
          under many hooves.

NOW
>   Over the horizon came Walk Two Legs.

>   And these they saw first
>>   but underneath was a Great Beast
>>>   with a strong head
>>>   and hooves that thundered on the earth.
>   And these Walk Two Legs
>>   were among the angry ones.

>   They came among us with great strength
>>   and sometimes their beasts knocked us down
>>   and sometimes they knocked us down with fists
>>   and they took what little food we had.
>   They took all the skins we carried
>>   and spoke angry words we did not understand
>>>   so that we knew we must go away.

AND
>   We turned North and East and North
>>   toward Walk by Waters
>>>   and had no wish to stay
>>   even though
>>>   some of our young lay still upon the earth.

>   As Snow on Top proceeded
>>   she struck one
>>>   with the staff she used for walking
>>   so that they had no wish
>>>   to guide their Great Beasts near her again
>>>>   and let us walk on.

NOW IT WAS
>   That many days were spent in walking.

>   The path was smooth . .
>>   many small things walked among the grass
>>   seeds and roots were many
>>   and there were no more Sitting High
>>>   so that we had no need to hurry.

>   The People grew strong again
>>   and walked with firmness.

AND EVERY NIGHT
>*All listened*
>>*to Snow on Top sing the Ancient Songs*
>>*so that what she learned*
>>>*would continue among the People*
>>>*after her Spirit had left us.*

And she never tired of the singing.

And those who were there said afterwards
>*that it was a happy time*
>*a good walking time*
>*a Learning Time.*

AND ALL WERE GLAD OF IT.

NOW
>The days grew longer
>>and the People sang their songs together.

>They found a new people
>>who also lived in rounded skin houses
>>>but who walked on their own feet.

>These were not an angry people.
>These were a sharing people
>>who taught us much
>>>of what was safe to eat
>>>>among the grasses.

>And this people
>>ate some of the flowers as well.

IN ALL THIS TIME
>We saw none of the Great Herds
>>and this was a wonder to us.

>But this people said . .
>>"They have gone North and will return
>>>When-the-World-Grows-Cold."

>And we had no wish to see them.

AND SO
We asked about Walk by Waters
and were told
it lay still to the East and North and East
and we would find it
as the land narrowed between Oceans
for it walked so far out into the waters
it could not be mistaken for another.

AND SO
WE ROSE ON THE LONGEST DAY
And went on
-- full of strength --
and carrying what to eat.

AND
IN JUST ONE TURNING OF THE MOON
WE CAME TO THE PLACE
WHERE THE LAND NARROWS.

AND THERE WE CAMPED
TO PLAN OUR JOURNEY.

How The People Learned
The Way Of Many Wisdoms

I. The First Wisdom

NOW
    I have told you
        that Snow on Top sang the Ancient Songs
            and all among us listened.

    But though many asked
        if she were First Among Us
            this question she would not answer
                but replied --

    "There are many things for you to learn
        and this shall be the last."

AND SO FINALLY
    None would ask her
        but would listen to her songs
        and learn a way to sing them to each other
            so that some would choose to please her
                by singing the songs to her in return.

    And the first among us
        to dare to sing her own song
            was a girl of eight winters

AND MANY SPOKE AGAINST IT.

    But Snow on Top said --

    "This One has shown me
        the true value of her listening
            and I am well pleased."

    And all the People
        were so astonished at her words
            that none could speak
        as it had come to be
            that First Among Us -- only they --
                now sang these songs.

But Snow on Top saw their mind
   and asked --
   "If only First Among Us sings these songs
     who will sing them next?"

AND WE SAW
   THAT THERE WAS WISDOM IN HER WORDS.

AND IT CAME TO BE
   That all vied each with every other
     to be the one to sing her . . her own songs.

Until Snow on Top became angry with our noise
   and spoke to us as one
     who would turn away from her People
   and said --

   "I shall walk on --
   Let none come to meet me
     until you have agreed among yourselves
      who shall sing next."

AND THE PEOPLE WERE AFRAID
   And some cried to see her going
     and struggled after her.

But Snow on Top raised her staff --
   all knew the level of her purposefulness
   and none would follow.

IT WAS THEN
   We sat despondent --
     none even rising to build a Central Fire --
     until at last She of Eight Winters
      rose up to speak for First Place.

And the People
   rose up to speak in an angry voice

And all spoke against This One
   and the din became so great
     that it is a sorrow to tell it.

For the People continued in this manner
   until She of Eight Winters --
      and others near her size --
         stood above us on rocks
            and clapped two stones together
               until this sound grew so great
                  that all else stilled.

AND WHEN AT LAST
   The Earth grew still --
      the youngest among them asked one question . .

      "IS IT YOU WHO WILL LEAD US?"

And it became so quiet
   that even the rustling of the grass was apparent
Until at last
   someone laughed -- and more -- and more --
Until all the People
   had to sit on the ground for laughing.

Until someone spoke . .
   "At last
      we know who will be First Among Us.'"

And more laughter
   until all the People were tired and happy
      and it seemed to them
         that they could see chinks
            in their black wall of despair --
               and sunlight beyond.

AND AT LAST
Someone said . .

"I think the Great Island That Lies Beyond
will be a good island

"Now how do we get from here to there?"

AND AT LAST
THE PEOPLE BEGAN TO COUNSEL TOGETHER.

AND AT LAST
THEY BEGAN TO FIND THEIR OWN WISDOM.

AND LATER
THEY SAID
THAT THIS WAS THEIR FIRST LEARNING . .

IF THERE IS NOT ONE AMONG US
WHO CONTAINS SUFFICIENT WISDOM
MANY PEOPLE TOGETHER
MAY FIND A CLEAR PATH.

II. *The Second Wisdom*

WITHIN THREE DAYS
    Then -- we found Snow on Top
        waiting for us on a high rock
           so she might know that we were coming
    Still in her hand remained the staff.

    And he-whom-we-had-chosen approached her first
        and spoke thus --

        "We have caused you great Heart Sorrow
           when you have endeavored only
               to allow us to learn.

        "We are a Following People
           and have learned to follow you

        "YOU HAVE BECOME OUR CENTRAL PLACE."

    And Snow on Top answered him --
    "You can see
        what may happen to a Central Place . .

        "AND SURELY
           I TELL YOU NOW
               MY SPIRIT, TOO, WILL BE SWEPT AWAY
               AND HOW WILL IT BE FOR YOU THEN?"

BUT THIS TIME
    No one cried
        nor even did any show distress.

    He Who Stood Forward answered simply . .

    "WE WILL TALK TO ONE ANOTHER."

    And Snow on Top looked
        as if she had seen something truly beautiful
           then turned and walked on
               toward Walk by Waters.

AND
    THE PEOPLE AFTERWARDS SAID
      THAT THIS WAS OUR SECOND LEARNING . .

    THOSE WHO ALWAYS FOLLOW
      ONLY LEARN THE SHAPE OF ANOTHER BACK.

III. *The Third Wisdom*

SO IT WAS
>That the People walked on
>>and began to vie with one another
>>>to see who would walk by Snow on Top
>>>>until again all became noise.

>Until at last
>>Snow on Top walked away from her People
>>and would let none near her.

AT LAST
>The People grew angry with her
>>and spoke much among themselves
>>>of her wisdom
>>and how she could not long be with them.

>Until at last
>>someone saw that among all the People
>>>only the young ones were not angry
>>and so they said --

>"Let us send the young ones
>>to listen to Snow on Top."

AND SO
>This was the manner of their going . .

>That during the day
>>Snow on Top walked in a circle of young ones
>>showing them how to learn
>>>from That Which Grew
>>>and from That Which Also Walked
>>>and from That Which Flew.

>And during the first of the Dark Time
>>she sang her songs that all might hear.

>And with the Next Light
>>those who could carry packs
>>>sang those same songs to each other
>>>>no longer seeking her listening.

SO THAT
   All the People learned all the old songs

   And by the end of their walk

      NO LONGER
         WATCHED THE BACK OF SNOW ON TOP.

AND
   THE PEOPLE AFTERWARDS SAID
      THAT THIS WAS THEIR THIRD LEARNING . .

   THERE ARE MANY WAYS OF CHOOSING
      BUT TO CHOOSE QUICKLY IS OFTEN BEST
      OR THE CHOICE MAY COME TOO LATE.

IV. *The Fourth Wisdom*

AND SO IT CONTINUED
    That the People
        sang their songs to each other
    And let the young learn from Snow on Top
        until one day
            a great dispute rose among them.

    And those of us in the rear
        thought at first
            that something had been found
                that required decision.

    But when we drew closer we learned
        that two
            argued the wording
                of one of the Ancient Songs
            and sought to resolve this issue
                between them.

    But all had this and that to say
        until some saw that Snow on Top
            stood alone away from her People
                and entered the dispute in no way.

AND THEN
    Someone saw her wisdom and said --

    "She is showing us
        that the answer is near at hand
            but must be sought."

    And at first some argued among themselves.

BUT AT LAST
    All saw this wisdom and asked Snow on Top
        what of this song was in her memory
            and learned to their surprise
                that it was neither one
                nor yet the other
                but a third
                    which none at all had spoken.

AND AFTERWARDS THE PEOPLE SAID
 THAT THIS WAS THEIR FOURTH LEARNING ..

ALTHOUGH MUCH MAY BE RESOLVED
 AMONG THE PEOPLE
 SOMETIMES
  AN ELDER VOICE IS BEST.

AND FROM THIS LEARNING -- AND THE FIRST --

THE PEOPLE LATER DERIVED
 THEIR GREATEST LEARNING ..

THAT NEITHER ONE WAY -- NOR THE OTHER
 BUT A BALANCE BETWEEN THE TWO
 LIGHTS A CLEAR PATH.

V. THE FINAL WISDOM

NOW AT LAST
    The People came to rest
        at the top of a high hill
            so that all
                might regard the path before them.

    The Place of Honor at the highest point
        they gave to Snow on Top.

And at her feet
    sat He Who Stood Forward
        whom the People had come to choose
            as Second Leader.

And at her side
    sat the Mother of She of Eight Winters
        who more and more acted as her assistant
            even lending her young support
                when Snow on Top grew tired
                    as was increasingly true for her.

NOW
    The People were soon prepared to go on
        as the path before them seemed sure
            and the first glistens of Ocean
            appeared at the edge
                of this great sustaining island
                on which they stood.

    But Snow on Top raised her staff
        inviting them to sit yet awhile
        and -- out of respect --
            they settled again to Earth.

SNOW ON TOP
  Gazed at the bright distant reflections
    on the water that lay beyond

And echoes of the gleaming water
    appeared in her own eyes
      which few were close enough to see.

  "Look beyond."
    -- she motioned --

  "For such is our destination --
    and beyond even that
      may lie our home.

  "Before we rise and descend this hill --
    thus losing sight
      of what we know is there --

  "I would speak to you my children
    about the nature of our path."

AND ALL KNEW
  That when she spoke as Mother
    she spoke with Wisdom

  For surely
    she was Mother to the Spirit of the People

  For surely
    she was Mother to their Chosen Path
      for how many more
        might lie still against the Earth
          for want of her Wisdom.

AND SNOW ON TOP SPOKE --

  "YOU HAVE SEEN HOW IT IS
    that we are a Strong People --
      one who has walked out
        from a thundering Earth
        and an Ocean that became sky.

  "YOU HAVE SEEN HOW IT IS
    that we are a Wise People --
      one who learns survival quickly
        against a changing circumstance.

"YOU HAVE SEEN HOW IT IS
    that we are an Enduring People --
        one who continues in the Chosen Purpose
            against great difficulties.

"YET YOU HAVE SEEN HOW IT IS"

    -- and she traced in the air
        the closing of the circle of her thought --

    "that we are a Young People --
        like small ones
            whose teachers go away
                before they have learned enough
            who quarrel
                over the resolution of this and that.

"SO
    LET US NOW LEARN HOW TO BE A PEOPLE
        WHO SEEK THE WISDOM OF ORDERED COUNCIL.

"LET US REMEMBER
    HOW QUICKLY ONE WHO LEADS
        MAY BE TAKEN FROM US.

"LET US UNDERSTAND
    THAT WHAT IS IMPOSSIBLE FOR ONE
        MAY BE POSSIBLE FOR MANY.

"AND IF ALL THIS ESCAPES YOUR MEMORY
    REMEMBER ONLY THIS:
        SEEK THE WISDOM OF ORDERED COUNCIL --

    "HOWEVER MANY
        HOWEVER FEW
            HOWEVER OLD
                HOWEVER YOUNG

    SEEK THE WISDOM OF ORDERED COUNCIL.

"Let even the youngest among you
sit and be heard.

"Do not do this because I advise it --
nor even in my honor --

"DO THESE THINGS
AS YOU SEE THE WISDOM
THAT LIES THEREIN.

"NOW
I speak as one of the People
who would like her People remembered.

"AND I SAY THIS . .
When other Peoples cross our path
When they sit with us awhile.

"LET THEM SAY
THAT THEY HAVE SEEN A PEOPLE

"WHO LISTEN TO ONE ANOTHER

"WHO TAKE COUNCIL TOGETHER

"WHO FOLLOW AN ORDERED PATH
TO WISDOM.

"I HAVE SPOKEN."

AND
THE PEOPLE'S HEARTS WERE TOUCHED
BY A WONDER

AT THIS PERSON

AT ALL THEY HAD SHARED TOGETHER

AT ALL THEY HAD LEARNED.

They saw Snow on Top
    begin to descend that high hill
        aided in her descent by one
            who increasingly eased her path.

And many understood the love
    that continues to flow
        from one who is Mother to her People.

And in their eyes too
    were the distant glistens of Ocean.

NOW
    He Who Stood Forward
        also arose and gave a great shout . .

        "WHO SEES THE DISTANT OCEAN?"

AND ALL THE PEOPLE
    Joined him in his glad cry

        "WHO SEES THE DISTANT OCEAN?"

They called to one another
    following the slow path
        begun by Snow on Top
    some passing her by
        in their eagerness to reach Ocean.

AND
    Only those who notice such things
        saw the hesitation in her step.

Water's Edge

As the Sharing People had said,
it was not difficult
to find Walk by Waters

For surely
it did walk farther out into ocean
than any other.

AND YET
THE PEOPLE HESITATED

What they had envisioned as a glad rush
toward the Great Island That Lay Beyond
became a careful decision.

For the ocean waters played against the rocks
in ways that made one think of storms.

And a People
who so recently faced an Ocean Mountain
had no wish to see even a little ocean hill
from a place grown precarious
amidst a rising ocean.

AND SO
THEY HESITATED.

Taking counsel one with another,
waiting for Snow on Top
whose pace had become so slow
that one by one
they went on to prepare her way,
leaving her assistant and two strong men
to walk with her.

AT LAST
Even these two arrived
and sat down to the council,
saying that Snow on Top was resting nearby
and would descend soon.

THESE TWO
Had listened much to Snow on Top.

He Who Stood Forward
had walked with the People
and knew their mind.

SO IT WAS THESE THREE
Who laid out the council circle
wide enough for all
close enough to Fire.

AS THEY WAITED
The People began to talk
of storms and shaking Earth,
slippery footholds and washing waters.

For many Go and See went out
and some now had returned,
bringing tales
of narrow rocks and washing waters.

ALL KNEW
The Great Cold would soon begin,
and with it
always walked as many storms
as men had fingers.

None had any wish
to greet such a storm from a wave-washed rock.

NOW
    Before Snow on Top arrived
        and after every Go and See had returned,
            bringing each some different learning,

    Another whom no one recognized
        came walking from this Ocean Path,
            a look was in his face
                which many saw and understood.

THEY SAW
    That he, too,
        had survived something
            no one wants to remember.

    He sat with them,
        nor even considered his own defense,
            so that they understood it was for him
                as it had been for them
            when they sat for three days without speaking.

    They saw his despair
        and honored his sorrow
        and waited for him to speak.

WITH PATIENCE AND KINDNESS
    They learned from him
        the Telling of a Strong People
            who decided to throw their sitting robe
                to the Great Island That Lay Beyond
            before that water crossing
                entirely disappeared beneath the waters,
        as every year
            more and more was already gone.

MANY DAYS
    Were required for this crossing
        and few were the places left
            where one might sit and eat.

    His People hurried,
        and he described with his hands
            how they carried those
                whose legs were not yet long
        and how they rested little,
            telling each other
                of the great rest that lay beyond.

They had chosen, he explained,
　　the time when few storms come,
　　　　ensuring further their success.

AND YET IT CAME
　　A great storm appeared on the horizon
　　　　and swept down upon them
　　　　　　with no time to return to a safer island.

Each found a place of their own
　　as secure as might be,
　　　　lashing themselves -- some of them --
　　　　　　among the protecting rocks.

THE STORM WAS NOTHING.
　　Not even the great winds
　　Nor the beating winds
　　　　could dislodge his People,
　　　　　　for they were strong.

BUT THE OCEAN WAS SOMETHING.
　　And the great waves
　　　　washing under the great winds
　　　　　　beat against his People,
　　　　　　　　causing rocks to dislodge
　　　　　　　　　　and fall against them, crushing many.

And the waves continued their beating,
　　tearing away protection,
　　　　these rocks
　　　　　　moving against each other
　　　　　　　　like great teeth chewing at the ropes,
　　　　　　　snapping them in two,
　　　　　　　breaking each life line,
　　　　　　　spilling out his People
　　　　　　　　into a raging Ocean.

AND THE TERRIBLE WAVES POUNDED.
　　After the storm was gone
　　　　and the sky a clear and warming blue,
　　　　　　these waves still pounded,
　　　　　　　　grinding what was left of his People
　　　　　　　　　　against unyielding rock.

So that when the ocean at last quieted
　　and he could leave his own sequestered place,
　　　　none near him were any longer there.

Up and down the rocks he clambered,
  careful at first,
      remembering the waiting ocean,
until he came at last to understand
    that among these rocks
      lay none of his People,
          save one or two washing under the Ocean,
            still held by their cord.

HIS FATIGUE AND HUNGER WERE SUCH
  That he felt his great sorrow
    as a numbing presence, devoid of reality,
      until he found at last a little one,
        a small one who had lately learned from him
          some trick of fishery,
          now gently washed beneath that same Ocean.

AND THEN
  His sorrow rose up to greet him
  and would not let him go.

  Salt tears obscured his vision
    so that he no longer knew his direction.

  Stumbling and tearing his hands
    on the out-stretched rocks,
        he came at last to a broader island
        and found himself -- he knew not how --
          seated next to our Central Fire.

THE PEOPLE CARED FOR HIM,
    nourished his body,
    heard his sorrow
    and waited to tell him
      of the many they, too, had left behind.

BUT
  Away From Ocean was his only thought,
    not willing even to wait
        until the People chose their own Path,
    not willing even to sit with them
      this close to Ocean.

And so the People -- understanding --
    set his feet upon a path
        toward the Sharing People,
    drawing for him patterns on the earth,
    speaking in spirit terms
        of the nature of direction.

THEN
    When he had gone,
        they sat in council
            over all that they had learned.

NOW
   I HAVE TOLD YOU HOW IT WAS FOR US . .

   A People shattered by a great sorrow
      slowly stood again
         and slowly chose a path.

   They followed this path
      with a great and wise woman
         through many learnings.

COME AT LAST
   To the edge of the pathway they sought,
      they heard the sorrowing descriptions
         of one whose People had failed.

   They sat among themselves now,
      discussing all they had heard,
      saying how they might prevent it,
      waiting for their wise companion.

   Against the setting sun
      they saw one figure coming toward them.

   It was the Mother of She of Eight Winters
      who now entered the council circle
         and sat again among the People.

   "I have come
      to ask what it is you have decided"
         -- she explained --
            and waited for their answer.

THE PEOPLE
   Formed a circle round the Fire,
      each showing an attentive face
         to every other person.

   AND THEY SPOKE,
      each waiting quietly
         till the other had finished,
            as they had learned to do,
      a circle of silent listening
         framing the wisdom each contained
      until the wisdom of all was spoken,
         contained at last
            by the Circle of the People.

And those who notice such things
  saw an increasing radiance
    on one listener's face.

Even as they described their lonely visitor
  and his great sadness . .

Even as they described the Great Storm
  and the greater loss,

Even then
  her face still had the look
    of one pleased with what she hears.

"She who sent me
  asked me to learn the People's decision"
    -- she began --

"And I not yet hear it,
  but I hear something
    which pleases me more.

"I hear a People
  who have learned to listen to one another
    and to take ordered council together.

"I HEAR . . SOMETHING BEAUTIFUL."

THEN
  All the People saw in their hearts
    the wisdom of her words.

Thinking again
  of those earlier days
    when much noise
      but little wisdom was heard,

Thinking now
  of the quiet circle of listening hearts,
    they were filled with an understanding
      of the value of their way.

AND A FIRM RESOLVE SWEPT THROUGH THEM.

A purpose
  other than attaining a second island home.

THEY DECIDED
  To be a People
    who would perpetuate and refine
      this manner of ordered council
        which they had achieved

  So that the children's children's children
    might benefit from greater understanding . .

  And their paths through joy or sorrow
    might be eased
      by the soft sounds of wisdom's voice.

  For they saw the People
    like a Great River --
      spreading out upon the land,
      spreading out across the waters,
      dividing down a thousand thousand paths
        not yet seen.

AND A SENSE OF TOMORROW
  ENTERED THEIR HEARTS
    AND NEVER AGAIN LEFT THEM.

SUCH WISDOM IS OUR GIFT
  FROM THOSE WHO WENT BEFORE.

MAY WE OFFER EQUAL MEASURE
  TO THOSE WHO FOLLOW US.

NOW
>*Truly did the People counsel together,*
>>*and that mutual counsel guided their hands.*

>*No single thought of staying with our People*
>>*had touched the Sorrowful Man.*

>*So now no thought of following him*
>>*touched the mind of the People.*

>*Rather, they reminded each other . .*

>>*"THAT WHICH IS IMPOSSIBLE FOR ONE*
>>*MAY BE POSSIBLE FOR MANY."*

THINKING OF THIS,
>*They wove ropes*
>>*which were long as well as thick*
>>*and with which those who were struck by Ocean*
>>*and washed from their footing*
>>>*might be restrained by others*
>>>*who were more secure.*

>*EVEN SO*
>>*MIGHT THE PEOPLE HELP ONE ANOTHER*
>>*TO ACHIEVE THEIR COMMON PURPOSE.*

>*For these ropes would endure an Ocean's pounding*
>>*and even the grinding of rock against rock,*
>>>*held as they were by the People,*
>>>*touching rock in no way.*

YET IN ANOTHER WAY
>Would the People
>>be independent of one another.

>For the Sorrowful Man had said
>>that the places to sit and eat were few
>>>and the People had heard him.

>"We shall neither sit nor eat in comfort"
>>-- they told one another.

AND SO
   Food was dried for each individual,
     and a small water skin prepared
       so that each walking person carried
        that which was necessary
         for only a few days.

   Nor need any wait for the water skin to come.

AND
   The People ordered themselves
     so that the strongest women
       carried those too small to walk,
     and those with less strength
       walked behind those too small
        to carry a pack,
     and those with least strength
       responsible only for themselves.

   The men also ordered themselves in such a way
     that those two already chosen as strongest
       would lead the People on their Water Path,
        with He Who Stood Forward coming last
         to assure the passage of all.

   Each of these
     carried heavy rope against a storm's mischance
       or a watery passage.

   Then the other men
     arranged themselves evenly among the women,
     and each of these
       took special responsibility
        for maintaining the long rope
         that would unite the whole People
          in their common purpose.

   And some of these carried more water
     than they might need
       so that those whom the Sorrowful Man
        called short of leg
         might have enough.

NOW
    As the People made these preparations,
        they watched the sky and sea,
           measuring the storms,
           counting their passage.

It seemed to them
    that little enough time was allowed
        between one and another
           to walk such a Walk by Waters.

And they spoke much of this,
    wondering what manner of decision
        might ensure a speedier transit.

Till one at last said . .

    "In the Mountains by the Sea
        we walked by sunlight.

    "Yet in the Great Dry Place
        we learned to walk with neither light
           nor heat from the sun.

    "Now perhaps the endurance which we prize
        will aid us.

    "Can we not learn
        to continue quickly by day
           and slowly by night?

    "And will this not relieve us
        of a search for islands,
           even as it encourages us forward?"

BUT
    Some among the People said
        that it is one thing
           to walk an even dryness
               during the dark time,
    and another
        to find a wave washed foothold
           with only the light cast by stars
               for counsel.

UNTIL AT LAST
    The People were agreed that Gives Light
        were worth the carrying
            for the safety and the speed
                they would encourage.

And so it was
        that these sticks which Give Light
        were the last things
            that the People prepared.

NOW DURING THIS TIME
    And with all these preparations,
        the Mother of She of Eight Winters
            came and went.

Sometimes she worked with the People
    and sometimes she left.

ALL UNDERSTOOD
    she cared for Snow on Top.

ALL UNDERSTOOD
    when she said
        that Snow on Top sat within herself
        seeking a special wisdom.

ALL KNEW
    such wisdom would be shared.

AT LAST
    No thing was left undone.
    No thing was yet to be prepared.

Many, many days had passed
    since anyone at all --
        except she who came and went --
           had seen Snow on Top.

They longed to see her,
    to hear her wisdom,
    and to share their pride
        in all they had accomplished.

YET SHE DID NOT COME.

The People waited and prepared,
    questioning She Who Came and Went
        whenever she sat by their fire.

AND YET SHE DID NOT COME.

FINALLY
Each thing planned lay ready to carry,
    bound by thongs into each tight carrying pack,
    protected even from the salt spray
        which would soon frequent their path.

AND YET SHE DID NOT COME.

AS THE PEOPLE GATHERED
To share their contentment
    at all they had accomplished,
        asking each other one more time
           if something else lay forgotten,

She Who Came and Went joined them at their Fire,
    listening
        as they discussed the possibility of storm.

    "If She Whom We Lack were here"
        -- someone said --

    "We could begin
        at the next storm's ending."

Some anger was heard from a People
    who had waited long indeed.

She Who Came and Went
    rose and met their anger
        with her own compassion . .

"You have waited patiently
    for Our Wisdom to come.

"She knows and understands
    your preparations.

"All that might be done
    you have accomplished
        without her counsel.
"Her words she found unnecessary
    and so she sought instead
        her own peaceful understanding.

"She waits now
    for word of your accomplishments.

"With First Light
    I will return with her words."

AND SO SHE LEFT,
    So quickly
        none could question her going
        or ask to understand
            if she whom they awaited
                would come at last.

The early dark
    was filled with counting.

Each who was strong enough
    carried their own pack,
        some with enough
            for those who were yet too small.

Ropes were again hefted
    and Gives Light judged a minor weight
        in view of probable need.

NOW THE PEOPLE WAITED
    Sang each other to sleep
        with some of the old songs,
            and spoke with pride and affection
                for the aging face they hoped to see.

• • •

HOW IS IT FOR A PEOPLE
　when purpose is within grasp,
　　yet they meet again the unexpected?

HOW IS IT FOR A PEOPLE
　who have sustained great sorrow, much loss,
　who come now to a sought-for crossing,
　　and yet
　　　who do not see their expectations?

　IS STRENGTH ENOUGH?
　OR SORROW GREATER?

　DOES PURPOSE SUSTAIN?
　OR DISAPPOINTMENT IMPEDE?

FOR
　She Who Comes and Goes
　　arrived with the morning sunlight . .
　　walking alone as she often had,
　　　and a sad murmur
　　　　washed through the People
　　　and disappointment
　　　　laid a hand on their hearts.

YET THEY WAITED
　patient another day
　　to learn what news approached.

YET THEY WAITED
　gathering close together
　　so that all may hear.

YET THEY WAITED,
　and watched the approaching footsteps
　　of one they knew.

At an unhurried pace
yet full of purpose
she approached . .

Her younger footsteps
in marked contrast
to those most recently remembered,
and a gentle fear began to touch
the thoughts of the People.

AND THOSE WHO NOTICE SUCH THINGS
Remembered a flagging step.

BUT
She Who Came and Went
continued her approach.

And the People saw in her a confident spirit.

THOSE WHO NOTICE SUCH THINGS
SAW EVEN MORE . .

For they saw
a woman grown firm and purposeful
in the shade of whitened hair.

And they understood
here came a daughter
for one they knew and so admired.

So that her approach
marked a change in the hearts of the People.

AND THOSE WHO NOW LISTENED
WERE NOT THE SAME
AS THOSE WHO HAD LOOKED.

FOR
    She Who Came and Went
        approached the People.

BUT
    Daughter of Wisdom
        now stood before them to speak.

    No one present was heard to whisper.

    Silent listening
        was the mark of their respect.

THE PEOPLE LISTENED
    Heard her speak
        of flagging footsteps
            and White Hair bent with age.

    Ocean crossing with no place sure for foothold,
        and new beginnings beyond an Ocean's flow.

    Salt tears greeted every word,
        and yet they listened in silence.

    For Daughter of Wisdom
        spoke of purpose and careful planning,
            ordered council and wise arrival.

    SHE SPOKE OF THE PEOPLE.

SO IT WAS
    The People learned
        that Snow on Top had watched them from afar,
            growing daily weaker,
                and more concerned
        that the People -- seeing her --
            might turn from their purpose
                to care for her
            or find another path
                more easily walked by a halting step.

SO
    Secure in the knowledge
        that She Who Came and Went brought to her,
            she had sat within herself
                seeking some parting counsel,
                seeking her own peace.

She had come to understand
-- Daughter of Wisdom now said for her --

How a People might achieve
even the most difficult task.

There was no wisdom she might show them
that they had not already shown one another,

So for their present purpose
she had no counsel,
save her judgment
that they were well prepared.

BUT
For their arrival on the other side of ocean,
she saw much
that might be taken with them . .

"Take with you"
-- she counseled --

"The habit
of ordered purpose . .

"Decide and Do
an early morning song . .

"Nor leave behind
the need for ordered council,
a careful ear
to hear your brother's heart.

"Do not let sorrow
be your only gathering.

"Arrive at purpose
in even pleasant times.

"Define some task,
and let the People answer it.

"Do not let skill in easefulness
slip away.

"SO THAT YOUR CHILDREN,
AND AFTER THEM THE CHILDREN,

WILL FIND A PATH
MORE EASILY DEFINED . .

"THEIR CONSTANT JOY
AN ORDERED WAY OF LEARNING

FROM ALL THEY SEE
AND EVERYONE AROUND."

THEN
>Daughter of Wisdom paused
>>-- and all understood
>>>they heard another voice through her --

>"There is more yet"
>>-- she told them --

>"But I am cautioned to speak again
>>beyond the Ocean."

AND THEN
>The People were glad
>>that they had made such careful provision
>>>for Daughter of Wisdom,
>>placed her among them
>>>so that she was well protected by strength,
>>>>for she now took a double place.

ALL UNDERSTOOD
>that Snow on Top
>>had released her spirit
>>>rather than be carried by the People.

FOR SURELY
>Daughter of Wisdom would never leave her
>>while she walked.

THEY FELT GREAT SADNESS.

AND YET
>Many days had passed
>>since they had seen their old companion.

>They had grown accustomed
>>to relying on one another.

ALL
>respected her decision,
>perceived the change in Daughter of Wisdom.

AND -- for all their love --
   None thought light the task
      of carrying even the most joyful bundle
        along the path
          that Sorrowful Man described.

AND SO
   They sang a gentle sorrow,
     for a life well lived and kindly given.

   Seeing the resolute face of Daughter of Wisdom,
     none questioned the wisdom by their side.

THEY SANG
   through the night of their sorrow . .

AND THEN
   THE NEXT STORM CAME.

The Second Principal Telling

The Crossing
A Forest of Mountains
They Walk Beyond
The Southern Path:

Two Strong Brothers
Circles on the Earth
The Way West
The Water Walking People
Ancient Songs
Beginning Song
Who Are the Human Beings
How We Came to Value Age
They Dwell in Round Houses
Ocean Again
Growing Woman

The Way East -- Sad Partings

The Crossing

FOR THREE DAYS
    The sky was dark over an angry ocean.

Winds carried a sharp and colder rain
    against all that intervened.

The People sheltered one another
    against this force,
        making no attempt to maintain an open fire,
            for soon their purpose would warm them.

"We will build our next Central Fire
    on the Great Island That Lies Beyond"
        -- He Who Stood Forward told the People
        as he walked among them.

Three days of cold
    made the People even more anxious to begin.

And the first visible sun rise
    was greeted by a glad shout.

    "Who sees the sun?"
        -- a small one sang out.

And many rose to dance this happy sight.

ALL UNDERSTOOD
    The foolishness of drying clothing
        so soon exposed to constant salton spray.

No word was spoken.

As if in ancient dance
    the People soon assembled,
        gathered all provisions to them,
        and ordered themselves
            according to their purpose.

Some wind still blew,
    but the storm was gone,
        and no one saw the wisdom of delay.

Gathering as they had devised,
the People made of themselves
a Great Rope,
stretching from one end to the other
of a Whole People.

Understanding themselves as interconnected,
they understood themselves as strong,
strong enough, perhaps, for Ocean.

JUST AT THE EDGE OF OCEAN
He Who Stood Forward
stepped toward the People one more time
and spoke --

"You see how it is"
-- he said --

"For one who ventures to stand forward?
He shall one day therefore come last!"

AND
All the People laughed,
laughed at a new beginning
with an old friend,
laughed at their understanding of how it is
that any who take a special responsibility
among the People
may, therefore, come last of all,
laughed at their own understanding
of themselves as a Whole People.

Their sense of purpose
and their willingness to begin
joined them in laughter
toward their chosen path.

"LET US BEGIN"
-- He Who Stood Forward called out --
and

"LET US BEGIN"
-- the Two Strong Men called back --
stepping out upon the rocks,
closer now to ocean.

AND
> *None thought of an Ocean Mountain,*
> > *but of the Great Island That Lay Beyond*
> > *and of how they strove*
> > > *with Daughter of Wisdom among them*
> > > *and carried Ancient Wisdom in their hearts.*

NOW
> THIS WAS THE MANNER OF THEIR CROSSING . .

Two Strong Men came first,
> carrying with them
> > enough of the woven rope
> > > to make a hand-held bridge
> > > > across any open waters.

Behind them in ordered sequence
> came the People,
> > with the strongest here and there
> > > to lend the strength they had
> > > > toward the survival
> > > > > of the Whole People.

It was their thought that a broken rope
> might once again be knotted,
> > providing only
> > > that someone with energy enough
> > > > stood nearby and filled with purpose.

Daughter of Wisdom
> walked the path set down by others,
> > describing with her own footsteps
> > > the path for those who followed her.

AND
> *although the People saw themselves*
> > *as keepers of this valuable person,*
> *so also did she see herself*
> > *as Keeper of her People.*

AND SO IT WAS
    That her strong hands,
        grown accustomed to a joyful burden,
            found easy now the task of helping others.

    And many whose legs were short
        or whose strength
            was overwhelmed by circumstance
                found those hands easing their Path,
                encouraging them on toward a Great Island,
                    lit as it should be by the Central Fire
                        the People purposed.

AND AFTER ALL OF THESE,
    after each of the women,
    after each of the men,
    after the weak and the strong,
        old and young,
    after all the varying people
        who called themselves One Together,
    after all these
        came He Who Stood Forward,
            as strong in his purpose
                as those who led,
            leading -- as Wisdom often does --
                from the last place among the People.

FOR HIS STEPS FOLLOWED,
    BUT HIS THOUGHTS PRECEDED THE PEOPLE,
        calling back and forth,
        signaling each other of an easeful path,
            a difficult crossing.

THEY ACTED TOGETHER
    to assure that none might meet surprise.

No sudden ocean washing here . .
    for surely
        some one would see it
            and -- thinking of the Whole People --
                call out of oceans coming.

AND SO IT WAS
  That the Two who came first,
  He who came last,
  And She who secured the middle
    set a pace
      the Whole People could maintain,
    called out
      to remind each other of the value
        of a Whole People's perception,
          the chanted notice of passage --
            secure or insecure . .

  REMINDING EACH OF THE UNITY OF ALL.

THE PEOPLE WALKED AS ONE --

AND AS ONE
  THEY FOUND CONTINUANCE.

NOW ALL KNEW
 That a steady, rhythmic pace
  was more easily maintained.

 And -- toward this end --
  the Two Strong Men
   maintained unceasing forward vigilance.

 For even in those crossings where water
  was without the benefit of convenient rock,

 Even in those places
  it was their purpose
   to maintain a steady pace.

AND SO
 The word went back,
  "A water crossing coming."

 And one of the Two Strong Men
  would walk or swim the path,
   lashing his rope
    to some beyond projection,
   assuring the People
    a guided, rope-taut path.

 And the other Strong Man
  secured the first one's passage,
   binding his rope to rock and to himself.

EVEN IN TIMES
 When water washed too strongly,
  sweeping the first beyond his chosen path,

EVEN THEN
 Did the purpose of a People evidenced by rope,
  binding all together,
   retain and gather to them
    the first of the Two Strong Men.

FOR
    If one rope would not hold,
        the other -- bound round his waist
            and around the waist of his brother --

    THAT ROPE WOULD HOLD.

    And his brother --
        held not only by his own strength
            but by the strength of all the People
                who purposed to leave no one behind . .

    That secured brother
        would pull him back --
            back from an ocean's washing,
            back from a very long passage home
                beneath the crest of Ocean.

AND SO
    Each water bridge
        was fashioned by Two Strong Men,
            assisted as they were by all the People,
        nor did even the smallest
            shrink from assisting his brother.

    For no one wanted to return,
        like the Sorrowful Man,
            bereft of a Whole People
                for want of timely care.

AND AFTER THEM ALL
    Continued to come He Who Stood Forward,
        nor did he permit
            even the most faint of heart
                to slow their step,
        but found some word to cheer them,
            or someone nearby
                to lend a help-filled hand.

    And Daughter of Wisdom
        sometimes sang a phrase from an ancient song,
            reminding the People who they were,
            reminding them of new beginnings
                for an ancient way.

AND
    THE PEOPLE STRUGGLED ON.

FOR SURELY I TELL YOU NOW
    THEIR STRUGGLE WAS GREAT!

Even the words of the Sorrowful Man
    were less than this new reality.

So much less
    that the People often thought his Great Storm,
      or perhaps the ones that followed,
        tore away more of a rocky crossing
          than That One had remembered.

SEVERAL TIMES
    Did the People meet a swimming pathway.
    No rock here to guide a tiring foot.

SEVERAL TIMES
    One or the other of the Two Strong Men
      strove forth,
        swimming against an Ocean current,
      carrying with him
        the hope of a Whole People,
      securing with rope
        the children's children's path.

FOR
    WHO WILL COME AFTER
    A PEOPLE DROWNED BY OCEAN?

    WHO WILL FIND FOOTPRINTS
    IN AN OCEAN'S SHADOWED DEPTHS?

AND
    WHERE ARE THE SONGS
    FROM YESTERDAY'S OCEAN SORROW?

AND YET
  NONE OF THE PEOPLE FELL.
    THEY WALKED ON.

    Struggling with ropes and sharpened rock,
    carrying packs
      filled with the possibility of Tomorrow,

    THEY WALKED ON.

    Clinging to rock and to each other,
      mindful of an Ocean's changing,

    THEY WALKED ON.

    UNTIL AT LAST
      the land broadened again
        and they had hope of enough.

NOW
   THE PEOPLE HESITATED.

Faced by a wider island,
   they hesitated.

No longer accustomed to an easeful pathway
   they hesitated,
      until He Who Stood Forward
         perceived their dilemma . .

"Let us say"
   -- he called out --

"That this
   is the first of our Ocean crossings.

"Let us say"
   -- he counseled --

"That many more lie ahead.

"In that manner"
   -- he suggested --

"None but pleasant surprises await us!"

AND
   The People laughed to hear such wisdom.

Their fatigue somehow diminished
   against the broadened pathway,
      they continued in their purpose,
         maintained their steady pace.

THREE DAYS
  Had passed
    in this first of the ocean crossings.

THREE DAYS
  Of washing waters and swimming forward,
  Of scant provisions and narrow footholds.

THREE DAYS
  Of constant movement toward their purpose,
    no less purposeful once sky grew dark.

  Their footsteps
    guided by the light they carried with them,
      stars to remind them
        of the distant Central Fire
          which lit their mountains by the sea,
          which might yet light
            another Great Island,
            another soft sand shore.

  Remembering the Sorrowful Man,
    none suggested they rest even here,
      here where the path grew broader,
      here where the ocean
        no longer touched their feet.

THEY WALKED ON
  But in this more easeful passage
    found more possibility of food,
      an easier way to share water.

  And still they measured their provisions,
    maintaining much to ease their future path.

  FROM LIGHT TO LIGHT
    THEY CONTINUED.

  AND THEN
    THE LAND
      NARROWED ONCE AGAIN.

What had become a group walking
became a line of people once again.

Footholds were once more painfully sought
and maintained with difficulty.

A path
that had become easy enough
for even the smallest to walk
required assistance
one to the other again.

BUT THE PEOPLE WENT ON
Comforted by the knowledge
of the great difficulties
they had met and yet survived,

THEY WENT ON
Secure in the thought
that the People might yet find a path
through any difficulty.

NOW
It was rock they walked,
nor any cushioned earth
to ease their footfall.

Sometimes still
the path seemed easier to walk.

Then jagged rock ensued
with few places for a foot of any size.

UNTIL THEY CAME AT LAST
to what seemed to be the end
of their long journey,
for ahead of them
lay only open water.

SEE HOW IT WAS FOR THEM . .

A WHOLE PEOPLE
   clinging to rock grown slick with moss
      and with an ocean's ceaseless washing,
   sustained each by the other,
   guided and assured by strength and wisdom
      from within and without,
   watching their bridges built before them
      one by one
         with rope and strength and purpose.

Suspended between sea and sky
   to watch Their Strength,
      bound fast to the People,
         carrying with him the Life Line
            that would secure their passage,
      washed from his footing
         to be at one with Ocean,
      pulled back by another Strength
         to go forth once again . .

SUSTAINING EACH OTHER
   ACROSS A HAND ROPE BRIDGE,
      the youngest, the oldest,
      the weakest, the strongest.

THE TWO STRONG MEN
   Already stood at the water's edge
      seeking some means of passage.

Rock lay beyond,
   but through a pounding surf
      and swirling waters.

Even the longest of the ropes
   woven by the People
      would be insufficient to this task.

BUT
   The People waited,
      assured by the many previous crossings
         that a way would be found,
      assured by the strength of these two,
         which seemed to grow with each passage,
            neither hunger nor fatigue
               taking their toll.

AT FIRST
    They only tested the waters,
        searching for sustaining rock below.

    Some means
        of passing the spray-filled waters
          must be devised
        and a stretch of rope long enough
          to accommodate the swirling waters
            must be assured.

THE TWO STRONG MEN
    Strove through the waters,
        sustaining each other
          through every danger,
        preserving the People's way
          by preserving each other,
        building a water path
          to sustain even the smallest one.

AND THE PEOPLE WAITED
    Clinging to slippery rock,
        lashed here and there as projections allowed,
          awaiting the sustained pathway.

    AND THE TWO MEN SEARCHED
        learning the nature of rock and ocean,
        discerning the pattern of Ocean washing,
        deciding the future of a rock-strewn path.

AND
    This was the nature of their discovery . .

    At the foot of the rock on which they stood,
        surf pounded on a shallow rock bed.

    The water here was strong
        and the direction of the surf so variable
          that little could be done
            to predict its way.

Beyond that pounding surf
    lay a shallow shelf of rock,
        ocean washing strongly over it
    so that to stand or walk thereon
        seemed improbable.

Beyond that
    lay a broader rock shelf
        over which ocean washed with less purpose,
    so that here a rope-taut bridge
        was all the people would require.

AND BEYOND THAT
    lay a short distance
        of few if any rocks at all,
            scattered here and there,
                providing no continuous footing
                    for any of the People.

AND BEYOND EVEN THAT
    lay another rock island
        similar to the one on which they stood,
            which might be approached
        only with extreme difficulty
            as the cliff face was sharp,
    and even the lower face in-set,
        ground away by an ocean's washing,
    so that the cliff above
        extended over the water below.

HE WHO STOOD FORWARD
    Came forward now
        and assisted the Two Strong Men
        in their search.

FOR SURELY I TELL YOU NOW
    that even as every previous water passage
        had been swum by just one man,
            sustained as he was by his companion,
    so could this passage
        never be swum by just one man . .
            however strong . .
    for the water washing and the length of rope
        made this beyond any man's reach.

BUT
  THAT WHICH IS IMPOSSIBLE FOR A FEW
    MAY BE POSSIBLE FOR MORE . .

  AND THESE THREE
    working together
      assisted often by any of the People
        who saw the possibility . . .

  EVEN THESE THREE
    devised a path across unceasing water,
    devised a path for the young and the old,
      the strong and the short of leg,

  DEVISED A PATH
    THAT A WHOLE PEOPLE MIGHT FOLLOW.

FOR I TELL YOU NOW,
  THESE THREE WISE MEN
    secured a rope
      to a rock outcropping submerged below Ocean
        at the edge of the broader rock shelf,
    secured this rope at a point
      where the water's washing was less
        and the hope of a foothold more,
    secured this rope
      beyond the reach
        of pounding surf and ocean running fast,
      beyond the reach
        of Ocean that tears foot from rock,
      beyond this danger.

  AND
    when the People saw this security
      they gave a loud cry.

FOR SURELY
  They saw the two Strong Men
    standing rock solid against an ocean's course
  And they knew
    that such security for strength
      might be replicated
        for even the smallest of the People
          with the assistance of all.

THE PEOPLE SAW HOPE
  BUT THEY NOT YET SAW POSSIBILITY.
For between them and this security
  lay surf and racing ocean.

How one might find passage
  through this barrier
    they not yet understood.

NOW
  HE WHO STOOD FORWARD
    placed himself at the highest point of cliff
      from which one might see.

Hauling in the other end of rope,
Pulling it with great difficulty
  through the ocean current,
    he began the process of securing this rope
      to the top edge of the cliff face.

THE PEOPLE NOT YET SAW HIS PURPOSE
  Thinking he planned to discover some other route,
    they waited.

But He Who Stood Forward
  continued in his task,
    securing the rope above the reach of water
  so that it formed a suspended curve
    from cliff top to rock shelf.

AND YET
  THE PEOPLE DID NOT UNDERSTAND.

NOW
 The People saw one among them,
  a man also noted for his strength,
   binding himself to this curved rope,
   allowing foot and hand and binding
    to slow his descent
     from high cliff to underwater shelf.

 Slowing himself in this manner,
  he walked rope through air,
   suspended
    from this hand-woven bridge over water
    to the safer shelf beyond.

NOW
 The People were puzzled,
  some giving a joyful shout
   seeing a new pathway,
  others seeing only danger
   and a sudden drop to ocean.

BUT
 when a second rope
  was laid across the broader shelf
 and a foothold
  found at the base of the next cliff face
   away from the strongest ocean waters,

AND
 when he who first walked a sky path
  found his way up the cliff face,
   securing rope for all the People,

AND WHEN THAT ONE
 stood on the top
  of Cliff-Face Beyond Reach . .

THEN
 did all the People give a great shout --
  nor did any doubt they would prevail
   and cross this one more water passage.

GLAD THEY WERE NOW
    For the careful planning,
        the arrangement of one person after the other
            so that appropriate assistance lay at hand.

    Those men selected first
        to give aid
            to women carrying or assisting
                the short of leg,
        now carried those same ones,
            and the women were glad of this change.

    For the People one by one
        filed down this sky path,
            clinging to the unity of the People,
        bound to their sustained purpose,
        aided one by the other.

    And when that broader, underwater shelf
        was reached . .
    The People clung to a second rope,
        this second hand-bridge to sustain the People,
            and made their way slowly through Ocean,
                waist deep in the moving waters,
        arriving at last at the foot of cliff --
            lifted, some of them,
                like loose bundles up the cliff face --
            others climbing with hands and feet and knees,
                coming at last
                    to the top edge of the next cliff,
                resting there
                    and aiding those who yet climbed.

    AND
        the last of the People
            to make this water crossing,
        the last to walk the sky path,
        the last to reach the rock shelf,
        the last to climb the cliff face --

    THE LAST OF THESE
        WAS HE WHO STOOD FORWARD,
            FOLLOWING AFTER HIS PEOPLE,
            ASSURING ALL WAS WELL.

IT WAS THEN
That the People saw the risk he had taken.

Untying the rope from its secure position,
he walked the sky path
along a less secure line.

Reaching the rock shelf,
three strong men pulled this sky path rope
until it loosened itself
from its rock mooring,
secured only by a sitting rock.

Gathering this rope to them,
they unbound the end
near which they stood
and swam, walked, and struggled their way
across the broadened pathway,
bringing the Life Lines of the People
as they came.

AND

ALL THE PEOPLE UNDERSTOOD
IT WAS WITH NO SMALL RISK
TO THEMSELVES
THAT THEY DID SO.

AND

The People grew silent,
touching their thanks
to the Three Strong Men
who climbed at last
this top of cliff.

Thirty-five of the People
    were strong enough to carry packs . .

Seventeen more
    were not yet so strong,
        and three of these
            must be always carried.

THESE WERE THEY
    who crossed Walk by Waters,

THESE WERE THEY
    whose unceasing movements
        carried the possibility of Tomorrow
            from one Great Island to another,

THESE WERE THEY
    who laid out our path
        on the back of Turtle Island.

FOLLOWING THIS WATER PATH
THEY GAVE US THE GIFT
    OF TOMORROW

Thirty-five of the People
    were strong enough to carry packs.

Seventeen more
    were not yet so strong,
        and three of these were carried.

NO MORE THAN THIS.

YET A WHOLE PEOPLE
    Who understood their unity,
        understood how it is
            when none
                are chosen to be left behind,

A WHOLE PEOPLE
    walked a slippery path
      through a washing Ocean,
        carrying each with them,
      assisting each
        as circumstance required.

THESE WERE THEY
    who now stood
      on the back of a rock island,
        looking toward Tomorrow,
    their Walk by Waters
      a song to be remembered,
    their difficult passage
      a thing they once had done.

FOR I TELL YOU NOW
    No further water paths
      stood between them
        and the Great Island beyond.

Along rock they climbed.

Sometimes water washed,
    but never again requiring assistance
      one to the other,
        save from time to time
      for those the Sorrowful Man
        called short of leg.

THEY THOUGHT MUCH OF HIM
That Sorrowful Person.

HOW MIGHT IT HAVE BEEN
    for him and for his People
      had only someone
        come to mark the path
          with cries of warning.

HOW MIGHT IT HAVE BEEN
    for the People themselves
      had no such person intervened.

FOR SURELY
    they would have prepared
        for little food and less water

AND SURELY
    the thought
        of slippery rocks and falling people
            would have caused the weaving of ropes.

BUT WHO AMONG THEM
    Would envision such vast expanses of open Ocean,
    the rise and fall thereof
        making every rock a torrent.

WHO AMONG THEM
    would choose such a path,
        save for the thought
    that the Sorrowful One's People
        survived all but a storm,
            carrying too little rope
                and too little unity with them.

BUT IT WAS THE PEOPLE'S THOUGHT
That a great joining of strengths
*   along a carefully woven rope line*
*   might sustain them each*
*   and, therefore, sustain them all*
*   toward the Great Island*
*   they sought together.*

AND SO
*   THEY WOVE THEIR ROPES*
*   LONGER*
*   THAN ANYONE HAD SEEN BEFORE.*

*   LONG ENOUGH*
*   to sustain a Whole People*
*   through a perilous water crossing.*

*   LONG ENOUGH*
*   to reach from one great island*
*   to another that lay beyond.*

*   LONG . . ENOUGH.*

*LET US DANCE
    THE ACCOMPLISHMENT
        OF A WHOLE PEOPLE.*

*LET US SING
    OF WISDOM
        AND OF PERSEVERANCE.*

*LET US REMIND ONE ANOTHER
    OF THE GIFT
        THEY HAVE GIVEN US.*

*FOR WE . .
    ARE THE CHILDREN'S
        CHILDREN'S
            CHILDREN.*

NOW
The People
continued to walk with great care,
as none could say
there were no more water pathways.

ALL KNEW
That as the oceans came and went
islands formed and went away again . .

So that all saw
their path might cross one more island --
and water beyond.

BUT NO WATER CAME.

Ocean grew closer and farther away
on either hand,

BUT NO WATER CAME.

AND WHEN AT LAST
The People reached a broad expanse of land,
covered with low-growing bushes,
it seemed to them a good place
to rest and gather strength
for whatever lay ahead.

BUT THE LAND CHANGED LITTLE.

FOR MANY DAYS
The people walked across this land
of nothing growing tall,

BUT THE LAND CHANGED LITTLE.

That which grows low and catches the feet
grew everywhere,
nor was water in any way lacking.

For the earth here was beyond damp.
Drops of water spangled all that grew
and pools of water lay everywhere.

NOTHING WAS DRY.

This far away from Ocean,
    each of the People
        tried to spread out their clothing in the sun
          whenever they were resting.

But the sun shone through a murky sky
    and the earth
        was so covered here and there by water
          that none of the People
        found that which is dry a possibility.

"Ocean does not want to let us go"
    -- someone said.

And all the People laughed.

BUT
    It was a sad laugh,
        for all sought the comfort
          of that which is dry
            and a warm fire.

YET
    Everything here was wet
        and would not burn.

Nor could the People see ahead
    anything more pleasing.

No place was found
    where the People
        might find comfort in which to wait
          while those who chose to Go and See
            might travel and return.

AND SO
    The People walked as one
        with little warning of what lay ahead.

Nor did the land in any way change,
    remaining the same
        with only a slight rise to the North
        and lessening damp
          that accompanied that rise.

STILL NOTHING WAS DRY

So that the People grew weary
 of the constant damp,
  and warmth was difficult to achieve.

AT LAST
 They came to rest
  just below the crest of a ridge.

 Here at least no standing water,
  and some shelter from wind.

 They made warmth for themselves
  with their own bodies,
   remembering a time
    when they did so out of lack of water
    and wondering which was best.

 For here comfort was less,
  but thirst was less also,
   and none lay still upon the earth
    of any part of Walk by Waters.

 FOR THREE DAYS
  the People waited for those among them
   who chose to Go and See.

 FOR THREE DAYS
  they sought food of any kind
   and wood dry enough to burn.

  AT LAST
   they learned
    that some of the thicker stems
     of that which grows low
      would make a small fire.

 But nothing they found
  grew flames large enough
   to dry their sodden clothing.

FOR THREE DAYS THEY WAITED.

AND IT SEEMED TO THEM
 The land they left
  was better than the land they found,
   though the difficulty
    of the achieved crossing
     still pleased them.

AND THEN
    The others returned,
        bringing with them
           what little food they found.

"Beyond this"
    -- they said --

"Lies again and again as much."

"This is a damp land
    and nowhere can you stretch out your hand
    and touch that which grows.

"Perhaps at the edge of what we can see
    lie the implications of mountains,
        but far enough off
           so that no one can be sure.

"No change in the land is anywhere seen,
    so that it is clear
        the People must learn
           to sustain themselves hereon --
    or learn to fly to the edge of mountain."

NONE OF THE PEOPLE
WERE GLAD TO HEAR IT.

    Even in their most difficult circumstance
    some sort of tools lay at hand.

YET HERE
    They saw none --
        or what they saw
           seemed less than apparent need.

BEFORE THEM
    Stretched a panorama of not enough,
        a bleak land hung with mist
           at the end of their long quest.

AND SOME AMONG THE PEOPLE
    Began to speak of return,
        for such a difficult pathway
           seemed deserving of a better end.

YET OTHERS
Would not consider
another such Walk by Waters,
and among these were those
with responsibility for the young.

"Shall the children's children's children
say we are a People
strong enough for Walk by Waters,
but too weak for a disconsolate march?"
-- one of these asked.

AND THE PEOPLE SPOKE MUCH TO ONE ANOTHER.

Yet no sound was yet heard
from any of those who stood forward.

AT LAST
The People were resolved
to continue to the implication of mountains,
so that all might judge the path.

And as they walked,
the food grew less,
as that which they gathered and dried
on the other side of Walk by Waters
began to disappear
and not enough was seen
to take its place.

FOR THE PEOPLE NOT YET KNEW THIS LAND.

NEITHER DID THEY UNDERSTAND
The nature of possible food.

Walking made it difficult to place snares
-- which must be returned to --
and the small things
that ran through that which grows low
were unfamiliar to them.

NEITHER DID THEY UNDERSTAND
The roots which might be edible,
but began to gnaw at this and that
to learn what might give benefit.

IT WAS NOT A JOYFUL MARCH
    For the sun was seldom seen,
        and the mists would not go away.

    Pools of water were fewer
        and the land showed them a slight rise.

    But that which grows low did not change
        and the People grew discouraged.

THEN
    They came to the implication of mountains,
        beyond which no Go and See had yet essayed,

    And the People gave a sad cry --
        for the implication was slight,
            nor in any way could the distance
                or the nature of mountains be judged
        for the land shaped in ways
            that were not familiar to them
                and their old understandings
                    guided them in no way.

SEEING THEIR INDECISION,
    Daughter of Wisdom sat down
        and began a quiet song . .

    "I wonder how far it is to mountain"
        -- she sang --

    "And which of the People
        shall be first to arrive."

BUT
    Some of the People grew restive.

    Seeing such a distance
        between them and possible change
            in this land of little food,
        their hearts grew empty within them,
            and their eyes grew sad.

    No possible way of finding enough
        occurred to them

And some
    began to talk again of return,
      leaving behind, perhaps,
        those of other purpose.

BUT
    Daughter of Wisdom looked in her heart
      and saw the people
        struck by an enervating sadness,
    too little food
      to sustain joy in such a dismal land.

She thought of Mountains by the Sea,
    as Snow on Top had shown her to do,
      and what might be learned therefrom.

"I AM THINKING"
    -- she said at last --

"Of how it was in our former land.

"Of how morning mist
    sometimes hung in the air close to ocean,
      but beyond ocean, toward mountain,
        the mists were not.

"I AM THINKING"
    -- she continued --

"That beyond these mists
    lay a vast mountain land,
      full of that which to eat,

"And beyond even this
    the land changed again
      to become
        what we call the Great Dry Place.

"AND I AM THINKING"
    -- she concluded --

"That any dryness at all
    might be greeted with greater joy here
      than any knew there!"

ALL THE PEOPLE UNDERSTOOD HER
When she spoke of change
and the great surprise
that sometimes
waited over the next ridge.

FOR THESE WERE A PEOPLE
who had walked far --
and across many difficulties.

THESE WERE A PEOPLE
who had achieved purpose
and a determined future.

THESE WERE A PEOPLE
who had learned to choose and to prepare,
with little time
for learning the nature of things.

THESE WERE A PEOPLE
WHO HAD LEARNED
TO LISTEN TO ONE ANOTHER.

AND YET THEY HESITATED.
Kinder possibilities
danced in their eyes.

AND YET THEY HESITATED.

DAUGHTER OF WISDOM SAW THIS
and knew to speak to their heart . .

"LISTEN TO ME"
  -- she arose and spoke at last --

"FOR I WILL SHOW YOU
  WHAT IS IN MY HEART.

"We have spoken little of Ancient Wisdom,
  each knowing she still moves in our hearts.

"Now I will share with you
  her concern for the People.

"She understood this People as Strong,
  and you have heard her.

"Even as she spoke of ordered council,
  even then, she understood this People
    as one which could learn from one another
      such a device.

"She watched you from her distant place
  and grew content with your proceedings.

"She understood this People
  as one
    who had learned to listen to one another.

"But she also understood
  the difficulty
    of a purpose sustained beyond expectation.

"And she wondered what might happen
  if the land beyond Walk by Waters
    proved more difficult
      than that which preceded.

"And a People
  who have overcome such great difficulty
    might find small difficulty
      harder to sustain.

"I AM THINKING NOW
  of how it was
    at the Great Water Crossing
  and how He Who Stood Forward risked much
    to retrieve a rope
      woven so carefully by the People,
    retrieved it with the thought
      that even more such water crossings
        might lie ahead.

"During this walk,
  his rope has carried us only over puddles.

"YET I SAY
  that this rope still binds a Whole People.

"I SAY
  that many greater water crossings
    may lie ahead.

"For in these implications of mountains
  may not great streams thunder?

"AND
  who will lack a rope to cross them,
    or a way of binding life to life?

"SURELY NOT THIS PEOPLE,
  NOT THIS WALK BY WATER PEOPLE."

DAUGHTER OF WISDOM
  paused to consider the changes
    in the faces around her . . .
    and then went on . .

"WHICH OF YOU REMEMBERS"
  -- she asked --

"How it was
  for us in the Great Dry Place,
    and who it was
      who spoke of Walk by Waters,
    and how it was she spoke?

"WHICH OF YOU REMEMBERS"
   -- she went on --

"The very words of Ancient Wisdom,
   how it was
     that hcr old eyes
       longed to see
         the Great Island That Lay Beyond?

"WHICH OF YOU UNDERSTANDS"
   -- she intoned --

"The great sadness which filled those old eyes
   when she saw how it was for her People,
     how a joyful bundle
       had become too much to carry,
       how a slowly diminished Walk by Waters
        had become too narrow to sustain her?

"YET IT WAS HER WISH
   THAT HER OLD EYES
     MIGHT SEE THIS LAND.

"I CANNOT GO"
   -- she told me --

"BUT
   perhaps these old eyes
     can make such a journey . .
   perhaps young legs
     can carry old eyes . .
   perhaps the potential of vision at least
     can accompany the People.

"She asked me to sit with her
   until her Spirit
     left its Earth Clothing behind.

"AND
       -- as she asked me -- so I did.

"Sat with Ancient Wisdom,
       she who was too wise to deter her People,
       too aware of the difficulties ahead,
       too understanding of limitations.

"As she asked,
       I waited, and
              -- as she asked --
       when that wise Spirit returned,
              leaving her Earth Self behind,
       I took with me that double gift of vision
              and promised them no ordinary place.

"Shall these eyes"
       -- she asked,
              drawing from her sacred pouch
                     a carefully wrapped package --

"Find a place such as this their home?

"FOR SURELY
       EVEN IF WE CHOOSE TO RETURN,
              THESE EYES
                     REMAIN ON THIS GREAT ISLAND.

"Shall they not find a mountain home
       from which one sees the land that lies beyond?

"Shall This One not keep her word,
       offering sight
              to a distant, valued Spirit?

"I TELL YOU NOW"
       -- she concluded --

"IF ANY OF THE PEOPLE HESITATE,
       THIS ONE DOES NOT!
       THIS ONE . . .
              WALKS TO THE MOUNTAINS!"

Gazing at each face among the People,
    assuring them of her purpose,
        she turned away at last . .
    and strode
        toward those implications of mountains.

   "WHO WALKS WISDOM'S PATH?"
      -- someone called.

AND MORE AND MORE
  THE PEOPLE SPOKE TO GO.

UNTIL AT LAST
  He Who Stood Forward
    -- seeing none were left behind --
     turned his eyes, too,
       toward the probability of mountains

   AND FOLLOWED WISDOM'S PATH.

A Forest Of Mountains

THIS IS HOW IT WAS
   FOR THE PEOPLE . .

Earth soggy under foot,
   clinging still to each forward step.

Sun dim overhead,
   shielding damp clothing
     from the possibility of comfort.

Carriers increasingly devoid
   of wherewith to sustain Life.

   YET OF WATER
   THERE WAS STILL ENOUGH.

Pools among which the People walked
   slowly began to diminish.

Chewing on bits and pieces of bark,
   on leaves with a pleasant taste,

   THE PEOPLE WALKED ON.

Twigs -- as yet too green to sustain fire --
   were placed each evening
     in the center of the Fire Circle.

   "REMINDING US OF PROBABLE TOMORROWS"
   -- Daughter of Wisdom said.

AND
   it was she who insisted
    that all those actions
     necessary to kindle a flame
     be taken
    even though all knew
     that sustained fire
      was impossible in such damp.

   "REMINDING US OF POSSIBLE WARMTH"
   -- she said again.

IT WAS THIS WISDOM
    That some of the People watched,

    This awareness of the possibilities of Tomorrow
        so filled the mind and heart
          of Daughter of Wisdom
        that the very nature of her presence
          disallowed
            those who might otherwise perceive
              only today's melancholy,
              only the sorrows
                of an aching stomach
                and a spinning head.

YET, DAY AFTER DAY,
    Daughter of Wisdom
        set a firm foot on today's path,
          speaking often
            of mountains covered with trees,
        surely those trees
          sheltered many creatures beneath,
        and surely berries and roots
          were there to sustain many of those creatures.

    "And we shall learn again by watching"
        -- she went on --
          asking who would perform this and that task
            when opportunity arose.

AND SO IT CAME TO BE,
    In this land of slowly decreasing waters,
        that Each One focused
          on some special task pleasing to them
            that they would undertake
              where circumstance allowed.

AND DAUGHTER OF WISDOM
    Walked among the People
        cajoling them away from present sorrow
          and toward tomorrow's possibility.

Remembering each self-selected task,
    she would inquire
        into the manner of this and that --
           how This One preferred to craft snares.

UNTIL ALL THE PEOPLE
    Discussed these tasks
        to the exclusion of all else,
           gathering from time to time
               into groups reflective of their focus.

AND
    There were some among the People
        wise enough to discern her purpose . .
        and first among these
           was He Who Stood Forward.

FOR I TELL YOU NOW
    That One understood
        that Daughter of Wisdom
           carried all the People
               across a trackless morass
                   with the strength of her purpose.

NOW IT BECAME HIS PURPOSE
    to carry them
        up the sides of mountains, across ravines,
        toward whatever better place
           might be found for a People
              who had come to prefer
                 sustained residence.

AND SO, FROM TIME TO TIME . . .
    Already accepting this responsibility . .

He Who Stood Forward would comment
    on the increasing proximity of the mountains
        which were at first only implied
           along a distant horizon.

And he began to talk about ascents and chasms,
    valleys and placid streams . .

UNTIL ALL THE PEOPLE
    looked at the same image . .
        a land of difficult crossings . . .
          and quiet rewards,
        strength-measuring climbs . . .
          and secure arrivals.

AND
    they began to discuss, one with another,
        the manner they might employ
           to sustain each other up cliff sides
             as they had sustained each other
                across slippery rock crossings . . .

AND THE TASK
    SEEMED EASIER ALL THE WHILE.

AND DAUGHTER OF WISDOM
Carefully watched each smallest person.

Perceiving a lagging foot,
    she would settle herself with a sigh,
        suggesting
          all might stop
            and wait for her to rest awhile,
        suggesting
          all might nibble a grain
            of this or that
        and drink freely of the so-present water.

Making much of vigorous chewing,
    she would comment on the distance achieved,
        on how a purposeful People walks quickly
          beyond probability,
          past possibility,
          toward achievement.

    "And yet more is achieved"
      -- she would add --
        until the pattern became a song.

"NOW LOOK . . .

"More is achieved
   by a Purposeful People
     than by those
       who see only today
"More Earth is crossed
   by a Purposeful People
     than by those
       who only count stones

"Safe valleys are reached
   by a Purposeful People
     which the purposeless
       never recognize"

MANY PEOPLE
   Sang this song of many verses and one theme,
     each inventing a new way
       to express their understanding.

And some among the People
   were wise enough
     to see the flow of action.

Their startlement
   that one as strong as Daughter of Wisdom
     found rest so frequently necessary
   slowly changed to an understanding
     of how a People
       with little food and less knowledge
         manage to cross a vast land
           of little food and less shelter.

WHERE ANYONE AT ALL
   saw an impossible purpose . .

DAUGHTER OF WISDOM
   perceived possibility . . .
     and carried the People with her
       on the threads of her thought.

NOW
 The horizon slowly rose up
  until it towered above
   each level-eyed person.

 Looking increasingly skyward,
  the People searched
   for Eagle's patterned spiral in the air . .

 Knowing to conclude from this
  the probable scurry
   of four-footed fur bearers --
  those who carry with them
   some food and some warmth
    for a people who hunger
     and who would take joy
      in some additional protection.

AND
 As the mountains slowly approached,
  He Who Stood Forward
   sought the attention of Wisdom's Daughter.

 Catching her gaze at last,
  he carried invisible food to his mouth.

SHE UNDERSTOOD HIS PURPOSE
  and slowly approached
   some of the eagle watchers,
  talking now and again
   about small berries and other fruits
    which might escape the notice
     of those who only watched the sky.

 Focusing in this way their awareness
  without encouraging expectation,
   she modified a sky-gazing people
    into one
     which watched both sky and earth.

AND SOON
   The first berries were found,
      fat and sweet and white in color.

   Too few to sustain a People,
      enough to give them hope.
   And each berry was carefully divided
      into as many pieces as gave each a share,
         leaving two for the Earth --
   so that all the People
      might understand this first gracious gift
         of a new Earth.

AND
   A great shout went up in recognition
      of the sky patterns
         traced by two outstretched wings,
   bringing the People an image of future plenty.

AND
   The hearts of the People were light indeed,
      lifted skyward on wings of perception
         to join Eagle
            in his search for Earth's other bounty.

Eyes now constantly searched the earth
   for traces of vines or four-footed travelers,
      seeking a place to stay and eat
         and gather strength for the mountains
            which walked rapidly toward them.

Few eyes turned to their advancing height.

AND SO IT WAS
   That the People looked at last with amazement
      at the towering rock around them.

   Eyes bent to the ground turned again skyward
      and understood at last
         where Eagle had begun his flight.

TWO EYES AT LEAST
    had watched the approaching mountains
        from the very first day,
            measuring their possibilities,
            understanding the nature
                of the task at hand.

THESE EYES
    had slowly selected the surest path,
        the best access to mountain structure,
    and had led the People instead
        into a rim of vertical rock walls.

Regarding these apparent limitations,
    so abrupt an end
        to so long and tiresome a march . .

THE PEOPLE CRIED OUT IN DESPERATION.

"How will we reach from here
    any accessible valley?"
        -- they asked and asked again.

FOR
    They saw the necessity of finding some space
        better endowed than any so far seen
            with roots and berries
            and the four-footed creatures
                of whom Eagle reminds us.

BUT HE WHO STOOD FORWARD,
    Watching Daughter of Wisdom
    and her careful path,
        had designed a path of his own.

"HOW WILL WE FIND A SOLUTION?"
    -- he asked.

UNTIL SOMEONE SUGGESTED --

"LET US COUNSEL TOGETHER"

AN AWARENESS
>   that safety
>   lay in the coalescence of the group
>   rapidly touched the thoughts
>   of each of the People,
>   gathering them together
>   around possible fire
>   to consult with one another.

AND IT WAS THEN
> That Daughter of Wisdom
>   gave the People one more gift.

"This Council"
> -- she explained --

"Has won its fire center."

AND WITH THAT
> She withdrew a bundle
>   of carefully gathered sticks,
>   guarded during these long days,
>   carried over so much water,
>   and struck fire into their midst.

"A GIFT
> from the Great Island we left behind"
>   -- she explained --

"Gathered for you by Ancient Wisdom.

"BEFORE WE LEFT ONE ANOTHER,
> That One gathered three bundles:
>   one to be lit
>   at the first secure place
>   we reached on land beyond water,
>   one to be lit
>   at our first valley home,
>   and one to be lit
>   when we choose a place to maintain.

"IT WAS MY THOUGHT"
> -- she went on --

"IT WAS MY THOUGHT
>   that until now
>   we had not left the waters behind."

AND ALL LAUGHED
 understanding the piquant humor of her words,
 valuing her apparent confidence
  in their ability to achieve a goal
   much too distant to be possible,
 looking once more
  at the magnitude
   of their present accomplishment.

AND THIS COUNCIL
 Began on just so secure a footing,
  laying out plans for tomorrow's progress,
  assigning tasks to today's children,
  devising a pattern of search
   for a wise mountain access.

FOR I TELL YOU NOW
   THEIR PRESENT LOCATION
     HELD NO GREAT PROMISE!

Dry stone walls reached up on three sides.
   No water ran between them.
     Few bushes and no food lay on every side.

IN NO DIRECTION
   did trees promise
     either shade or a higher place
       from which to view this part of Earth.

"I have been thinking"
   -- He Who Stood Forward said at last --
     seeing dismay in many faces.

"WHAT A GIFT IT IS
   TO BE WHERE WE ARE.'

Satisfied with the startled looks
   he saw around him,
     he went on.

'FOR SO LONG NOW
   we have stood in mist and spray.

   "No thing we recognized was dry.

   "Little protection from any wind
     could be found.

"YET HERE WE ARE NOW"
   -- he continued --
     "Secure against rock walls.
     Protected from any wind.
     Water near at hand.

"A People
   who have only been somewhere
     between damp and dripping
   stand at least on the edge of warmth,
   drying their dampened Spirits
     before the sun's gift of heat
     these walls have so carefully gathered for us."

AND ALL THE PEOPLE SAW
THAT THIS PERCEPTION -- TOO --
WAS PART OF THE WHOLE
WHICH THEY ADDRESSED.

THOSE WITH THE WISDOM TO SEE IT
Gave thought to the careful patience
which enables one of the People
to encourage all of the People
toward a purpose they alone perceive.

THESE ONES GAVE CONSIDERATION
to the quiet thought
that often precedes
the apparent accident of success.

THESE ONES GAVE THANKS
that such persons
as Daughter of Wisdom
and He Who Stood Forward
had been born and learned
and survived among the People . .

THAT THE WHOLE PEOPLE
MIGHT ALSO SURVIVE.

BUT THESE ONES UNDERSTOOD
That daily living
also requires a Whole People to survive.
They saw a water path
crossed by no one at all
had not the Whole People
made that journey.

AND THESE ONES SAW
that sometimes
an individual vision
and sometimes
the general wisdom
are required for survival.

BUT THESE ONES ALSO SAW
  THAT, AS IT REQUIRES TWO FEET
    TO WALK FROM ONE PLACE TO ANOTHER

SO DOES IT ALSO REQUIRE
  TWO WISDOMS
AND THE ONE AND THE OTHER
  COME FROM DIFFERENT SOURCES . .

AND YET
  THEY BOTH COME FROM THE PEOPLE.

AND SO IT IS
  THAT SOME
    LEND A SPECIAL VISION . .

  THAT THE WHOLE PEOPLE
    LEND MANY FEET . .

  THAT THE ONES
    WHO SEE BOTH POSSIBILITIES
      TRULY SUSTAIN A PEOPLE.

  FOR IT IS THESE
    WHO RAPIDLY FOLLOW
      AND THEREFORE ALSO LEAD.

AND
  WITHOUT THESE MIDDLE PERSONS
    OUR PATH
      WOULD BE A HELTER SKELTER
      OF DISPARATE MOTION.

  SO BE IT . . .
    FOR I TELL YOU NOW . . .
      IT IS SO . . .

NOW
    The People
        sat in the middle of a reality
            they seemed only dimly to remember.

    Warmth surrounded them.

    And the pervasive damp
        which had followed them everywhere
            slowly rose skyward
                and returned to its Ocean source.

    Their Council
        seemed filled with accomplishment
            for as they heard one another
                everything around them slowly dried.

AND
    IT WAS THE THOUGHT OF THE WHOLE PEOPLE
        Once all they carried with them
            was dry enough for comfort
                and for preservation --
        to choose a center place closer to the stream.

    IT WAS THEIR THOUGHT
        that whatever might grow
            that could sustain life
                might more easily flourish near water.

    IT WAS THEIR THOUGHT
        that in this land of less accessible water --
            the four-footeds that Eagle implied
                might more easily find their way
                    toward snares set along water trails.

NOW
    The People specified a patterned exploration
        with stream as its center.

    One way and another they searched,
        seeking out roots and berries . .
        slowly evaluating
            the nature of the gifts of a new land.

    Those short in leg
        set snares along water paths,
            learning the nature of those recognizable only
                in that they also lived within a fur skin.

Their patterns, too, were slowly identified.

Similarities to and differences from
    those previously known became slowly apparent
      to those who carefully watched such things.

Those of longer leg
    sought signs of the hard of hoof,
      those for whom Eagle had no regard.
      those who might sustain a Whole People
        for many days.

SLOWLY
    The implications of bounty began to accrue.

Those few stores left to the People
    at the end of such a long crossing
      were still apportioned over many days.

FOR SURELY
    those who survived
      the crossing of the Great Dry Place
        understood the possible effects
        of too rapid a transition
          from one food to another.

Still saving this previous bounty,
    the People were able now
      to sit in the midst of future stores,
        slowly drying
          underneath a more cooperative sun.

AND SLOWLY
    They were able now
      to increase today's sustenance,
        giving each Earth Self time
          to accept the nature of this change,
        remembering the pain
          of those who ate too quickly
            in the New Grass Land.

And strength increased
    and dryness became a custom.

Small creatures came -- from time to time --
    to offer themselves to snares.

But none of the hard of hoof
    were yet located.

AND THIS WAS A GREAT PUZZLE.

"We not yet know"
    -- one of the People pointed out --

"The Nature in this place of the Long Cold
    that must surely follow.

"Yet there is value in preparation.

"And surely
    a People who wove ropes longer
        than ever before envisioned
    have a need to identify shelter
        and the greater stores
            that the hard of hoof provide."

AND SO IT WAS
    That some of the People
        more carefully
            explored the rock walls around them.
                seeking the nature of a sheltered place.

And others of the People
    walked far along possible trails,
        seeking an understanding
            of the possible sustenance
                this New Land might provide.

MANY DAYS PASSED
    And the surrounding air became cool indeed
        before any too large for snares
            were perceived.

There was motion on a distant mountain
    and the memory of this image
        matched markings along the ground
            once this mountain was attained.

JUST BEYOND
    The nature of rock made it difficult
        to follow the patterned wanderings
            of an unseen being.

Yet the markings perceived
    followed dimmer markings
        and the nature of a trail was perceived.

Some among this group of Those Who Sought
    followed the direction
        taken by the last hoof marks,
    their purpose
        to identify possible destination.

Some followed these same marks
    in reverse direction,
        their purpose to identify possible origin.

Some took up watch
    along this first identified trail,
        waiting to learn what might approach
            and offer itself to pointed spears.

BUT IT WAS THOSE
    who sought purpose
    who first began to learn the nature
        of those hard of hoof
            who might inhabit this New Great Island.

For they found solitary marks
    slowly increasing toward a valley
        which only these marks showed them.

AND THEY FOUND
    In a valley of sparse grass --
        a number past twice two hands
            of creatures not before seen.

Twice the weight of Sharp Tusk each carried,
    so that any two of them
        might provide sustenance
            for the Whole People for many days.

Neither could it be seen
    whether these creatures carried with them
        as much of the soft part of meat
            as Sharp Tusk provided
    as an added gift for the Long Cold.

Yet their fur was shaggy
    --indicating a Great Cold yet to be --
        and promising relief therefrom.

It was their nature
    to scatter throughout this valley . .

And since it seemed they had arrived individually,
    it was the thought of those who watched
        that they might all too easily leave
            in a similar manner.

IN NO WAY
    Bringing themselves to the attention
        of those eaters of grass . .

    Two among the watchers
        took word of circumstance
            to the watchers along the trail.

AND SO
    Word gradually reached those
        who sought the origin of the first trail marks . .

    Reached even the Fire Circle by the stream,
        so that all the People
            now sustained a watchful waiting,
                in expectation of the return of those
                    who sought the hard of hoof.

AND THOSE WATCHFUL WAITERS
    At the edge of the grass valley
        maintained a patient silence.

    Waiting for the Great Shaggies
        to show them the nature
            of their movements through the day,
                their patterned dance through Life,
        with which
            these seekers after a different nourishment
                might cooperate
        so as to bring back to the People
            both the reality of Enough Today
            and the possibility of Enough Tomorrow.

FOR SURELY I TELL YOU NOW
THESE ONES UNDERSTOOD
THEIR PRECARIOUS STAND
ON THE EDGE OF A GREAT COLD.

BEFORE THEM
  They saw more than enough
    to sustain a People.

They not yet saw
    any manner of probable transition
      from grass valley to fire circle.

AND THEY UNDERSTOOD
THE POSSIBILITY OF LOSS . .

Great Shaggies disappearing down many paths
    to find other, more distant grass valleys
      which none of the People might ever see.

THERE WERE THOSE
    who spoke for a deep dug pit
      Great Shaggies
        disappearing as if down some chasm.

BUT OTHERS
    spoke of difficulties
      inherent in digging at the edge
        of creatures you chose not to disturb
    and wondered
      about the manner of maintaining quiet
        with such a task at hand.

OTHERS
    spoke of waiting along a chosen pathway,
      pointed spear set firm in the ground.

BUT OTHERS
    spoke of the sounds of alarm
      and how creatures once disturbed
    may develop a certain wariness of action,
      making tomorrow more difficult
        than today.

FROM THESE QUIET DISCUSSIONS,
    The nature of the Need Of the Whole People
      became apparent.

Over many days and much searching
    no other hard of hoof had been seen.

YET
    Where these were found
        surely somewhere there must be others.

So that sustenance for the Whole People,
    until other Great Shaggies were found
        and their nature understood,
    became a long rope
        -- stretching from here to there --
    which must be carefully and quietly woven
        by those who presently devised ways
            to carry enough of the hard of hoof
                from this valley to the Fire Circle.

THEY DISCUSSED
    the nature of silence, of spears,
        and of the digging of pits . .

UNTIL ONE AMONG THEM --
    turning these images
        this way and that way in his mind --
    created a new image,
        never before seen among the People.

Crafting it slowly in his mind,
    he added this element and that
        until he was satisfied within himself
    that such a pattern would enable,
        would form a bridge
            from this valley to the People.

AND YET
    he knew his task was not complete.

UNDERSTANDING THE NATURE OF DISCUSSION
    AND OF THE MANY-VOICES-WISDOM
        THAT CAN ENSUE

He saw his present task
    as that of designing in the air
        a replicate image of his vision
            that all might see.

"Let them then speak"
-- he said to himself --

"Seeing perhaps some reality
that has escaped my thought."

AND SO THEY SPOKE
  ONE AFTER THE OTHER
    in consonance with the pattern of his thought,
      polishing this or that action
    until the whole design
      lay before them --
    a design
      which they never had known before . .
    and yet each element of which
      was recognizable to them.

AND SO THEY DUG -- QUIETLY --
  Not one great pit for shaggies,
    but many small depressions in the earth.

  Each such depression
    was edged with fallen trees and branches,
      gathered slowly
    so as to disturb the Great Shaggies in no way.

  Soft grass was also gathered
    and laid in mounds
      beside the low wall of branches.

AND WHEN AT LAST
  Some familiarity
    with this patterned dance had been gained . .

THREE AMONG THEM
  were selected to watch the whole,
    waiting to see
      when Great Shaggies might stand beside
      each shallow depression,
      each such low branch wall.

AND WHEN AT LAST
   These three adjudged themselves capable
   of wisdom in this regard . .

EACH SEEKER
   settled himself
      within his hollow depression,
   settled himself
      behind his low branch wall,
   settled himself with his spear
      to listen
         for the triple call of Eagle's voice . .

FOR THE DECISION
   to take those steps necessary
      to carry enough Great Shaggies
         from valley to fire circle
            to sustain a Whole People
            through the Great Cold to come.

AND YET LISTEN
   The wisdom inherent in this patterned action
   may be easily seen from here.

In the center of that valley
   it was more difficult to perceive . .
      and understanding grew more slowly
         than the telling of it.

FOR IT IS ONE THING
   to turn patterns
      this way and that in your mind,
         seeking some new combination . .

AND QUITE ANOTHER
   FOR A WHOLE PEOPLE
      TO PERCEIVE SUCH AN IMAGE . .

QUITE ANOTHER
   FOR THEM TO SELECT TO WORK TOGETHER
      TOWARD THAT END.

   • • •

AND SO IT WAS
   That the Seeker of New Patterns
      first lay himself beside a fallen tree,
         waiting the approach of Great Shaggy,
       discovering the necessity
         of some shallow depression.

   Again and again he lay beside a tree,
      showing with his action
         the possibility of success.

THEN -- AND ONLY THEN --
   Did all seekers of the hard of hoof
      gather to watch his actions.

   ONE BY ONE
      they abandoned
         the pattern of their own thought
      to watch this search toward a new pattern
         which still lay beyond anyone's reach.

   ONE BY ONE
      THEY SAW THE VALUE
         OF SUCH ACTIONS.

   ONE BY ONE
      THEY SAW
         THE EDGES OF PATTERNS OF THEIR OWN.

THEN -- AND ONLY THEN --
   After much watching and many attempts
      did they sit quietly together,
         in mutual recognition of emerging wisdom,
      sit quietly together above the valley,
      sit quietly watching the Great Shaggies
      and carefully craft a new approach . .

   Weaving together a long, sure rope
      to stretch from a valley
         dappled with great creatures here and there
      to a fire circle
         around which sat a Whole People
            looking into the dark eyes
               of the Long Cold in a new land.

AND SO IT WAS
  That the personal vision
    of one seeker after the hard of hoof
      was gradually shown
        to each other seeker.

Slowly drawn toward this new vision,
  each in turn understood it as he might,
    saw the value of a new way
      and some possibilities of variation.

UNTIL AT LAST
  they formed a circle on the Earth
    and spoke to one another,
  modified a personal vision
    toward a general purpose,
  wove a rope
    that sustained a Whole People
      toward the warmth
        that lay beyond the Long Cold.

FOR
  once in place,
  once the triple call of Eagle was heard,
  once the patient waiting
    in each shallow depression
    behind each branch wall
      for each Great Shaggy's slow approach
        toward succulent grass
  once this patient waiting
    had accomplished enough of their purpose
      to secure one end of the long rope
        woven for the People . .

THEN *DID EACH SEEKER*
  rise at the triple sound of Eagle's voice
  rise and address the Great Shaggy near him
  rise and with joy for the People
    and sorrow for the hard of hoof
      find a sudden place for each spear
        beneath that shaggy coat.

Beginning a long journey
  from valley to Fire Circle
    for enough of this Great Shaggy People
      to sustain their own People
        past probable cold
        toward possible Tomorrow.

THERE WAS JOY
　　IN THE HEARTS OF ALL THE PEOPLE

WHEN KNOWLEDGE
　　OF THIS CAREFULLY BRAIDED ROPE
　　FIRST REACHED THEM.

JOY IN THE DAY
　　WHEN ENOUGH
　　　　FIRST REACHED THE PEOPLE
　　　　IN THIS NEW LAND.

JOY IN THE CAREFUL LABOR
　　THAT ASSURED TOMORROW.

JOY IN THE NEW WISDOM
　　THAT THE SEEKERS FOUND.

AND THERE WAS SORROW, ALSO

SORROW
　　For the many of the Great Shaggy People
　　　　who lay still upon the earth . .

SORROW
　　That something which they not yet understood
　　　　had struck down perhaps
　　　　　　as many from among that People
　　　　as had been tossed like pebbles
　　　　　　by a trembling earth
　　　　or washed toward ocean like so much foam
　　　　　　from among a People
　　　　　　　　which walked on two legs
　　　　　　　　and learned new paths
　　　　　　　　　　toward possible Tomorrows.

FOR IT SEEMED TO MANY
　　That a People
　　　　who suddenly rise up from behind such walls
　　　　　　and find sudden paths
　　　　　　　　under shaggy coats for spears
　　　　must seem as Ocean become a great wall
　　　　　　to wash the many away from the few.

AND
   Some of the People began songs
      asking that this Great Shaggy People
         also learn the wisdom of new ways,
         learn to sustain itself
            toward possible Tomorrows . . .

   So that they and the People
      might dwell side by side
         living in the same land.

   And so that occasional mounds of succulent grass
      might give thanks for a valued gift
         and even more occasional spear
      might begin another rope
         stretching across another Great Cold.

AND AS THE PEOPLE LABORED TOGETHER,
ASSURING MANY TOMORROWS . .

EVEN SO
   Did they also retrace
      the many patterns of the days
         since Walk by Waters.

   The difficult, toilsome path across the waters
      was spoken of quietly, and only with respect.

   The Walk by Little Waters
      --being as it was more painful in the mind --
         was spoken of little at all.

   Yet the days since arrival at the three rock walls
      were well understood,
         and the patterns traced again and again.

FOR
   It was in the mind of each Far Walker
      that much had washed away from the People
         with that Ocean Wall.

   Of the First Among Us
      not one was left
         to cross the rope bridge,
         to Walk by Waters.

   And what might be left
      of all that ancient wisdom
         no one was yet sure.

SO THAT IT GREW TO BE A GREAT DETERMINATION
AMONG THEM . .

   THAT NO WISDOM
      LEARNED SO PAINFULLY
         WOULD GO UNRECOGNIZED.

   THEY SANG TO ONE ANOTHER
      of the patterns in the mind
        which we call thought,
      of how these might be rewoven
        by each new arrival at the Fire Circle . .

   SO THAT NOT AGAIN
      NEED ALL OUR WISDOM WASH AWAY
        IN ONE GREAT TOSS OF OCEAN.

IF ANY OF THE PEOPLE YET STAND
  let those two legs
    carry an ancient treasure,
  let those two legs
    lift a carrying pack
      past any previous value,
  let those two legs
    lift a Sacred Pouch
      of the gathered wisdom
        of a Whole People.

  NOT AGAIN
    WOULD THE PEOPLE
      TRUST SUCH MEMORY
        TO ONLY A FEW AMONG THEM.

                  • • •

AND SO IT WAS
  That the People spoke with one another
    over the slow process of separating fur robes
      from future sustenance.

  SPOKE WITH ONE ANOTHER
    as they patiently severed many narrow strips
      from the great quantity before them.

  SPOKE
    as they laid these strips
      on the carefully crafted drying racks
        already prepared.

  SPOKE
    as they watched this future plenty,
      patiently turning one side and another
        toward the warmth of sun,
      scanning the blue arch above them
        for any who fly
          and might covet this plenty,
      watching the bushes
        for any of the four-legged
          who might find such plenty
            irresistible.

  Discouraging these,
    setting small offerings elsewhere
      when necessary,
    they painstakingly crafted a way of life
      responsive to this new land.

WEAVING FOR MEMORY
   WHAT WAS A MOST CAREFUL NET . .

THEY STORED WITHIN
   THE VALUED TREASURE
     OF THE WISDOM OF THE PEOPLE

AND IT WAS AT THIS TIME
   THAT THE PEOPLE
     LEARNED ANOTHER GREAT LESSON.

THEY LEARNED
   that the cold and much snow
     of itself gathers the People together,
       gathers them to talk with one another,
       gathers them toward shared wisdom.

AND IT WAS AT THIS TIME
   That the People learned from one another
   a manner of crafting songs
     which evoke memory
   -- short sounds which carry great meaning --
   and to which the People can respond
     with limitless detail.

AND IT WAS IN THIS MANNER
   THAT THE PEOPLE
     BEGAN THE SONGS AND PATTERNS
       THAT YOU HEAR FROM ME TODAY.

FOR
   WITHOUT THIS CAREFUL WISDOM
     THERE WOULD BE MUCH LESS THAT YOU . .
       AND I . .
         MIGHT SAY TO ONE ANOTHER.

LET US THEREFORE
   PERCEIVE THIS WISDOM.

LET US JOIN
  The long line of patient People,
    carefully crafting a woven rope
      which reaches farther . . and farther,
      across Walk by Waters,
      down a long chain of mountains . .

A ROPE
  THAT TRULY STRETCHES
    FROM A DAY
      WHEN ROCKS FELL LIKE RAIN
      AND OCEAN CAME LIKE A GREAT WALL . .

  TO THIS MOMENT
    WHEN I SPEAK WITH YOU . .

    TWO MORE TWO LEGGEDS
      WHO UNDERSTAND
        THE NATURE OF WEAVING.

  SO BE IT . . .

ALL DURING THAT LONG COLD
   The People
      gave careful thought to every action
         before they decided
         after it was done.

   FOR
      even as the manner of the People
        had changed
          from living
            only in their Central Place
         to living among mountains,
      even as this and that
        required modification,
      even so did they now understand
        that they devised among them
         a new pattern for a New Land.

THE MEMORY
   Of deep dark places in the earth
      and of the crushing nature of rock on rock
        was so clear to them
          that many chose a colder bed
            under an open sky.

   OTHERS AMONG THE PEOPLE
      remembered the woven round dwellings
        they had first understood
          as some Gathering of the Great Beasts.

   SOME OF THE PEOPLE
      began the weaving
        of more and more pliant saplings
        more and more reeds and small branches
      until it was known among them
        which weavings
          held against wind,
        which weavings
          modified the direction of rain,
            leaving a dryer, warmer place within.

YET
   The fire built to warm the People
      was still built within the deep dark places
        or within the sight of stars

Until some one among them
      remembered ashes on the floor . .

And it seemed to him
    that these ashes held the possibility
        of warmth away from wind and rain
        warmth away -- also --
            from the possibility of crushing rock.

And what with one thing and another
    This One designed a small Fire Circle
        within his woven round dwelling
    and a manner of releasing smoke
        from the net
            in which woven branches held it.

AND SO IT CAME TO BE -- AT THIS TIME --
    That some among the People
        chose woven dwellings for the fewer in number
    And some
        chose the deep dark places for their bed.

AND IT SEEMED TO THEM
    That this was different in no way
        from the Two Ways Life they had chosen before,
            with some of the People
                living along the sand at the Edge of Ocean
        and others
            here and there among mountains.

AND SO IT WAS
    That certain of the tasks
        so common to the Long Cold
            were given to dwellers in the deep dark places
    And others
        to those choosing woven round shelters.

THOSE WITHIN THE DEEP DARK PLACES
    had special responsibility
        for keeping all but some of the sustenance
            carefully dried to last
                till Earth warmed again.

AND THOSE WITHIN THE WOVEN SHELTERS
    Had special responsibility
        for the finding of wood
            and the occasional sustenance
        which can be found
            even when snow lies deep on the ground.

AND
    When all was arranged
        each dried strip cut from under the fur
            of Great Shaggies and small four-footeds,
        each dried herb and root and berry . .

When each of these was carefully laid away,
      protected from rain and even damp
      protected from other Peoples
         the four- and many-legged . .

When each fur was trimmed
      and softened toward greater comfort,
         clothing made and wrapping robes folded
           so as to deter no foot . .

When wood was stored and future wood located --

THEN DID THE PEOPLE BRING, EACH OF THEM,
WOOD AND KINDLING
    TO A GREAT CENTRAL FIRE . .

THEN DID THE PEOPLE JOIN, EACH AND EVERY ONE,
THAT SAME CENTRAL FIRE

THEN DID THE PEOPLE
SING THEIR GRATITUDE

    For Earth
      who provides the possibility
      of food and shelter

    For the ambient air around us,
      from which pour the waters --
        rivers, streams, and oceans

    For the Great Shaggies
      who were patient with our intrusion
      and giving of themselves

FOR ALL OF THESE POSSIBILITIES

FOR THE PROBABILITY OF TOMORROW

THE PEOPLE SANG THEIR GRATITUDE

Their thoughts
 turning to a great panoply of change . .

From trembling rock
 to rock washed by Ocean

From the Great Dry Place
 to more damp
  than pleased anyone at all

From slender stores
 to racks
  bent under the shape of Enough

AND FROM THIS MUCH SINGING
 THE PEOPLE SLOWLY GREW TIRED . .

ONE AND ANOTHER
 Began a quiet song
  of all they had learned . .

  Of Ancient Wisdom
   and her purposeful walking

  Of Daughter of Wisdom
   and her patient footsteps

  Of He Who Stood Forward
   and the Two Strong Men

  OF ALL
   THAT THEY HAD SEEN AND HEARD
    DURING ONE GREAT WALK

 AND IN THE SONG
  THAT ALL THE PEOPLE SANG

 AT LAST
  THEY REMINDED ONE ANOTHER

  LET US REMEMBER

   LET US REMEMBER

    LET US REMEMBER.

THE NATURE OF EARTH BEING WHAT IT IS,
Many of the People understood
from the thickness of Great Shaggy fur
the probable Long Cold to follow.

Nor was the understanding different
from the reality which followed.

FOR I TELL YOU NOW
THE COLD WAS INDEED GREAT.

The protection of rock walls
catching the nature of sun
visible more and more briefly to the South
was greatly valued.

Valued also was the protection
afforded by these same rock walls
against the many great winds
descending from the colder North.

Storms washed in from the Ocean also . .
and these brought much snow, but less cold.

SO IT WAS
That the People
found their careful preparations
were in no way irrelevant to circumstance.

During the storms bringing the most snow
those of the People
living in woven round dwellings
found the thought of the possibility
of crushing rock walls
less meaningful than the reality
of tumbling, drifting snow.

For the great white mounds in this land
rivaled the woven round dwellings themselves,
many disappearing
beneath too many individual flakes.

Yet as each such storm would pass --
   those now dedicated to a clear sky overhead
      would return,
         moving gathered snow
            from one place to another,
   and re-enter their rounded dwellings,
         protected in part by their drifted snow.

AS THE GREAT COLD CONTINUED
   The sustenance carefully provided
      gave the People increasing strength.

Neither was there any lack
   of fuel or fur or many things to eat.

And -- as snow caught in a skin container
   and warmed near the fire quickly melts --
      there was no need to find a careful path
         between shelter and stream.

                    ⋄ ✕ ⋄

AND THE PEOPLE
   Who had learned to live with little and less,
   Who had learned to walk
      even almost while they also slept . .

THIS PEOPLE
   Learned the meaning of Enough
      and of comfort which seemed improbable
         in a land of so much snow.

AND THE PEOPLE
   SANG THEIR NEW SONGS . .
      telling each other of yesterday,
      wondering -- sometimes -- about tomorrow,
      valuing today
      until one and another saw the value
         of the living together,
         of counseling where every voice was heard,
  AND
      of designs crafted in air
      of possibilities not previously seen.

THE PEOPLE SAW THAT THIS WAS GOOD
AND THERE AROSE IN EVERY HEART
A NEW AND STRONGER PURPOSE.

"LET US PRESERVE"
  -- they told one another --

"Not only the nature of our path,
  but also the nature of the coming together,
  the talking one to another,
  the designs in air
    that we have learned to follow.

"LET US PRESERVE ALL THIS
  SO THAT NOT AGAIN
    SHALL THE CHILDREN'S CHILDREN'S CHILDREN
WALK UNAIDED
    THROUGH A STRANGE AND NEW LAND.

"FOR WE HAVE SEEN"
  -- they continued --

"HOW IT IS
  that much counseling together of every voice
    can lead to Wisdom,

"AND HOW THE PATTERNS
  perceived by this one and that
    can weave a new way
      through difficult circumstance.

"AND HOW THE PEOPLE
  can survive the apparently unsurvivable
    with these two strong legs to stand on.

"SO LET US NOW'
  -- they said at last --

"REMEMBER THE NATURE OF THIS PATH
  SO CLEARLY

"THAT THE CHILDREN'S CHILDREN'S CHILDREN
  CANNOT FAIL TO SEE IT
    IN THE MANNER OF OUR WALK
      AND THE NATURE OF OUR SPEECH.

"LET THEM LEARN FROM US
  WHAT WE HAVE SO PAINFULLY LEARNED
    FROM ONE ANOTHER."

AND DAUGHTER OF WISDOM HEARD THEM.
  And those who notice such things
    saw her smile --
      and understood it.

FOR I TELL YOU NOW
  THAT NEVER SINCE THAT DAY
    HAVE THE CHILDREN'S CHILDREN'S CHILDREN
      FAILED TO LEARN THESE GREAT LESSONS,

SO THAT . .
  even if some
    learn it more slowly than others --
      this way has been preserved,
    even as you
      learn it from me now . .

  As you hear these words from me --
    let your children's children
      hear such words from you.

SO THAT . .
  EVEN SHOULD THE EARTH SHAKE
    and the sky drop down stones
    and the ocean rise to meet mountains

  EVEN SHOULD SUCH THINGS OCCUR
    as had never been before seen

  EVEN THEN . .
    WILL THE CHILDREN'S CHILDREN'S CHILDREN
      carry with them a flame brighter than fire
      and an understanding more secure
        than any circumstance . .

EVEN THEN
   WILL THEY KNOW
      TO WALK FROM ONE LIFE TO ANOTHER . .

   sure that somewhere among them
      lie the possibilities
         of a long rope bridge
            across improbable changes . .

SECURING WHAT WAS
   TO WHAT WILL BE . .

ASSURING
   THE SURVIVAL OF THE PEOPLE.

LET IT BE SO . . .

SOON THE COLD LESSENED.
   Earth was seen here and there
      through the diminishing cover of snow.

   The first green appeared at last
      through the mud brown of melting snow.

   Of food there was still enough,
      so that only the most adventurous
         need search out new paths
         and new possibilities

AND YET THEY WERE LEARNING.

   The nature of rock and earth
   green leaves and wandering fur creatures,
      was different in this land
         than had been so
            in the Central Place left behind.

NOW
   ALL TURNED THEIR ATTENTION
   TO THESE NEW LEARNINGS . .

   Searched out the burrows and keeping places
      of all these new Four-legged.

AND YET
   another place not yet seen
      might hold greater comfort, newer learning.

   Perhaps snow sits less deeply
      on another mountain edge,
   Great Shaggies and other hard of hoof
      walking in greater numbers
         down its valleys.

AND IT CAME TO BE
   A GREAT DISCUSSION AMONG THEM . .

   Whether to choose present ease
      or the possibility
         of finding some wiser place.

NO ONE KNEW
   what might lie beyond this Edge of Mountains.

Valleys remained to be explored
and one to be chosen
down which to search
for the other side of Mountain.

ALL THE GO AND SEE
who walked for many days
in this direction and that
brought back no resolution.

The nature of Ocean told them
that neither South nor West
held any save a water path.

The nature of the Long Cold gave warning
of any path followed too far North.

WHATEVER PATH THEY CHOSE
must find its end
on the South side of a mountain
protecting against winds from the North.
Perhaps such a mountain
might give access toward the South.

AND IT WAS THIS LAST
THAT FINALLY LED TO A DECISION
BY ALL THE PEOPLE.

FOR IT WAS THEIR WISH
TO GIVE A FURTHER GIFT
TO THE CHILDREN'S CHILDREN'S CHILDREN.

IT WAS THEIR WISH
to find an edge of Ocean
washed by warmer waters.

One lying, then, toward the South . .
though East seemed the only way
from here to there.

AND YET
IT WAS THEIR WISH
to keep for today's children
some of the comfort so recently achieved
after so much painful walking.

AND SO IT WAS THEIR DECISION . .

That a small group
   might search out
      the most probable valley
         of a South-facing Mountain . .

One which would provide shelter for the People,
   shelter from the coldest winds,
   rock walls to catch the warmth of lessening sun,
   easy paths to deep, dark places
      which maintain a dry nature
         even in melting snow
      and which provide easeful access
         to level places where rounded dwellings
           might be built for those
         who found such ways preferable.

SUCH A SMALL GROUP HAS CHOSEN AT LAST . .

A valley which extended from the valley
   in which the first Great Shaggies were found.

And although this valley walked away from Ocean,
   it was the thought of all the People
      that farther East
a path might lead toward the South,
   from which a path toward Ocean
      might again be found.

Provisions were gathered
   from the More Than Enough which still remained
      after the Long Cold was past.

Those who remained
   busied themselves with early preparations
      for the coming warmth . .
   and with even earlier preparations
      for the Long Cold that lay beyond even that.

ANOTHER DECISION
   WAS MADE BY THE WHOLE PEOPLE . .

Of the seeds of this and that
   brought across Walk by Waters,
      each nature was divided
         toward three purposes.

One such seed
    was buried in appropriate Earth here
      near their Winter Place . .

One was taken toward the possibility
    of a new Edge of Mountain beyond . .

And one was carefully stored
    against the possibility
      that neither one place nor the other
        might prove an appropriate home
          for these Growers of Seeds.

IN THIS MANNER
    Did the People prepare for two possibilities,
    and one more
      which lay even beyond that.

IN THIS MANNER
    Did the People
    assure the possibility of Tomorrow
      for those who came after them.

LET THOSE
    who lead a long line of the People
    always remember
      those who follow.

LET THE PEOPLE
    IN THIS MANNER
      SURVIVE THE EXISTENCE
      OF EACH AMONG THEM.

NOW I HAVE TOLD YOU
That preparations for the warming days
and for the next Long Cold beyond
were begun in two places.

NOW IT WAS
That the People waited
to learn which of these places
might prove more appropriate for living.

FROM TIME TO TIME
Some one from among the People
whose curiosity exceeded a desire to stay
would walk toward those who preceded
and find their searching camp
to return and tell of their wanderings.

FOR I TELL YOU NOW
that those
who had chosen this wandering path
maintained no less determination
than those
who had crossed Walk by Waters.

And those
who allowed their curiosity
to move them from one place to another
became a way of the People
talking to one another . .

So that each
might continue to learn from the other,
as had increasingly
become the nature of their learning.

IT WAS THEN
THAT THE PEOPLE
CAME TO UNDERSTAND

The value of the short camps
which the First Among Us
made among the Mountain People.

The purpose of these camps
was a search for Sharp Tusk
and a concern for the Long Cold.

YET
WHAT ALSO OCCURRED THEN

AND
WHAT OCCURRED NOW . .
WAS A UNITY OF PEOPLES,
DISTANT IN LOCATION
FROM ONE ANOTHER,

AND
THE PEOPLE UNDERSTOOD THIS VALUE

And designed songs
from which Those Who Come After
might learn for themselves . .

The gift
that the curious in nature
bring to those
who prefer an easeful place by the fire.

FOR THE PEOPLE LEARNED NOW

THE NATURE
OF THE SEARCH
FOR ANOTHER PLACE
APPROPRIATE FOR THE LONG COLD.

They Walk Beyond

MANY DAYS
  Were required for forward exploration
    and even then
      wisdom could not be assured.

Who can tell
    whether melting snows
      might not fill a deep dark place
        presently filled with summer warmth?

Who can know
    which of the Four-legged
    and which of the sliders-on-belly
      might prefer this place
        -- or that --
          for their winter slumbers?

AND YET
  A place must be chosen,
    secured against the changing year
      and provisioned for the Great Long Colds
        which seemed natural to this place.

NONE OF THOSE
    preferring rounded dwellings
      had joined this group.

THESE WERE THEY
    who found transit
      between one place and another easier --
    there being greater possibility
      in carrying some of the weaving sticks
    than in lifting any of the deep dark places.

THOSE
    who preferred the deep dark places
      were at one place or the other . .

WITH THOSE
    who wove dwellings
      traveling between one and the other,
      learning of valleys and mountains in between
      and the variability of dwellings
        which might be quickly prepared.

THESE WERE THEY
who began to untangle
the nature of the paths followed
by the Great Shaggies.

THESE WERE THEY
who first learned of others
among the Hard of Hoof
who might be found here and there.

THESE WERE THEY
who traced the nature
of these paths also --
so that when any gathering occurred
with a focus
toward gathering any of the Hard of Hoof
toward present sustenance
and the future nature
of soft fur robes . .

THESE WERE THE VOICES HEARD FIRST
as to which valley paths to follow
and the manner of approach.

AND YET,
Those whose location was more fixed
were learning also.

THESE WERE THEY
who traced the paths of the small Four-legged,
who searched out
the nature of fruit
growing from trees and bushes,
the nature of succulent under-earth roots.

THESE WERE THEY
who learned to set snares near at hand
and to encourage berries
toward next year's crop --
some also for this year's stomachs.

YET
Among all creatures seen from time to time,
no one yet
saw any of the nature of Standing Bear.

IT WAS WELL UNDERSTOOD
    that Bear had slowly walked away
        from all the deep dark places
           in which the People dwelt.

YET HERE
    No sign of any Two-legged was found,
        nor of Bear either.

THIS WAS A GREAT PUZZLE AMONG THEM.

Some similarities -- here and there --
    with some creatures previously known
        were found.

Similarities to Bear were expected also,
    but none yet found.

           . . .

NOW,
    As to the nature of dwellings,
        it was during this year of exploration,
           this year of new thoughts
               on the nature of dwellings,
           this year of new paths
               for old ways
        that many ways were employed . .
           many ways
               of weaving the rounded dwellings,
           many ways
               of arranging this and that
                   within the deep dark places.

BEFORE,
    In the Great Center Place,
        the People had become so many . .

That varying purposes
    seemed appropriately set apart from one another.

YET HERE,
    Where the People were few . .

    And where that few
        was divided into this place -- and that --
        and the woven dwellings in between . . .

HERE
    There seemed little purpose in such separation
    and -- as the divisions were less . .

    THE UNITY OF THE PEOPLE WAS MORE . . .

SO THAT
    old and young found more purpose together.

    Persons both male and female less reason
        for different locations.

    AND IT WAS NOTED
        THAT IN THIS MANNER
        MORE LEARNING WAS ACHIEVED.

MOREOVER,
    Between this place and that
        there were as many differences
          as similarities.

    And those who walked between,
        living in woven dwellings,
          brought differences greater yet.

SO THAT
    whereas there was greater Unity
        within this small People
          spread out to many explorations,

    Yet there were also greater differences
        in the manner of their days . .

SO THAT
    the varying ways of life
        within this small People
          seemed greater in number
    than the differences between
        the First Among Us by the Ocean's Edge
        and the Mountain People.

AND YET,
  UNITY WAS ALSO GREATER.

MANY
  PUZZLED OVER THE NATURE OF THIS CHANGE.

  How it was
    that Unity could be greater
      while the differences were more.

AND DAUGHTER OF WISDOM
  Sat long over this seeming variance,
    patterns in the fire
      speaking to her
        of the Nature of There . . and Here . .

HE WHO STOOD FORWARD
  Also wondered
    at the many changes in living,
      and the greater cohesion
        they also seemed to beget.

UNTIL
  It was suggested by one and another
    that once the next winter was assured
      with the storage of much sustenance,
        fur robes and wood for fire,
      that same Winter
        there be an Asking Question.

  "As the snows fall"
    -- Daughter of Wisdom began to say --

  "Let the thoughts of each of the People --
    young and old --
    male and female --
      turn to the nature of our Path.

  "Let each Fire be surrounded
    by much individual thought
      and many shared words.

  "Let us ponder
    the nature of this seeming difference.

"WHY IT IS
THAT THOSE
WHOSE DAILY MANNER
SEEMS SO DIFFERENT
FIND THEREIN GREATER UNITY."

. . .

AND
   During that well-provided Winter
      the thought
         and the many gatherings
            of spoken thought that followed
      came back again and again to this focus.

FOR
   A People who had walked through such variance
      did and did not
         find the present variance in their days
            surprising.

"SURELY"
   -- one said --

"Those who walk through
   such rapidly changing circumstance
      for more than the turning of a year
         can find little value
            in maintaining the same manner.

"Those who walk a Great Dryness
   to soon be drenched in too much standing water
      can find no inherent value
         either in the saving of water
            or in its throwing away.

"RATHER"
   -- he went on --

"Will they not find value
   in the willingness to change itself?

"May it not be those who would not change
   who lie still against the earth behind us?"

AND MANY SPOKE IN AGREEMENT.

Then another replied --

"Yet the People have in one way
   never changed, never varied.

"Was it not"
   -- she continued --

"Our unvarying purpose
   to walk to this Great Island
   and to find upon it
      a secure place for living . .
   so that
      the children's children's children
         might find joy
            in the manner of our days?"

AND THE PEOPLE ANSWERED HER
   IN AGREEMENT ALSO.

SO THAT
   IT CAME TO SEEM TO THEM
      THE NATURE OF UNITY LAY IN PURPOSE,

   AND
      IN THE NATURE OF PATH
         LAY THE POSSIBILITY OF DIVERSITY . .

SO THAT
   They came to understand
      that many paths lead to the same purpose
      and that there may be much mutual learning
         as between those paths,

AND YET
   Without the nature of purpose
      they would have become
         only one more wandering people,
      following -- as some do --
         the wanderings of the Great Herds.

IT SEEMED TO THEM
   THAT THEY PREFERRED
      TO CHOOSE A PATH OF THEIR OWN.

AND SO IT WAS
> *That during this time*
>> *of Earth-lies-beneath-Snow*
>>> *there were many Learnings.*

FOR
> Sitting around the fire became a time
>> for much sharing of new explorations.

> The nature of many paths through the mountains
>> was discussed,
>>> each path becoming a careful focus.

> The nature of the land in every direction
>> -- and much distance had been walked --
>> was carefully discussed,
> each understanding shared
>> among all those around the Fire Circle.

> It was the nature of their days at this time
>> that many of the People
>>> lived within the first deep dark place
>>>> chosen by the People,
>>> and many lived in the second such place.

FROM AMONG THE PEOPLE
> ONE IN THREE
>> had chosen the woven rounded dwellings

> AND THESE
>> had chosen to locate themselves
>>> -- as the Great Cold approached --
>>> near one or the other
>>>> of these Earth locations

> SO THAT
>> The People were very nearly evenly divided
>> between one place and the other.

DURING THIS GREAT COLD
> Snow lay so deep on the Earth
> that there was no thought
>> -- even on warmer days --
>> of travel between one place and another.

SO IT WAS
  That the Learning in one place
    was not the same as in the other.

ALL SAW
  This was the nature of their Learning,
    and that -- once the warming of Earth
      allowed or encouraged travel once again --
        there must be another great sharing.

AND YET
  ANOTHER THING WAS TRUE.

AS BEFORE
  Many days were so thick with falling snow
    or with the sharp snow carried on strong winds

  That those within the woven rounded dwellings
    sought greater shelter
      within the deep dark place
        which was home to others of the People.

ALL KNEW
  The last washing of cold from the North
    had found the Whole People
      warm and well fed on every day.

  Nor was there any reason
    to suppose it would be other
      during this second Great Cold
    for those
      who dwelt in the second such place chosen.

  But whereas all the People together
    had dwelt within the first such place,
      knew it well,
    and understood what Great Cold
      might be withstood therein . .

  Only some of the People
    had seen the second such place
    or understood its security.

AND SINCE NO ONE AT ALL
    Had yet survived a Great Cold therein . .

    SO IT WAS
        that as the light and warmth
            shared with Earth by the distant Sun
            became each day greater . .

    SO WERE THOSE
        who dwelt within the first deep dark place
        each day
            more desirous of learning the well-being
            of those who dwelt in the second such place.

ALL DURING THIS GREAT COLD
    There had been no word,
        no footfall between one place and the other.

    IT SEEMED TO MANY
        that the Great Stinging Winds
        came more often
            during this Great Cold
                than during the last
    and concern for those
        in the forward location
            became greater with each passing day.

    "So small a People"
      -- someone said --

    "Will find the loss of half its number
        great indeed."

AND
    No one spoke the frequent thought
        that it was the most venturesome among us
        who had chosen to walk beyond.

    Without them,
        it seemed increasingly likely
            that those in the first deep dark place
                would become a sedentary People,
                    venturing no further explorations
                    for many Walks of Days.

BUT
　　Daughter of Wisdom counseled them.

FOR I TELL YOU NOW
　　She had chosen to dwell in the first place
　　　　even as He Who Stood Forward
　　　　　　chose to stand forward once again . .

And her counsel was of this nature . .

　　"It seems to me
　　　　that anyone at all
　　　　　　hearing what this small People
　　　　　　　　has already accomplished
　　　　　　would deem survival improbable.

　　"Yet we sit now
　　　　around this fire
　　　　　　unconcerned with any lack.

　　"KNOWING THIS,
　　　　is the probability
　　　　　　not greater rather than less
　　　　that those who walked ahead
　　　　　　know so well
　　　　　　　　the patterned dance of survival
　　　　that what with one thing and another
　　　　　　they will find a way
　　　　　　　　to greet the warming of Earth?

　　"HOW WILL A PEOPLE
　　　　who remember
　　　　　　the long walk on water-washed rocks,
　　　　　　the crossing of the great Ocean itself . .

　　"HOW WILL SUCH A PEOPLE
　　　　forget survival
　　　　　　merely because the wind blows a little
　　　　　　and carries ice crystals with it?

　　"I TELL YOU NOW,
　　　　This One
　　　　　　expects to find a Whole People
　　　　　　　　surviving even the greatest cold."

AND IN THIS MANNER
　　The concern of all was abated . .

UNTIL
    Earth began to warm again and snow to melt,
        but no word was yet heard
            from those who walked ahead.

    Talk began again and concern grew
        until Daughter of Wisdom spoke once more . .

        "I WAS THINKING"
          -- she said --

        "Of the nature of exploration
          and the possibilities
            of a home to the South.

        "AND I WAS THINKING"
          -- she went on --

        "Of how it is
          that another exploration
            must be undertaken."

    Many spoke in consternation . .

    "How may we plan another exploration"
        -- they asked --

    "Without the willing counsel
          of those who walked ahead?

    "Or indeed"
        -- they continued --

    "Without any understanding
        of what the Great Cold may have left behind
          in the deep dark place beyond this one."

BUT
    Before too many imaginings
        occurred to the People . .

    Daughter of Wisdom spoke again.

    "You misunderstand me"
        -- she explained --

    "This exploration
        is of a different nature.

"ALL REMEMBER"
    -- she went on --

"That our Ancient Wisdom
    had a great desire
        to see this Great Island
            Beyond Our Home That Was.

"YOU WILL RECALL
    that I still carry with me
        those possibilities of vision
            she entrusted to me
                when she left us to Return.

"IT IS NOW MY THOUGHT
    to begin to search for an edge of mountain
        from which much beauty may be seen
        and a distance as vast as may be.

"*IT IS TO JUST SUCH A PLACE*
    that all that remains to us
        of the Friend to us all
            might wisely be entrusted.

"IT WAS MY THOUGHT"
    -- she continued --

"To walk toward our Brothers,
    our Sisters to the East --
        once the snows begin to melt
            and the earth turns firm underfoot . .

"*Searching along the way for a great Mountain*
    which might become home at last
        to the vision of Ancient Wisdom."

AND THOSE WHO NOTICE SUCH THINGS
    Saw how it was
        that the concern of the People
            had turned from one thing to another.

Those who had seen only a frantic haste
    to discover the rest of their small People
        -- drowned, perhaps, by too much melting snow --
    now searched also in a deliberate manner
        for a mountain large enough
            to contain the gratitude
                of a Whole People.

AND THOSE WHO NOTICE SUCH THINGS
Saw how it was
that a rapid walk through thawing mud
toward a vision of possible disaster
had become a careful preparation
for a search that could not fail.

FOR SURELY SOMEWHERE
Already lay a path around a great mountain . .

AND SURELY
that great mountain would become one
with all that remained to the People
of their Ancient Friend.

AND THOSE WHO NOTICE SUCH THINGS
Saw also
that this great change had been wrought,
these cheerful preparations engendered,
by the few words of Daughter of Wisdom.

FOR I TELL YOU NOW
That none of the People
would allow any other
to discover that mountain without them.

So that all of those dwelling
in the first deep, dark place
packed remaining food and every fur,
thinking -- perhaps --
to give relief to those
who dwelt in the second such place
thinking also
of the sustenance and warmth necessary
for those who seek mountains.

AND THOSE WHO NOTICE SUCH THINGS
Saw how a few words
had changed a People
who would wait anxiously for word from those
who explored along the forward path,
into a People
who would not be stopped from going forward.

AND THOSE WHO NOTICE SUCH THINGS
WONDERED MIGHTILY
   at the change a few words may bring
   when spoken with wisdom
   and with a kind compassion
   for all the People.

NOW IT WAS
  THAT THE PEOPLE
    made deliberate preparations
      to walk forward,
        forward along a mountain-seeking path,
        forward toward whatever may remain
          of those who walked ahead.

  Gathering together all those who walked . .
  Carrying all those not yet able,
    the People awaited an Earth
      firm enough after the melted snow
        to bear the weight of so many footfalls.

WHEN AT LAST
  The sun spilled its warmth
    over just such an Earth,
      the People began their exploration.

  Only one among them
    had visited the second deep dark place --
      being as it was a walk
        of many, many days from their beginning.

  The first steps
    were along a path that was easily followed,
      with many of those
        who chose the woven rounded dwellings
          recognizing this and that.

AS THEY WALKED,
  They crossed paths increasingly new
    to more and more of the People,

  UNTIL AT LAST
    five and then three and then one alone
      were the number of the People
        who saw anything at all they recognized.

  Much discussion and disagreement
    preceded the selection of each path . .

  UNTIL AT LAST
    more was recognized and agreement reached.

YET NOW
    Standing at the point that three recognized
      and gazing beyond
        to a path none but one had ever walked,
      the People felt sad at heart
        that more had not chosen
          to walk this long and difficult path . .
      and sadder yet
        that no voice they recognized
          yet answered their occasional cries.

    "Think of it this way"
      -- Daughter of Wisdom suggested --

    "How would it be for us now
      if none at all
        had walked this lengthening path?"

AND ALL LAUGHED
    Seeing present possibility greater
      than the one she described.

AND THOSE WHO NOTICE SUCH THINGS
SAW THE TURNING OF THOUGHT
A FEW WORDS ENGENDERED.
THEY SAW WISDOM AT WORK.

Proceeding along the path selected
　　by the last Far-Walker
　　　　was a journey of many days.

This One found greater difficulty
　　　in recognition of the way previously walked
　　　　　than he expected . .

And many wanderings here and there,
　　　many searchings for marks left behind
　　　　　were necessary
　　　　　　　before an assured path was discovered.

AND SO IT WAS
　　That a several-days-walk
　　　　became even more . .

And the People began again
　　　to feel that same painful concern
　　　　　for the well-being
　　　　　　　of the rest of their expanded circle
　　　　　that had so marked many previous days.

NOW
　　No words from Daughter of Wisdom,
　　No search for nearby mountains
　　　　could give quiet thoughts
　　　　　　to those who saw the warming of the Earth
　　　　　　　passed by many days,
　　　　　　and no other voice of the People yet heard.

FOR SURELY
　　　as these from the first Island Home
　　　　sought those from the second --

SURELY
　　　some from among those
　　　　　who had walked ahead
　　　　　　also now returned
　　　　　to find those who remained closer to Ocean.

AND YET NO VOICE WAS HEARD.
　　This one and that
　　　　climbed mountain edges to a greater height,
　　　　　calling out to any who might hear,

AND YET NO VOICE WAS HEARD.

UNTIL AT LAST
 The People came to the edge of mountain
  which the Forward Walker
   said contained the deep dark place
  wherein they would find
   their Sister People,
   their Brother People --
   those others who completed
    their expanded circle.

 Around the base of this mountain all walked,
  climbing when that proved necessary
  and clambering down when that way lay the path.

UNTIL AT LAST
 The last edge of the mountain was walked beyond
  and before them
   lay the opening to the deep dark place
    which He Who Walked Forward recognized.

 Cold were the hearts of those who looked . .
  and those who saw.

 Cold indeed were the thoughts of all the People
  as they gazed at an entrance way
   choked with ice and snow.

 On all sides
  lay only the massed and frozen drifts
   of what had once been
    individual crystals
     of falling, blowing snow.

 Cascades of melted snow
  stood frozen against the mountain,
   denying even entrance
    to this deep, dark place.

AND YET THEY MUST ENTER.
 None would turn their back
  on this chilling vision,
   forgetting to learn which of the People
    lay buried beneath this icy torrent
   and which might still be sought
    between sheltering mountains.

It was a work of great difficulty
identifying access to entrance --
and beyond that to the interior
of this deep, dark, ice-filled place
at the edge of mountain.

Only the strongest
were able to penetrate this frozen shelter . .

And only they
returned to describe this and that.

How this place must have seemed
during summer's warmth.

How it may have been an excellent shelter
-- even --
from the chilling winds
that began each Long Cold.

But how it was
that slight gaps and cracks in interior walls
seemed only to provide access
for dripping, running waters
that began -- perhaps --
with the coating of snow
that marked the true beginning
of any Great Cold.

ALL KNEW SUCH PLACES.

On that Great Island they left behind
such as this was found from time to time . . .
and quickly abandoned.

What remained here was to learn
whether the direction of ice
had been perceived in time --
or whether a sudden flood
had trapped the People,
as had been known to happen,
in the inaccessible reaches
of deep, dark places in the Earth.

Those who searched the inner reaches
came out from time to time
to reassure those remaining at the entrance.

Much chopping was heard now and again --
    the clearing away
        of ice blocking passages clearly indicated.

Those at the entrance
    divided themselves so that some remained,
        preparing a warming fire at least
            for the return of those exploring
                and perhaps for those they might find.

Others spread out in each direction
    looking for signs
        that might indicate the passage
        of those they sought.

With rare exceptions,
    none at all were found,
        and even those few
            indicated no particular direction.

AT LAST, ONE BY ONE,
    These seekers returned.

AND AT LAST, ONE BY ONE,
    The seekers within
        forewent their patient chopping
            and returned to sit among the others
                of their disconsolate People,
            warmed by their echoing sadness
            and by the small fires set.

NO SIGN AT ALL
    Of any habitation had been found within . .

AND YET
    Every discernible area and opening
        had been explored.

This was indeed the proper place
    -- He Who Walked Forward observed --
        the memory of its configuration
            still clear in his mind.

AND YET
    NO SIGN OF THE PEOPLE WAS FOUND.

NO ONE AT ALL . .
  Not even Daughter of Wisdom . .
    suggested any move.

All sat in silent contemplation
  of the difficulty at hand.

ALL KNEW
  that no indication of direction was found.

ALL KNEW
  that ice might yet hide
    all the rest of their People within.

No clear path lay before them,
  nor any preferable direction.

Anywhere at all -- or nowhere --
  might hide the rest of their expanded circle.

NONE
  Had any desire to return to their first place.

It had been their thought
  some forward progress
    toward a more southerly edge of ocean
      might be made.

NONE
  HAD ANY WISH
    TO RETRACE SUCH STEPS.

NONE
  Had any desire to wander from here to there
    seeking that great mountain
      Daughter of Wisdom described.

No mountain found along a wandering path
  would properly join with Ancient Vision.

RATHER,
  such a place could only be found
    overlooking the probable future path
      of all the People,
        however many they might be.

AND SO NO WORD,
    No description of possible future
        was yet heard on any side.

    RATHER,
        The People sat together in increasing quiet --
           quietly sharing
                their awareness of present circumstance.

LONG HAD THEY SAT THUS,
    Speaking no word one to the other,
        until a sudden sound was heard.

    It seemed a vision call --
        someone announced to the general air
            that something was perceived.

    And yet the sound
        was too distant to be sure.

    The People sitting together counted one another,
        looking to learn whether some one
            might have walked farther away
                than any other
                    and only now returned.
    None such seemed missing.

    Perhaps -- they said --
        it was only the echo of their own heart,
            hoping to hear
                a Brother voice,
                a Sister voice
                    over the ice.

BUT NOW THE CALL CAME AGAIN.
    Surer this time . .
        and closer.

    Twice it came . .
        and then redoubled --

    Two voices called
        where one before had faintly come.

AND THEN -- I TELL YOU NOW --
    All the People in that disconsolate circle
        rose as one -- and gave a mighty shout.

    A shout so great indeed
        as to drown any and every answering cry.

    Only with great difficulty
        could they still their voice to listen.

    Yet this was done.

AND ONCE MORE
    The People heard a vision call
        resounding from more than one --
           and echoing from each wall of ice and rock.

    This dance of voices
        continued
           from one indeterminate place to another . .

UNTIL AT LAST
    The first dim outline of one they might recognize
        appeared over the edge of mountain
           they had themselves walked
               toward this icy chasm.

    Soon this increasing image
        was joined by another --
        and yet a third . .

UNTIL ALL THE PEOPLE
    SAW THREE WHOM THEY RECOGNIZED
    FAST PACING ALONG THEIR VERY PATH.

AND THEN I TELL YOU
    The din was such
        that no one at all could be heard.

And the rejoicing was great --
    for whether or not any others of the People
        remained to be found,
           these ones at least were here,
        providing some possible access
           to anyone else at all.

       . . .

"It was your pounding we heard"
    -- these three new arrivals explained --

"It has beckoned us
    for most of this latter part of day.

"And so we hurried in your direction.

"We have recently come"
    -- they continued --

"From the very place
    in which you spent the last two Snow Times,
    and in which we spent the first.

"We followed behind you
    ever since our arrival there.

"This time of year your tracks
    were made in earth soft enough
        -- from time to time --
    and no snow at all
        to hide them from our vision.

"We came by a different mountain path
    than this one"
        -- they explained --

"And never saw you until this day.

"Our paths were near, but never crossing"
    -- they went on --

"And so we walked the full length
    to where you were,
        finding all too slowly
            the way to where you are.

"NOW ALL IS JOINED.

"And let us say
    that none at all has disappeared
        beneath either snow, or ice,
    or any mishap
        when last we saw the rest of our People.

"They sent us to you
    to explain the nature of their path.

"For soon into the Dark Cold
    we discovered the poor nature
        of the shelter chosen . .
    and knew of others
        searched out over the warmer months.

"And it was from these
　　that we chose a wiser residence --
　　　　moving all as quickly as we may
　　　　　　between the first and second great storms
　　　　　　　　of the Long Dark Cold.

"Now all the People
　　are gathered together in that second shelter,
　　　　waiting
　　　　　　that we bring word of your thoughts
　　　　　　and your direction.

"Yet we have learned to our chagrin
　　that both your thoughts and your direction
　　　　were quicker than our feet!"

ALL LAUGHED
　　At the image of slow-paced feet
　　　　and faster-paced concern . .

Seeing how it was
　　that those who expected
　　　　only the well-being of all concerned
　　　　　　might indeed be content with a slower pace
　　than those
　　　　who held on the edges of their thought
　　　　　　the possibility of disaster.

IT WAS A QUICK MATTER TO WALK ON.

>   Nor was evening camp
>   made in this same location.

>   The struggle over ice and still-melting snow
>   slowed their pace.

And yet
>   Three days walk
>   placed their feet on the nearer path
>   to the second home of this second community.

>   Nor was there any sadness
>   in the reunion.

>   Some had and some had not
>   expected this meeting.

>   *YET ALL WERE GLAD OF ITS ARRIVAL.*

>   An open air camp was established,
>   secure enough against still-changeful weather,
>   and council was begun.

FOR
>   THESE WERE THEY
>   who would again decide
>   the Future of the People.

>   THESE WERE THEY
>   who walked before all those who came after.

>   THESE WERE THEY
>   who would choose to stay in some nearby place,
>   living among things now recognized,
>   or seek to find a better home
>   within a few Season's Circles
>   -- the apparent dance
>   of Sun from North to South --
>   or choose a longer purpose.

FOR
  WHO COULD SAY
    how many times of Earth Beneath Snow
      might come and go
    before the People searched the Earth
      with steps careful enough
        to carry all the People
          to the edge of a more southerly ocean?

  WHO COULD SAY
    What nature of Those Who Walk might be met --
      both Two and Four-legged
      and those like Bear
        who changed from one to the other
          as seemed appropriate to him?

  WHO COULD KNOW
    what waters might need walking,
    what mountains might require toilsome climb . .
    what chasms call out
      for the lengthening stretch of rope
        some of those who explored here and there
        found increasingly useful?

FOR
  The People had not forgotten,

  Nor had they allowed to fall into disrepair,
    the longest of ropes
      prepared for Walk by Waters.

AND IT CAME TO SEEM TO THEM
  That a stretching out of that rope
    and a stretching out of the People
      across mountain circumstance
        toward a southerly ocean
    was appropriate
      for those who walked away from falling rock,
        across a vast dryness,
        and over a water pathway.

IT BECAME A FIRM RESOLVE WITHIN THEM,
  So mutually shared
    that few at all were the words spoken
      to reach a resolution of this next step --

UNTIL
  ONE AMONG THEM ROSE AND SAID . .

"Let us learn
    how far our longest rope may stretch
    and how well along its length
      our People may learn to walk.

"Let us proceed across mountains,
    however high, however many,
      walking always to greet the sun,
    until a pathway South
      and a way again to Ocean may be found."

AND
  As he seated himself again,
    another rose to say . .

"Let us learn the wisdom of this place.

"Let us continue to explore
    that which may be eaten
      and where and how we may live
        maintaining health.

"Let us watch and learn
    how the young among us
      may best learn to teach themselves
        the nature of well-being."

AND
  As she sat
    the People spoke among themselves

UNTIL AT LAST
  The oldest among them rose and said . .

"As a rope
    is woven together of many strands,
      now let us weave this path of ours
    so that it stretches far, including Wisdom.

"Let us learn from our two-fold path.

"Let the People
    establish a place for snow-living,
      securing survival during the Great Cold.

"Let many go out
    searching this place and that
        until the world around
            is better understood.

"Then let some of the People
    choose a forward path and a new location
        until that place, too, is well-secured.

"Then let those who remained behind
    walk forward
        to join their distant Brothers, Sisters.

"From time to time
    perhaps we will choose
        to cross together another great difficulty.

"BUT LET US GAIN
    FROM WHAT WE HAVE LEARNED.

"LET US RETAIN THIS WISDOM.

"Let our forward progress
    toward an edge of Ocean
        no one at all has yet seen
    be a two-foot path,
        first one . . and then the other . .
            with an occasional two-foot stance
        when a great chasm must be leapt across.

"Let first one and then the other
    of these Brother Peoples,
    these Sister Peoples step forward.

"Let those who wander here and there,
    exploring other paths,
        be the memory between them --
    tying the Whole People together
        as sure as any long-woven rope.

"Let us proceed
    in this sure-footed manner along a path
        which may -- I tell you now --
            require more Walks of Days
                than anyone here possesses."

AND
   All heard the Wisdom in the words
     this Eldest One spoke.

FOR
   Although less
     than the turning of a Season Circle
       had been required for the difficult walk
     from their Great Central Place
       disappearing underneath rock and water
         to the edge of the Ocean
           they then walked . .

   Although the very next Great Cold
     found them
       on the other side of Walk by Waters . .

   Even so had they all understood
     where lay their purposed destination.

   They all knew that this one and that had
     -- from time to time --
   gone and returned
     bringing back tellings of just such places.

AND YET NOW THEY WALKED
THEY KNEW NOT WHERE.

NO ONE AT ALL
   Had returned
     with tellings of Ocean to the South.

   East, they said, and South which follows.

   But if any found Ocean at the edge,
     none at all had heard of it
       and none at all
         knew how far it might be.

AND SO IT WAS
   They chose a deliberate path -- East.

   And after East -- South.

   And after South, some toward-Ocean direction,
     if that could be learned.

THEY HAD CAST THEIR GREAT ROBE
TO THIS GREAT ISLAND . .
AND HERE
THEY WOULD STAY.

AND YET
The gift they chose to give
was a searched-for pathway
to an edge of ocean far to the South,
where the gentler winds might blow
and the colder northern winds
cast themselves
against protecting mountains.

MAY THOSE OF US
WHO FOLLOW IN THEIR FOOTSTEPS
PROVIDE SUCH CAREFUL THOUGHT
FOR THOSE WHO FOLLOW US,

LET US CHOOSE THE SANDS WELL
IN WHICH THEY WILL PERCEIVE
THE MARKS OF OUR PASSING.

NOW THE PEOPLE
Who were firm in their decision
turned their thoughts
to this Sun is North task.

Establishing open air camp here and there,
gathering wherewith to live,
they sent out this one and that
searching for the Great Mountain
which would appropriately join
with Ancient Vision.

EVEN
AS THE DAYS CAME AND WENT,
bringing increasing thoughts
of yet another Great Cold . .

Some returned with tellings of a Great Mountain
which stood over a gorge so deep
that none at all might cross it.

Nor had any yet found a way
-- North or South -- along its edge
which led to an easier passage.

"NOW"
-- some one said --

"This Great Mountain sounds to be one
which may appropriately mark
the arrival of Ancient Vision.

"And is the gorge beyond
any more dismaying in its depth
than Walk by Waters
was in its breadth . .
and occasional depth beneath Ocean?

"Might not this mountain
especially be
the one for which we search?"

AND ALL SAID IT MUST BE SEEN,
Both the nature of the Mountain itself
and also of the gorge beneath.

For if its limits were as great
   as some described,
      perhaps they were already come
        to the easternmost land.

AND YET SOMEONE SAID . .

"Somewhere at last
   even the greatest river meets Ocean.

"And might not that joining be found?

"Perhaps a People who Walk by Waters
   may choose to walk them again."

AND ALL LAUGHED
   At the image in their mind
      of walking the waters of a great river,
        spilling all its thundering turbulence
          into an equally thundering ocean.

"Perhaps instead we may choose
   to walk an airborne pathway,"
      -- some third one suggested --

"But this at least --
   let the People see,
      Each One,
        this Great Mountain."

AND SO IT WAS
   THAT ALL THE PEOPLE
      rose again as one
      and set their face toward the mountain,
        following a certain purpose
        along an uncertain path.

NOW
>*When that Great Mountain*
>>*walked toward them*
>>>*none doubted its appropriate nature.*

FOR SURELY
>*it rose towering overhead,*
>>*seeing in every direction*
>>>*more than any other Mountain.*

AND
>*When the nature of the chasm was perceived,*
>>*all the People knew*
>>>*that surely here*
>>>>*would Ancient Vision*
>>>>>*happily join with Earth.*

>*For the Mountain was Great . .*
>>*and the chasm itself*
>>>*might still the heart*
>>*of any who had never Walked by Waters.*

AND SO IT WAS
>*That the People chose an edge of mountain*
>>*from which*
>>>*one might look indeed a long way East*
>>>*and yet a long way South as well.*

>*From this place*
>>*anyone at all might easily watch*
>>>*a Walk-by-Water-People*
>>>>*decide the nature of their current path.*

>*For surely*
>>*only East across the chasm --*
>>*or South along its edge --*
>>>*were even considered.*

THEN,
>As the People
>>discussed the nature of their pathway
>>>-- saying this and that
>>>>about purpose and possibility --

AT LAST
>One of the People
>>rose to fill a quiet place in the talk.

It was She of Eight Winters,
   who had attained now Ten.

And these were her words
   which the People came to treasure
      beyond any other gift . .

"I have watched a People learning"
   -- she explained --

"The nature of many difficult crossings.

"I have watched a People"
   -- she went on --

"Teaching themselves
   new ways in a new land.

"I have heard much listening
   to all that's spoken
      and seen many ways of daily life.

"I have watched a People
   turn away from easeful living
      with thoughts only
   of the children's children's children . .
      and where they at last may walk.

"I speak for them now,
   for those whom some of you will never see . .
      and yet I may,
   for those beyond even them
      who will escape my vision . .
         to be seen only by those who follow me.

"GRATITUDE COMES . .
   FROM ALL OF US
      WHO FOLLOW SUCH A PEOPLE.

"GRATITUDE COMES
   FROM EACH OF US
      WHO WILL FOLLOW YOUR THOUGHTS.

"THIS ONE, AT LEAST
   WILL PRESERVE THEM."

A quiet humming was heard among the People,
  and many eyes dimmed
      at words
          they knew came from many not yet born.

No lack of resolution had existed --
    and yet I tell you
        all resolution now was doubled . .
    and a People who already purposed much
        came to purpose even more.

"LET US PROCEED"
    -- some one said --
    and yet She of Ten Winters still stood.

"I REMEMBER"
    -- she went on --

"HOW IT WAS
    across Ocean Running Fast . .
        And I wondered how anyone at all
            might put even one footstep farther
            toward the new sun.

"AND YET
    as I watched
        the Two Strong Men strode forth,
            secured by He Who Stood Forward.

"*AND AT LAST*
    a Whole People walked air across an Ocean
    no one at all could walk alone.

"IT SEEMS TO ME NOW"
    -- she continued --

"JUST SUCH A PATHWAY
    might be devised
        across the depth of a chasm
    as we devised
        across a powerful sweep of Ocean."

AND
    Many echoes of her words were heard . .
        so that all knew
            this was their mutual purpose.

AND SO IT WAS.

Two Strong Men
  began the slow and painful descent,
    supported once more
      by He Who Stood Forward.

As they progressed,
  each and every shred of rope
    was woven into place --
  not the strong Ocean washing
    but the weight of the rope itself
      their greatest difficulty.

NOW AT LAST
  A call came back
    that the Two Strong Men
      had reached the lowest part of the chasm,
    only the crossing of a great river remained.

Again and again they tried the crossing,
  until at last
    the People grew discouraged.

The last of the rope was gone
  and strips had been cut from many robes
    and lashed in place.

Now He Who Stood Forward
  chose the Three Who Walked
    from one deep dark place to another
      to take a careful heed
        of this beginning of a rope pathway --
  and he himself began the painful descent.

When he arrived
  The Two Strong Men were rested again --
    and as before each helped the other
      over this greater-than-Ocean torrent,
    working their way from rock to rock
  until the other side of the river was attained.

A GREAT SHOUT
  WENT OUT FROM THE PEOPLE.

AND THEN
> Another rope bridge was laid down
> > for He Who Stood Forward
> > > so that he, too, might find a path
> > > > from one side of the river to the other.

THEN
> Three Men Together slowly climbed
> > the face of the sharp-edged cliff beyond --
> > achieving . . at last . . its summit,
> > working the rope slowly up this other side,
> > shortening its length as appropriate,
> as the Three Messengers
> > gathered all that was no longer necessary.

AT LAST
> A ROPE BRIDGE THROUGH AIR
> APPEARED BEFORE THEM.

Only the sturdiest lengths of rope
> were now used in this span --
> > all the sections of lesser strength,
> > all the cut strips of warm furs
> > > were culled -- one by one --
> > > > from the greater strength
> > > > that remained.

AND YET IT DID NOT SEEM SECURE.

A rope woven with great care,
> twisted again and again and braided,
> > seemed but a wisp
> > > when suspended over so great a chasm.

AND YET IT WAS CLEAR
> Watching the slow and difficult progress
> > of Three Strong Men on so steep a cliff face --
> > that only a few of the People
> > > were capable of this transit.

NO ONE AT ALL
> Now spoke of the southern route
> > along an increasing river
> > > as it leapt at last to join with Ocean.

A quiet murmur sounded among the People,
  echoing their concern
    for an apparently difficult transit . .
      until one at last spoke.

"I REMEMBER"
  -- he began --

"How the People looked with dread
  on the last such crossing.

"The fall was shorter,
  but the end just as sure.

"Washed sideways by a thundering Ocean,
  any such
    would have quickly been far beyond
      any possibility of survival.

"It is equally so here"
  -- he went on --

"Any fall
  leading quickly beyond survival.

"Yet there is this
  that seems better here . .
    all is more direct
    and more easily seen.

"If any may fall,
  no one at all
    will wonder where you are."

AND ALL LAUGHED
  At this image of the value of certainty,
    until another spoke.

"When we essayed
  to walk rope through air
    across a turbulent ocean,
  This One, at least, was carried.

"Yet I tell you now
  the passage of two more winters
    tells me this need no longer be.

"This One, at least,
    will walk rope through air unassisted.

"Perhaps he who carried me
    may well assist another."

AND NOW
  All gave thought again
    to size and strength,
    to ability to walk through air unassisted

  And each reminded the other
    of sustaining short ropes
      which assured safe passage
    for even those whose hand or foot
      refused to remember the rope bridge
        from time to time.

  When all had been secured,
    packs made of necessary sustenance,
      each of those who would be carried
        assigned to one whose strength
        was equal to the task,

THEN
  The People gathered at the beginning
    of one more rope bridge
      across great difficulty
      toward a future none could guess.

  All paused in some hesitation before the task.

  Daughter of Wisdom
    stepped to the edge of a higher level
      and spoke . .

    "Now Ancient Wisdom"
    -- she began --

    "You may watch a People
      who have chosen their path to Tomorrow.

"NOW ANCIENT WISDOM"
   -- she went on --

"YOU MAY SEE FROM HERE A VAST ISLAND..
   AND SOMEWHERE ON THAT ISLAND
     YOU WILL REMEMBER
      TO FIND YOUR CHILDREN.

"For you
   whose wish began our journey
    will watch us from this place
     as we learn this new land.

"REMEMBER US,
   MOTHER TO US ALL,
    AS WE REMEMBER YOU.

"We leave here now,
   at the edge of this great chasm,
    all that is left to us
     of your Earth Nature.

"LET IT BE SO."

AND WITH GREAT CEREMONY,
   Daughter of Wisdom
    placed her carefully wrapped
     and herb-filled bundle
      just below the edge of mountain,
       covering it with one great stone.

THEN SHE TURNED..
   and in silent memory
    all the people remaining on this side
     of that great chasm
      began the task
       of walking a rope bridge through air
        from one side to the other.

One by one they filed across that bridge
   carrying -- some of them --
     packs of this and that
   carrying -- some of them --
     those not yet able
       to essay such rope walking . .
     those the Sorrowful Man called Short of Leg.

They continued in this task
   throughout the day.

UNTIL AT LAST
   Daughter of Wisdom effected her own crossing,
     leaving behind her precious bundle.

Only the Three Messengers
   remained on this first edge
     of another great crossing.

And these, one by one,
   also walked air across a great chasm.

Nor did anyone venture --
   as He Who Stood Forward had done --
     to loosen this end of rope
       so that the whole might be recovered.

RATHER,
   ALL THE PEOPLE TOGETHER
     left this carefully crafted, narrow passage
     at the foot of the rock which marked the place
     from which Ancient Vision may yet watch
       to learn the chosen path
         of a Whole People
           who walked together
             through great difficulty.

           walking through water,
           walking through air --
           and arrived
             on another Great Island,
           arrived
             on the farther side
               of a Great Chasm.

AND
   WHEN ALL THE PEOPLE
      STOOD GATHERED ON THIS FURTHER SIDE . .

   Daughter of Wisdom
      turned and called back across this depth . .

      "WATCH US, OUR WISDOM
      WATCH US, OUR MOTHER

      "HERE
         ARE A WHOLE PEOPLE
            WHO HAVE LEARNED
               TO WALK THE EARTH AS ONE."

AND
   WITH NO FURTHER WORD

   THE WHOLE PEOPLE
      TURNED . .

      AND SOUGHT
         TOMORROW'S PATH.

The Southern Path

NOW
    You may wonder
        how it was for us then,
            seeking a Southern path toward Ocean.

YET LITTLE HAS BEEN PRESERVED
OF THOSE DAYS.

There are songs of mountain wanderings,
    down this way and that,
        songs of seeking a southward direction.

Yet no exact thing
    has been recorded of finding the way
        until the People came to the eastern slope
          of a great series of mountains.

They called them
    The Mountains That Never Stop,
        for it seemed they never should.

YET THE PEOPLE CONTINUED.

It was in their mind
    that East
        had been more often their direction
      than South.

For this reason
    it seemed to them that somewhat West
        was necessary to find Ocean.

And for this reason
    they sent small groups out again and again
        to find a westward path
          through these never-ceasing mountains.

AGAIN AND AGAIN
    These groups returned
        to the Place That Sustains Life
          kept by most of the People.

They brought sad tales of mountain passes
    grown even more difficult with every day's walk.

YET THE PEOPLE WERE NOT DISCOURAGED.

"Those who go quickly East
    may find the way West a slower process"
        -- someone said.

And all the People laughed at this Wisdom.

AND SO
    The People devised a way of living
        that allowed comfort for many.

Seeds of this or that
    were encouraged into Earth
        near each new For-Awhile Community.

Thus assured of continuance,
    individual groups went out again and again,
        seeking westward transit.

NO ONE ANY LONGER
REMEMBERS HOW MANY WINTERS
*   PASSED IN THIS MANNER.*

ALTHOUGH
    These changes of the seasons since Walk-by-Waters
        were counted,
    The winters spent in For-Awhile Communities
        were not.

You and I must say, therefore,
    that many such seasons passed -- or a few --
        as the People tried again and again
            to find their westward march.

• • •

NOW IT CAME TO BE
    That two young men who were brothers,
      grown strong
        during this time of constant searching,
      asked to be sent
        on a particularly long and difficult mission.

    "Send us farther South
      than anyone has gone before . .
        and farther West also.

    "Do not ask us to return
      in even two or three Season Circles.

    "Let us go so far
      we cannot return in time . .

    "Then, when we have found our way,
      let us return East
        of these Mountains That Never End
      and walk North
        to find you wherever you may be."

THE PEOPLE SPOKE TOGETHER.
    It was not in their mind
      to do without these strong young men
        for such a time.

Yet surely,
    it was in their mind
      to find a westward path to Ocean.

They had found no one at all
    who seemed to know an Ocean Path.

Indeed, those they met had no awareness
    that Ocean might lie beyond.

For those few people they met
    concerned themselves only with Great Shaggies,
      catching smaller Four-leggeds
        when they could,
      and encouraging no seeds at all
        toward Earth.

These ones still let chance encounter
    determine the manner of their food.

After a day and night of discussion,
 the People at last decided that edge of Ocean
  held greater possibilities
   than two young and strong men
    might afford the community.

AND SO IT WAS
 That, when the weather turned again
  from Cold-and-Hard to Warm-and-Soft,
 These brothers
  gathered a Long-Traveling Pack
  and set off South . . .
   and were not heard from again
    for many Winters.

NOW THIS IS HOW IT WAS
    FOR OUR PEOPLE.

Living was not difficult.

Our Brothers and Sisters on the Earth
    were few,
    and were of a nature we did not recognize.

AS I HAVE SAID,
    They let chance
        determine the nature of their food . .
            though in this
                perhaps we misunderstood them.

Surely it was so, however,
    that they kept no one place
        for any length of time,
    in that manner
        seeming much like the Followers After
            we remembered from before.

Neither was any group of any great number.

Smaller yet than our greatly reduced group . .

No one at all living in the great numbers
    we had known before Walk-by-Waters.

These ones were not unfriendly,
    yet neither were they friendly,
        seeming to prefer to keep to themselves.

For this reason,
    little was to be learned from them,
        save we understood
            they knew the ways of the Four-leggeds.

AND YET THEY SOUGHT
    To prevent us watching the manner
        of their search for food . .

Neither was it clear to us why.

No group we met
    seemed aware
        there was anywhere in the world but this.

SO SMALL A SPACE
TO CONSIDER ONE WHOLE EARTH!

No oceans were known to them,
only lakes which might easily be walked around.

IN THIS MANNER
They could not understand our talk of Ocean,
thinking such only a great lake
taking some few days to walk around.

It seemed to some of the People
our talk of things
not understood in their way of being
might be one root cause
-- as roots predict the tree --
of their discomfort with our presence.

SO IT WAS
That the People moved
-- from time to time --
further South
along this Eastern Edge of Mountains . .

Until we found a place of great comfort,
a valley just long and wide enough,
sheltered to North and South by low hills,
open to the East,
and with the Never Ending Mountains
to the West.

Down this valley ran several small streams,
making islands here and there.

The Earth here was low and fertile.

HERE
  The People stayed
    for what they considered to be a long time . .
      sending out groups
        to search the westward path,
      wondering
        about the two young and strong brothers,
      singing songs of Walk-by-Waters
        and the Remembered Land beyond
          for those too young to remember . .

IN THIS WAY, TOO,
  ASSURING
    THE CONTINUANCE OF THE PEOPLE.

Two Strong Brothers

NOW BEGINS THE TELLING OF TWO BROTHERS.

IT WAS THEIR STRENGTH
 THAT LED US AGAIN TO OCEAN,

THEIR WISDOM AND DETERMINATION
 THAT LED US SAFELY THERE.

Where many
   might choose a path closer to the People,
These ones . .
   walked away toward an unknown Tomorrow.

Winding back and forth
   between these Never Ending Mountains,
      they sometimes lacked for food.

No seed encouraged toward Earth
   might bear fruit under their watchful eyes,
      eyes moving constantly South or West --
         or South and West,
      feet searching a path for Tomorrow's People.

YET
   These Brothers moved and moved again.

   Back and forth between possibilities
      they threaded their path.

   Again and again
      they searched out apparent ways
         between these Never Ending Mountains,

   UNTIL AT LAST
      They found the way too difficult
         for the many to travel.

      Some few ways possible for them
         were impossible for those
            who walk from one winter to another
               with many short of leg.

AGAIN AND AGAIN
   The Brothers sought out ways . .

UNTIL AT LAST
    They found themselves
        at the edge of a great cleft,
            looking down into a rushing river
            moving West or South or both.

For many months
    these Brothers found their precarious way
        along this river,
            seeking always the easier path
                that smaller feet might follow.

Ways easy enough for a Whole People
    were walked again and again
        to assure memory.

IN THIS MANNER
    They made their painstaking way,
        moving more and more West.

        • • •

A TIME CAME,
    In the first-warm season
        when things begin to grow . .

That these two purposeful men
    made their way
        up a cliff face beside the river
            and -- when they reached the crest --
    looked West over No Mountains at All . .
        hills of decreasing height walked West.

HERE, PERHAPS, LAY OCEAN

HERE, PERHAPS, LAY A PLACE
    FOR THE CHILDREN'S CHILDREN.

Walking resolutely forward,
    these two
        continued to follow the river,
        continued to search
            for an Ocean each knew must be there.

"We are an Edge of Ocean People"
   -- they told one another --

"Surely
   here we will find a place
     we may recognize."

As the river walked West,
   it grew in size and continuing strength.

No one at all
   might choose to swim therein
     to find whether it might be done.

No one at all
   might want to craft another rope bridge
     across this purposeful river.

FOR THIS REASON,
   The Brothers
     kept to the southward edge of river,
       walking West or South,
       finding a way a Whole People might follow.

DURING THIS TIME
   They met no one at all of the Two-leggeds.

The land grew more and more open
   as they walked the river's course,
     until the river widened.

FROM TIME TO TIME
   Ripples could be seen
     making their way up river.
   Sounds and smells changed also
     until the Two Brothers knew
       they neared the sea at last.

Crossing the last ridge,
   the blinding light of sun reflected on sea
     dazzled their eyes --

AND
   perhaps for this reason,
     they wept.

NOW
  I HAVE TOLD YOU HOW IT WAS
    FOR THESE TWO STRONG BROTHERS,

  HOW IT WAS
    they crossed many mountains,
      and crossed them again,
    so that Never Ending Mountains
      saw at last some distant edge.

  I HAVE TOLD YOU
    of ripples traveling upstream
    and of Ocean shining.

  I HAVE TOLD YOU
    HOW IT IS
      to arrive at some distant purpose,
        unaware
          of how great the distance may be.

NOW
  I WILL TELL YOU HOW IT IS
    THAT ARRIVAL AT PURPOSE
    MAY BE ONLY ONE SMALL PART
      OF THE WHOLENESS OF CIRCUMSTANCE.

IN FOLLOWING THEIR PURPOSE,
  No matter what personal energy it required,
    These Two had forgotten
      the relevance of counting days
        to measure distance.

They had not done so
  out of ignorance
  or lack of thought.

Rather,
  the circle dance of many seasons
    spent in vain pursuit
      of a westward passage
    had taught them the probable cost
      and encouraged them
        to forget to count it.

IT WAS THEIR THOUGHT
    that, whatever the requirement
      of the turning of the seasons,
        it was their purpose to continue.

IT WAS THEIR THOUGHT
    that too careful a count
      of the cycles of change
        spent outside the circle of the People
    would give them too much thought
      of Home and Fire and of the children
        who might now sit patiently before them.

IT WAS THEIR THOUGHT
*   TO BE FATHERS TO THE WHOLE PEOPLE,*
*   LOSING THEREIN, PERHAPS,*
*   THE OPPORTUNITY*
*   TO BE FATHERS TO SOME.*

They spoke much of this between them,
    laughing at what woman
      might encourage such aged men
        to sit beside them.

For surely they saw themselves as aged
    before they could return.

AND SO
    they had not counted
      the turning of the days,
      nor the changes of the moon,
      nor the circles of the change of seasons --
        trusting in their own ability
          to find their way back to the People
            once Ocean was attained.

NOW THEY STOOD,
    Eyes dazzled by a glistening Ocean,
      only a few winters passed since walking West,
        and no awareness of probable distance.

AND YET
*   THEY UNDERSTOOD*
*   WHAT HAD BEEN GAINED.*

The mountains, streams, and valleys crossed
were, indeed, well-learned --
stored in each memory.

NOW
It remained to find a path more directly East,
as surely the People
would have moved gradually South
during this time . .
and would continue to do so.

NOW IT BEGAN AGAIN.
The ceaseless pacing
up every possible valley
and down again . .

Weaving possible pathways
for a Whole People,
Measuring now
both the walking day-count of distance
and the probable distance covered by a People
among whom also walked many short of leg.

BACK AND FORTH
These Brothers
wove their awareness of possible travel

UNTIL AT LAST
the probable crest
of these Many Mountains was reached
and the land began to descend again
toward the grassy flatness they remembered.

Aware now of a broader reality
-- day count distance,
the possibility of sustenance
for a larger number,
locations here and there
where many might make short camp
to recover strength --

They wove in their minds
an image of possible passage
to bring back as a gift
to a Whole People.

NOW THIS WAS THE WAY OF IT.
  The People
    thought often of those Two Strong Brothers
      who had left them,
    thought how it was
      that they had given up
        an easeful place beside the fire.

  Such men
    might easily have earned
      a respected place by any fire . .

  Yet they spilled out this possibility
    upon the Earth . .
      and walked across it
        toward a more distant possibility.

NOW ALL KNEW
  HOW IT WAS WITH SUCH THINGS.

  Many might seek
    -- over some few changes of the moon --
      to understand something not yet known.

  Yet few enough walked out from the People
    for a full circle of the change of the seasons
      toward some possibility.

  And none at all
    since Rocks Fell Like Rain,
    since walking out from our Center Place,
      had ventured more than one such circle.

YET
  THIS WAS THE WAY OF IT NOW.

  These Two Young Men
    had walked out from among the People,
  Winters came and went,
    and yet they were not seen again.

  None considered them lost forever,
    yet those rapidly gaining age
      began to wonder
        whether they might again
          see those two faces.

AND
    THIS ALSO WAS THE WAY OF IT.

Those who encouraged the People
    during perilous times
      -- across a water bridge,
        a rope bridge,
        a great sky walk --
These ones now became
    one more of the People moving slowly South.

The pattern of their days was such
    that, as each accomplished
      whatever task was theirs,
        it was enough.

Moving slowly on their southward dance
    required some meaningful effort,
      but few great decisions
        requiring the wisdom
          of a Whole People assembled --
        the advice of Ancient Wisdom.

AND SO IT WAS
    That some among the People
      began a pattern of days,
Some sharing their memories of this or that,
    that those who would
      might listen.

AND
    IT CAME TO BE UNDERSTOOD

That some among the People
    held things more easily in their thoughts
And some understood the telling of it in such a way
    that feet
      felt the slippery rock by water's edge
    that eyes
      saw for the first time the Great Shaggies
        which were the first Four-leggeds
          on this Great Island
            they had taught themselves
            how to wait for.

AND SO THE PEOPLE DECIDED
*   THAT THESE*
*   MIGHT BE GIVEN A SPECIAL TASK.*

"Let them sit together"
   -- some one said --

"And let them speak with one another.

"Let those
   with the best ways of remembering
      speak first . .

"And let those
   who understand
      the nature of speech-for-action
         confer.

"Then let them tell all these songs
   to the Whole People
      so that each may speak their mind.

"IN THAT MANNER WE WILL TEACH OURSELVES
TO KEEP THE MEMORY OF A WHOLE PEOPLE
FROM ONE GENERATION TO THE NEXT,
*   BEYOND THE MEMORY OF ANYONE HERE."*

AND ALL SAW HOW IT WAS,
THAT WISDOM SPOKE THESE WORDS.

So, as what to eat became enough
   and winters assured,
      many of the People
         turned themselves to the task
            of crafting for a Whole People
               . . a Whole Memory.

AND
*   The joy of it was such*
*   that many not involved*
*   sat at the edge of the Circle*
*   while those seated within the Circle*
*   taught each other the many memories*
*   that are possible within a Whole People.*

Slowly they crafted songs for every generation
from then till now . .

Sang them for each other,
and -- when each among them
was pleased with the singing --
sang them for the Whole People.

NOW IT MUST BE SAID
That even this great fulfilling of a task
was not enough.

For as the songs were sung,
this one or that would remember
what had almost been forgot
and -- standing forward --
would ask for its inclusion,

AND IN THIS MANNER
THE MEMORIES OF A WHOLE PEOPLE
WERE CRAFTED INTO ONE GREAT SONG,
WHICH YOU AND I SING NOW . .

FOR
THOSE THAT LISTEN
-- TRULY LISTEN --
SING THE SONG
IN THEIR HEART.

NOW IT CAME TO BE
   That, as these songs
      were sung again and again . .

  Those among the People born so short a time ago
     that they never at all
       had seen the face of the Two Strong Brothers
     began to ask --

     "Where are they now?"
       and
     "Will our eyes ever behold them again?"

  Those who remembered These Two
     began to answer . .

     "Such Purposeful Young Men
       will not be turned away
         by distance only,
           nor by the dance of days.

     "They will find us.

     "One day we will wake
       and find two seeming strangers
         on the hill beyond
       and discover -- they are our Brothers."

AND ANOTHER THING OCCURRED.

  In answering these questions
    from the very young,
       those of more winters
          taught themselves to remember
      how it was that these Two Brothers
        had come to take upon themselves
          so great a task.

  They began to talk with one another
    about two young boys,
       curious always as to what had happened
       before they joined the Circle of the People.

    HOW IT WAS
      that their curiosity was so great
        that their questions never seemed to end,
      so that even the most patient among them
        found that patience running out.

Not a few, they came to understand,
    felt some relief at the going out
        of these Two Purposeful Men.

At least, they thought,
    questions would no longer dance
        so constantly on the wind!

YET NOW
    Here were the very young
        wondering every day
            about these Two Young Men.

AND IF THEY UNDERSTOOD IT BEFORE,
THEY UNDERSTOOD IT BETTER NOW.

It was the curiosity of the young
    which is the true gift
        to Tomorrow's grandchildren.

THE TRUE GIFT ALSO
TO TODAY'S POSSIBILITY.

FOR THEY SAW NOW,
    If they had not seen before,
        this questioning after past difficulty
            had firmed into a present purpose.

Those
    who had not bound themselves
        to a Whole People
            with rope longer
                than any had seen before . .

Those
    whose feet
        had never slipped on moss-slick rock,
    whose shoulders
        never had withstood a rock's pounding . .

These same ones
    had been strengthened by the telling,
        walked with mind's feet
            that narrow, water-washed crossing,
    bound themselves
        to the purpose of a Whole People.

Strengthened in this way,
   These Two had walked away from easeful living
      toward No-One-Knows,
         a land of little probability
           and much hoped-for purpose,
        an Edge of Ocean home
          for this Edge of Ocean People.

IN THIS MANNER
  They came to understand
    how much one may learn
      from what was never seen,
  save with the eyes that lie within.

AND IT CAME TO BE
  That the People valued more and more
    their songs of What Many Yet Remember,
      seeing the value it had
        for those whose feet
          had never walked that way at all.

NOW IT CAME TO BE
> That the very young
> > devised among themselves
> > > a thing they found of value.

> Each morning
> > one would go to the top of whatever hill
> > > lay to the South
> > and look further South
> > > to see if any two figures coming North
> > > > might be seen.

AND -- AFTER AWHILE --
> Some of these young and newly purposeful people
> > began to talk of going out further to look.

AND SO IT WAS AGREED
> That, when the finding of sustenance allowed,
> > seeds well encouraged into Earth . .

> Those few who chose
> > might walk a Great Circle to the South,
> > > looking to see
> > > > what might be learned of circumstance
> > > and whether or not four legs
> > > > divided between two people
> > > > > might be seen.

> It became a kind of celebration,
> > our Early Winter Circle to the South
> > > in search of Two Young and Purposeful Men
> > > > whose only thought
> > > > > was of the well-being
> > > > > > of the Whole People.

BUT WINTERS PASSED
> And -- whereas from time to time
> > some others of the Two-leggeds were found --
> > > our Two Brothers were not.

> So that those among the very young
> > who had reached additional Winters
> > > began to talk
> > > > of greater Circles to the South,
> > > extending into the Never Ending Mountains.

Those who had attained so many winters
  they remembered how few a People may become
    if many leave
      advised against this.

"How will you find"
  -- they asked --

"Four legs divided between two persons
  in the changing patterns
    of such Never Ending Mountains?"

"Perhaps, when each of you is grown,
  we will decide together
    a group that may go."

AND IN THIS MANNER
  The very young were something like content.

AND IN THIS MANNER
  THE PEOPLE HAD LEARNED ANOTHER LESSON.

GREAT PURPOSE IS NEEDED
  for the few
    to spill possibility upon the Earth
  and walk beyond for the benefit of all . .

YET TOO MUCH PURPOSE
  may shatter a Whole People
    against a quarrelsome rock of possibilities.

AND SO IT WAS
  THAT THEY CAME TO UNDERSTAND
    THE NEED FOR BALANCE
      BETWEEN CONTINUANCE AND PURPOSE.

NOW
What a People have learned
and what they therefore decide
may be two dissimilar things.

Understanding
the shattering force of Too Much Purpose,
a People may decide for less.

YET,
Understanding how it may be
for a People
in an unforeseen and adverse circumstance,
the People
never at all decided such a thing.

INSTEAD,
They chose to design other celebrations,

Celebrations
which led distant wanderers
back to the Circle of the People.

AND SO IT WAS
That after the Early Winter Circle to the South,

The People
came to mark the turning of the Winter
as a Great Celebration,
a celebration
of Ancient Songs and New Wisdom,
a celebration
of purpose and of return,
a celebration
of curiosity and of the Circle
in which that curiosity is nourished.

AND SO IT WAS
They began to learn
to balance strength of purpose
with stability of place.

"Our Circle on the Earth may move"
    -- they sang to one another --

"Yet it is the same Circle."

"Dancers may come and go"
    -- they sang --

"Yet the Circle must remain
    for the children's children's children."

AND IN THIS MANNER,
    And with the agreement of the Whole People,
      they decided a pattern
        whereby
          those who go out from among the People
            need seek their agreement to do so.

"With songs and rejoicing
    they will go forth . .

"With wherewith to eat
    and the possibility of water
      they will go forth . .

"With the understanding
    of the Whole People,
      they will go forth."

AND
    Such decisions came to be made
      at the Turning of the Year celebration --
        after this last season circle
        was understood,
        after the learnings therein
          had been pondered,
        after the purposes
          of each and of all the People
            had been considered.

THEN AND ONLY THEN
    SUCH DECISIONS WERE REACHED.

AND IT CAME TO BE
  A GREAT CELEBRATION . .

A CELEBRATION
  OF ACCOMPLISHMENT AND PURPOSE . .

A CELEBRATION
  OF CONTINUANCE AND CREATIVITY . .

A VERY GREAT . . CELEBRATION.

Circles On The Earth

NOW AS THE WINTERS TURNED . .

And those too young
to remember the faces of Two Strong Brothers
grew in stature,

IT CAME TO BE
that they asked and were allowed
a special responsibility
for Circles to the South
and this came to be understood
as the Circle of Growth.

AND YET THERE WERE OTHER CIRCLES.

CIRCLE TO THE NORTH
became Wisdom's Way,
the way the People had come,
the way the oldest among them remembered.

CIRCLE TO THE EAST
became the Dawn Greeting Circle,
the New Day Coming Circle,
it was dark and now I see Circle.

This Circle, too,
was seen as having a great value.

CIRCLE TO THE WEST
became the Quest for Understanding Circle,
even as the Two Strong Brothers
had circled West, expecting to return,
so others circled now
in celebration of such wisdom,
the need to learn and to understand.

NOW IT CAME TO BE
That these circles, too,
were added to the Circle of the People,
which became the Center Circle
of these other four.

AND THE PEOPLE SAW
THAT THIS WAS GOOD.

NOW
It came to be part of the Great Celebration . .
so that this one or that
would choose the circle to walk
which was most appropriate
for their learning that year.

As the People saw the value
of this circle of circles . .

IT CAME TO BE
that the center circle was understood
as that which contained
the learning and resident Wisdom
of the Whole People,

WHEREAS
those four circles dancing at the edge
became the personal circles
of each of those
who together constitute that People.

AND IT WAS SEEN AND UNDERSTOOD
THAT THE CENTER CIRCLE
NOURISHED THE WHOLE PEOPLE . .

WHEREAS
FOUR-CIRCLES-AROUND
NOURISHED INDIVIDUAL GROWTH
WHICH -- RETURNING TO THE CENTER CIRCLE --
NOURISHED, IN TURN, THE WHOLE PEOPLE.

AND IT CAME TO BE
That an understanding grew among them
of a double circle,
constantly walked.

The first of these
    the Whole People
        walked in a continuous direction.

The second of these
    was walked,
        as appropriate and needful to each one,
        as if it spun off from the Center Circle
          -- which indeed was so --
    so that
        it was walked in the opposite direction,
          returning each such individual
            once more to the Center Circle.

AND FOR A LONG TIME
    The People kept this Pattern on the Earth
        as a recognition of their understanding . .

The needs of each,
The needs of all,
    are appropriately walked
        in a continuous direction,
          each circle leading to the other
    so that all and each
        may continuously dance
          the Circle of the People
            and the Circle of Growth Within.

AND FOR THIS REASON
    You and I walk today
        this continuous double circle
        at the Turning of the Seasons,
        when Earth begins to turn again
        toward the light of growth.

AS IT IS SO . .
    SO LET IT CONTINUE . .
        SO THAT THE CHILDREN'S CHILDREN
        MAY LEARN THIS WISDOM.

NOW
   YOU HAVE HEARD
     HOW IT WAS FOR US THEN . .

   HOW THE PEOPLE
     patiently waited
       for the return of Two Strong Men . .

   HOW IT WAS
     that they designed a way
       of keeping the memories of each,
         in the memory of all . .

   HOW IT WAS
     that they designed a Great Celebration
       for each Return of Light Celebration.

NOW KNOW . .
   That patient waiting
     sometimes comes to fruitful end.

FOR
   As the Early Winter Circles to the South
     grew greater with each succeeding circle,
   So one year
     did five go out yet seven return.

AND THIS WAS THE WAY OF IT . .

   FIVE
     who asked for and were given responsibility
       for this Early Winter Circle
     took their first direction
       as South and also East.

   IN THIS MANNER
     they described with their feet
       a broader circle than the winter before.

   IN THIS MANNER
     learning the nature of the land
       as a gradual progression
         from winter to winter.

EACH DAY,
>as they walked this circle,
>>they crested every hill in eager anticipation
>>>of what might lie beyond . .

AND
>if no image
>>of four legs divided between two persons
>>>greeted their sweeping gaze . .

THIS MUCH WAS SO --
>each crested hill gave them access
>>to new understanding of the nature of Earth
>>>on the southward pathway.

Eager eyes sought the new location
>which the People might
>>from time to time require
>>>on their slow march to the South.

AND SO,
>As they sought their Two Strong Brothers
>>they sought also Tomorrow's home.

They learned accessibility of water
>and fertile earth for encouraged seeds,
>shelter from the winter winds,
>and the probable path of rain-met-with-earth
>>that may undercut the staunchest support pole.

AND IN THIS MANNER,
>Nothing was lost on their southward march
>>and much inevitably gained . .

So that More Than One Purpose
>also came to be the manner of the People.

NOW DURING THIS WINTER,
  I have told you,
    those who walked South were five . .
  Yet those who walked North were seven.

AND THIS WAS THE WAY OF IT . .

  Having reached the furthest southward point
    on the Earth Circle they walked,
      these five young men
        began the arching circle North --
        North toward their Home Place,
        North toward the People.

  Yet such is the nature of circles
    that this North was also West.

AND IN THIS MANNER
  These five walked closer than ever before
    to the Never Ending Mountains.

  Each crested hill found eager eyes gazing South,
    searching
      for four legs divided between two persons --
    yet none was seen.

  Day after day,
    feet turned West as well as North,
      these five watched the Southward path
        and searched the Westward mountains
          with unrewarded eyes,
        save that they learned with each glance
          more than they knew before.

YET IT BEGAN TO SEEM
  That their Northward journey
    would soon turn also East,
  Returning in that manner to the People
    with no more of Earth's Two-leggeds
      than had left the People many days before.

THEN IT WAS
  That they crested the highest hill yet found --
    one sitting close against the mountains.

  This was to be their westernmost point.

  Clearly, too, it was their highest.

So, with eager eyes,
    each young man crested this westernmost hill
        and searched the land to the South.

Who among them would be first
    to see four legs dance the far horizon
        under two separate beings?

THEN IT WAS
    That the first hill-crester
        breathed a sorrowful sigh . .

And, as he turned his eyes toward the path home,
    shared his thoughts with his brothers.

    "It would seem"
        -- he said --

    "That we must return once more
        in disappointment --

    "FOR SURELY
        these eyes see no moving image to the South
            which might become Two Strong Men
                as they approach.

    "AND SO
        I turn these eyes North and also East,
            beginning within myself the Song of Return
                with which we will share
                    all that we have learned
                        with the Whole People.

    "FOR SURELY
        even if we bring no returning brothers,
            we bring new learning
                of new possibilities to the South."

As his eyes swept North --
    and also East --
        he paused in this speech
            for a meaningful time,
                and then began again.

    "Cease your fruitless searching of the South,
        my Brothers,
            for I tell you now
                you will gain little from it."

AND
> As they grumbled their wish to search further
>> this one last time,
>>> he added --

> "Cease your fruitless searching to the South,
>> my Brothers,
>>> for it is ill directed.

> "These eyes can,
>> I think,
>>> assure you nothing will be gained,

> "For these eyes tell me
>> our two lost Brothers
>>> precede us to the North
>> and -- if we do not hurry --
>>> may reach our Home Place
>>>> before these ten feet can catch them!"

THEN ALL TURNED
> And -- one by one,
>> as their eyes separated from the land beyond
>>> two moving forms with two legs each beneath,
>>>> joined in a joyous shout
>>>>> and a much tumbling down the hill
>>>>>> in that general direction . .

• • •

AND SO IT WAS
> That ten feet did, indeed, move quickly enough
>> that -- hill by crested hill --
>>> four other feet were not so far ahead . .

UNTIL AT LAST
> Four ears heard the joyous shouting
>> and ceased their forward progress

UNTIL
> Ten feet and four
>> became at last twice seven on the Earth,
>>> forming the Circle of Mutual Recognition.

AND THIS WAS THE WAY OF IT . .

    What had been learned to the West
      was slowly shared . .

    As what had been learned to the South
      was shared.

YET
    These Many Feet Together
      sought the homeward path so eagerly
        that little enough was learned
          before the last nestling hill was crested
            and Where We Are Now lay below
              that these many eager eyes
                might see it.

THEN,
    I TELL YOU NOW,
      THERE WAS NO SMALL CELEBRATION!

    "This will be"
      -- someone said --

    "The greatest
      Turning of the Earth Circle
      we have yet known."

AND IN THIS
    THERE WAS NO DISAGREEMENT.

    For this was the year
      when nearly all the People
        chose the Circle to the West
          for their individual learning.

The Way West

THIS IS THE WAY OF THINGS . .

   As one Circle is danced,
      yet another becomes appropriate.

   So the return of the Two Strong Brothers
      closed the circle of their journey,
         making the next arc of a larger circle
            more apparent.

ALL KNEW
   That from Walk by Waters
      the People had walked usually East and South.

NOW
   West was the apparent next direction,
      making of their travels
         one great circle closed only by Ocean.

   For when the People
      heard of the bright, shining Waters to the West,
         a great shout went up.

   "Now this"
      -- someone said --

   "Begins to sound
      like a home place
         for the children's children."

YET
   AWARENESS AND COMPLETION
      ARE TWO DIFFERENT THINGS . .

   As the People came to understand
      as the Two Strong Brothers
         described their Earth Dance,
            a Circle to the West with many weavings . .

   One not easily walked by the whole People
      from Winter to Winter.

AND THIS WAS THE WAY OF IT.

Those who thought at first to begin at once
were rapidly disabused of the notion . .
too many mountains lay ahead,
too many canyons down which to walk,
too many rivers crossed with difficulty . .
and nowhere a great rope bridge
to cross from here to there.

YET THE PEOPLE HAD NEW HOPE
OF A MORE PERMANENT PLACE
AND WOULD NOT BE DISSUADED.

SO IT CAME TO BE
That they agreed among them
that this winter began a season of growth,
during which much would be kept
toward a variable future.

Drying racks were planned in every mind --
and carrying packs,
ways . . of moving with them
more than anyone would need
for many months.

For there were those among the People
who still remembered
the long and hungry walk
past Walk by Waters
and none at all were anxious
for such a learning to reoccur.

SO IT WAS
That all agreed to a variable plan . .

This changing of the seasons from Winter to Winter
would be spent in the much piling up
of things that ease rapid transit.

Wherewith to eat
that was easily carried
would be put aside for just that purpose . .
that which was not easily carried
would provide today's nourishment.

All gave thought to packs
　　that were easily accessed and as easily carried,
　　　　to ways that more might accompany the People
　　　　　　than ever before.

Yet the manner of their leaving
　　was not certain . .

For all agreed
　　that the following winter
　　　　was the time for measurement.

So that all that was stored
　　against a variable tomorrow
　　　　might be measured against the path
　　　　　　Two Strong Brothers described.

And perhaps early winter
　　might find the People on the move . .

Or perhaps another cycle
　　of much storing up of things
　　　　would be required.

AND IT WAS DURING THIS TIME
　　That the People taught themselves
　　　　how much might be carried
　　　　　　between two poles dragging over the Earth,
　　　　and how those same two poles
　　　　　　might provide ready protection
　　　　　　　　against a changing sky
　　　　　　　　　　even along such a distant path.

　　AND
　　　THIS NEW UNDERSTANDING
　　　CHANGED THE WORLD FOR THEM.

FOR YOU SEE HOW IT IS . .

How one person might carry more
than two might otherwise carry . .

And how the shortest of leg
or those bent low by whitened hair
might from time to time
join the bundles
between those two long poles.

AND -- IN THIS MANNER --
require less delay
than would otherwise be necessary.

AND SO AT LAST
THIS WAS THE WAY OF IT . .

Enough might be carried
by a Purposeful People
for even so distant a journey.

At the close of the time
for gathering in the things of this Earth --
those that walk
and those that walk with rooted feet . .

IT WAS DECIDED
that enough was here for Winter . . .
and for the Winter beyond --
so that the People might walk a distant path
with some sure purpose.

IT WAS DECIDED, THEREFORE,
BY ALL THE PEOPLE,

That an early Winter move to a new location
learned from the last Circle to the South --
near the highest hill
nestled against the Never Ending Mountains --
was an appropriate beginning
for the long walk West.

AND SO IT WAS
  THAT ALL THE PEOPLE ASSEMBLED..

Gathered at last in their old Home Place,
  packs filled with the promise of Tomorrow,
  skins stretched from pole to pole.

Carrying much
  that would be required
    for a winter against the mountains..

EVEN THIS PEOPLE
  SET THEIR FACES SOUTH AND ALSO WEST,
    SEEKING THAT TALLEST HILL
      AND THE BEGINNING OF TOMORROW.

NOW
    This was a decision
        which did not lack Wisdom . .

    For the People found their winter place,
        learned in that shorter walk
            which preceded the one to follow
                much that was useful thereafter.

*   And -- in the winter's quiet --*
*   gave themselves learning time*
*   with which to design their approach*
*   to Tomorrow.*

    For much of their thinking changed . .
        how to bind poles one to another
            for greater strength,
        which protection from a changing sky
            was most easily assembled,
        and which assembly brought best protection.

    Those things
        which showed signs of least long-keeping
            became that which the People ate
                during that long winter.

AND EVEN THIS LONG WINTER
SEEMED HARDLY ENOUGH.

    For the People discussed,
        again and again, how
            many people together
            might most easily make
                a rapid mountain transit.

AND IT WAS AGREED
    That all the People together
        would find an After Many Days camp,
            where many would remain
        while stronger others sought the next,
            carrying with them
                more than they might need . .

So that beginning camp was established by some
    while others returned
        to enable the same journey
            for the Whole People.

AND IN THAT MANNER
    They would enable greatest use of strength,
        that strength carrying with it
            those at the beginning
                and at the end of life

AND ANOTHER THING WAS LEARNED.
    How two who were strong
        might lift either end of two long poles
    And -- in that manner --
        enable crossing of rougher terrain
            than dragging poles might accommodate.

AND SO IT WAS
    This winter was spent
        in walking a future path
            with inward feet,
            learning what might be learned therefrom.

AND AS MORE WAS LEARNED,
    TOMORROW SEEMED MORE ASSURED . .

AND ALL THE PEOPLE
    FACED IN THAT DIRECTION
        WITH INCREASING EAGERNESS.

• • •

As mountain ice began to melt
and Earth soften beneath each foot . .

The People arranged stored goods for one last time,
packing all they planned to carry,
and began to climb the mountains
that would be their home
for at least another Winter.

The going up was relatively easy.
This side of mountain crest was somewhat known
and few flagged in the march,
relying still on resident energy.

YET
As the long march progressed,
more and more
chose to stay in each Many Days Camp,
while stronger others sought best routes
and assured best camp.

Nor did the Two Strong Brothers oppose this.

Better than any
they understood how many mountains
lay between them and the shining Sea.

Better than any
they understood how many camps
might form and disappear
before any foot grew wet with salton water.

AND SO IT WAS
That the People
slowly moved in incremental steps
toward their purpose.

Each chasm crossed was considered to be less
than one they crossed by rope.

And, as they discussed this among themselves,
those who were young
learned to value the efforts
of those who went before.

Especially were those so young
    they were carried across that rope bridge
        singled out for celebration.

"See how it is"
    -- someone would say --

"Who carries this one now?

"Rather,
    give this one a heavier pack,
        for they have earned the right to work
        for all the People."

"Here, let this one or that
    carry the Still So Young
        as they once were carried."

AND IN THIS MANNER
    did the People make slow march
        through the Never Ending Mountains,
        to which the Two Strong Brothers
        had indeed found an end.

• • •

NOW
    IT WOULD PLEASE ME TO TELL YOU
    That the People
        found great difficulty in this transit.

IT WOULD PLEASE ME TO TELL YOU
    IT WAS SO . .

SO THAT MORE MIGHT LEARN
    WHAT MIGHT BE OVERCOME
        BY A PURPOSEFUL PEOPLE.

YET I TELL YOU NOW
    IT WAS NOT SO.

I TELL YOU ALSO
  What the People learned from this.

THEY LEARNED
  That sometimes great difficulties
    are best overcome
      by some patient preparation.

AGAIN AND AGAIN
  SOMEONE WOULD SAY . .

"You see how it is --
  my Brothers, my Sisters --
    how we fail to run out of things!

"We have brought insufficient burden
  to those who hunt the Four-legged
    and to those who hunt our rooted brothers.

"Surely they will in turn
  fail to perceive we need them.

"IN THIS MANNER,
  we are ill prepared to want!"

AND
  All the People laughed and clapped their hands,
    joining in new songs about the value
      of slow preparation and slow eating . .
        slowly walked paths and distant purpose.

So that they saw
  they learned a tolerance for gradual progress
    to balance
      their tolerance for momentous tasks.

AND THEY SAW THAT THIS WAS GOOD.

• • •

It had been many days, now,
    since the People had begun this slow march.

Moon had turned and gone and come again
    four, nearly five times
        and already the crest of mountains
            lay beneath their feet.

Beyond lay more mountains than had now been crossed,
    stepping in a seeming nearly endless progression
        toward the West
    so that all minds turned to the thought
        that Never Ending Mountains was, perhaps,
            as good a name from East to West
                as it had been from North to South.

YET ALL KNEW
    That Two Strong Brothers
        had stood thigh deep in a salton Ocean.

AND YET ALL KNEW
    The Winter count of absence . .
        seven years in going out
            and five in the return,
    so that the youngest Always Carried
        counted thirteen Winters since that time

AS IF WITH ONE MIND
    The People wondered how many similar Winters
        might disappear in too much walking . .

UNTIL AT LAST
    one among the People
        clambered on a rock outcropping calling . .

"I was thinking.

"If only I were taller,
    perhaps I could see Ocean at the edge . .
    perhaps we should climb up
        to see the shining sea."

And all laughed at this Wisdom
    which said what it did not say
        and encouraged the People toward Tomorrow
        and away from lagging feet.

NOW
    The Two Strong Brothers stepped forward,
      indicating many mountains,
        and began to describe once more
          their travels.

    "There"
      -- they would say --

    "Is the chasm
      we crossed on such and such a day . .

    "And there"
      -- they would say again --

    "Lies the great river
      whose path we followed.

    "From here to there
      lie only many mountains.

    "Yet near that river lay many difficult edges
      with little place for feet
        between swift moving river
          and vertical rock.

    "Yet that way
      lies our closest route.

    "No long ropes,
      binding a whole People together
      are necessary here.

    "What is required here
      is great thought
        as to where each foot is placed
      and great care of the very young."

Without any further hesitation
    the People began their downward path,
      asking as they went
        the location of this and that,
    so that during the many tomorrows
      when mountains towered overhead
        they would remember when they lay below
      and remember
        their many patterns and directions.

        · · ·

NOW THIS WAS THE WAY OF IT.

    A People
        who would have wandered
            from one place to another,
                seeking some forward purpose,
        were guided instead
            by two of them who had made the journey.

    And the Two Strong Brothers made much of this . .
        calling out from time to time
            when they recognized this or that
                as if it were an old friend.

AND THE PEOPLE UNDERSTOOD HOW IT WAS
    That These Two told them over and over again
        they had been this way before,
    So that more among the people
        might gain a sense
            of guided and purposeful direction.

    Night camp found them sitting around a Central Fire
        telling how it had been for them,
            how this or that canyon
                was traversed from end to end,
                    looking for a better way.

    So that the People came to understand
        how travel from one winter to another
            might at first take many more.

AND IN THIS MANNER
  Were they assured
    of the probability of Ocean soon.

AND IN THIS MANNER
  They learned to value
    the gift these two had brought them.

AND FOR THESE REASONS
  They were increasingly honored
    among the People.

                • • •

NOW IT WAS AS THEY SAID.
  Many moons came and turned and left,
    the People finding themselves
      always further to the West . .

UNTIL THEY CAME AT LAST
  to a place where the sound began to change.

  Water,
    they heard.
  Water
    moving in many ways
      past many different things.

AND
  When some sought to rush ahead . .

  The Two Strong Brothers suggested
    that those for whom such travel
      had been most difficult --
    those bent low with years
      or still so close to Earth on growing legs --
    let these,
      who had in many ways
        made a more difficult journey,
          be first along this river to the sea.

AND
  ALL SAW THEIR WISDOM.

For surely patience along the journey is easier
  for the strong
    and for those whose long legs cover much earth
      than it is for those
        whose gait is slower and less sure.

So that all the People
  encouraged these ones forward,
    over the next rise,
So that their eyes might be the first
  to hold the image of the rapidly moving waters.

AND IT WAS SO.

• • •

NOW
  Much of this passage was,
    as the Two Brothers had said,
      of no great difficulty.

YET, NOW AND AGAIN,
  A place was reached
    which demanded great care
      where every foot was placed.

So that in these places
  those strongest and best skilled went first
    to mark the foot falls . .
  those with less strength went, then,
    between those with more.

AND IN THIS MANNER
  The People helped one another
    past each obstacle.

Working their way slowly along this great river,
  whose breadth became vast indeed,
    they learned a great respect
      for its rapid water.

Many narrow valleys --
  down which lesser streams sometimes flowed
    marked their path from time to time --
  so that these offered some small respite
    from an often vertical passage.

Yet camp was often difficult to make
in such narrow valleys.

AND
  The People traveled now as one . .
  slowly along a difficult path.

NOW
  The river widened yet again,
    giving some greater breadth of vision --
      transit along its edge grew easier
        as the height and slope along its edge
          grew less --
    so that night camps of greater comfort
      could be arranged.

IT SEEMED, NOW,
  Like a good time for a long camp . .

  Yet even the most weary among the People
    longed to see the shining Ocean.

    "These old feet"
      -- someone said --

    "Long for the rush of salt water once more."

    "If we only had a mountain"
      -- someone said --

    "Surely Ocean could be seen from here."

AND ALL AGREED IT COULD BE SO.

    "Watch"
      -- the Two Strong Brothers said --

    "Watch the ripples."

  And many understood,
    casting glances toward this widening river,
    seeking the telltale sign.

• • •

Two more camps
    and an easy transit followed.

The very young often ran ahead
    to study the river surface, making -- sometimes --
      their own contrary ripples --
        indications of a Two-Legged Ocean.

THEN AT LAST,
    MANY THINGS OCCURRED AT ONCE.

Someone said
    the salton smell grew apparent . .

Someone else
    that un-engendered ripples could be seen . .

Some climbed a hill
    and claimed a view of distant gleaming.

UNTIL
    All the People began to run,
      dip their hand in river water
        testing for the taste of salt.

Those with the greatest energy
    would leap up from time to time,
      claiming a distant vision.

The Two Strong Brothers held back.

    Direction was clear from here
    and they who had first seen
      this side of the Great Ocean
      need not be first again.

ALL NOTICED HOW IT WAS.

Sand appeared with wetter earth.

Ripples on running water
    more and more found every direction.

The river broadened
    to a shallow depth.

Birds of every nature
    called from the sky and dotted the water.

One last crest of sand lay before them --
    and the roar of Ocean beyond.

ALL PAUSED
    BEFORE THIS LAST BARRIER
      AND CELEBRATED
        THE NEARNESS OF COMPLETION.

THEN -- AS ONE PEOPLE --
They began a slow march
    over this last sand crest
      before the nearness of Ocean . .

And,
    when they reached its top,
      paused in breathless wonder
        at the world that lay before them.

A gleaming Ocean
    stretched away in every direction,
      river running slowly toward its home.

Birds of every manner sailed the skies
    and stalked its sand beaches,
      searching for continuation.

The young
    tumbled
      in this unaccustomed plenitude of sand,
    casting great handfuls in every direction.

No one was sure what to do next
    until one of the oldest among them said . .

    "I shall not believe it
      until I taste the salt."

And a rush began toward the pounding waters
    until all of the People who chose
      stood hip deep in salton water --
    evidence of this long-intentioned meeting.

NOW YOU SEE
  HOW IT WAS FOR OUR PEOPLE.

Long intentioned meeting with Ocean
  was today's task,
    leaving no task for Tomorrow.

Yet a People
  grown accustomed to slow-moving camp
    sustain themselves
      from one day to another
        with old habits.

SO IT WAS AT THAT TIME
  That those grown accustomed
    to a search for place
      began their usual dance.

Those grown accustomed
  to a search for continuance
    taught themselves
      the nature of River and Ocean
  so that sustenance
    might be procured therefrom.

NOT ALL KNEW
  That the dissimilarity
    between this Edge of Ocean Place
      and that other still remembered was such
        that the mere presence of Ocean
          seemed somehow insufficient --
            after awhile.

AND SO IT WAS
  That a Purposeful People --
    now met with their chosen circumstance --
      shifted that purpose slowly,
    so that more and more
      followed the edge of Ocean South,
        as well as North.

Those
  whose feet
    found the early Winter Circle to the South
      something appropriate,
    found now a similar circle.

AND SO IT WAS
   That the People's gathered understanding
      of this Edge of Ocean Place
         grew daily larger . .

AND IT WAS CLEAR TO THEM
   THAT THIS MANNER OF LIVING
      LAY A FIRMER BASE FOR TOMORROW.

Such
   is the nature of understanding
      and its value
   that much energy
      from each and all of the People
         is wisely invested therein.

SO --
   IN THIS PLACE
      OF SHALLOW WATER MEETS THE SEA,

   THE PEOPLE
      LEARNED A NEW PLACE

   AND TAUGHT THEMSELVES
      ITS VALUE.

. . .

NOW I WOULD SAY,
    IF IT WERE SO,

That the People found this land Enough . .

That its plenty so delighted their Spirit . .

That no thought of change came to them.

YET IT WAS NOT SO.

For a People
    who sought a mountain place against the sea
        found this land of low beach access
            disquieting.

All knew it was so,
    yet no one spoke.

UNTIL AT LAST,
    After a great storm and its pounding waves,
        someone rose and spoke.

"We remember how it was"
    -- he said --

"When mountains shook
    and rained their dust upon us
        in increasing slow cascades.

"We remember how it was"
    -- he went on --

"When Ocean disappeared to return again
    beyond our expectations,
    beyond our possibility of survival.

"I HAVE BEEN THINKING
 how it is in this place . .
 how it is that no mountains near at hand
  can shake their debris upon us.

"AND YET HOW IT IS
 that any great Ocean at all
  flows over this low land
   according to a variable circumstance,
 so that those resident thereon
  may seek in vain for any dry foothold.

"How would it be, in such a place,
 should Ocean rise once more
  and sweep all before it?"

NONE AMONG THE PEOPLE
 Found this an easy mind image.

All had heard from those who saw it
 how it was
  that all our Wisdom washed away.

NO ONE AT ALL --
 remembering
  the difficult passage of Walk by Waters,
  the newness of such Great Cold,
  the long walk South past many chasms,
  the Seven Winter Walk of Two Strong Brothers.

NO ONE AT ALL
 had any wish
  that such a purposeful People
   find themselves an under water home!

AND SO IT WAS
 That many searched the land around,
  looking for a convenient place
   that might survive great Ocean washing.

This hill and that
 was studied and found too low.

Yet "toward the mountain"
 was far, indeed, from Ocean.

IN THIS MANNER,
The People taught themselves
that no place near here
bore adequate resemblance
to the Center Place
that had been home
for so long no one remembered how long.

IN THIS MANNER
They also learned
they were not content with where they were.

"You see how it is, my Brothers, my Sisters"
-- someone said --

"We who have come a long way,
we who have arrived at long-thought purpose,
we who stand on the place we sought . .

"WE ARE NOT CONTENT!"

AND SO IT WAS
That the People explained to one another
that Purpose may be better than Finding . .

HOW IT WAS
That accomplishment of Purpose
may only show the way to Purpose Beyond.

AND THEY SAW HOW IT WAS
THAT THIS WAS IN NO WAY SORROWFUL
AND IN EVERY WAY GOOD.

"You see how it is"
   -- an Old One said --

"We have come to be a People
   who are comfortable with Purpose.

"Living from day to day
   is not enough.

"Nor even Winter comfort
      is any longer enough.

"We have come to be"
   -- she went on --

"A People
   whose nature is better shared
      with the Not-Yet,

"A People
   who select a Path
      the children's children may yet follow.

"NOW
   let us select such a Path.
   let us choose to search the edge of this Great Ocean
      for a place
         that gives our Spirit greater comfort . .
      one which allows
         a looking-down view of Ocean,
         a possibility of escape
            from too much water."

AND SO IT WAS --
   ALL AGREEING --
      THAT THE GREAT SEARCH BEGAN.

⋈⋈

NOW
 Few at all
  sought the Northern path.
   Though a place at Ocean's Edge
    fills the air with greater warmth,

 Yet all remembered
  the many snows of previous winters
  and none at all
   chose to sustain such winters.

SO IT WAS
 That South was better than North.

 Those who walked South found many streams,
  less broad though no less shallow
   than the one they knew.

 Here and there
  high elevations greeted the open water.

 Yet no Place was found
  which was judged similar enough
   to the general purpose of the People.

 Some Season Circles passed
  in this widening search.

UNTIL AT LAST
 The People began to discuss the possibility
  of some mountain valley close to the sea.

 No Sea-Meets-Mountain place was found
  that offered shelter from the open Ocean,
   yet access to all the Ocean holds.

AND THEN ONE DAY
 The last South Circle party returned.

 And these ones brought
  a Telling of Earth and Ocean,
  a Telling of Others Walk These Shores,
  a Telling so wondrous
   that all paused in their many doings
   to join the listening circle.

AND THIS WAS THE WAY OF IT.

> Bright shores met green hills to the South
>> so that the patient undulation of the land
>>> rose in no way sharply,
>>>> as the Center of our World had done.

> And yet Looks-Over-Water access
>> was to be found, here and there,

> Land level enough
>> for a Whole People to join in community,

> High enough
>> so that a distant view of Ocean was possible,
>>> access to Ocean a somewhat walk away.

> Farther South they went in searching
>> until a river of some greater proportion
>>> was reached,
>> this river flowing more swiftly into Ocean.

> Beyond it was a rise of land
>> and beyond that
>>> others of those
>> who walk the land on no more than two legs
>>> might be seen.

NOW
> THIS WAS THE AMAZEMENT.

> Between here and there,
>> along the surface of this swifter river,
>>> this People stood to cross it.

> I DO NOT TELL YOU
>> that they walked toward water,
>>> feet disappearing underneath.

> I TELL YOU
>> they stood upon the water --
>>> those that did not sit --
>> and traveled its surface
>>> on a kind of platform we might use over land
>>>> whose surface
>>>>> grew too wet for central fire . .
>> yet this platform was curved,
>>> enclosed so that no foot at all was seen.

YET,
   reaching river's edge,
      all stepped out upon the shore,
      hardly at all dampened by their river crossing.

AND SO IT WAS
   This Circle to the South
      thought they would return --
         share this understanding --
      wondering whether it was our thought
         to encounter such a Water Walking People.

AND SO DISCUSSION BEGAN.

AGAIN AND AGAIN
   Those who circled to the South
      on a narrow coast pathway
         described all that they had seen --
            narrow rivers and level hilltops,
            distant Ocean and ease of access,
            wider river and standing platforms . .

   UNTIL AT LAST
      each mind image
         gleanable from this Circle Path
            had been shared . .

AND AT LAST
   Someone rose and spoke.

   "It seems to me"
      -- he said --

   "That no one at all
      will truly understand what has been seen
         until each of the People sees it also.

   "I understand"
      -- he went on --

   "The nature of wood floats on water.

   "I understand"
      -- he continued --

   "How anyone at all who swims
      can benefit therefrom.

"Yet I fail to understand"
-- he finished --

"How anyone at all may stand thereon
for the purpose of water crossing.

"And so these eyes at least
will seek a southward path."

AND
The memory of Other Eyes
sat clearly in the hearts of the People.

So that they saw Wisdom's Path
lay to the South,
where all might learn . .
the manner of this water walking.

AND SO IT WAS DECIDED.
Those with greater curiosity
to know and understand
formed a second circle to the South.

While all others
remained in their present place,
gathering to them wherewith
for all the People
to make such a journey.

. . .

AND
    It was this latter group
        who learned to their sorrow
            the summer dance of a sand place.

    For small things that fly came among them,
        disturbing both tranquility and pleasure,
           so that South
                seemed increasingly the wiser path.

    Those who could
        organized themselves
           to live and gather continuance in the hills,
             away from small things flying.

    Those who must
        remained at water's edge,
           gathering its sustenance
           and discouraging small things flying
             with frequent splashing
                and dabblings of mud . .

    So that those who became one with Earth
        had the greater comfort . .

    And their Brothers to the hills laughed mightily
        at those who chose to leave the People
           and join the Earth . .

    And yet they knew
        that a fool's dance has frequent value.

    These Earth Brothers were they
        who caught and dried those who swim
           for the long Southward journey.

"Let us celebrate"
  -- some one said --

"A People
  who have the Wisdom to join Earth
    so that a Whole People
      may more easily
        find Tomorrow's Purpose."

AND
  SHE BEGAN A SONG
    THAT OUR PEOPLE
      REMEMBERED FOR A LONG TIME,
      A LONG TIME ..

"Let the Nature of Earth
  and the Nature of Water
  and the Nature of the People
    so combine

THAT TOMORROW
  MOVES TOWARD US
    ALONG OUR CHOSEN PATH .."

    SO BE IT.

The Water Walking People

NOW
    Those who found sustenance
        among water-washed rocks,
        among the hills,
        and from the waters
            were joined again
                with those whose Circle to the South
                    provided Second Wisdom.

They came
    with greater understanding
        of this Walking Water People.

They came
    full of awareness
        that a People we found so amazing
            might easily find us so.

They came
    bringing thoughts with them
        of a small river North of this
            that might make a Winter camp
                for a People seeking understanding . .
    so that by small increments
        they might gain this sought-for wisdom,
    and, by small increments,
        meet at last this Walking Water People.

. . .

AND SO
    THIS WAS THE WAY OF IT.

Before the greater cold
    of this milder winter country began,
        the Whole People rose up,
            gathered wherewith to live,
            and established a new Winter camp
                on a rise above one narrow river.

Two days travel carried anyone who chose
   close enough to the wider river
      so that they could begin to understand
         this Water Walking People.

Sustaining themselves where they were
   and traveling South from time to time
      they began to understand
         how it was with them,
         how water
            was a way for them
               from here to there,
      whereas for our People
         a stream great enough
            for their water walking
               might be for us too great to cross.

UNTIL AT LAST ONE DAY
   Some one said . .

   "YOU MAY SEE HOW IT IS,

      "How we are a People
         who stand up and walk
            anywhere at all
               a firm foothold may be found,

      "How we are a People
         who Walk by Waters,
         who walk sky bridges,
            carrying Tomorrow with us.

   "YOU SEE HOW IT IS FOR THEM,

      "How they are a People
         who stand up and walk . .
            to the nearest water,
               sitting thereon . .
                  on their platform.
         In some manner
            we not yet understand,
               water becomes the path."

AND ALL THE PEOPLE
SAW THAT IT WAS SO.

How for us what was a barrier
became for them a path
and how our paths
made light of their barriers.

AND IT CAME TO BE
That the People saw a possibility,
how we might live with the Water Walking People
by walking the forest around them.

AND SO IT WAS DECIDED
AND A NEW WAY SOUGHT.

FOR
This Earth Walking People
had no wish to chase logs across the river
and so a passage further upstream
was patiently sought for . .

And an approach
toward this Water Walking People was designed
which walked through the forest,
which they did not value,
rather than approach by water,
which they saw as their own path.

AND SO,
As the Earth warmed,
this inland path
was walked by the Whole People,
approaching slowly
from the East and also South,
making camp far enough away
so that too many mouths
might not be seen as empty,
so that only those chosen by the Whole People
might approach this Walks the Water People.

. . .

When all was arranged
   as for a summer camp . .

Those who were chosen
   went out toward the community
      built by those who Walk the Water.

Coming upon the edge of this circumstance,
   they were rapidly met by some who were men.

You need not know,
   for it is easily guessed,
      what difficulty comes between two Peoples
         neither of whom is used to communication
      beyond the immediate group.

AS IT WAS,
   SO LIFE CONTINUES.

Yet, through this circumstance
   the People learned a great lesson . .

How much thought and effort are wisely invested
   in the possibilities of such communications.

Three days were required
   to establish some mutual understanding.

We were as wondrous to them
   as they to us . .

Yet our People
   showed less concern
      for the differences in manner.

It was the very young
   who first began
      to learn the nature of their speech.

Listening quietly
   from the privileged position
      a lack of stature earns you,
   they rapidly learned the patterns
      of this new speech.

Bringing this learning with them,
   they settled around our Central Fire
      and became those from whom we learned,
Sharing in this manner their new-found wisdom.

AS WE LEARNED
    We began to ask this nearby People
        whether or no
            our living near them in the forest
            seemed appropriate.

IT WAS OUR THOUGHT
    to learn from them,
    as they from us.

IT WAS OUR THOUGHT
    to come to understand
        their Walk the Water ways.

AND YET
    They wondered less about us . .
        it seeming to them strange
            only that we had arrived by land
            and not by water.

THEN
    We asked them in this manner,

    "How is it
        that you have come to live in this place?"

    "It is our place"
      -- they replied --

    "And how came you here?"
      -- we asked again --

    "Our Old Ones understand this."
      -- they replied and sent us to inquire.

    "LONG AGO,
      LONG AGO,
        LONG AGO,"
      -- these ones began --

"THERE WAS NO EARTH,
  BUT ONLY WATER.

"On the face of the waters
    in every direction
        nothing at all could be seen.

"The People were afloat
   in the midst of endless Ocean,
      with water falling down
   so that air and Ocean were nearly one.

"And then the water ceased to fall
   and the Ocean extended around us
      in every direction.

"Nor was there any understanding
   as to where we might go.

"And the People wailed their sorrow
   calling out
      for some assistance
         in the naming of direction,
      for some small piece of Earth
         on which to stand.

"But no answer came.

"Then on the third day
   a messenger came.

"Black Bird came
   and brought land out of the water,
      on which land we presently stand,
   so that we know
      this was a land Black Bird brought us
   and we are a People
      who celebrate this understanding."

WE CAME TO UNDERSTAND
   That their world
      had been brought to them by Black Bird,
      out of an endless Ocean.

Even as our path to this place
   had wound down the valleys
      of the Never Ending Mountains.

"You see how it is"
   -- we told one another --

"An Endless Ocean
   has an end at last,
      and Never Ending Mountains
      also greet the sea!"

YET
  THE NATURE OF BLACK BIRD
  LAY BEYOND OUR UNDERSTANDING.

NOW IT WAS
  That this Water Walking People came to us
    and said
      that if we would do this and that for them,
        they would agree to our nearby presence
          and bring us some of those that swim
            that grow to large size.

AND THIS WAS AGREEABLE TO US.

AND
  This was also the nature of our discussion.

  It was their wish
    that we call them
      by what they called themselves,
        and this was Black Bird's Children.

  Then they asked at last
    where we had come from.

  We told them how it was
    that we had walked around the northern edge
      of this nearby Ocean.

  Though we said in many ways
    what length of days
      this crossing had required,
        they seemed unwilling to know
          how great a land this may imply.

  "You see how it is"
    -- we said to one another --

  "These ones also see the world
    as islands
      surrounded by a greater sea.

  "Yet their islands
    seem clearly smaller in their mind
      than this great island on which we stand
        seems to us.

"So it is
    that their mind
        will not expand to match this great size,
    and yet
        they say the Ocean is without limit."

"We have come"
    -- we finally told them --

"From farther away
    than you might imagine . .

"And --
    since we lack your skill with Water Walking,
        we placed one foot
            in front of the other
                all the way."

This was a great amazement to them.

It was spoken of from one to another many times,
    until at last one said . .

"We hear how it is for you . .

"How walking is your way
    as travel on the water is ours.

"WE SEE . .
    YOU ARE A WALKING PEOPLE."

AND
    IN THAT PLACE,
        THIS BECAME OUR NAME.

NOW
    Our days were spent in slow learning
       and no great care.

    The nature of this forest
       was different than those we knew . .

    Yet many of our skills were still appropriate
       to this new circumstance.

    Far beyond this place
       we dug into the Earth
         and encouraged our seeds.

IN THIS MANNER
    We thought to avoid too much learning
       for this Water Walking People.

    The nature of their minds
       seemed to resist new learning.

    Yet their ways were various and effective
       for this place.

    Plenty was the nature of all they had,
       with more than enough to share,
         so that our encouraged seeds
           were kept for our own People,
        and this other People found them
        seeds
           too small for consideration,
           too soft to be valuable as nuts.

    Neither did this offend us.

WE SAW HOW IT WAS FOR THEM,
    How being unwilling to expand their thoughts
       to the size of this vast Island,
         they had little interest
           in learning what lay beyond their world.

THEIR WORLD WAS WATER
    WITH BLACK BIRD BRINGING EARTH.

They had lived here, they said,
  "Since the beginning."

  And that beginning
    was wrought by Black Bird.

OUR WAY --
  Walking as we did on one foot
    and then the other --
      seemed to them inferior.

    "Clearly"
      -- they said --

    "Wiser people travel as do we."

    Oceans exceeding such possibility,
      streams too narrow,
      and vast mountains
        held for them little interest.

AND SO
  WE CONTINUED AMONG THEM,
  LEARNING THEIR WAYS.

  AND THEY LEARNED LITTLE FROM US.

              • • •

NOW ONE DAY
　　There arose an extraordinary commotion
　　　　at the edge of their wider river.

　　Neither were we allowed
　　　　to approach the direction of this commotion.

SO IT WAS
　　That all we know of these events
　　　　came to us through one of our own
　　　　　　who now counted twelve Winters.

　　This one found an infinite fascination
　　　　in the manner of Water Walking.

　　Whereas none of us fully grown in height
　　　　were encouraged in this direction,
　　　　　　these younger ones were permitted
　　　　　　　　and spent much of every day
　　　　　　　　　　in contemplating
　　　　　　　　　　　　the nature of Water Walking.

　　In this we encouraged them,
　　　　relieving them of any alternate tasks.

IT WAS OUR PURPOSE
　　To learn to understand the how-ness
　　　　of what they did
　　　　　　to cross their many rivers.

FROM THIS
   WE LEARNED TWO THINGS . .

  These were an every-day People.

  Living in a land of little change --
    save it rains or it does not --
      their preparations from winter to winter
        were less than ours.

  Their rivers, filled with those that swim,
    never seemed to lack.

  Their supplies of seeds and nuts --
    gathered from time to time --
      were never depleted
        before they were refilled.

  And one season seemed to lay over another
    so that one kind of gathering
      began before the last was complete.

IN THIS MANNER,
  This People over continuous generations
    had had no reason
      to learn the value of Tomorrow --
        carrying wherewith to live
          past a Winter's limitation.

FOR THIS REASON
  They had little concern
    past the reliability of today.

  This being their custom,
    it did not seem among their thoughts
      that those
        who learn during their Twelfth Winter
          will soon have passed their Twentieth.

  Perhaps, since they had not seen us
    nor any other differing People,
      before the day we walked among them --
    it was not in their mind
      that we would be here winter past winter.

WHEREAS
These seemed limits they refused to exceed . .

IT WAS SPOKEN OF AMONG US
AND DECIDED . .

That we would learn to understand
these thoughts,
this way of thinking,
and allow the pattern of their days
to ease the pattern of our own.

AND SO IT WAS
That we encouraged our young
to spend their time in unopposed learning,
all the People benefiting therefrom.

NOW I HAVE SAID
    That the day came
        when a great commotion arose.

AND I HAVE SAID
    The young among us
        were the only of our People
            allowed as witness to it.

    This One of the twelve-winter count
        was first in understanding of
            the manner of Water Walking.

    It was even he
        who had first put words to our amazement --
            seeing these ones
                pace back and forth over apparent water.

    It was he
        who pointed to whereon they walked
        and named them platforms.

NOW
    It was he
        who brought to us day by day,
            careful descriptions
                of the crafting of these platforms.
    These were brought
        as his gift to our Central Fire.

    Carefully laid out and carefully described,
        he spoke of how it is
            a People may require Tree as transit,
        how these trees
            may be encouraged to Earth before their time,
        how they may be cut and carved and shaped . .
            often much as our own People
                crafted smaller things.

    This crafting was sometimes from one tree
        and sometimes from more . .
            but many whole trees
                were indeed consumed in this manner . .

    The handling of resultant wood
        yielding, perhaps, the greatest lesson.

AND ALL THESE LEARNINGS
    WERE CAREFULLY KEPT.

NOW WE COME ONCE MORE
    To the day of great commotion.

He of the twelve-winter count sat by the waters
    studying the nature of construction,
        when another of these platforms
            with the curved up edges
                formed itself in the distance
                    and began to approach.

Since from time to time,
    these platforms came and went,
        He of Twelve Winters
            was puzzled at the noise.

Never before had any such been greeted
    by other than small amounts of joy.

Here
    there seemed both fear and consternation.

AND THEN HE UNDERSTOOD.
    These were not from among the People here,
        but were unknown to them --
            unknown from any previous time.

And he began to understand how it was . .

A People who understand
    that Black Bird brought land from water . .

A People who have no wish
    to listen to the vastness of this land . .

Such a People
    may have no way to explain arriving others,
    no way to tell themselves
        whether Black Bird again
            brought land from water
            or brought forth the newly arrived.

Such a People
    may have no wish to contemplate newness.

YET
    These new arrivals
        sought some welcome,
        sought some permission to stay.

AND WHEREAS
    This People who abjured the new
        and found communication difficult . .

    Our young,
        having newly learned their language,
            found it easier
                to understand one language more . .
            finding also some similarity between the two.

    Since their presence went unnoticed
        and their attention was not sought,
            they waited patiently
        until the issue of where to be was resolved
            sending word to our Walking People
                of the new arrivals.

AND IT CAME TO BE
    That some agreement was reached,
        but friendship was not.

    These new arrivals
        were allowed space on the beach,
            but not in the houses.

    They were allowed time to replenish their keepings
        for the long Ocean Walk they seemed to plan.

    And when they described this leaving,
        none sought to dissuade them,
            but relief from concern touched every face.

            . . .

NOW
    He of Twelve Winters
        made this learning his special task.

    As soon as no one restrained him,
        he gained access to this new Ocean platform,
            studying more closely than before
                the nature of its construction.

    It grew rapidly clear to him
        that the relation between these two people
            was closer and closer . .
                not only the manner of their crafting,
                not only the patterns of their language,
                but the manner of their behavior
                    was in many ways similar . .

    So that
        He of Twelve Winters saw they were related,
        these new arrivals saw they were related . .

YET
    This People who abjured the new
        saw no relation at all . .

    They saw only difference . .

    And the difference more disturbing
        because of the similarity.

SO IT WAS
    That they offered little help
        to these new arrivals.

    Those that swim were easily obtained
        and drying racks appeared on the beach.

    Seeds and nuts were sought,
        but gathered only with difficulty
            as these ones who disliked the new
                were concerned
                    lest too much familiarity with place
                      incline the new arrivals to stay.

IT WAS THEN
    THAT WE SAW OUR OPPORTUNITY . .

THEN
    That we understood
        the nature of this possible exchange.

    Through our young
        we offered these new arrivals an exchange.

    If they shared their learning with our young
        with a willing and open heart . .

    We would share our more-than-enough with them . .
        enabling thereby their long Ocean Walk.

AND THIS WAS PLEASING TO THEM.

    They were puzzled
        as to why those they considered brothers
            grew so anxious for their going away.

    Yet they were not puzzled
        by our presence.

    They had met, they explained,
        many different Peoples . .
            and walking as a way of life
                was not unknown to them.

AND THIS WAS THE WAY OF IT.

    He of Twelve Winters
        returned at opportune times to our Central Fire
            to share what he had learned --
        seeking to hear wonderings
            from the Whole People --
        and from these wonderings
            to design the next day's quest.

SO IT WAS
    That he asked one day
        the nature of their arrival.

    They had come, they said,
        over a Great Water
            which was well known to them,
                seeking land they knew must be there.

THE MANNER OF THEIR KNOWING
   WAS THIS . .

It was well known among their People
   that a Great Land
     lay beyond the Great Water.

The manner of this Ocean Crossing
   was also well known . .

Yet for this or that reason --
   great storms and changing circumstance --
     no one at all
       had returned from any Great Ocean Circle
  so that fewer and fewer left,
    until no one living
      any longer remembered such an outgoing.

Yet it was well known among them
   that such had been the manner of their people
     for time beyond time.

NOW
  It was a great amazement to them
    that we understood whereof they spoke,
      yet their brothers
        understood them not at all.

AND IT WAS AT THIS TIME
  That we explained
    how Black Bird brought this people,
      pulling land out of the water.

AND
  THIS PUZZLED THEM GREATLY.

"The manner of this Ocean
  has been well known among our People
    since time beyond time"
      -- they said --

"There never was an only-water time.

"Rather, Ocean and Earth
　　relate to each other
　　　　in ways we find convenient."

AND
　　They described once more
　　　　their Great Ocean Circle,
　　　　　　arriving at this Great Island,
　　　　　　traveling south along its edge,
　　　　　　　　then out again to Ocean,
　　　　　　　　　　to arrive at islands of no great size
　　　　　　　　　　and which they called Ha-va-i-kay.

Now these islands offered little
　　save a chance to gain unsalted water
　　　　and some new continuance,

But much was gained
　　in learning that the appropriate way
　　　　was followed
　　　　and to assure this
　　　　and to encourage all subsequent others
　　　　　　soft rocks were marked with symbols
　　　　　　　　which identified
　　　　　　　　　　He Who Led each Water Walking group
　　　　　　　　and a great celebration was held
　　　　　　　　　　before continuing this Ocean march.

AND THIS WAS THE WAY OF IT.

Only one
　　who had made this Great Circle on the Ocean
　　　　would be given responsibility
　　　　　　for a new community.

People and goods
　　would be subsequently laden
　　　　onto his Great Ocean Platform
　　and a new way toward a new land
　　　　was his to learn.

And he who led this group
　　willed the establishment
　　　　of such a new community.

　　　　　　• • •

NOW
There grew up among our Peoples --
these new arrivals and our own --
many great friendships . .

So that as they prepared
for their long Water Walk
and tried their platform on the water,
some of our people went with them.

And the manner of this travel
was so pleasing to them
that they asked if they might join them
for their Great Water Walk.

And when all understood
that no possibility of return was here . .

Then two from among our People
were allowed to walk the water with them
as two of their People
had been lost during their travel
and space and need were there.

BUT
He of Twelve Winters,
despite his forever curiosity
about all manner of water walking,
chose to remain with the Walking People,
chose to remain with his own.

AND SO IT WAS
That -- after several moons had appeared
and turned and disappeared --
these new arrivals left,
as did two of our own People,
and were never seen again.

NOW
    We did not foresee --
    And yet it was so --
        that our purposeful interaction
            with these new arrivals
                was perceived by this Water Walking People
                    as a great gift.

For reasons not yet clear to us,
    their fear of this similar People was very great
    and their fear of us very little.

WE SAW IT WAS
    that we were not a Water Walking People,
    nor one skilled
        in catching the great river swimmers.

WE SAW IT WAS
    that we did not build either houses
        or water walking platforms
            with the great trees that abounded here.

WE SAW THAT IT WAS ALSO
    that those possibilities
        at which we were accomplished --
            finding ways across endless mountains
                and around vast seas,
            encouraging seeds toward Earth,
            learning how to learn . .
    these were things
        which were neither regarded
            nor understood among them,
    things from which they turned away
        before the mind image occurred to them.

YET NOW
    THEY SHOWED US GRATITUDE.

Not only were they like a People
    relieved of a great burden . .

But also we came to understand
    that those two from among us
        who chose a water walking way
            had fulfilled a request to them
                from the new arrivals.

These additional hands and feet
　　were necessary to such a long journey . .

And the new arrivals
　　had chosen our eager interest
　　　　over the unwilling experience
　　　　　　of this other People . .
　　who in their turn
　　　　had feared the sudden and unagreed-to loss
　　　　　　of two of their own People,
　　　　　　　　bound all unwilling
　　　　　　　　　　against some part of the platform
　　　　　　　　until much too far from shore
　　　　　　　　　　for any reliable change.

OUT OF THIS GRATITUDE
CAME MANY THINGS.

We were allowed a permanent place
　　on land they did not value
　　　　at the edge of land they valued,
　　providing always
　　　　that we continue in our ways
　　　　　　which strove not against them.

Neither would they permit use of their great trees
　　either for the building of houses
　　or for the building of water walking platforms.

THEY CONTINUED
　　To allow our young to watch their every move,
　　　　still failing to apprehend somehow
　　　　　　that the young grow tall at last.

Further, however, no participation
　　in the nature of their building
　　　　by hands that were ours was permitted.

Gradually our women were permitted
　　access throughout their community,
　　　　though they were still regarded
　　　　　　as a separate group.

The result here was inevitable,
　　yet unforeseen by them.

FROM TIME TO TIME
    One of their men chose to join
        with one of our women in a continuous way . .

    So that a growing community within a community --
        evidencing both ways of living --
           came to be.

AND YET . .
    As our men
        were permitted no access to the community
    And their women
        showed no wish to live in any other way . .
           there came to be
               no similar community within our own.

AND WE CAME TO UNDERSTAND HOW IT WAS . .

    How it was their thought
        that should any other new arrivals
           suddenly appear,
        it was we
           who would protect their People
               from any change.

    And for a People for whom little changes,
        perhaps this is wise . .

AND WE CAME TO UNDERSTAND THIS.

YET WE WERE BECOME A PEOPLE
*   FOR WHOM GREAT CHANGE*
*   HAD BECOME A DAILY CIRCUMSTANCE.*

AND SO IT WAS
 That our learning
  from all circumstances
   came to have an infinite value.

AND HEREIN LIES WISDOM ALSO . .

 FOR SURELY
  we have been and still are
   a People
    for whom some stability
     within the context of rapid change
      contained the seeds of survival.

 AND THESE SEEDS ALSO
  WE KEPT WITH ASSIDUOUS CARE . .

NOW SOME WINTERS PASSED --
With much rain and little snow --
  but not many.

As I have said,
  an increasing number of our women
    lived among them,
      gaining a new kind of learning.

Although to us nothing seemed to change,
  indeed some change occurred,
    for a comfortable circumstance
      became increasingly uneasy.

As new arrivals failed to appear,
  perhaps our usefulness
    to this changeless People
      seemed of lesser value . .
  perhaps also this community within a community
    began to encourage some movement
      toward change.

HOWEVER THAT MAY BE,
  It became apparent to us
    that many councils were held
    and that great agreements
      were in the making . .

And yet no one at all
  shared the nature of these councils with us.

Only our women who lived among them
  reported great anger and consternation
    on the part of the men from these People
      with whom they lived.

                • • •

SOME TIME PASSED,
  Discussions still clearly held
    from time to time . .

UNTIL AT LAST
  Some cohesion became apparent.

A People still arguing with one another
   slowly changed to a People
      with some saddening purpose . .

So that we began to wonder
   whether this Water Walking People
      might have decided
         to follow the new arrivals across the sea.

YET IT WAS NOT SO.
   The focus changed
      and turned and shifted in such a way
         that it became apparent to us
         that we were the focus of their discussion.

Angry looks
   were increasingly cast in our direction
      and those who had come to greet our words
         with kindness, ceased doing so.

Our women from among them
   also reported great change.

A comfortable place by the fire,
   earned through hard work,
      no longer seemed assured --
         so that they seemed uneasy.

. . .

NOW
   Consternation among our People
      turned into an inward query.

Unwilling to ask questions of these People
   who seemed averse to curiosity,
      we asked each other,
         searching for causes.

Had we transgressed
   against our agreement?

Taken great swimmers from the water
   or great trees from the forest?

IT WAS NOT SO.

Had our men wandered through their community
  against advisement?

IT WAS NOT SO.

Had our young shown curiosity too great
  or too little restraint
    in the handling of tools.

IT WAS NOT SO.

No question
  turned in the direction of our own behavior
  or of our agreement with this People
    yielded any understanding
      which explained
        the focus of these many councils
        or of the saddened anger they evoked.

AND SO WE WAITED,
  Unwilling still to question
    where questions were unwelcome . .

  Unwilling to disturb
    even this disturbing circumstance.

*UNTIL AT LAST
  CHANGE CAME.*

IT BEGAN WITH A GREAT CEREMONY
Which we neither recognized nor understood.

Neither
was it part of their accustomed circumstance . .

Yet it was clear
that any from among our People
were both unwelcome and uninformed.

Even those among our women
who lived among them with great content
during these years
were neither welcome nor informed.

SO IT WAS
With a certain sense of dread
that we awaited news
of a shifting circumstance . .

Explaining to one another
what differences there may or may not be
between a trembling Earth
and a trembling People.

In either circumstance,
things may shift and change
in unrecognizable patterns.

SO IT WAS
That we who were accustomed to change
reminded each other it was so . .

And discussed when circumstance enabled
how we might meet this or that change,
principal among which
was our thought of a possible leave taking
in which these ones might follow
an Ocean pattern long forgot.

YET I TELL YOU NOW IT WAS NOT SO . .

Neither did they leave
nor discuss the possibility of leaving.

Rather, after the last of their ceremonies
　　to which we remained uninvited,
　　　　a great delegation from among them
　　　　　　came out to us in ceremonial progress --
　　　　leaving behind each of the men among them
　　　　　who had as his first companion
　　　　　　one of our women.

AND IT WAS THIS
　　That first changed the direction of our thought,
　　　　leading us to expect no news of their leaving.

. . .

AND IT WAS SO.

　　Their decided message
　　　　was delivered without preamble
　　　　　　or any other explanation.

　　"It has been decided among us"
　　　　-- they said --

　　"That your way and ours
　　　　do not live easily on this land.

　　"Though we have striven"
　　　　-- they went on --

　　"To separate your way and ours,
　　　　your way yet intrudes upon our daily manner.

　　"Especially is it so"
　　　　-- they added --

　　"That those among your women
　　　　who live among us
　　　　　　have come to be regarded
　　　　　　　　as less than welcome.

　　"It is not their first companion
　　　　who usually says this,
　　　　　　but it is our women and our other men.

　　"Your women are more like men than women.

"And for this reason -- and for others --
we ask now that you leave us.

"You who are so good at gathering sustenance
where we find none
may gather it now
and depart in any direction you choose.

"BUT LET IT BE SOON.

"Let no further winter storms
fall upon you in this place."

• • •

SO IT WAS ANNOUNCED
AND SO IT WAS DONE.

Much had been learned with each passing winter.

Yet, if we were not allowed access to river
or to the possibility
of building in their manner,
opportunities for use of these learnings
were rare.

Much of the world lay devoid of any community
walked by those whose two legs carried them.

Neither was our general unwelcome
pleasing to us.

Neither was it our pleasure
to be understood
as some defense against change.

AND . .
As they had no wish
that their young
learn curiosity beyond the known . .
So had we no wish
that our young
learn their seeming lack of curiosity.

As to the women and the men,
we understood them at once.

Those among our People who were women
   walked with quiet purpose wherever
      they were not specifically proscribed,
   sat at any fire expecting to be heard,
   listened as well as spoke,
      then spoke again.

This same sense of self
   they taught their children,
      so that our young also expected to be heard,
         listened as well as spoke,
            then spoke again.

Their councils
   never involved the Whole People,
      but were limited only to several among the men.

This same limited wisdom
   had obtained among those new arrivals,
      whereby sometimes the decision of one
         determined the act of the People.

AS IT WAS SO AMONG THEM,
IT WAS NOT SO AMONG US.

WE WERE A PEOPLE
   Who had learned to value
      each individual wisdom,
         carefully gathered
            from around the Circle of the People,
         nourished among them
            toward some central purpose.

IT HAS BEEN OUR GREAT LEARNING
   that any individual wisdom
      may be swept away in an instant,
         disappeared beyond reach
            of a hungering People.

IT HAD BEEN OUR GREAT LEARNING
   that whatever wisdom remains
      rises on two feet
         after any calamitous circumstance . .
            and walks toward Tomorrow.

IT HAD BEEN OUR GREAT LEARNING
  that any
    who might be chosen as First Among Us
    might just as easily be lost,
      leaving only the resident Wisdom
      of an unaccustomed People.

IT HAD BEEN OUR GREAT LEARNING
THAT NO ONE AMONG US
CONTAINS ALL WISDOM.

RATHER, EACH AMONG US
CONTAINS SOME PART.

IT HAD BECOME OUR MANNER
TO GATHER ALL SUCH ADVICE
  INTO A CENTRAL COMPREHENSION.

$\bullet\ \bullet\ \bullet$

AND SO IT WAS AT THIS TIME
  That we gathered once again,
    consulting each,
    consulting all . .

UNTIL
  each shred of possible understanding
    was gathered into the perception
    of the Whole People.

AND THIS WAS THE WAY OF IT.

From those
  who had learned of the path to the East
    came descriptions of an endless dryness,
      devoid of water.

And from the Water Walking People
  little else was learned.

To travel East
    was to invite a choking end to daily walking
        and no return at all, they said,
            nothing at all
                any of them chose to contemplate.

YET IT WAS KNOWN AMONG THEM
    that some other People
        were settled to the South,
    that these were related
        to this Water Walking People,
    and that these lands
        were understood as a continuing place
            for too-many-among-us
                as from among this Water Walking People.

IT WAS THEIR THOUGHT
    That we would go East and also South . .
        as we had arrived.

We had no wish to go North,
    the land we had so recently left.

AND SO THIS WAS OUR THINKING.

It was known to us
    that toward the East
        lie the Never Ending Mountains.

As we had found a way from there to here,
    so might we find a new way back.

Yet this precipitous leave taking
    allowed no Brothers at all
        their careful wanderings
            to choose a way for us.

Land yielding so little water
    would yield less sustenance.

ALL REMEMBERED
    how it had been in the Great Dryness
        from before,
    how much purposeless wandering,
        searching for water,
            had preceded our determination
            for the North.

ALL REMEMBERED
    how many lay still against the Earth
        for lack of water.

A People slowly grown in number since that time
    had little wish to see the number less
        for lack of planning.

AND SO IT WAS
    That we decided for the East
        as the probable shortest transit past mountains
            toward probable water.

What we could carry would be carried,
    yet *rapidly*
        is the best crossing for so much dryness . .
    so that carrying poles were forgotten
        and only individual packs mutually allowed.

Seeds for tomorrow
    and sustenance for today were planned,
    and carrying sacks for water also added.

Travel by night was agreed on
    and all the People had learned
        from the Great Dryness
            was discussed over and over --
        morning dew and small creatures,
        energy expended neither in cooking
            nor in gathering wood . .

    ALL WAS AGREED TO.

AND THEN
    A new delegation formed among us.

Those whose many winters
    bent them closer to the Earth,
        so that they could better listen
            to her thoughts,
                came among us as one body.

    "How will you travel quickly"
    -- they asked --

    "If we travel with you?"

    AND NO ONE HAD AN ANSWER,

UNTIL AT LAST
    carrying poles and easy riding
        were discussed again.

    "Let those of you
        who consider riding such poles
            an easy exercise
        spend one day in such travel"
           -- one of them said.

    "We say
        that the better answer
            is for us to stay here,
            or to travel South
                if that is not allowed.

    "In this manner,
        we too will nourish the future,
            enabling quicker transit."

AND SO,
    After much discussion,
        it was agreed that a delegation
            would approach the Water Walking People
                from among our Many Winters folk.

    And it was learned at this time
        how difficult the Never Ending Mountains
            had been for those bent closer to Earth,
        for none of them
            had spoken of this until now.

    It was learned
        how little wish they had
            to cross these mountains again.

AND IT WAS ALSO THEIR THOUGHT
    That the very young
        might be left with them,
            to nourish a probable future.

AND SO IT WAS
    That three of our oldest ones
        approached the Water Walking People,
            saying they would soon leave
                this Earth existence anyway
        and had little wish
            to lay out their lives on mountain crags,
                impeding the forward progress
                    of their People.

AND BECAUSE
    This Water Walking People also respected age

AND BECAUSE
    They still saw
        how we had rescued them from their own terrors,
            they allowed this possibility.

AND
    When they also asked
        that those one must carry
            be allowed to stay with them,
        full of their awareness of obligation,
            they also agreed.

AND IT WAS AT THIS TIME
    They learned
        we had not come from the South and East,
            but from the North in a circular manner.

    But their mind resisted this information . .
        so that it was clear to us,
            as it was not clear to them,
                that they thought
                    they sent us back to our previous place.

    WHEREAS
    WE CHOSE INSTEAD
    A NEW DIRECTION.

• • •

IT WAS LEARNING FOR US,
  BUT ONE WE HAVE REMEMBERED EVER SINCE.

  Those who resist information --
    however improbable
      in the context of their own perceptions --
    limit themselves to those perceptions,
      greatly reducing their own learning.

  Perhaps a People
    for whom little changes
      can live easily within such limitations.

BUT A PEOPLE
  WHOSE DAILY SONG IS CHANGE
  CAN ILL AFFORD IT.

AND SO IT WAS
  That the limitations of the Water Walking People
    indicated new paths to our own learning
      which we were not eager to walk.

  YET WALK WE MUST.

AND SO
  The People
    gathered in a great celebration . .
      of unity and separation,
      of learning much
        and knowing too little . .

  A CELEBRATION
  OF WHO WE ARE.

AND IT WAS AT THIS TIME
 That one of the oldest among us
  rose to speak.

 "I remember"
  -- she said --
 "Walk by Waters.

 "I remember"
  -- she went on --
 "Slippery rock and washing Ocean.

 "I remember"
  -- she concluded --
 "How a Whole People
  bound themselves together
   with a twisted, braided rope longer
    than any had before seen
    or even considered.

 "Now let us twist and braid a rope
  that will bind us together
   across this Great Island
    we gradually come to know.

 "Let us twist the strands
  of individual memory.

 "Let us braid these gathered thoughts
  into a rope so strong
   it will bind us together
    no matter how separate.

 "LET US CRAFT A ROPE
  OF SUCH FLEXIBILITY
   THAT IT WILL STRETCH
    BETWEEN ONE PLACE AND ANOTHER,
   TOUCHING EACH HEART
    WHEREVER WE MAY BE."

AND SO IT WAS
    As the People saw great value
        in the continuance of memory
            they spent three days
                telling each other once more
                    everything I tell you now.

SO IT WAS
    They came to understand
        that this oldest among us --
            she who now counted eighty-six winters --
            had at one time counted only eight.

SO IT WAS,
    AFTER ALL ELSE WAS SAID
        AND TOLD ONCE MORE
            SO THAT MANY MIGHT REMEMBER . .

ALL SAT TO HEAR
    WHAT THIS ELDEST,
        MOST PURPOSEFUL MEMORY
            MIGHT CONTAIN.

Ancient Songs

THESE ARE THE SONGS
of the Eight Winter Child.

THESE ARE THE SONGS
of one who listens and remembers.

THESE ARE THE SONGS
of one who brings wisdom and purpose
to a discontinuous People.

FOR IN THOSE DAYS
When others sought only attention or approval
from Ancient Wisdom . .

This child of the People
listened,
listened to all Ancient Wisdom spoke,
to all she did not speak at all,

AND -- as they heard her words --
They began to understand the quiet patience
with which this Daughter of the People
had shaped and encouraged their lives.

Was she not Daughter of Wisdom's Daughter?
Granddaughter in that way
to Ancient Wisdom?

AND
When Daughter of Wisdom
was lost beyond reach
in the deep river crossing,
had this one not stood forward
that we should go on?

GO ON
to complete the purpose of a People
who had learned to listen
to Wisdom's voice,
whatever its source might be.

NOW
    This one sang songs
        of listening and remembering,
            songs we have woven
                into the Song of the Whole People.

    Yet there were three
        which Ancient Wisdom had sung to her one day,
        which no one else seemed to remember.

AND
    These were the songs she sang.

            . . .

Beginning Song

NOW I MUST TELL YOU
    That our People had their beginning
        long before our Edge of Ocean home . .

SO LONG AGO
    That no one at all can count the time.

    YET
        THESE ARE THE TELLINGS
          THAT HAVE COME DOWN TO US.

LONG AGO,

    LONG AGO,

        LONG AGO . .

Our People lived in loose groups
    and wove the pattern of their days
        through trees so tall sun was seldom seen.

IT WAS AN EASY TIME,
    A time when the mere extension of an arm
        was greeted by some ripened fruit . .

A time when water
    was as often gleaned from trees
        as from earth,
    as its constant cascade was captured
        in leaves and the forks of branches --
          the ground below
            being often sodden and dangerous.

SO IT WAS
  THAT THE PEOPLE LIVED CONTENT
  FOR TIME BEYOND TIME --
    UNTIL THE WORLD BEGAN TO CHANGE.

Understanding came back
  that the place where-trees-were-not
    grew closer,
  so that great trees fell to earth
    and were not replaced by new.

These massive giants,
  so dependable for so long,
    rooted firmly to Earth,
  began to lose their earth connection
    and toppled -- one after another --
      toward a receding forest.

IN THIS MANNER . .
  Trees which had been our refuge
    became our great danger.

And those who saw the nature of this change
  learned to walk out on the grassy places.

And yet the way to live here was so difficult
  that many retained their forest home
    until the trees themselves
      shook them loose in falling.

            . . .

NOW IT WAS
  That those who teach themselves new ways
    with greatest ease
      gave wondrous gifts to the People.

THESE WERE THEY
  Who learned new ways of continuance,
    finding that which is not fruit
      and yet nourishes,
    learning ways of finding water.

For rain came less and less often,
  catching here and there on the Earth
    and seldom at all in trees.

SO THAT
    Some among the People
        would find some high place --
            a rock or hill --
        and search all distant places for signs
            of the gatherings of great beasts
                which indicated water.

AND
    Those who were most clever in this pursuit
        came to be valued by us.

. . .

NOW
    It was the nature of our People
        to move in loose groups
            in a nearly northerly direction.

As this pattern continued
    we learned the ways of this new land
        so that not all was eaten,
            but some was saved --
        not all was drunk,
            but some water retained.

AND
    THESE THINGS FOR US WERE A GREAT LEARNING.

Yet our manner of living
  . was simple at this time . .

Neither did we build any way
    to shelter ourselves
        against inclement weather,
            but found only what shelter
                Earth might provide.

Neither did we protect our bodies in any way,
    but sat in the pouring waters
        until no water fell,
            gathering all we could carry.

NOW
   THE NATURE OF THE LAND BEGAN TO CHANGE.

   It rose to the North and West
      in increasing ways,
         until East was the only direction
            which held no increasing height.

NOW IT WAS DECIDED AMONG THE PEOPLE
IN THE MANNER OF THAT DAY

   That East was the lesser direction
      and that North was the continuous path.

SO IT WAS
   That the People slowly climbed this elevation
      in a northerly and also west direction
         until after several days
            they reached a point high enough
               to see what lay beyond.

AND
   What lay beyond was an amazement to them.

   To the edge of the horizon
      toward the North, the West,
         and even to the South
            nothing was seen but water --
            water so great it covered everything --
         so that the People wondered mightily
            how much it might rain in this place.

NOW
   Seeing how it was for them,
      how water had come to be
         so carefully maintained among them
            that they considered the value
               of climbing to look beyond,

   Here, then, was more water
      than all the People together
      and all other creatures
         could ever consume.

NOW
    The People began a careful descent,
        the way too steep for eager rushing,
           and slowly reached the lower elevations,
      coming out at last on a dry and grainy earth
        in which feet were easily buried
          but -- unlike dampened earth --
             which did not cling as one walked.

It was this
    the people did not understand --
      how at the edge of so much water
        the earth could be so dry.

          . . .

NOW
    They walked forward -- one after the other --
      toward the edge of this Great Water . .
        which was so great the ripples at its edge
          made a thunderous noise.

They walked toward the water
    and discovered more than they hoped.

FOR
    as they approached this rumbling water,
    as they sought the ease of plenty,
      they discovered a water
        no one at all had ever known.

FOR
    this water had a bitter taste,
      unpleasing
        to tongue, to mouth, to stomach.

AND SO
    the People came to understand
      that their plenty was nothing --
    a tree with bright fruit appended
      whose bitter taste
        gives neither tongue nor stomach
          any pleasure.

AND SO
    the People sat and wondered,
        hoarding the water brought with them,
        wondering how long another climb
            over the great elevation might require
            and whether this water might be enough.

AND YET IT IS KNOWN
    Some of the people sought North and South
        along the edge of this Great Water
  for easier access
    to the other side of the elevation
        recently crossed.

In so doing,
    two small but rapidly moving streams
        were found
            which led down toward the Great Water,
        the taste of neither being bitter,
            but fresh and pleasant to the tongue.

AND SO IT WAS UNDERSTOOD AMONG THEM
    That while this more pleasant
        water could be obtained
            and if survival
            was as easily found here as elsewhere . .

This would be the center of their living,
    edged on the East by great elevation,
    on the west by Great Water,
    and on the North and South
        by unknown grainy earth.

NOW
  The manner of living in this place
    became easeful.

FOR,
  As the People discovered its nature,
    they learned
      what might be obtained from elevations
      and what from the Great Waters.

  All the while
    two streams cut across this Edge of Waters,
      yielding pleasant water in abundance.

  Since the land beyond the elevations was dry,
    the People came to see
      more wisdom than understanding
        in their decision
          to climb the elevations.

AND IT WAS THEIR THOUGHT
  That being in this place
    was of a much pleasanter nature
      than the constant search for water
        under the feet of great beasts
          had been before.

· · ·

NOW IT CAME TO BE
  That a People who had been few
    began to become many.

  Sands to the North and South
    long ago had been walked
      so that the limits of this place were known.

  Here was a great body of water
    washing into a great curve in the edge of Earth
      so that from one seaward end of land
        to the other,
      one could sometimes see the nature
        of that other rocky promontory.

IN THIS MANNER
    The People came to understand
        that this Great Water
            was only a part of a Greater Water beyond
            which was also bitter to taste.

AND THIS CAUSED WONDER.

All still remembered the walk past many lives
    from trees-that-were to no trees at all,
        reaching at last this Ocean Edge.

All remembered, therefore,
    how great the land might be.

Now they wondered
    how great might be the bitter water.

Small groups went out
    so that it was learned
        that both North and South
            yielded much sand-and-rock walking --
    and past each such scalloped edge
        the Great Water continued --
    so that the People began
        to understand the Water
            as greater than the land.

AND THOUGH --
    As light and dark followed each other
        over many lives --
    They began to learn
        that both to North and South --
            walking far enough --
                the land gradually
                    turned West and West and West.

EVEN SO,
    they did not lose their understanding
        of Water as the greater part.

• • •

NOW
    The nature of things being what they are,
        the number of the People
           along this Edge of Ocean
              began to increase
    so that living was not as easy as it had been.

ALTHOUGH
    Those who walked North and South
        along this edge of Ocean
           established new communities
           here and there
              with ease --
    understanding as we now did the nature of Ocean
        and the possibilities of sustenance . .

    EVEN SO
        the numbers of the People grew greater
        than we might wish.

IT WAS WELL UNDERSTOOD
    that some answer must be sought and also found.

IT BECAME APPARENT
    that different views were held
        as to the cause of this increase in numbers.

SOME THOUGHT
    it was the natural change of seasons,
        which caused flowers to blossom
           after winter rains
              and never later.

SOME THOUGHT
    this could not be so,
        as all flowered plants bloom
           and yet not all who are female
              beget young with each season.

OTHERS THOUGHT
    that plants might be found here and there
        showing the possibility of blossoms
        and yet no blooming occurs.

STILL OTHERS THOUGHT
> that the cause might be the Earth dance
> > between those who are male
> > and those who are female.

AND YET OTHERS THOUGHT
> some combination of each element
> > might obtain.

AS IT WAS UNDERSTOOD
> Some answer must be found
> > so some way of walking alternate possibilities
> > must be found.

SO IT WAS AGREED
> That the nature of the land
> > would decide the nature of the walk.

As the sands were divided
> by two sweet water streams . .

SO WOULD THE PEOPLE BE DIVIDED.

SO THAT FROM WINTER RAIN TO WINTER RAIN
> one in four of the People,
> one in two of those of the People
> > who were male,
> > > would live together
> > > > North of the northernmost stream.

IN A SIMILAR MANNER
> one in four of the People,
> one in two of those of the People
> > who were female,
> > > would live together
> > > > South of the southernmost stream.

AND IN A DIFFERENT MANNER
> two in four of the People,
> one in two of those who were female
> and one in two of those who were male,
> > would live together in the usual way
> > > in the land between the streams.

AND ALSO
> watch was kept along each stream
> > to assure
> > > that agreement and living
> > > > would match one another.

AND SO IT WAS.
>   *From one winter rain to another*
>   *this was, indeed,*
>   *the manner of the living of the People . .*

>   *And all was carefully watched to assure*
>   *that the learning would derive*
>   *from the actual pattern of their days.*

. . .

NOW
>   This was the result
>   of this changeful living . .

>   Among those of the People who were female,
>   not one among those
>   living South of the southernmost stream
>   brought out any young among the People
>   at any time during the following season.

>   Among those among the People who were female
>   and who lived between the streams together
>   with some from among the People who were male,
>   many of these women -- and yet not all --
>   brought out young among the People
>   during the following season.

THUS IT WAS LEARNED
>   *That the Earth Dance*
>   *between those among the People*
>   *who are female*
>   *and those among the People*
>   *who are male*
>   *does not assure*
>   *and yet is requisite to*
>   *the bringing out of young*
>   *among the People.*

STILL,
>   TO ASSURE THE ACCURACY
>   OF THIS LEARNING . .

Some from among the People who were female
and who had lived South
of the southernmost stream
were asked and also agreed to continue
this manner of living
past another winter's rain.

AND IT FOLLOWED AGAIN
that from among these
no individual brought out young
during the following season,
even though some of these
had brought out young
in previous seasons.

NOW THE PEOPLE CAME TO UNDERSTAND
THAT A NEW WAY
OF MODIFYING THEIR LIFE
LAY BEFORE THEM.

Like walking North . .

Like crossing the great elevation . .

Like learning the nature of Ocean living . .

So did this understanding provide
some greater purposeful flexibility
in the manner of living of the People.

AND YET,
A sure understanding
of this new learning
was clearly necessary . .

AND SO
Some from among the People who were female
and who had brought forth young
after that first season
were asked and agreed
after these young no longer drew milk
to take up one season's living
South of the southernmost stream
with those who had lived there
since the first season.

And from among these
no young were brought forth
during the following season.

AND YET,
When all the People
subsequently lived again together,
many of these and many of those
who had lived South since the first season
now brought out young.

AND SO IT WAS LEARNED AS A SURE THING
That -- whereas the great Earth Dance
between those among the People who are female
and those among the People who are male
will not necessarily
cause the bringing out of young . .

YET IT IS ESSENTIAL TO IT.

AND
THIS WAS A GREAT LEARNING
THAT OUR PEOPLE HAVE KEPT EVER SINCE.

NOW
>It was also a continuous learning,
>>this living at Ocean's edge . .

>So that the People learned better and better ways
>>of moving through water in such a manner
>>>that many areas
>>>>beneath the surface of the waters
>>>>became known to them.

FOR
>The small creatures most easily consumed
>>often attached themselves in various ways
>>>to rock surface below water
>And even did others -- more prone to travel --
>>bury themselves in certain ways in sand or rock.

>So the seeking out of these creatures
>>required some time under water.

FURTHER,
>Gathering most easily took place
>>in the following manner . .

>With arms and legs,
>>cause your body
>>>to be much beneath water surface.

>As you find an appropriate place to seek out
>>those that swim and those that scuttle,
>>>hold carefully still.

>Shortly there is great chance
>>some may begin again
>>>their own search for sustenance
>and -- in that manner --
>>you may find some appropriate creature
>>>walking or swimming toward you.

>At that time
>>take hold of such a creature in such a way
>>>that they come home easily with you.

· · ·

NOW
As these things were being learned
another thing began occurring.

FROM TIME TO TIME
Great Swimmers came --
and these were nearly as great as we
and sometimes larger.

AT FIRST
the People were wary of these new swimmers
as they were unknown.

AND YET
greater familiarity caused us to learn
that little concern was merited.

RATHER,
These ones seemed to take great pleasure
in swimming among us,
so that we began to swim willingly with them
and to learn from them
some of the nature of Ocean.

FOR
IT WAS THESE ONES
from whom we learned
the deeper nature of Ocean
and how to help the young ones swim.

THEY AND WE
being of different configurations
it was not possible for us
to move nor swim exactly as they,
and yet much that they did
was possible for us.

FROM THEM
we learned to forget to breathe
for longer times of swimming
and to survive this circumstance
with increasing ease.

THERE WAS SOMETHING
about the patterns of their communications
which stirred in us some wonder.

ONE UNDERSTOOD FROM ANOTHER
AND YET
the manner of it was not clear to us,
so that we began to wonder
about how we might seem to them.

The manner of our communications
was mainly shaped in the open air --
as theirs was mainly in the open water.

YET
each might transpose this
to the opposite circumstance
with less, yet meaningful, efficacy.

SO THAT THROUGH ALL THIS
WE BEGAN TO UNDERSTAND OURSELVES
IN WAYS
NEVER THOUGHT OF BEFORE.

AND WE SAW HOW IT WAS
THAT THESE GREAT SWIMMERS AND WE
DID NOT SEEK EACH OTHER
FOR SUSTENANCE
BUT FOR COMPANIONSHIP
AND FOR LEARNING.

AND
WE SAW THIS AS A GREAT VALUE

AND
ASKED OURSELVES
TO REMEMBER THE VALUE OF SUCH LEARNING,

REMEMBERING ALWAYS
TO ASK THE QUESTION,

"HOW MIGHT WE SEEM TO THEM."

NOW
    Through all this learning
      and modification in manner of living . .

    Through even the ways
      we learned to moderate
        the increase in numbers of the People . .

    EVEN SO IT CAME TO BE
      that too many feet
        came to walk the sand
          of what had come to be
            one Central Place among many.

NOW FROM TIME TO TIME
    A group of the People
      gathered themselves together
        and walked away from Ocean over high places
          into an unknown part of Earth.

    It came to be such
      that one group or another
        left from time to time.

NOW AT LAST
    A NEW THING OCCURRED,
      for one such group formed
      and -- with great reluctance --
        decided to walk out over the high places
          toward an unknown Tomorrow.

AND WHEREAS
    This was in no way
      different than before,
        it was different in this way . .

    THIS FORMING GROUP
      CONTAINED
        THOSE WHO WENT BEFORE US.

AND
    FROM THAT TIME TO THIS
      NONE OF OUR PEOPLE
        HAS EVER AGAIN
          SEEN OUR CENTRAL PLACE.

Who Are The Human Beings?

NOW
> *THIS WAS THE WAY OF IT.*

WHEREAS
> *Space on the Earth*
> > *was one of the thoughts of the People*
> > > *in deciding for a new land,*
> > *learning was in their mind also.*

> *For much had been learned and was preserved, still,*
> > *from along the northward path*
> > > *and great and equally preserved*
> > > > *was our Edge of Ocean learning.*

HOW MIGHT IT BE TO ADD TO THESE LEARNINGS
> *An awareness*
> > *of the nature of land to the East of before?*

THEREFORE
> All the People were alert to change . .
> > water or lack thereof,
> > variations in the nature
> > > of what might be consumed,
> > rises and falls in the land,
> > stretching out of valleys.

> All this was expected.

AND YET
> *ONE VARIATION WAS UNEXPECTED*
> *AND THAT VARIATION*
> > *LAY IN THOSE*
> > > *WHO WALKED THE EARTH.*

AMONG THE PEOPLE
> There was some variance . .
> > some were taller, some shorter,
> > some darker, some lighter . .

YET
> The variance here
> > exceeded these limited possibilities.

HERE
   Variations in height were so great
      that some
         who walked the Earth with two legs
           might seem as too young
              to be full grown . .
      others seemed to tower over us
         as if they stood on some rocky outcropping.

Variations in light and dark were also greater,
      some disappearing long before dark
         with others almost as marked by moonlight.

Variations in hair or lack thereof
      were also marked.

AND EVEN
      the two legs with which they walked the Earth,
         some being straight and long
         with others curved toward the Earth.

SOME
      seemed to communicate with each other
         through patterns of sound
           we did not recognize.

OTHERS
      seemed not to possess this capacity,
         but shook themselves before each other
           in ways that might contain communication.

THE PEOPLE WERE AT A LOSS
*   TO UNDERSTAND THESE MANY WAYS OF BEING*

AND BEGAN TO CONFER
*   AMONG THEMSELVES*
*   AS TO HOW*
*   THEY MIGHT RELATE TO ONE ANOTHER.*

Which are our Brothers, our Sisters?

Which are related to us
*   and in what manner?*

How may we understand them?

Is it possible, desirable
    to form communities with them?

Or will our living be better
    separate from them?

ALL THIS
    Was discussed at length,
        comparing this and that,
    Until the People moved beyond the variations
        between those
            who walked the Earth with two legs only.

THEY LOOKED NOW
    At the variations between all two leggeds
        and those who walked the Earth with four
            or those who swam the waters
            or those who sailed the sky.

So many variations.
So many similar patterns
    across these apparent differences.

UNTIL AT LAST IT WAS DECIDED . .
AND IT WAS A DECISION
    OUR PEOPLE
        HAVE HELD FROM THAT DAY TO THIS . .

If we can learn from the Great Swimmers
    and understand our relation to them . .

Surely we can learn
    from any who walk the Earth with two legs,
        whether they share understanding
            through sound patterns
            or patterns of movement
            or through something
                we not yet understand . .

Surely we can learn from them
    as they from us.

Surely they are all our closest brothers,
    tall or short, dark or light.

And surely
    they merit our awareness of the relation.

AS WE ARE THE PEOPLE,
  So are they also their own People
    and --
  As there are so many apparent differences --
    we should honor these,
      as well as the similarities,
        and learn from both.

SURELY
  ONLY WISDOM
    LIES IN LEARNING

AND SURELY
  GREAT LEARNING
    ALWAYS DOES CONTAIN
      GREATER POSSIBILITY OF SURVIVAL.

Let us learn from those
  who have not known an Ocean edge.

Let them teach us
  the manner of each new place
    and -- if they are not so comfortable
      with all that we have said --
      let us learn quietly and from a distance
        so that we do not give offense.

AND -- AS I HAVE SAID --
  From that day to this
    our People have learned to remember
      who are our Brothers, our Sisters
        from whom we may best learn.

WHATEVER WE CALL OURSELVES
  That is greater than one People,
    we call them by this name as well.

ALL . . . ARE BROTHERS, ARE SISTERS

YET
  ALL WHO ARE TWO LEGGEDS
    ARE GREATER BROTHERS, SISTERS,
      THAN THIS.

SUCH IS THE NATURE OF LIFE.

         ◦ ◦ ◦

NOW
>The People gathered in great wonder
>>to hear all this ancient woman had spoken
>>>of the beginning of things for us . .
>And they studied its implications.

>*How easily*
>>*such things may be forgotten*
>>>*and yet how clearly*
>>>>*they describe our future path.*

A PEOPLE
>Who had learned to live at an Ocean's edge
>>and walked out from that place
>>>toward the East,
>>learning from all Brothers, from all Sisters . .

>Became an Edge of Ocean People
>>once again in a new Center Place . .
>>>still seeking learning.

>Driven from that place
>>by a changing circumstance,
>>>they still sought an Edge of Ocean home.

YET, AGAIN
>Because of too many People here . .

AND YET ALSO
>Because of too little brotherhood
>>and mutual learning . .
>They were leaving their Edge of Ocean home
>>after too few years,
>>>walking East
>>>>to seek another Ocean, however far.

FOR SURELY
>THIS WAS A GREAT ISLAND
>>AND ONE NOT EASILY CROSSED.

• • •

NOW
    All had a wish to know why --
      during all the years of walking together --
    None had heard this Telling
      of the Beginning for our People
        and how it came to be
          that one woman now sang them this song.

AND
    She explained how it had been . .

    How Ancient Wisdom had at one time
      counted only eight Winters . .

    How it was at that time
      that she was one of the Mountain People --

    How it was
      that her natural curiosity and will to learn
        drew her to every fire
      so that she might learn whatever thoughts
        drew those there together.

AND
    SHE WAS NOT WELCOME.

    These fires often
      were for the First Among Us --
    Those that kept the Ancient, valued wisdom --
      and -- as she was not First,
        she was not welcome at their fire.

AND SO IT WAS
    That she taught herself stealth.

    She hunted the hunters among the First Among Us,
      secreting herself in some nearby place,
        rarely seen and sometimes tolerated
          by those who did see --
      with much laughter
        about night eyes and listening ears . .

EVEN SO
    Did she listen to every perceivable word,
      unwarmed by any fire or by any bulky robe,
        shivering out her cold with sharpened ears.

AND THE PEOPLE THOUGHT GREATLY
    About young and listening ears,
        and reminded themselves of their value.

    For had not He Who Counted Twelve Winters
        been the one who brought us understanding
            of the nature of Water Walking?

    Was it not he who best learned
        the manner of building these Water Platforms,
            so that the beginnings of understanding
                began to appear in every mind.

    And was it not he
        who first returned to explain
            how it was
                Black Bird brought Earth
                    from the limitless waters?

SO IT WAS
    That all asked him
        who now counted Sixteen Winters
            to explain again this Great Learning.

AND SO HE BEGAN.

Black Bird's Children

YOU KNOW HOW IT WAS
    When we first came here.

    How the Water Walking People
      explained their arrival.

    How it was they were on a Water Platform
      in the midst of limitless Ocean
        with nothing but water around.

    How it was they cried out with a great cry
      for some place to be that was not water
        and how Black Bird appeared
          and brought land out of the waters.

NOW HEAR
    What was learned from the new arrivals . .

    How it is their nature
      to travel the Great Ocean.

    How it is that some of them
      know the water path
        from one place to another.

    How it is that some among them
      know the water path from their home to this
        and to those islands
          they will next call home
        and from there
          to the place they call their first home.

I HAVE ASKED THEM
    If all know these water paths
      from one place to another --
        and they have told me it is not so.

    Only three among them truly know these paths --
      so well do they know them
        that it does not matter
          no one has walked them
            in a number of lives --
    And two among them
      begin the learning.

What would happen
    if you lost these three people,
        I have asked,
    for surely great storms or little water
        must make that possible.

AND THEY HAVE TOLD ME
    That if these three were lost to them
        by storm or illness or too little water . .

And especially
    if the two who learn were also lost . .
        then surely the Whole People
            would be lost on a faceless Ocean.

AND I HAVE ASKED THEM
    Whether the path to this place
        is clearly marked to the river itself.

AND THEY HAVE ANSWERED ME
    That they know the general path
        and how to find land out of Ocean
        before it can be seen.

Then it is
    that they follow these signs
        to the land itself.

AND
    When I asked what these signs might be
        they seemed puzzled among themselves
            as to how to explain,
                as I have never walked the Ocean.

THEN AT LAST
    One among them pointed toward the sky
        and -- looking up --
        I saw a great bird flying East.

    "WE LOOK FOR OUR FRIENDS"
        -- he explained --

    "AND FOLLOW THEM."

AND SO FROM ALL THIS
    I have learned another way to describe
        the arrival of the Water Walking People
        to this place.

I see that there was a great storm
   with much tossing of waves,
      pouring rain, and strong wind.

Even such an Ocean storm
   as destroyed the Sorrowful Man's People,
      whose telling we know . .

I see that during that storm
   they lost whatever persons among them
      knew these water paths . .

So that -- when the storm cleared --
   this People was truly lost
      in the midst of a limitless, faceless Ocean.

I see that after much calling out
   that a better place be found,
      Black Bird appeared . .

AND SOMEONE KNEW TO FOLLOW HIM . .
   so that this People
      came out from a faceless Ocean
        to a new and unknown shore.

AND
   THE CHILDREN'S CHILDREN
     forgot the home place,
     forgot the lost understanding
     and remembered only how it was
       a People lost in a faceless water
         were brought out to land by Black Bird.

              * * *

AND
   ALL THE PEOPLE SAW HOW IT WAS
      AND HOW IT EASILY MIGHT BE SO . .

   HOW IT WAS
      THAT MUCH WISDOM MAY BE LOST
         FOR A LACK OF LISTENING EARS . .

   AND GAVE THEMSELVES RENEWED PURPOSE.

"Let us choose"
   -- they said --

"TO BE A PEOPLE
   WHO REMEMBERS.

"Let us choose"
   -- they went on --

"TO BE A PEOPLE
   WHOSE YOUNGEST EARS
      ARE WELCOME AROUND ANY FIRE.

"And let us choose"
   -- they concluded --

"TO BE A PEOPLE
   WHO STUDY MEMORY IN SUCH A WAY
      AS TO REMEMBER
         BLACK BIRD
            AND WATER AND STORM
            AND THOSE WHO ARE LOST
            AND WHERE WE CAME FROM.

"LET US REMEMBER
   OUR BEGINNING."

AND
  A great shout went out
    that echoed against every tree.

  Groups gathered here and there
    telling and retelling
      all that was remembered.

AND
  FROM THAT DAY TO THIS
    WE HAVE CHOSEN TO BE A PEOPLE
    WHO LEARN FROM CHANGE . .

  A PEOPLE
    WHO REMEMBER
      THEIR BEGINNING.

How We Came To Value Age

NOW
THE PEOPLE REASSEMBLED
FOR A COMMON PURPOSE.

They had told and retold
each of their understandings
until all knew the content thereof,
even those too young to express it.

NOW
They gathered together
to learn any other understanding
which lay hidden in the memory
of anyone there.

AND AGAIN
She who had Eight Winters
and who counted now eighty-six
sat forward and began.

• • •

I HAVE TOLD YOU HOW IT WAS
FOR OUR PEOPLE . .

How they had traveled North and then West
across great height . .

How they had learned
to be an Edge of Ocean People . .

How they learned
from each other,
from the land,
and from the Great Swimmers . .

How the People grew too many on the sands . .

And how those who went before us
came out at last across the great height,
learning new ways, new Peoples,
and a new understanding of Brother.

KNOW NOW HOW IT WAS
    That they crossed an island greater than this,
        traveling always East . .

  How they crossed
      many great level places, many streams,
        and three great braided chains
          of standing mountains
            running from North to South.

  Stopping here and there for awhile,
      they would rise again
        and travel further East,
    until they came to a place
        where great and endless mountains
          lay to the South.

  And we lived there for a long time,
      as Wisdom
        washed down the stream valleys toward us,
        and we were grateful for it.

BUT BEFORE THAT TIME
    There is a Telling which must be shared.

    It is the Telling
      of how we came to value age
      and of how we came to wear clothes
      and they are the same telling.

          ◊ ✕ ◊

NOW AT THAT TIME
THE MANNER OF THE PEOPLE
WAS THIS . .

  Walking always East and staying seldom,
      they followed one among them
        who showed always excellent judgment
        as to all that was new --
    so that she led her People safely
      from one place to another
        and her presence among the People
        was greatly valued.

And this woman had a father
  who had been valued among the People,
    but whose strength was less
      now that his Winters were many . .
  and it was he
    who was first to follow his wisest daughter,
      showing by his own actions
        the respect he felt she had won.

NOW
  This daughter also had a son
    who was greatly valued by her father --
      as he saw in him some image of himself.

NOW AT THIS TIME ALSO
  There was some new continuing change
    so that each winter
      was colder than the one before
    so that the People
      wondered whether East or North were colder,
  but they told one another
    that it was in their memory
      that Edge of Ocean was warm.

AND SO IN THAT MANNER
  They thought to walk
    through greater cold toward greater warmth . .

  For surely
    Ocean lies at every edge of each island,
      however great . .

  And surely
    A purposeful People can find it.

BUT EACH WINTER GREW COLDER
  So that even a warming fire was not enough,
    nor was sleeping clustered together,
    nor were the stiff skins
      they used to bundle and carry
        any great quantity of sustenance,
    nor the thongs and fibers
      they used to tie them . .

So that it came to be
    a matter of some laughter among them
        that this or that person
            would go to join the four leggeds . .

For surely
    they provide their People
        with fur against the Winter Wind,
            whereas we two leggeds are not so wise.

MUCH DISCUSSION
    WAS FOLLOWED BY FEW ANSWERS.

Weavings of branches
    were placed between the People
        and the Winter winds.

In this manner also
    they sheltered their warming fire
        and yet even this was not enough.

On the coldest days
    many awoke with frost on legs as well as arms --
        sometimes causing great pain

So that the People had little wish
    to leave shelter during any storm.

Yet here there were no mountains
    against which the winds might blow,
        leaving the People untouched.

AND
    No further answer was found
        until one day
            this young son of Leading Woman
                did not arise to greet the morning sun.

AND
   The sorrow of Leading Woman was great,
      but the sorrow of her father was greater,
         so that he walked out from among the People
            toward the North,
            toward great cold.

AND FROM SUCH WALKS
FEW EVER RETURNED.

               ◦ × ◦

NOW
   This man of many Winters
      walked North.

Nor did he intend any particular thing.

RATHER,
   He wept and pondered in his mind
      the nature of cold that prevents walking
         and the nature of his own sorrow.

Neither had he any intention
   of returning to the South.

South for him
   held only the memory of a still, small shape . .
      the shape of his own sorrow.

NOW
   He chose a place for sitting
      which was at the edge of a stream
         running from North to South --
            from greater cold to greater warmth.

And he thought of the nature of warm and cold . .
   thought of how it was
      that one extreme and the other
         were uncomfortable
   and how it was
      that warm is moderated by water . .
         as cold may be also.

He sat and wondered
   how water might be used
      as a limitation for cold . .
   yet found no answer.

FIRE, OF COURSE, ALSO WAS.
    Yet very hot
        is the nature of fire too close
    and hardly felt
        is the nature of fire too far,.
    so that he saw no answer here.

Neither is sleeping close any guarantee
    against the coldest nights . .
        and whether it was the Eastward direction
            in which they walked
        or whether
            there was a slight rise in elevation
        or whether it was a time
            when the world was changing again
                he did not know . .
            but all knew the world grew colder
                with each succeeding winter.

NOW
    He turned his thoughts to the small shelters
        the People sometimes made
            with the stiffened skins
                of small four-leggeds,
            much of which had been eaten
                for the warmth of food.

He thought of the various ways
    such shelters were set against the wind,
        so that greater warmth
            was retained by the People.

He thought of how these skins were
    before their taking . .

And laughed gently at the thought
    that perhaps
        the People should grow their own furry skins,
    for surely such skins on a walking being
        were soft and supple
            and provided secure warmth
                against the bitterest wind.

NOW
   As he contemplated these things,
      he saw his daughter's son
         covered with a new soft warmth,
      perhaps also burrowed in earth
         against a north wind's access.

   His hunger came at last . .

AND AT LAST
   He began the quiet chewing of seeds
      the People gathered and ate as they walked.

   As he slowly chewed these hard, dry seeds
      into a softened mass . .

IT OCCURRED TO HIM
   That life would be simpler for the People
      could they only soften the stiffened skins
         of those who walked once,
            yet walk no more . .
      soften them perhaps in a simple manner.

   Turning this image of softened skins
      covering the unfurred nature of the People
         over and over in his thoughts,
      he found it pleasing -- so pleasing
         that at last he laughed.

   Taking a corner
      of one small stiffened skin used for carrying,
         he began to chew one edge
            to test its nature.

   He found the taste no longer pleasing . .

   And so he developed a way
      of washing the skin in the stream at his feet,
         then chewing one edge
            until the taste no longer pleased him,
      then washing again . .

   So that -- as he continued in this way --
      he decided to leave one small skin
         always washing in the stream
            while he gently chewed the other.

NOW
    By the time light left that day
        he was aware
            of a great softening in these skins . .
        and began in earnest
            setting himself certain tasks
        so that he explored different possibilities
            in different ways.

NOW
    The passage of days became precious to him.

Now he worked
        to prepare one full skin of some size
            in this manner.

HIS CONCERN WAS THIS . .

He might prepare any number of such skins,
        carry them South to his People,
            and never again be able to find them
                on their constant march East.

AND HIS CONCERN WAS ALSO THIS . .

He might allow possible distance to encourage his return
        before enough skins
            grew soft under his constant attention
                to show the People clearly
                    what possibilities were here.

FOR SURELY
    A People grown used to stiffened skins
        would only slowly understand the possibilities
            that danced in his mind . .

Of the People
    covered
        against North wind and cracking earth,
        covered perhaps completely
            with such softened skins.

FOR SURELY
> The People valued their nature . .

> Saw how it was
>> that those who walked the Earth on either leg
>>> were different
>>>> from those who walked the Earth on four.

> And one of the ways
>> in which these differences were most marked
>>> was the lack of any covering
>>>> that might be called fur
>>>>> on the bodies of the People.

YET NOW
> This aged man purposed to cover the People
>> in just such skins,
>>> proof against any bitter wind.

SO IT WAS
> He saw the necessity of returning to the People
>> as quickly as he may,
>>> yet with enough softened skins
> So that the People might quickly see and understand
>> the nature of the gift he brought them.

NOW HE WORKED QUICKLY
> To prepare three skins of good size
>> softened enough
>>> that his own skin found comfort thereunder . .

> And one of these skins he softened yet further
>> in order to discover the other edge
>>> of this possibility.

> It was his thought
>> to wear two skins over his own body
>>> and carry the softest third
>>>> to pass from hand to hand
>> so that the People
>>> might easily experience its softened nature.

NOW
  His walk South was brisk, indeed.

  A sorrowing man was so filled with purpose
      that it carried him quickly over rocks and crags
          to the last fire he remembered.

NOW
  As he knew so well to do,
      he followed the traces his People left,
          followed them East at a pace too rapid
              to be matched by the very young,
          followed them without stopping
              to search for food . .

  And in this manner
      hoped to overtake the People
          within some few days.

NOW ON THIS PATH OF RAPID PURPOSE
  He discovered already little need
      to build a fire at night --
          and this, too, hastened his purpose.

  These softened skins already gave him such warmth
      that nights were warmer for him
          than huddled without them
              near some small fire.

  How might they be with fire as well?

AND THIS THOUGHT
  Also quickened his pace,
      so that in only some few days
          he saw fresher references
              of people being here.

  And this as well quickened his pace.

                    ◊ ✳ ✳

NOW
    In his haste to find the People
        he had given much thought
            to the nature of this learning
        and little at all
            to the nature of his appearance.

    So that on the morning
        his glad eyes were greeted
            by the rising smoke of last night's fire,

    So were they soon greeted
        by the sight of his People
            running in every direction,
                trying to escape this great lumbering beast
                    who used no more than two feet
                        in the process of walking --
        and yet
            was greatly covered
                with various and shaggy fur
    so that some new and not yet known form of Bear
        was suspected.

    Yet here apparently
        was a Bear more dangerous than ever before --
            one who clearly had no fear of fire.

NOW
    As this aged and shaggy man
        saw the People running
            and the young men coming out in defense . .

    So did he understand the nature of Almost-Bear
        and the nature of his own predicament.

    For if he turned and ran,
        these purposeful young men might pursue him
            and bring a rapid end
                to his purposeful walking --
            thinking they brought the People
                a great gift.

    And if he continued in his approach,
        surely they would be even more concerned
            at the great proximity
                of such a monstrous Bear.

Even his words
were lost in the general shouting,
for it was the custom of the People
to allow a general din
to frighten off unwanted visitors.

AND SO
This aged man
sought an alternative course.

He neither turned and ran,
nor did he approach further.

MOREOVER
He ceased his shouted attempts
to explain the nature of this new-found Bear.

Rather, he ceased all motion,
remaining transfixed in place
as if suddenly a part of Earth herself,
rather than one of those
who move over her surface.

AND SO
The purposeful young men
approached him with lesser purpose,
forming a slow circle around him . .

Until they were close enough
to see an unexpected face
over such fur-covered shoulders
and a staff at the end of one arm.

NOW
He began to move slowly . .

And as slowly laid his staff along the Earth,
thereby abandoning this defense
and also giving to those nearby
time to understand its nature.

Now he slowly sat upon the Earth
so that the defense of running
or any sudden leap
were also in this manner laid on the ground.

Now he slowly began to pull away the skins
loosely tied over his shoulders . .

AND
    A great cry went up from all
        who saw this great Bear
            pull away his own skin.

    Whether this caused him pain none could say,
        yet clearly something never before seen
            sat before them
        and the People murmured to one another
            in wonder and in some fear
        and in a lack of general understanding
            of what was here and what to do.

NOW
    This aged man
        carefully folded his precious softened skins
        and slower yet stood up --
            so that all might see who he was.

YET AGAIN
SOMETHING OCCURRED
THAT HE HAD NOT FORESEEN.

    Since it was well understood among the People
        that one who walked North
            and was not seen for three subsequent days,
                was never seen again.

    Yet here was one -- emerged from Bear --
        whom they had not seen for many days
        and the wonder of it was too great.

    They turned and ran --
        this seldom fearful People . .

    Turned and ran away
        from too much strangeness,
            too much unexpected circumstance.

          ◊ × ◊

AND SO IT WAS
> That no one at all
>> came to lay this Bear Person
>>> still against the Earth.

NO ONE AT ALL
> came to speak to him.

All ran when he approached
> so that the possibility of explanation
>> disappeared with them.

AND SO IT WAS
> That he maintained a quiet vigil
>> at the edge of each camp,
>>> warmed by no fire,
>>> warmed by his softened skins.

No food was shared with him
> and all
>> kept the greatest distance possible from him.

As no one was sure of his nature,
> so no one chose any action against him,
>> thereby easing his days . .

Yet none chose any action for him either,
> thereby making his days more difficult . .
>> so that all that he ate
>>> came from his own hand and no other.

• • •

NOW
    All continued in this manner for some days
        until the People --
           who grew no friendlier --
               grew at least less fearful.

SO AT LAST IT WAS
    That he purposefully found his daughter
        at some distance from the People --
           where none could see She Who Led
               speaking quietly to one who might --
               or might not -- be Bear.

AND AT LAST
    All WAS EXPLAINED

HOW IT WAS
    That sorrow led to new understanding
        so that subsequent others
           might stand and walk
               after the coldest night.

"You see how it is, my Father,"
    -- she answered now --

"The People do not know
    whether these skins
        you stretch across your shoulders
           are truly separate from you
               or are the skin of your body.

"Neither do they know
    whether you are he who left us
        many days ago
    or whether you are some residue
        of that Person.

"These eyes see you
    and know who you are.

"You are my Father
    from whom I learned so much
        and now learn again.

"These ears hear you
    and understand your sorrow and your search.

"For surely
    This One as well
        has sought some different path strewn
            with fewer who no longer rise
                to greet the sun.

"Yet these ears
    have heard other words as well . .

"How your sudden standing at the People
    caused such consternation among them
        that they will not soon sit quietly by you.

"AND SO THESE ARE MY WORDS.

"Take off your skins.
    Carry them if you must,
        but as if carrying some bundle of provisions.

"No longer sit fireless at the edge of the People
    nor yet approach our fire.

"Rather,
    build a small fire
        in the manner of the solitary traveler,
    sit by it in the manner of the People.

"Seek your own sustenance.
    Neither offer nor request any such
        from the People.

"Live -- at the edge of our moving camp
    as if you traveled alone.
        Neither seek conversation with anyone.

"Proceed in this unvaried manner
for many days --
until I make a sign to you.

"This sign will mean
that the People
begin to suspect you are
who you now seem to be.

"When I make this sign,
do you on the next evening
begin to sing the old songs . .
of how it was for our People
long before this place.

"Sing
the old songs of new learning.

"Sing them quietly to yourself at first
so that the People
will only hear familiar patterns.

"Then -- after some days --
sing them somewhat louder,
so that the words themselves become apparent.

"Change this behavior in no other way.

"When it is clear to This One
that the People
begin to listen for your voice
with recognition which contains no fear,
then and only then will I on the next morning
offer you some sustenance.

"Do you take what is given
and sit quietly by our fire until it is eaten.
Then return to your own place.

"IN THIS MANNER OVER SOME DAYS
I hope to change the thinking of the People . .
leading them as I might lead them
over some great mountain,
with slow and careful steps.

"This I will do and no other, my Father.
For all the love I bear you,
it is the Whole People
who demand my greatest concern.

"If they cannot be brought by such steps
    to a willing acceptance of your return --
        then you must walk North again.

"FOR --
    much as these eyes will sorrow in the going --
    it is the well being of the Whole People
        that must be my special concern."

AND SO IT WAS AGREED BETWEEN THEM
AND SO IT INDEED OCCURRED.

OVER MANY DAYS
    This One folded away his soft skins
        and huddled close to a small personal fire
            for warmth.

    In all the usual ways
        he rose to greet the sun,
            spent his day gathering wherewith to survive,
            followed the People at a slow and steady pace
                when they moved from one place to another.

    Throughout these days
        neither did he approach too close
        nor did he in any other way
            attempt communication with the People.

ON THE FIFTEENTH DAY
    He rose to greet the sun,
        facing East
            toward this shining orb of gathered light
            and toward the smaller gathering of the fire
                round which the People slept.

ON THIS MORNING
    As on no other
        he faced East toward She Who Leads
        and saw now a beckoning hand.

    With no hesitation and with absolute purpose
        he paced toward her,
            sat at a cleared space beside that fire,
            and accepted from her hand
                in the usual manner
                    First Sustenance for the day.

Chewing slowly, he finished his meal,
   rose and returned to his own small fire
      with no further word.

Now he waited . .

Waited to understand his daughter's understanding
   of the mind of the People --
      whether acceptance was there
         or none at all.

THROUGHOUT THE DAY
   He proceeded in the usual manner,
      seeing no sign one way or the other,
      gathering sustenance --
      following the People at a measured distance.

Nor was any sign seen that day.

RATHER
   As he rose to greet the sun once more,
      his eyes were once more greeted
         by his daughter's welcoming gesture.

Again he approached,
   accepted First Sustenance from her hand,
   and sat at the cleared space
      until it was consumed.

NOW
   He returned once more to his own fire
      and the day was as the previous day had been.

Five such mornings were counted,
   each seeming to him
      to hold greater promise of acceptance,
         fewer hints of another journey North.

UNTIL ON THE SIXTH DAY,
   When he rose to leave the larger fire,
      his daughter gestured
         that he should sit again.

"Stay, my Father"
  -- she suggested --

"Stay yet awhile
  that I may ask you
    how it has been for you
      since last we met --
  for I hold within myself
    a great desire to understand
      the nature of this walk of days
        since you left us to walk North,
    yet seem to follow us now
      with patient steps."

Her voice was neither loud nor soft
  as she asked her questions.

It was such that those nearby could easily hear,
  yet those at some great distance
    could easily turn away and hear no more.

IN THIS MANNER
  Did she invite those who will
    to listen . .

Yet those
  for whom this questioning still seemed ominous
    might easily turn away --
  leaving some greater space for the new thoughts
    that may occur in older minds.

NOW THIS WAS THE MANNER OF IT.
  For three days
    did She Who Leads ask questions of her father,
      then release him to his solitary day.

When it was her judgment
  that many still listened,
    yet soon would not,
      her questions ceased.

An entire day elapsed
  before any new question was asked.

NOW ON THE FOURTH DAY,
  When it was her judgment
    that many still carefully listened . .

And when little time for appropriate answer
    had elapsed,
        she rose and suggested
    that was -- perhaps -- enough
        to satisfy her curiosity for one more day.

"But not enough for mine"
    -- some one said --

"Go on, Old Father, finish your telling
    and let This One leave if she wills."

AND SO IT WAS
    That She Who Leads left the circle
        to the questioning of the People . .

Her father never more than answering
    any specific question,
        those among the People coming and going,
    so that curiosity or discomfort with the new
        were equally accommodated.

Gradually the People learned --
    each at their own pace --
        the nature of the path
            of one who walks North . .
            and yet returns.

UNTIL AT LAST
    Someone asked the nature of shoulders
        that are --
    and are not -- covered with fur.

NOW
    This one whom they called Old Father
        sat in silence,
            remembering
                the cries of fear and of amazement
            that both his image
                and his softened skins evoked.

Nor was he anxious to learn
    whether some chance word
        might find him
            suddenly invited Northward once more

And so
    he said quietly only very little.

    "It was a thought that occurred to me
        as I sought some greater protection
          for the young among us
            as these nights grow colder."

AND
    Seeing
        that he had no great wish
          to discuss it further,
    Seeing also
        that he suggested in no way
          any change among the People,
        save some greater protection for the young,
          they were content to leave it . .
            for awhile.

        • • •

NOW AS THE DAYS PASSED
    Old Father continued in the usual way.

    Save now
        he sat at the Great Fire round which all gathered,
          answering from time to time
            some new question,
          or answering again
            some other asked before.

    Nor did any ask again
        about changeful shoulders.

AND YET
    The nature of the world changed by increments
        toward that which is colder . .

    Until one morning
        two of the very young were slow to waken
          and complained of great pain
            in hands and feet,
        though all slept together
          and protected from North Wind by shelters.

NOW AS THE DAYS PROGRESSED
    The mother of one of these
        grew steadily more anxious . .

    And -- as night camp was made --
        concerned herself
            with every manner of evening protection
        so that her son
            might more easily rise in the morning.

AND YET EVEN THIS
    Was not enough to assuage her concern.

    Finally she approached Old Father,
        wringing her hands, one with the other.

        "Old Father"
          -- she began --

        "You see how it is . .
       how my son arose this morning
          only very slowly,
            complaining of great pain.

        "It is my thought"
         -- she continued --

        "That tomorrow
          he may be even slower."

        "Knowing this"
         -- she concluded --

        "I was wondering
          whether you have any use
            for that softest skin
         which you carried with you
           when your purposeful steps
              carried you from North to East."

AND
    ALL LAUGHED AT THIS SIMPLE REFERENCE
      TO A PROFOUND CHANGE
        IN THE THINKING OF THE PEOPLE.

AND
    Two other women rose quickly
        to ask for the two remaining softened skins . .

So that soon three of the very young
  slept easily beneath these water softened skins.

And many laughed as others asked
  whether these very young
    might shed these new skins
  as easily in the morning
    as Old Father had peeled them
      from his shoulders many days before.

AND OLD FATHER . .
  No longer the center of attention,
    circled the fire
      making much of his hairless shoulders
      and basking in the easy acceptance
    which had at last
      replaced initial fear and consternation.

                    ❧ ◇ ❊

AND IT WAS AS YOU MIGHT EXPECT.
  None rose as easily the next morning,
    nor with greater comfort,
      than these three very young.

Neither were any of the early morning pains
  among them --
    so that they leapt easily and with alacrity
      from one place to another.

Much was made
  of putting on of skins and taking off . .

So that all could see -- and see again --
  that the mere wearing of softened skins
    did not easily become a permanent condition.

FOR ALL STILL REMEMBERED
  HOW IT HAD BEEN FOR OUR PEOPLE . .

How the many Season's Circles beside the Ocean
  had slowly washed much hair away
So that the nature of our being was changed --
  only this one and that born among the People
    still reminding them how it had been.

AND
This Edge of Ocean learning --
as all the others --
was still so clearly coveted
among the People . .

And their amazement at their later learning
that not all among the two legged
had learned this lesson was so great . .

That they had no wish to change and change again
for the mere presence of a little more cold
than before.

YET THEY SAW NOW HOW IT WAS
That they had a new learning . .
such that warm days
might lead
to the carrying of such softened skins
and cold nights
to their appropriate distribution
in a manner that assured
not only greater comfort,
but greater survival as well.

FOR
WHERE IS TOMORROW'S PEOPLE
IF THE YOUNG
DO NOT SURVIVE TODAY?

⬧ ⬧ ×

NOW EACH AND ALL OF THE PEOPLE
Sustained a great desire
to learn the nature of softened skins . .

So that Old Father
found his voice grown harsh
with too much telling
and his jaws grown sore
with too much demonstration.

So that now he asked the first three mothers
　　to tell for him
　　　　this oft repeated explanation
　　and to show for him . .

How it is
　　one may soften skins
　　　　both with washing
　　　　and with purposeful chewing.

AND SO IT WAS
　　That the Whole People
　　　　taught themselves a new skill . .

And learned the balance
　　between softening skins
　　　　in an appropriate manner
　　and softening them so greatly
　　　　that many extra openings appeared therein!

AND -- AS IS ALWAYS SO --
　　Some learned this skill more easily
　　　　and some less . .

YET
　　All taught themselves this new convenience,
　　　　assuring thereby
　　　　　　the continuance of the People
　　　　　　　　through many winters to come.

                              ⋄ ⋄ ×

NOW
　　This would be the ending of this telling,
　　　　save that the People listened to one another,
　　　　　　learning therefrom another lesson.

FOR ALL NOW UNDERSTOOD
　　The value of the learning
　　　　Old Father's sorrow brought them.

ALL KNEW
    how easily they had assumed
        that his Northward footsteps
            carried him forever from them.

ALL KNEW
    that soon his slowing steps
        might be encouraged again Northward,
    so as to hinder the Whole People in no way.

NOW
    ALL DISCUSSED THESE MANY THOUGHTS

UNTIL AT LAST
    one rose and said . .

    "Let us learn from this.

    "Let us learn"
        -- he suggested --

    "That a slowed step
        may yet predict a quickening of new thought.

    "Let us see"
        -- he continued --

    "How one too old for usual tasks
        may yet spend his time
            inventing new tasks for us.

    "And let us decide"
        -- he concluded --

    "FROM THIS DAY FOR AS MANY DAYS
        AS THIS PEOPLE MAY ENJOY

    "Let us remember
        to value the gifts
            Great Age may bring us.

    "Let us hesitate --
        and hesitate again --
            to encourage any step
                toward the North."

AND ALL SAW AND UNDERSTOOD
  THAT ONLY WISDOM SPOKE HERE.

SO THAT IT WAS SAID AMONG US . .
AND SAID AGAIN . .

   "HERE WE HAVE LEARNED
   A DOUBLE LESSON.

   "LET US LEARN IT WELL

   "LET THE CHILDREN'S
   CHILDREN'S
   CHILDREN
      HEAR OUR VOICE . . .

   "AND UNDERSTAND."

   SO BE IT.

They Dwell In Round Houses

NOW
> *The People saw such value*
> > *in all these many learnings*
> > > *that they asked once more*
> > > > *that each share any gift*
> > > > > *that memory contained.*

AND SO IT WAS
> That one among the People who was male
> > and who was of middle years rose
> > > and said . .

> "I have heard none discuss
> > how it was we came to assist
> > > those who dwelt in the rounded houses,
> > and yet it is a thing that I remember."

WHEN WE FIRST MET THE WANDERING PEOPLE,
> Those on this Great Island
> > on which we now stand
> > and who live to the East
> > > of the Never Ending Mountains
> > and who follow after the great herds
> > > gathering this and that . .

> One among the People
> > who came to lie still against the Earth
> > > explained how it was
> > that other People may learn other ways
> > > from a similar circumstance.

> For after those
> > who rode the Great Beasts with the long heads
> > > drove us off from the rounded dwellings,
> > after we saw such dwellings
> > > we greatly feared to approach them.

AND YET
> Some days' walk
> > toward the Ocean we purposed to cross . .
> Some who walked, did not ride,
> > and yet also greatly covered their bodies,
> > > approached us.

As such things often are,
    it was difficult to understand their purpose.

They walked -- again and again --
    toward some stream,
        wading in and beckoning.

Still, we did not understand
    until one day
        one of our short of leg misjudged his step
            and was swept away by the waters.

Understanding his ability
    to make his way through such waters unassisted,
        all laughed.

Yet these People
    who greatly covered themselves
        saw disaster here.

SO MUCH WAS CLEAR TO US.
    Where we see water
        as a means from one place to another . .

They saw
    lungs filled with no air at all
    and an Earth self sinking slowly beyond reach.

Their fear and consternation was evident,
    as was our jubilation
        when our Young One
    swam easily to the bank along the moving waters
        and walked quickly back upstream.

Then these new ones
    poured many sounds over these young shoulders,
        even shaking him a little,
            and gesticulating greatly
    until we easily understood their fear
        and more slowly understood their purpose.

IT WAS THIS ABILITY
    TO RESCUE OURSELVES EASILY
        FROM A WATERY CIRCUMSTANCE
            WHICH HELD THEIR SPECIAL ATTENTION.

We came to understand over some days
    that it was this skill they sought from us
      and it was for this reason
        they followed us now.

AND SO IT WAS THAT -- FROM TIME TO TIME --
We showed them
    the nature of our movement through water.

Yet it was their tendency --
    when trying to replicate our action --
      to greatly drown!

Coughing and spluttering,
    they rose from any water place
      on feet
        unwilling to find any other way of motion
          than that learned from walking,
    so that their knees bent
      as if climbing through the water,
  nor were they able to learn
    the straight leg motion
      our People use in water.

AND THERE WAS MORE.
  For no matter how we sought
    with great demonstrations
      to teach them the value
        of fewer clothes in such a circumstance,
      even removing every skin
        as we did for fastest motion,
    no coaxing or demonstration
      elicited from them any willingness at all
        to remove even the least necessary garment.

NOW OVER THESE MANY DAYS
  We had begun to learn this and that
    about this new People.

They had come, they told us now,
    moving always East
      along the Southern edge
        of something very high.

WE CAME TO UNDERSTAND
  That these were the great ice walls to the North.

AND
   WE CAME TO UNDERSTAND
     how it was for them,
     how such contiguity with ice walls
       led to great unwillingness to remove clothing
     how every such removal
       and lying still against the Earth
         were one and the same to them,
     how it was that this
       was such a sure thing in their mind
         that sinking below water
           seemed to them the wiser choice.

SO IT WAS
   That -- in small ways over many days --
     we showed them how it was
       they might never learn the manner
         of our movement through water
       in such a way as to assure safe arrival.

   Yet, the best among them
     began to be able
       to cross at least narrow streams
         through movement too rapid
           to allow for much sinking,

   And we, in our turn,
     learned how much water might be displaced
       by such flailing action.

NOW
   These ones -- some of them --
     continued to return to our moving camp
       from time to time,
     until we came at last to Walk by Waters
       and saw our purpose
         stretch out ahead of us.

NOW IT WAS
   That these ones from time to time
     had coaxed some of our People South with them,
       giving them slowly to understand
         that they purposed their own crossing.

AND THIS WAS THE WAY OF IT.
It was clear from their behavior
that this People
had crossed to various islands
to the South of the main land
and that this crossing
had grown more difficult
as Ocean grew higher on the land.

IT SEEMED TO US
THAT THIS PEOPLE, TOO,
RETAINED A MEMORY OF EASE OF ACCESS
AT AN EARLIER TIME.

Now it became apparent to us
that this People fled, also.

Not from Ocean coming like a Great Wall,
but from those
who rode Great Beasts with long faces
and had little regard for the ways of others.

NOW
This gentle People with forever clothing
sought the other side of a water
proof against such beasts and their riders.

Yet they would gladly be crushed under hooves
before they would risk an icy, frozen path
to that Great Quiet.

SO IT WAS
That those few of our People still with them
sat puzzling,
thinking through all they had learned,
sifting and sorting,
wondering what learning
might here find a new purpose . .

Until at last
their thoughts turned to the nature
of the rounded dwellings this people built
and to the nature of water.

SO IT WAS
    That those few of our People still with them
        sought logs dry enough to float,
           large enough to sustain some weight.

    Trying this and that --
        first with themselves
           as their self-rescue
                was easily accomplished --
        then with the strongest
           among this other People,
        they developed a way
           of tying each to an appropriate log.

    Kicking and spluttering
        they taught themselves
           how to cross to other islands --
              and the strongest returned . .

    Learning this difficult skill,
        until they learned a way
           to carry across even the very young,
              propelled by some strong man.

IN THIS MANNER
    Did all this People --
        so unwilling to risk a change in dress --
        nonetheless cross an open water.

SO IT WAS
    Our People came to understand
        that much may be done --
           despite self-imposed limits --
              to meet a new circumstance.

    Swimming across one last time
        in our easy manner . .

    They gave -- one People and the other --
        equal wishes
           for renewed purpose
           and expanded ability
              to meet a new circumstance.

Then,
    showing their leave-taking was purposeful . .

Our People
    returned to the main land
        in their easy manner
    and rejoined our People
        at the edge of Walk by Waters.

Ocean Again

NOW YOU WILL UNDERSTAND
  HOW IT WAS

  That there was one more Telling
    yet retained by Eight Winters Child,
  She who yet remembered Walk by Waters,
  She who had listened
      to the many words of Ancient Wisdom,
          asking only
              that these words
                  find a new and a younger home.

  AND
      This was the Telling of Ocean Again.

FOR AS I HAVE TOLD YOU,
    Our People were a Forest People,
      and yet
          learned to be a People of the open plain.

  This Open Land People
      learned to live by the Edge of Ocean
          whose bitter water yielded sustenance,
              none of which was liquid.

NOW
    THIS EDGE OF OCEAN PEOPLE
        CROSSED ONCE MORE
            THE HIGH LANDS TO THE WEST OF BEFORE
            AND BECAME . .
                A WALKING PEOPLE.

  FOR SURELY
      THAT MUST BE OUR CONTINUING NAME.

THIS WALKING PEOPLE
    Maintained
        their self-sustaining walk to the East,
            learning always,
            learning at last
                the cold winter wisdom of clothing
                    and the value, therefore, of age.

THIS LEARNING PEOPLE
   Continued their walk past mountains
     and over the level places,
       finding at last a new Learning Place
        at the northern edge
         of many high southern mountains,
       waiting eagerly for wisdom
        to wash down the valleys,
         carried by stream waters.

NOW WITH REGRET,
   THIS PEOPLE
     re-commenced its slow march East,
      seeking always another Ocean.

It was their thought
   that there at last
     they might find an Edge of Ocean home
So that the children's children's children
   might learn and grow with some surety.

WE DO NOT KNOW,
   FOR IT HAS NOT BEEN RECORDED,
    THE THOUGHTS
     THAT PRECEDED THIS DECISION
     TO MOVE ON EAST,
      AWAY FROM WISDOM WASHING DOWN.

Perhaps again winters grew colder --
   or perhaps it seemed enough had been learned.

Perhaps other Peoples came to live so nearby
   that sustenance grew more difficult to find.

WE DO NOT KNOW
   WHAT THOUGHTS THEY SHARED

AND YET WE KNOW
   They did again begin their eastward march,
   which led them at last to another Ocean
   as they expected it should.

THIS, THEN,
is Eight Winters Child's Telling
of yet another Ocean arrival . .

HOWEVER IT WAS
that our People
found their way to another Ocean,
this is what is recorded about their arrival.

×∞∞×

FOR SO LONG
THAT THERE WAS NO COUNT . .

The People had maintained an eastward direction,
sustaining themselves
as the land best allowed.

NOW ALL CHANGED.
Rivers which had flowed only north
began to flow in every direction,
many flowing in a wandering eastward way.

It was one of these
the People chose to follow,
exploring this way and that,
learning the nature of the land.

AS THEY PROCEEDED
The Winters grew warmer
so that habits learned before
began to change,
and some among the People
spoke against this.

"Will we lose"
-- they asked --

"Skills gained at such great price?
Will the children's children's children
confront the need to devise again
such a manner of finding comfort
within the context
of a changing circumstance?

"Or will we learn a way
to encourage understanding
of the presently unnecessary?

"Who prefers
the risk of hoping one who remembers
survives from one cold Winter
to whenever we find such winters again?"

AND THE PEOPLE DEVISED A WAY
In which new eyes
could be opened to these possibilities,
sharing the nature of changing circumstance
and the varying behaviors
that may relate thereto.

It was found among them
that certain ones seemed best skilled
at helping these new eyes
look clearly at unapparent possibility.

And it was these
who had special responsibility
to assure clear-eyed vision.

YET
All shared this responsibility,
singing from time to time
about old ways and cold winters,
discussing as if they had been there
the thoughts of the People
at this or that time
that led to subsequent decision.

AND SO
YOUNG EYES SLOWLY OPENED

AND
SLOWLY SAW HOW IT HAD BEEN
FOR A PEOPLE
WHO HAD LEARNED
TO SURVIVE A VARYING CIRCUMSTANCE.

• • •

NOW
As the People maintained a wandering path
along the course of one great river,
moving East or South,
the river grew in waters
as many small waters
joined this larger stream.

NOW
The People felt an eager anticipation,
for surely such a swelling river
presaged the birth of some great water.

NOW
All sustained a great will to learn
whether this great water
would be some great lake,
repository of many rivers,
or whether it might yield at last
the ocean's edge
anticipated by so many of those
who went before.

AS THE RIVER GREW GREATER,
It passed from time to time
through steep mountain gorges,
difficult to cross,
And much time was spent
finding this way or that to rejoin the river.

AND YET
Their purpose was not lost,
the river found again after each separation,
Until at last
the river lost itself in many channels,
great reeds, small buzzing things,
and no ease of access.

"You see how it is"
-- someone said --

"How a mountain pass
leads you to yearn for flatter land,
and yet flatter land
may lead you
to yearn for yet another mountain pass."

AND ALL LAUGHED

Disheartened by apparent inability
either to decipher these many channels
or to learn in any other way
the best direction toward the great water
which must lie beyond,
they spoke together
and decided at last
to turn somewhat North,
finding their way -- perhaps --
through some low mountains
to an edge of this Great Water.

AND AFTER SOME DAYS
Of finding their way North and also East,
toward the low mountains
which lay in that direction,
their feet grew at last dry
and an easy path was found.

NOW I WOULD TELL YOU,
IF IT WERE SO . .

That the People found at last their Ocean Place
and -- with a glad cry -- rushed toward it,
well aware of its probable bitter nature.

YET IT WAS NOT SO.

For a gradual incline
led to one rise after another,
Until the People
were looking down on a small bay
with water and water and water beyond.

IN THIS WAY
Did they assure themselves
that Ocean at last had been found.

Yet there was no place at the edge
for a new People.

For below them at the Edge of Ocean
were a numerous People.

AND -- AS FROM AMONG THE TWO-LEGGED --
These were the most different they had seen,
or of whom the memories had been kept.

For these ones
were short in stature,
darker in hue than the People
yet not the darkest yet seen.

Their hair above a thickened face
was of its nature short --
or cut in some way --
and with a thickness that often comes
from some intrinsic constant bend
in its nature,
so that from here to there
each hair travels a variable path.

Their bodies were covered with more hair
than the People yet retained --
and it was this
that gave us to think this was a People
newly arrived at Ocean . .
for surely none who live there long --
over many, many lives --
find such covering convenient.

SUCH IS THE NATURE OF TWO LEGGEDS
That some are open and unafraid
of meeting others . .

And yet some
approach any variation in their lives
with fear.

AND SO IT WAS
That the People
watched quietly from where they were,
waiting to learn whether circumstance
would show us a manner of approach
that would be pleasing to them.

AND YET NONE OCCURRED.
Finally, after much discussion,
three from among the People
were chosen to descend to the beach.

It seemed that three new People
would be no great concern
for such a numerous group.

AND YET IT GAVE CONCERN.
For when our young men approached them,
the noise was great --
and much brandishing of sticks ensued --
so that the three from among us
who went to meet this people
crouched down in un-defiance,
settling quietly
at one end of this beach near fresh water.

AND THIS IS WHAT THEY LEARNED . .

This People
had a great fear of anything strange.

It was not only our People --
pale and tall and straight of leg
compared to them --
who caused them great disquiet.

Even when we left implements --
which were different for them than for us --
within easy reach,
yet they feared to touch them.

Any from among our People, even the smallest,
would have approached slowly
and with increasing curiosity.

Yet none of these People approached,
even starting back
when we moved forward
to place some implement at their feet
for their inspection.

FOR IT WAS IN THIS MANNER
That a slow approach to strangeness
was often made easier
between disparate Peoples.

Those among this People who were male
    seemed always to stand between us and
    those among their People who were female,
    and only with the latter
        were the young ever found.

Those who were female
    seemed even more fearful than the men,
        nor was it clear to us
            whether they were fearful of us
            or of their own men.

Although the women
    seemed to argue with their men as a group,
    we saw no individual woman
        ever make issue with any male.

THIS PUZZLED US GREATLY
    As, if the respect we consider essential to life
    were shown by any of these,
        we were unable to discern it.

Their manner of communication
    seemed a great puzzle to us.

No sound patterns emerged
    whose meaning seemed predictable to us.

Rather, they seemed to make a great sound
    to gather attention,
        then with gesticulation
            make known at least
                the direction of their thoughts.

YET IT SEEMED TO US
    So much more was communicated
    than could be predicted
        from either sound or motion
    that we resolved to study them carefully
        so as to understand their pattern.

AT LAST
    These three caused such continuing consternation
    that they chose to leave,
        resolving to find another way
        to ease an understanding
        between our Peoples.

• • •

In studying the manner of these sand dwellers,
    we came to know
        they varied sustenance little
            from what Ocean provides.

Once we discovered one from among them
    who was female and carried a very young one.

She had crossed the low mountain
    to its western side
        and gave every evidence
            of looking for that which may be eaten.

Being very careful of her natural reserve,
    two of our People slowly approached her,
        when, to our great surprise . .
    one of their men
        walked rapidly over this same mountain
            and -- finding this woman --
        brandished his stick at her,
            ignoring our close approach --
        stalked angrily after her,
            returning her to the eastern side
                of this low mountain.

WHY THIS PEOPLE
    Would forego the possibility
        of increased sustenance --
            and sustenance of a more varied nature --
        merely to keep the women close
            was a great puzzle to us.

IT WAS DECIDED AMONG US
    That we would sustain ourselves
        on the western side of this low mountain
            until we understood two puzzles . .

Why this People
    behaved as they did, male and female . .

And how it was
    that more was apparently communicated
        than we found any way at all of predicting.

EITHER
  WE WOULD ANSWER THESE QUESTIONS

OR WE WOULD DECIDE
  WE COULD NOT FIND THE ANSWERS.

IN EITHER EVENT,
  since soggy ground and a great river
    lay to the South
  and since this People
    seemed all unwilling
      to share their Ocean's Edge,

WE WOULD SEARCH
  TO THE NORTH
    FOR A PLACE
      IN WHICH TO CRAFT TOMORROW.

          • • •

NOW
  WE TRIED AGAIN.

Three of our People who were men
    took gifts of varying kinds
      and laid them at the edge
        of their fresh water stream.

Rather than accept these gifts,
    this seemed to cause them to hesitate
      even to drink,
    though we left our gifts and returned quickly.

FINALLY,
  We brought back all our gifts
      and even found a place along the soggy ground
        where the water ran freely
          for our own water . .
      though the walk was long and many ill
        before the freely moving water was found.

NOW
   ALL SEEMED TO BE AS IT WAS BEFORE.

None among this People seemed disturbed
   if we retained our position
      on the western side of this low mountain.

None of them came again to that side.

They seemed so unconcerned
   with our distant presence
      that we wondered
         whether their vision was as sharp as ours.

Those who had been closest to them
   saw that their eyes had a tendency
      to search out their own nose,
   and we wondered whether they had the ability
      to see beyond their immediate concern.

We wondered further
   whether this might not be the cause
      of their great concern over our presence.

SO IT WAS
   We resolved to study this People
      in a manner inoffensive to them.

We chose those from among us
   with the sharpest sight
      and gave them the sole obligation
         of learning from afar
            all that might be learned.

FIRST
   They chose to test
      whether approach and appearance
         had some discontinuance with one another
            for this People.

They tried -- day after day --
   various distances and means of approach.

They discovered that --
   if they maintained a certain distance --
      all was as if they were not there.

FURTHER, THEY LEARNED THAT,
If they managed a closer approach all unseen
and then remained carefully still . .
it was also as if they were not there.

AND IN ONE MANNER OR THE OTHER
Many days
were spent in learning about this People
while in no apparent way disturbing them.

As light and dark followed one another,
our People
learned how rarely this People used fire.

Perhaps the warmth it gave
seemed of lesser value
to a People living near the warmth of Ocean.

AND YET
They also wore some clothing of their own design.

Perhaps the softness engendered in some roots
by a proximate fire
seemed of little use to those
whose sustenance came mainly from Ocean.

YET WHATEVER THE CAUSE,
Fire was less used
and no Central Fire ever built.

MORE THAN THIS.

Those who watched began a careful count --
as much to fill their days
as for any learning purpose.

As they counted and counted again
they learned a thing
that was greatly surprising to them.

WHEREAS AMONG OUR PEOPLE
A balance between those who were female
and those who were male
was usually the way of things . .
some few additional People being female.

AMONG THIS PEOPLE
  NO SUCH BALANCE OBTAINED.

Rather, a careful many-times count told us
  that among this People
    there were three males
      for every two female persons.

We thought then of the female
  who wandered
    to the western side of the low mountains
    and how one among them who was male
      chased her back to the other side.

WE BEGAN TO WONDER
  Whether this imbalance in itself
    predicted the angry care
      given by the men among them
        to the women among them.

AND ANOTHER POSSIBILITY OCCURRED TO US.

If they would not accept as friends
  the men among us,

If they would not accept our gifts,
  then perhaps
    they would accept
      some from among us who were women,
        either as guests or as friends.

AND THIS WAS GREATLY DISCUSSED.

Perhaps any so going down
  might find joining such a People
    easier than the leaving of it.

AND YET
  all were eager to learn more of this People,
    eager also to accomplish the learning
      and to find our own place to the North.

SO IT WAS
  That three from among us who were women
    chose to go down.

AND IT WAS AGREED AMONG US
   That these three
      were also among the most strong
   And -- since our women
      were not in the habit
         of cowering beneath sticks,
      perhaps this strength
         would carry them away from this People.

AND
   A sign for such a time was agreed among us . .
      as our People had no difficulty at all
         in seeing the watchers,
            both those at a distance
              and those who sat still.

AS IT WAS ALLOWED,
   SO IT WAS AGREED
      that some one from among them
         would seek water at the stream
         and convey at that time
            the general condition of each.

AND SO IT WAS.

   Our three women were accepted with hesitation,
      but with some ease,
   Some few from among their men
      rapidly herding them toward the other females
         where they settled carefully.

FROM TIME TO TIME
   It was clear to the watchers
      that some altercation arose
         as between our women
            and those from among the other People,
   and yet altercations seldom arose with the men.

  Daily
      one or more of our women approached the stream
         and signaled
      either content or some distemperate safety.

NO INDICATION OF THREAT WAS SEEN.

MEANWHILE
  Our watchers
    learned the manner of their hunting.

  They searched for creatures below the water.

NOW AND AGAIN
  Some one from among them
    would send up a great cry,
      pointing with his stick . .

  And would communicate his purpose
    in such a way that --
      before they could in any way we understood
        communicate --
    it was apparent
      all followed some general agreement.

  Nor was the manner of it
    ever clear to us during this time.

YET
  Within moments of the first loud summons,
    all acted in a coherent manner
      for the purpose of catching
        some large underwater creature.

  Neither did they have any great skill at swimming,
    so that all helped one another
      with this general task.

                  ◇ ✕ ◇

NOW AS DAYS FOLLOWED ONE ANOTHER,
  These were their patterns,
    until one morning
      one of our women signaled from the stream
        that they would soon be leaving.

  They gave us three days
    to prepare to head north
      and we responded that this was enough.

NOW ON THAT THIRD DAY
    A great furor arose among this People,
        with much calling and chattering,
           so that we knew
                some great event was occurring.

FINALLY,
    Our three women
        separated themselves from the others,
           who seemed to be chasing them away.

    Although they did our women no great harm,
        their purpose was clear . .

    And in that way
        their leaving was even easier
           than their going in.

◦ ◦ ◦

NOW THIS WAS THE WAY OF IT.

    It had been agreed among us that --
        given the evident varying skills
           in communication
                this People seemed to possess --
    an ability to bring out with us
        one of their young
           might be appropriate.

    It was also seen
        that the easiest way of accomplishing this
           might be for our women
                to bring these young with them
                    in the usual manner.

    Given the nature of these men,
        it was not a thing that was asked . .

    AND YET
        IT WAS A THING THAT WAS GIVEN.

FOR WE NOW LEARNED
    That these three women from among us
        had agreed among themselves to leave
            as soon as it was clear
                that at least two
                    expected to bring out young.

IN THIS MANNER
    They were likely to live among this People
        long enough to learn much,
            but not so long
                as to sorrow greatly in the parting.

THEN IT CAME TO BE
    That two of them
        had acquired this extra benefit of nature,
    Yet all three
        had come to be so valued
            for their industriousness
        that the willingness of the leave taking
            concerned them greatly.

AND SO IT WAS
    They decided to so arouse the People against them
        that their going out
            would be greeted with cries of joy

AND
    as they had carefully studied this People
        so as to accommodate their manner to them,
    so they also studied them
        so as to fail to do so.

IN THIS THEY WERE GREATLY SUCCESSFUL.

AND FOR THIS REASON
    The great noise we heard on the third day
        had arisen.

NOW EVEN SO,
   The men they called friend
      were loath to part with them,
   And only by arousing all the women against them
      were they able to free themselves easily.

IT WAS THEIR THOUGHT THAT
     had this People known they took with them some future young,
       neither would this have been allowed.

AND SO
   They took great care
     to fail to share their knowledge,
       even sharing with the one in three
         who carried no young
           those signs of such connection.

  In this,
     they found themselves wise,
       as this People herded their young
       as the men herded the women,
         seldom allowing them to stray.

  This closeness, too,
     they thought related to their vision.

A PEOPLE
   who do not see easily over any great distance
     are likely to be unwilling
       to allow wandering.

IT WAS ALSO THOUGHT POSSIBLE
   That the difference
     between the number of men
      and the number of women
     might indicate some wandering away too far . .

  Or perhaps a similar People
     acquiring effective direction over some female,
       much as one might pick up and carry away
        some crafted tool.

IT WAS THEIR THOUGHT
   That these women were unused to arguing.

NOW, MOREOVER,
 What the watchers had noted
  was noted at some great proximity
   by our three women.

FOR
 A regular pattern was one
  in which all but these three
   knew what to do . .

 Some precipitate and apparently understood action
  began,
   including all but them.

THESE THREE WERE CONVINCED
THAT NEITHER SOUND NOR MOTION
EXPLAINED THIS UNDERSTANDING.

RATHER,
 IT WAS THEIR VIEW
  that this People shared thoughts
   on such occasions . .

 It being only necessary
  to be sure you had the attention
   of those
    with whom you sought such sharing.

ALSO,
 IT WAS THEIR VIEW
  that on other occasions
   a general view
    evolved in the thinking of this People
   which all shared
   and which led to some general action,
    agreement to which
     was unperceived by our three women.

ALL OF THIS BEING WHAT IT WAS,
It remained now only
to await the arrival among us
of these two young ones
and to come to understand
the gifts they bring.

AND FROM THAT DAY TO THIS
THERE HAVE OFTEN BEEN BORN AMONG US
THOSE OF THE STRONG SPIRIT EYE
WHICH LOOKS OFTEN INWARD . .

AND IN THESE ONES
IS USUALLY BORN A NATURE
TO LISTEN
WITHOUT SPEECH
AND TO HEAR
WITHOUT WORDS.

THESE AND OTHER SUCH ABILITIES
are valued among us as a gift
given us by three strong and wise women,
who walked away from their People
into an unknown circumstance,
earned their way among a strange People,
and found a path home
crafted from their own wisdom.

LET US
CELEBRATE THEIR WISDOM,

LET US
WALK THE NORTHWARD PATH.

⋈⋈⋈

Growing Woman

LONG AFTER WE FOUND
  OUR EDGE OF OCEAN HOME

AND YET
  LONG BEFORE WE LEFT IT

  THERE LIVED AMONG THE PEOPLE
    ONE WHO WAS CALLED AT THAT TIME
    GRATEFUL DAUGHTER . .

FOR SURELY
  THIS ONE
    SHOWED BOTH GRATITUDE AND RESPECT
    TO THE ONE SHE CALLED MOTHER.

YET
  This Mother had recently sickened,
    suffering from the bending disease
      which stoops shoulders
        and bends both fingers and hands.

SO IT WAS
  That this woman,
    one who had been renowned
      for quick motion and purposeful search,
        slowed in both step and motion.

  No longer able
    to bend in the old familiar way,
  She found some convenient gathering place
    and lowered herself slowly to Earth,
      shifting sideways
        from bush to bush, root to root,
      still gathering for herself at least
        that which is necessary to sustain life,
      yet no longer able to gather for the many
        who once had eaten round her fire.

IT WAS THIS
  That her Daughter found most difficult.

  How one who had fed many,
    inviting any hungry person to sit with her,
      now barely fed her own bent self.

AND SO
>This Daughter did all she could
>>to ease her Mother's path . .
>>>cut her a staff to aid in walking,
>>>worked a soft skin to lay on the earth
>>>>for one who sits
>>>>>to search each bush and rooted place,
>>>brought gifts of this and that.

"Too much found today"
>-- she said --
And
>"I fail in understanding, my Mother.

"Why is it
>that you who fed me
>>during many young years
>>>may not now be fed by me?

"Is it
>that you wish to limit my skills
>>as Mother?"

YET
>No cajoling,
>No reference to a personal wish for efficacy
>>could convince this Bending Woman
>>>to allow others to provide for her.

Still, nearly every day,
>she rose with slow and purposeful motions --
>>leaning heavily on her staff --
>and, having risen,
>>went out to search one more day
>>>for sustenance.

NOW
>Her Daughter,
>>watching these slow and painful steps,
>>>knew her own pain,
>>and had a great wish
>>>to ease the differing pains each felt.

SO IT WAS
    That she convinced others
        to leave gathering places
            which were near at hand
            untouched
        so that this bent and aging back
            would have less distance to travel.

YET,
    Even these were at last depleted,
        so that once again
            those painful feet
                walked farther and farther.

AND ON THOSE DAYS
    When storms were great or pain exceeded purpose,
        this Was-Able Mother
            lay by the fire, wrapped in robes,
        and eating only that which she had gathered . .
            so that more and more often
                this was nothing at all.

                ⋄ ⋄ ⋄

NOW
    Grateful Daughter saw this,
        saw how little weight her mother now carried,
            and her eyes were often misted
                as if rain had followed her home.

YET
    Her Mother would allow none to feed her,
        saying those who cannot feed themselves
            must learn the consequences
        and seeing -- as far as anyone could tell --
            none of the pain this caused others.

        "Blindness comes in many manners"
          -- someone said.

AND ALL AT LAST AGREED
    That this Bending Woman
        should be allowed her own course in life,
            even if that lightened her weight
                past survival.

Yet all were sure to leave this and that about
which assured survival
and to complain often of Too Much.

AND YET
Sorrowful Daughter could not be content.

For on warm and sunny days
Bending Woman even then
found the path toward sustenance difficult.

And on cold and stormy days
she found it impossible.

AND -- WHAT WITH ONE THING AND ANOTHER --
FROM TIME TO TIME
There were more of one than of the other,
and this came to determine the health
of Bending Woman.

⋄ ⋇ ⋄

NOW, AS I HAVE SAID,
Sorrowful Daughter was not content
with the manner of these things,

Yet she was unwilling
to cause her Mother
the different pain of dependency
for one who had been depended upon.

AND SO
Her mind wrestled greatly
with one possibility and another . .

UNTIL ONE DAY
Staring at some offending plant . .
she asked why it chose to live where it was.

She asked further
whether it might not decide a different thing
and come to live closer to the People,
closer even to her Mother.

SHE UNDERSTOOD HOW IT WAS
that too much gathering close at hand
discouraged our rooted brothers
from living near us.

SHE UNDERSTOOD HOW SOME SAID
that great care must be given
to leaving some of every rooted family,
leaving especially some of their seeds.

AND YET NONE WERE SURE
that our four legged brothers were as kind.

Perhaps they --
or someone from among the Two-Leggeds
too hungry to remember tomorrow --
had taken the last seed,
destroying tomorrow
for one more of our rooted brothers.

SO IT WAS, AT THIS TIME,
That all walked farther and farther
to find every kind of sustenance.

Only the rains
provided a constant supply of liquid,
though more in some times than in others.

AND SORROWFUL DAUGHTER
Sat by the side of one of her rooted brothers
and studied the nature of things . .

Turning all I have said
over and over in her mind
like a determined Bear
searching for grubs under fallen leaves
or a crayfish
worrying a rock
until it releases some morsel.

AND AT LAST
Sorrowful Daughter
spoke to the Earth and the Sky
and all her rooted brothers
and asked . .

*"If these ones here
cannot walk to some more convenient place
and live there in peace
while providing us with plenty . .*

"LET THESE FEET WALK FOR THEM."

AND SO -- IN A RESPECTFUL MANNER --
She gathered three of the podded seeds
with no intention of eating
and found a muddy place nearer their fires,
encouraging each at last into Earth.

AND -- THE SEASON BEING WHAT IT WAS --
It was not long
before some small green showed,
and a trailing plant followed,
and the thoughts of Sorrowful Daughter
filled with joy.

        ❦ ❦ ❦

NOW IT MIGHT SEEM
That an easy solution to a difficult problem
also took root here.

BUT I TELL YOU NOW IT WAS NOT SO.
For Grateful Daughter well knew
that the thoughts of the People
were various and many.

EVEN AS SOME
Had failed in cooperation
with those rooted brothers
already near at hand,
so also might they fail in understanding here.

Therefore,
This One saw a long path
from first roots to sustained growth.

It was her first purpose
to cause some few of the People
to understand this possibility of solution.

It was her thought
to learn to understand
which persons from among the People
might most easily grasp
the nature of this possible change.

TO THAT END
She began asking occasional questions
about the nature of roots and growth

Until she rapidly learned
how difficult it would be
for some to accept the possibility of seed
walking from one place to another.

SHE CHOSE AT LAST
Two friends
who had lent willing ears
to her cries of concern for her Mother.

Taking them with her,
she showed them the new plants in muddy earth.

Yet they, too,
were unwilling to see in their minds
the steps from one place to another.

SO IT WAS
That Grateful Daughter
took them with her once again,
finding some vine growing of itself
in a distant place . .

She carried three seeds
    from one pod close by their living place
        and -- as her friends watched --
    buried these three seeds
        behind a rock placed close to the cliff
            in which their living place occurred.

"How long may it have been"
    -- she asked --

"Since any rooted brother lived this close?

"You see how it is"
    -- she went on --

"How many feet
    have pounded the earth beyond growth.

"Yet I now"
    -- she finished --

"Place three seeds beyond sight
    to learn what may yet grow."

ALL THIS
    Was quietly done.

ALL KNEW
    How quickly
        the People may learn in a new circumstance
    And how slowly
        they may learn in the old.

    None had any wish by intemperate action
        to encourage hardened thoughts
            in their Brothers, their Sisters.

EACH DAY
    These three came out to casually look
        between rock and cliff wall . . .
            and found nothing.

    UNTIL AT LAST
        only one pair of eyes
            strayed in that direction.

WE KNOW NOW,
   AS NO ONE KNEW THEN,
      how long may be the wait
         at certain times of year
            between the encouraging of a seed
               and the reality of growth.

SO IT WAS NOW . .
   And Grateful Daughter waited long.

UNTIL ONE DAY,
   when Earth brightened again,
      she thought she saw
         some disruption to the earth
            near rock and wall.

NOW AT THIS TIME,
   Some thought she had earned a new name,
      and called her Stares at Earth,
         laughing greatly at the thought
            Earth was moving . .

FOR,
   Although they did not understand her purpose,
      it seemed to them she stared at Earth
         in anticipation of its moving.

Nor did Grateful Daughter
   stare only at Earth near rock.

Her preoccupation with growth became such
   that now she carefully watched the growth
      of all our rooted brothers,
         pointing out this and that.

NONE KNEW,
   BUT MANY LATER LEARNED,
      THAT SHE SOUGHT TO PLANT ANOTHER SEED . .
      THE SEED OF UNDERSTANDING

      . . .

NOW AS I HAVE SAID,
　　Earth brightened
　　　　and the days warmed
　　　　　　toward another growing time.

　　Grateful Daughter
　　　　studied all growth . .

　　And every morning
　　　　studied the unmoved Earth
　　　　　　near their living place.

AND AT LAST -- AS YOU AND I WOULD NOW EXPECT --

　　The first green
　　　　of a new twining plant appeared . .

　　And then the second.

　　Quietly,
　　　　so as not to arouse curiosity . .

　　Grateful Daughter invited her two friends
　　　　to reexamine the place
　　　　　　they both remembered.

　　Each in her turn did so.

AND NOW FROM AMONG THE PEOPLE
THERE WERE THREE
　　who began to understand how it was
　　　that seed might sprout sudden feet
　　　　and move from one place to another.

AND YET THEY WAITED.

Their thought was to assure so much growth
that few would argue about seedlings.

So, when these two rooted brothers
had achieved some height . .

These three women
went in to their living place
and invited Bending Woman
to come with them,
on this day
when Earth was warm
and Sun kind to all.

AND SHE CAME -- ALL UNWILLING --
Describing her slow steps.

But these three explained
that they had much to tell her
and her steps might not be slow enough.

One and then the other,
they moved their feet
in step with Bending Woman,
describing as they went
the many purposes of Grateful Daughter.

NOW
Bending Woman had been valued
since her earliest years
for a certain quickness of mind
which moved her feet
in an appropriate direction
quicker than most.

Now although her step moved slowly,
her mind still danced.

And it danced now past their words,
often anticipating what they would next say.

SO IT WAS
>   She held no questions in her mind
>   when first she saw these trailing plants.

>   It was clear to all three women
>   that she expected
>   to find them there.

>   Given their explanation of procedure,
>   she understood
>   the probability of success.

>   And they were reminded again
>   of why this woman
>   had been valued among the People
>   since her youth.

NOW
>   Four women regarded two trailing vines,
>   asking each other the questions each held . .

>   How to explain all this to the People,
>   when and how quickly,
>   how to assure the fullest growth
>   to each of these two trailing vines.

IT WAS BENDING WOMAN
>   Who now described the next events . .

>   "Go you and cut two light staffs.

>   "For one
>   who needs to lean on a heavier staff
>   recognizes those with a similar need.

>   "These two trailing plants
>   are wont to climb
>   through bushes and over rocks.

>   "If they wander far here
>   it will be too far
>   and many feet
>   will beat their purpose into Earth.

"So let us help these two stand as I stand.
      In this
            they will require less space.
      In this
            they may survive."

AND SO IT WAS AS SHE SAID.
      Light staves were cut and brought to her.

NOW
      Bending Woman did something
            that amazed them all.

She beat with her heavy staff on a nearby rock
      and called out in her loudest tones
            for everyone to hear her.

All came,
      for she was one
            who had earned great respect,
            and earned now
                  their concern and their attention.

When all were gathered
      who were near at hand . .

She pointed with her staff
      to those two small plants.

Making no attempt at all
      to explain the process,
            she announced . .

"My Daughter has prepared a task for me,
      one equal to my skills.

"She asks me to sit and guard these two plants
      so that none may touch them
            until they are full grown.

"She has a great wish
      to learn how well they may do
            so close to our living place.

411

"*I ask*
    that all respect their right to be here.

"So that you will know precisely
    what we ask,
        we now place
            these two thin staffs near them."

AND
    With that she ceased,
        crossed toward the staffs
            which the other women
                now settled firmly in Earth,
        carefully spread out her soft sitting skin,
        and settled herself slowly to Earth
            with a clear and firm purpose.

ALL STOOD AMAZED AT THIS,
    Not least the three women
        who best understood this circumstance.

THEN
    Grateful Daughter began to smile.

    "This at least"
        -- she said to her friends --

    "BENDING WOMAN
        IS SETTLED TO EARTH.

    "You see how it is,"
        -- she went on --

    "She has given herself a purpose,
        one which requires little motion.

    "And look"
        -- she added --

    "*How many draw close to her,*
        seeking understanding."

    "I think we will now be allowed
        to bring her food"
            -- another added --

"AND OUR TWO TWINING PLANTS
    ARE SAFE
        AND WELL ASSURED OF SURVIVAL."

AND SO IT WAS.
   Bending Woman, in her Wisdom, understood
     that such great change in thinking
      is better left to questions
       than to explanation.

FOR THOSE WHO ASK . .
   often, if not always, seek answers,
     and have already prepared some place
      for a new understanding.

IN HER WISDOM
   she understood
     that many such questions --
      as each became willing to ask --
     was better than four women
      deciding for a Whole People.

SHE SAT NOW PATIENTLY
   from each light to each dark
     watching the growing vines,
     crowing with joy
   when a third green sprout appeared,
     shouting for another thin staff.

NOW
   she allowed her three daughters
     to bring her sustenance.

INDEED, IT BECAME THE CUSTOM
   For a curious people
     to bring something they had gathered
      to share with Bending Woman . .

As they asked once more
   to hear the Telling
     of Seeds That Sprout Sudden Feet.

AND IN THIS MANNER
  Did Bending Woman spend her days . .

Seated under a warm sun
  or by a sometimes warmer fire . .

Recounting the gathered wisdom
  of a long and useful life . .

Sharing with the children's children
  some of that which they had gathered . .

REMINDING ALL THE PEOPLE
  OF COURAGE . .
    AND PURPOSE . .
      AND CHANGE.

  and Grateful Daughter
  often remembered
  to smile.

. . .

NOW
  THIS IS ALMOST THE END
    OF THE TELLING OF GROWING WOMAN.

HER NEED
  ENGENDERED A GREAT LEARNING
    WHICH IS STILL A GIFT
      WE GIVE OUR CHILDREN,
    AND ITS END IS NOT YET.

FOR
  seeds prosper in New Earth,
    brought there sometimes
      by past pain.

  Brought there also
    by compassion
      and by concern for others.

THE PEOPLE
  did not accept this Wisdom at first,
    considering it more a curiosity
      than a Learning.

AND -- AS BENDING WOMAN HAD FORESEEN
    Some were so amazed at walking seeds
        that they sought destruction
           of three rooted brothers.

It was then
    that they learned
        just how fierce an old and bent woman
           with a heavy staff can be.

AND
    Since the love they all bore her
        was greater even
           than their fear
              of swinging staffs . .

ALL DECIDED AT LAST
    TO ALLOW
        THESE THREE ROOTED BROTHERS
        TO GROW AND PROSPER.

BENDING WOMAN
    would allow no seed to be eaten,
        but rather declared for herself
           a larger and more convenient place,
        encouraging each seed toward Earth,
        watching them daily.

AND FROM THAT DAY TO THIS
    There have always been among the People
        some few
           with a special love
              for our rooted brothers
           and a special understanding of them.

AND BIT BY BIT,
    ALL LEARNED TO LIVE
        WITH ENCOURAGED SEEDS.

Though in some times
    that living was easier
        than in others.

For it is difficult, indeed,
    for most
        to modify their understanding
           of the Nature of Things,

AND HARDER YET
   TO UNDERSTAND
      WHETHER POSSIBLE CHANGE
      WILL TRULY BENEFIT
      THE CHILDREN'S
        CHILDREN'S
          CHILDREN.

YET
   Those of us standing here
     join Grateful Daughter
      in her thanks
        for her Mother's need --
    and join each other
     in thanks to them both.

FOR
   WITHOUT THEIR WISDOM,
   NO SEEDS AT ALL ..

   Would have walked past
    an Ocean's Edge ..

   Survived moss-slick rock
    and washing water ..
      bound with the People
        by a lengthened cord.

AND FROM THAT DAY TO THIS,
   WE REMEMBER
    GROWING WOMAN
      AND HER STUDIED PURPOSE.

><><><

The Way East -- Sad Partings

NOW THIS WAS THE WAY OF IT.

FOR THREE DAYS
  All had sat and listened or sang
    every ancient song,
    every memory anyone knew.
    sharing these realities
    one with the other.

ALL UNDERSTOOD HOW IT WAS,
  How those weighed down by too many years
    to cross a Great Dry Place with rapid feet
    would stay here in respected isolation.

How those too young
  to have legs long enough
    to match the taller pace
would live with them,
  sharing tasks too difficult
    for aging hands,
  sharing Wisdom gained from a long life.

AND THE PEOPLE WERE CONTENT WITH THIS.

YET NOW
  Came one of the Water Walking People,
    carrying with him
      the thoughts of his People . .
        and these thoughts had changed.

FOR NOW
  This People so uncomfortable with change . .

So uncomfortable with the nature of the balance
  we had established between
    those among the People who are male
    and those among the People who are female . .

Uncomfortable even
  with the balance we had established
    between aged wisdom and new eyes wisdom . .

UNCOMFORTABLE WITH ALL THIS . .

THIS PEOPLE NOW
    Sought some foreseeable end
        to the realities we presented . .

And therefore asked
    that whereas the aged among us
        might yet stay,
    the young among us
        must also go . .

So that as each from among us
    who were past possibility
        of such a desert crossing
            lay still at last against the Earth,
                our presence might at last
                    completely disappear.

They did not understand, this People,
    or appeared not to do so,
        that nothing that Is entirely disappears.

There would never be, for them,
    a time again
        when the strangers
            had not come from over the waters,
        when this Walking People
            would not have arrived.

ALL WAS CHANGED . .
    AND IT SEEMED TO US WISDOM'S PATH
    TO RECOGNIZE IT WAS SO . .

YET RETURN TO WHAT WAS . .
    SEEMED THEIR EXIGENT PURPOSE,

AND NO WORD FROM US
    WAS ABLE TO DISSUADE THEM.

NOW THE PEOPLE SAT TOGETHER
    Pondering this change in circumstance . .

For their inability to understand
    the nature of change
        forced greater change upon us.

Yet it was our purpose
to meet that change
and take it willingly with us.

NOW WE DISCUSSED HOW IT WAS.
How short legs do not keep pace with long.

How many from among the People
lay still against the Earth
in that Great Dry Place
crossed by fewer than began the crossing.

How it was
that lack of expedition
engendered many such partings.

For neither what to eat nor the air around us
were critical during such crossings.

Especially the long of leg unbent by years
could walk many, many days
and only that which we drink is required.

ALL KNEW
That liquid --
whether rain or dew or runs-in-streams --
was the element
without which no such crossing
is accomplished.

ALL KNEW
The limits of enclosing water in skins.

ALL KNEW
A slower step adds one day to every three
in such crossings . .

And it was their estimate
that no more than ten days walk
were allowed by the nature and possibilities
of such water carrying.

AND IT WAS SUCH ALSO
That the Water Walking People
had a great and an abiding foreboding
for any who set foot on this great dryness.

Though it seemed to them
 none of our People
  would survive such a crossing,
 it was our purpose to do so.

NEITHER WAS IT CLEAR TO US
 Whether this dry place was as difficult
  or as large as the one crossed before.

It might be
 that this Water Walking People
  looked with unseeing eyes
   on all that lacked water.

AND YET OUR GO AND SEE NOW AND AGAIN
 Had walked out into this new dry place
  and returned devoid of any water,
 and yet
  with no implication of mountains beyond . .

SO THAT WE KNEW
 The path from here to there
  was farther still.

SO IT WAS THAT --
 As the People counseled together --
  they determined the nature
   of such a long and apparently dry walk.

Seeking to give the children's children's children
 the gift of survival,
  required a path today
   none wished to follow . .
   and yet follow it they did.

For it was apparent
 that the short of leg among them
  could neither stay nor go,
 and the resolution of this reality
  was painful to perceive.

YET IT WAS DECIDED AMONG THEM
 That if this Water Walking People
  promised no survivors
   from among any young left behind . .

THEN WE OURSELVES
  WOULD TAKE RESPONSIBILITY
  FOR THAT ACTION . .

And, in gentleness and in love,
  would give the young from among us
  the long sleep drink which --
  when given in excess --
  would cause that sleep
  to be the longest of all.

NOW MANY FROM AMONG US
  Spoke against this action,
  especially He of Twelve Winters,
  who had now sixteen.

IN THIS HE WAS ADAMANT.

IT WAS HIS VIEW
  THAT THOSE YET YOUNG AMONG US
  WERE WISELY INCLUDED
  IN SUCH DISCUSSIONS.

"It is their lives
  about which we decide,
  more
  than we decide about our own.

"Does not Wisdom
  require the inclusion
  of the thoughts
  of those most affected?"
  -- he asked.

AND YET
  Few were willing to include the thoughts
  of those whose thinking
  might soon be ended.

AND SO IT WAS DECIDED AMONG THEM
  That no such consultations were sought

And the decision was nonetheless made,
  against which
  He who had attained Sixteen Winters
  still spoke.

AND SO IT WAS
    That a great feast was prepared . .

    A celebration of community
        and a recognition of separation
        and -- as such -- both the joy of laughter
        and the sad sounds of weeping were heard.

AND -- AS AGREED --
    At the end of that celebration
        cups were passed,
            from which
                those long enough in leg
                knew not to drink.

AND -- AS ONLY THE YOUNG DRANK --
    He of Sixteen Winters -- this Wise Head
        with so much understanding of change --
            rose with one such cup in his hand
            and spoke . .

    "TAKE WITH YOU MY WORDS"
    -- he said --

    "FOR SURELY
        THEY ARE ALL OF ME
        THAT WILL GO WITH YOU.

    "Understand well
        the cost of your survival
            for you kill Tomorrow
                in favor of the day following.

    "I have lived
        among this Water Walking People
        long enough
            to understand their lack of respect
                for any thoughts
                other than theirs.

    "It is for this reason
        that they do not value New Eyes Wisdom.
    It so often differs from theirs.

    "Now, for the same reason,
        you have closed your ears
            to New Eyes Wisdom
                from among your own --
        as you feared a similar difference.

"I respect your purpose"
  -- he went on --

"I know
  you will reach the mountains to the East
    as we have reached
      so many destinations before.

"WHEN YOU HAVE ARRIVED,
REMEMBER MY WORDS.

"PONDER THEM.

"ASK YOURSELVES
  WHETHER IT IS TRULY YOUR PURPOSE
    TO BE THE PEOPLE
      YOU ARE BECOMING."

AND WITH THAT,
  HE LIFTED THE CUP
    CONTAINING THE LONGEST SLEEP OF ALL
      AND DRANK ALL CONTENTS.

THEN,
  Looking around to assure himself
    that all of the young from among us
      already slept . .

He added these words
  to the others he had given us . .

  "It is my understanding"
    -- he said --

  "That this Water Walking People
    values my wisdom more than any other.

  "I go therefore"
      -- he went on --

  "To sit before the place
    they built
      in recognition of their ancestors.

"When they waken"
    -- he concluded --

"They will find this form
    lying still against the Earth.

"IN THIS MANNER
    I INVITE THEM TO RECONSIDER
        THEIR GREAT FOOLISHNESS . .

"HOW A PEOPLE
    unwilling
        to look beyond their own perceptions
        may yet find themselves crushed
            by an impending circumstance . .

"AND HOW IT IS
    our actions may predict events
    we then find less than pleasing."

AND WITH THIS,
    THIS WISE HEAD
        TURNED AND LEFT THE CIRCLE OF THE PEOPLE,
        NEVER TO RETURN . .

TAKING FROM US A MOST VALUABLE LIFE.

GIVING THAT LIFE AS A GIFT . .

AS SEED
    for our growing understanding . .

AS SEED ALSO
    for the understanding
        of this Water Walking People
    who now -- out of concern
        for the maintenance of their ancient way --
        caused some of our own way
            to disappear.

NOW
> The aged among us also spoke . .

> "Neither will we stay in such a place
>> teaching
>>> those who will not learn.

> "RATHER,
>> we will move South,
>>> taking all with us --
>>>> far enough away
>> so that this Water Walking People
>>> will know that we are gone --
>>>> and spend our days
>>>>> in whatever place that may be."

AND ALL KNEW IT WOULD BE SO.

NOW
> From among the People --
>> four who were recently mothers arose.

> "We ourselves
>> must walk toward the mountains to the East"
>>> -- they said --

> "For our greatest responsibility
>> is to the children's children's children.

> "YET
>> we would not see you"
>>> -- they went on --

> "Alone in this circumstance
>> with no one to learn from you
>>> and no one to ease your steps
>>>> as age slows them.

> "For this reason"
>> -- they concluded --

> "We give these very young ones
>> into your care . .
>>> so that you may nurture them,
>>> so that they may learn from you,
>>> so that they may nurture you
>>>> in your turn."

AND SO IT WAS.
    Four of the very young from among us
        found new mothers,
            too old to have borne them,
        and one of these
            was She of Eight Winters . .

SO THAT -- FROM THAT DAY TO THIS --
    We have often wondered
        where that southern path
            might lead
        and who might live there still,
            gifted with such wisdom

YET IT WAS AS IT WAS.

AND WE DO NOT KNOW.

NOW I WOULD TELL YOU,
  IF IT WERE SO,
    that after the next day's ordered progress
      so many similar days followed
    that no short of leg,
    none bent with age,
      could have walked
        from one place to the other.

YET IT WAS NOT SO.

FOR THE PEOPLE DISCOVERED
  AS THE DAYS PROGRESSED
    that just beyond
      the farthest place
        yet walked and returned from,
    just shortly beyond,
      the implication of mountains began,
        and grew with each day's walk
          into great reality . .
    so that not ten days, but nine
      were the number necessary
        from one place to another.

AND THE PEOPLE
  REACHED THIS EDGE OF MOUNTAINS
    WITH LESS JUBILATION THAN SADNESS
    AT WHAT HAD BEEN DONE
      IN THE NAME OF SURVIVAL.

YET ALL KNEW
  THAT THE UNKNOWN HAD NOT BEEN KNOWN.

ALL KNEW
  That the time allowed
    for decision by the Water Walking People
      was less than a day's span.

THIS OR THAT POSSIBILITY
  WAS DISCUSSED AT LENGTH.

UNTIL
    We came to understand
        that there were possibilities . .

    Which time and our haste to walk quickly
        toward the Eastern Ocean which must be there
            and which yet held a place, perhaps,
                for a New People --
                    undeterred by others

    The haste of our decision
        and the haste of our steps
            had blinded us to farther vision . .
        how a return to northern mountains
            might be preferable
                to the numbing sadness we felt now.

AND THE PEOPLE
    Continued their disconsolate march,
        glad at least
            that some young from among us
                walked South on aged feet.

NOW
    They came at last to the eastern mountains
        and began their slow ascent,
            thinking now that aged feet and shorter legs
                might be happier elsewhere . .
        until a great commotion arose ahead,
            and roaring and yelling were a part.

    And all quickly learned the nature
        of this new circumstance.

FOR
    Those leading our forward march
        had nearly stumbled on a great Bear . .

    As great almost as the huge black skin
        still carried by the People
            from the great dwellers
        within the deep dark places of the Earth
            near our Center Place so long ago . .
        nor had this valued skin
            been left behind through any circumstance.

Yet it was now still carried
and gave the People
some continued understanding
of this great new Bear
whose coat was silvered as by frost.

FOR THIS WAS THE WAY OF IT.

This sudden stumbling over an angry Bear
had caused some altercation
between That One and our Forward Persons.

In order then
to protect those behind him
as well as himself,
First Person had struck out . .

And -- as it came to be --
had caused at last that Great Silvered Bear
to stretch his length out on the Earth.

AND NOW THE PEOPLE
Laughed and wept at once . .

Laughed at
"Perhaps Bear was only waving greeting"

Laughed at sudden unforeseen changes
in circumstance
for those who only seek to climb mountains.

Laughed and wept also.

Wept for Bear lying quiet.
Wept for too many lying quiet.
Wept for separation and for lack of wisdom.

WEPT UNTIL AT LAST
one from among them stood and spoke,
and it was First Person who did so . .

"Some say"
-- he began --

"That perhaps Bear was only waving greeting.
Yet I tell you now,
I, who stood closest,
did not have that impression!

"Rather,
  I, who stood closest,
    thought he waved away my life
      and that of others.

"Now perhaps it was so"
  -- he went on --

"Or perhaps not.

"YET THINGS ARE WHAT THEY ARE.

"Perhaps Bear came to tell us
  that our greatest fears
    are less than circumstance --
  as no one expected Bear just there.

"Or perhaps he came to tell us
  our fears are greater than circumstance.

"FOR SEE HOW IT IS . .
  this Great Silvered Bear
    is not at all so great
      as those we left behind,
  rapidly disappearing from our Center Place.

"So perhaps this Bear tells us
  this Great Island will at last
    be an easier place
  than the Great Island we left behind."

AND ALL CONSIDERED THIS
And saw how one thing or the other
  might equally be so.

AND
  When he saw and heard
    that all this had been considered,
      First Person spoke again . .

  "Did not He of Sixteen Winters
    ask that we consider his words
      when we reached Mountains to the East?

  "Perhaps Bear has come to remind us
    of sudden decisions toward survival.

"I remember those words
and speak them now
to these Eastern Mountains,
so that they might also hear them.

"AND THIS IS WHAT I REMEMBER . .

"'Understand well
the cost of your survival . .
for you kill Tomorrow
in favor of the following day.

"'You have closed your eyes'"
-- he said --
"'to New Eyes Wisdom from among your own,
as you feared
it would differ from your own.'"

AND ALL THOUGHT NOW
Of the many meanings of these words,
remembering this or that he had also said,
until all thoughts were centered
on learning too late
what tomorrow might bring.

"Let us learn from this"
-- First Person said --

"Let us not again
choose to be a People
who fail to listen
to New Eyes Wisdom.

"Let us not again
choose to be a People
who fail to listen
to those
most affected by the decision.

"Let us not again
choose to be a People
who allow themselves
sudden decisions
in a circumstance
that need not be sudden.

"LET US LEARN.

"LET US REMEMBER."

AND ALL THE PEOPLE SAW HOW IT WAS . .

How First Person spoke only wisdom . .

How the children's children's children
might benefit
from the many gifts of understanding
brought by too much sadness.

AND FROM THAT DAY TO THIS
WE HAVE ALWAYS CHOSEN TO BE . .

A PEOPLE WHO LISTEN
TO NEW EYES WISDOM . .

A PEOPLE WHO LISTEN
TO THE LEAST AMONG US . .

A PEOPLE
WITH THE PATIENCE
TO CONSIDER MANY POSSIBILITIES . .

A PEOPLE
WHO REACH BEYOND TOMORROW,
YET CARRY
BOTH TODAY AND TOMORROW WITH US.

LET US CELEBRATE THE WISDOM
TOO MUCH SADNESS MAY BRING . .

LET US CELEBRATE
THE MANY GIFTS OF NEW EYES WISDOM.

LET US REMEMBER
THOSE WE LEFT BEHIND.

SO BE IT.

Three Mountain Tellings

Sees Beyond:
How Vision Is One Thing
and Understanding Another

Fly Like Eagle:
The Telling of One
Who Could Not Walk

Sheltered Valley

Sees Beyond:
How Vision Is One Thing
And Understanding Another

NOW BEGIN TWO TELLINGS
  WHICH HAVE FOR US GREAT VALUE.

   A People
     who withstood Rocks Like Rain . .

   A People
     who wove themselves across Walk by Waters . .

   A People
     who found again an Ocean Home
     and who were turned from it . .

   Even this People
     found themselves now
        threading their way South
           along an Endless Ridge of Mountains.

LITTLE IS PRESERVED
  FROM THAT TIME . .

FOR SURELY
   Many lives
      were consumed in the Walking.

YET
   THESE TWO TELLINGS REMAIN.

AND
   THE FIRST OF THESE
      IS SEES BEYOND . .

      HOW VISION IS ONE THING
         AND UNDERSTANDING ANOTHER.

$$\bowtie\!\!\!\bowtie$$

NOW
   DURING THIS LONG TIME
      THERE CAME TO BE AMONG THE PEOPLE
         ONE RENOWNED FOR HIS VISION
            AND FOR THE WISDOM IT ENGENDERED.

FOR THIS ONE
   had shown from his earliest days
      the particular vision
         that sees beyond.

THIS ONE
   had sat within himself,
      teaching himself focus . .

FOR AT THAT TIME
   there were none among the People
      who made this their general purpose . .

AND OVER A LONG LIFE
   had clarified within himself
      this possibility of vision

   UNTIL ALL THE PEOPLE
      GAVE HIM THE USUAL NAME,
      SEES BEYOND.

AND THIS WAS THE WAY OF IT . .

THIS ONE
   Would sit in any open space at all
      and Look Forward,
         searching out
            the general path of the People.

Looking Forward
   as he knew how to do . .
      This One might see a clear path
         or a coming mountain.

Around that mountain
   he might see a rocky but reliable path
      to the North
   and an easy path
      to the South
         dwindling to nothing.

NOW
    It had become his preoccupation
        to learn the accuracy of his own vision . .

AND SO,
      even when the People
         had learned over tens of season circles
            to value his Vision as absolute wisdom,
      even so
         would he not allow it.

RATHER,
      he asked some from among the People
         to test the North path
    and some
         to test the South . .
    and only when those walking South
         returned to tell of an easy path
            dwindling into nothing,
    only then
         would he, himself,
            rise to walk the northern path.

FOR THIS WAS THE WAY OF IT.
    The People
         still purposing some eastward Ocean,
            mainly intended to cross these mountains
                in an easterly direction.

AND YET,
      winters being what they were --
         especially in the higher mountains --
    from time to time
         they tended also South.

NOW IT IS NOT RECORDED
    How much of their walk was East
        and how much South,
    But South
         was thought the principal direction,
            searching as they did
                through these Never Ending Mountains
                for easier winters.

AND ONE THING IS KNOWN --
   that during all this time
     they met no other People --
  so that it was their thought
   that they had at least
      these Never Ending Mountains
     to themselves,
    others preferring, it would seem,
     the flatter land.

. . .

NOW AS IT WAS SO
  That This One -- Sees Beyond --
   could look within himself
    for the distant image of mountain,
  so could he also look within himself
   for the distant image of tomorrow.

SO THAT FROM TIME TO TIME
  Some possible tomorrow
   would hover in his mind --
    clearer and clearer as he examined it --
  that he would store in his memory
   as a reference
    against which to measure all Tomorrows.

THE SEASONS
  Might turn and turn again . .

YET SURELY
  some morning light would arrive
   to clarify a today
    whose image had preceded it
     in the Vision
      of That One we called Sees Beyond.

SO IT WAS
  That the People began asking
   more and different questions of That One,
    waiting patiently for an answer.

AND
  That One knew within himself
   increasing disquiet . .

FOR THE PEOPLE
  acted in accordance with his mind image,
    grumbling mightily
      at his continuing insistence
        that all paths be tried.

  Was his accuracy
    not a continuing thing?

  Who remembered a time
    when That One failed the People?

AND YET
  He, himself,
    felt this responsibility more heavily
      than any other.

  And the quavering within himself
    as the People stepped out boldly
      on paths of his devising
        grew more intense . .

  Until he found it necessary
    to surround himself with ceremony
      to deter precipitate action on their part.

AND SO
  IT BECAME HIS CUSTOM
    to sit in some ceremonial place
      in absolute concentration
        unbroken by any usual activity.

  IN THIS MANNER
    he neither ate nor drank
      unless the concentration required this day
        was so great
          that occasional sips of liquid
            were requisite for continuance.

NOW
  Two things
    were accomplished in this manner.

  His capacity for concentration
    and the clarity of his vision
      were enhanced.

Yet also did this manner of his
cause the People to understand
the investment of daily energy
necessary for such vision.

AND SO
They began to cease their many questions,
asking only those things
of particular value to the People
and to their decisions,
leaving all personal What Might Be
aside for eventual learning.

. . .

NOW AT THIS TIME
The People entered a new part of Earth,
as different from yesterday
as yesterday had been from the day before . .

So that new learnings were required
and as what had been gathered for sustenance
was no longer here,
so was new potential here in its place.

Yet it was a potential heretofore unknown.

AND IT CAME TO BE
That one morning began
with brilliant sun and new discovery . .

For one of the People
found and gathered into great heaps
pungent berries from low bushes
that bit the reaching hand.

NOW ALL THE PEOPLE
Wondered whether this new nourishment
would prove a benefit to the People . .

And -- as this seemed to them
a valuable thing to know --
so they came to sit by him
they called Sees Beyond,
asking him his Vision.

AND -- THAT ONE,
SITTING WITHIN HIMSELF --
held the image of this berry before him
and sought for an answer.

Seeing no image
either for benefit or lack thereof
through this berry itself . .

He sought instead
for an image of Tomorrow
as he had taught himself how to do.

AND,
Searching through the possibilities of Tomorrow,
he saw at last
a Strong Vision
which seemed to carry within it
the answer they sought.

FOR
he saw this People, his People,
secure against a different mountainside
than any had seen . .

some stooped low with age,
some now of middle years
turned all white of hair . .

A SECURE AND PROSPEROUS PEOPLE,
SURE OF TOMORROW.

AND SO IT WAS,
    Looking at this Clear Vision,
      that he opened his mouth and spoke . .

    "I see"
      -- he said --

    "A People
      beyond Tomorrow,
    A People
      secure in their understanding
        of this place,
    A People
      grown old with this Wisdom."

AND
    In his heart
      he was so amazed at this Tomorrow
        that he failed to look at Today . .

FOR,
    As he sat entranced with this mind image,
      the People gave a glad shout --
      some of them --
      and began an eager eating of this new berry.

AND YET OTHERS,
    Remembering how it was
      this aging and visionary man
        always asked some few
          to walk the southern disappearing path . .

    Remembering also no previous time
      when anything at all that is consumed
        had been judged in this manner . .

THESE ONES ATE NO BERRY,
    BUT LET THEIR HUNGER
      SHARPEN THEIR QUEST
        FOR MORE FAMILIAR FOOD.

AND SO IT WAS
THAT ALL CHANGED
WITHIN THE TURNING OF ONE DAY.

FOR I TELL YOU NOW
That all those
eagerly eating this new nourishment
found satisfaction at first
and agony at last
as this new nourishment
turned into bitter gruel within.

For the much writhing on the ground
these ones suffered
was nearly as painful to watch
as it was to endure.

Those not yet in such pain,
Those who had ingested no berry
yet remained at camp . .

These Ones carried water from a nearby stream,
hoping
to ease the pain,
to dilute the contents of each stomach,
to so overfill each stomach
as to cause a retching up of contents,
losing in that way these bitter berries.

NOW ALL WAS A SORROWFUL IMAGE
For many of the People
already lay still against the Earth,
no stream water dilution
having any capacity to rescue them
from this Great Silence.

Others
still lay in agony-pools of their own retching,
crying out for the Great Silence.

Still others
were sitting in some agonized discomfort
and yet their pain was less.

NOW IT WAS
 Through this scattered camp
  that those who sought the southern path,
  those who sought some other sustenance,
   it was to this camp that they returned . .
    glad of their hesitant wisdom,
    sorrowful for the thrashing pain
     that lay in every direction,
    saddened also by the dull and lifeless eyes
     retained by him
      they called Sees Beyond . .
   He, whose clear vision
    had been so rapidly applied
     to so many hungry stomachs.

  Those eyes
   now held no promise of future vision . .

And some understood this at once,
  saw how those wise eyes
   would look no more for what the People
    too eagerly applied
     to present circumstance.

AND
 All those who ate sparingly
  of this new and untried berry
   suffered great pain . .

And some of these
  rose to walk again after many days
But more did not -- in such a way
  that neither size nor age seemed relevant . .

So that it was thought
  some natural proclivity for survival
   in this circumstance
    either was
    or was not
     for any individual.

And some of those surviving
  carried with them continuing pain
   so they did not always
    consider survival too great a gift . .

And the sorrowing eyes around them
   watched their slow pace
     until one by one
       those who continued in this pain
        came to join their quiet brothers.

AND A SHATTERED PEOPLE
CONTINUED ON A SOUTHWARD PATH.

. . .

NOW THIS WAS THE WAY OF IT.

Some from among the People
   saw how it was
     and sounded the perception.

"You see how it is"
   -- they said --

"A People who has learned the wisdom
   of causing none
     to lie still against the Earth
       by their purposeful decision
   has yet caused
     many such quietnesses
       by a purposed decision . .
        one unaware of its eventual cost."

AND THIS WAS ALSO THE WAY OF IT.

For many days
   Sees Beyond spoke no word
     and would allow none to touch him.

His white hair
   cresting vigorous shoulders
   now crested only a saddened, burdened person,
     bent low by one too many winters.

Such was his seeming,
   nor spoke he any word.

Moon came and turned and left
   again and again . .

Yet no word
   came from Sees Beyond --
so that his usual name changed
   as all called him
      with saddened respect
         His Voice is Still.

ALL UNDERSTOOD
   THAT THIS SILENCE
      CAME FROM THE MANY GREAT QUIETS
      HIS EARLIER WORDS
         HAD ENGENDERED.

· · ·

NOW
   The People who were left
      continued on a Southern Path,
         seeking greater warmth down some valley
      until they came to a mountain
         which required some new decision
            as it barred a Southern Path,
               requiring either North as well as East
                  or mainly West.

Here they stopped for some time
   to gather strength
      as many season circles
         had been constantly walked . .
      the place of Many Quiets left far behind.

AND
   WITH NEXT FIRST LIGHT
      ALL CHANGED
         AND THIS WAS THE WAY OF IT.

He whose vision
   had been central to the People
      sat in his continuing silence
         at the edge of the Circle of the People.

NOW -- AS FIRST LIGHT CAME,
   Bringing a different vision
      a great cry struck the air --
      and all looked North
         to find this Silent Man
            the source of such commotion.

NOW AT LAST
   Bitter tears
      followed one another in constant progression
         down those aged cheeks . .

Some light also entering those eyes
   as the tears left them at last
      free of some of their sorrow . .
      for, as all know, tears carry with them
      some of the burden of sorrow.

FOR SOME TIME
   the constant path of tears,
      precipitate from either eye,
   found increasing ways over this old face . .

   UNTIL AT LAST
      the shoulders seemed lighter
         and the eyes more willing to focus.

SOMEONE FROM AMONG THE PEOPLE
WISER THAN MOST . .
      touched knee to Earth beside this aged man
      and said . .

"We sorrow with you, my Brother,
   and yet are glad to see your sorrow
      after such a time.

"For we would hope now
   to hear perhaps some words from you
      at last,
   or any sound at all past sobbing."

AND
    The old eyes lifted to this face
        with some touch of gladness at the sight
            and -- rising at last --
                he spoke to all the People . .

"You see how it is,
    my Brothers, my Sisters.

"So long ago
    I saw an image of mountain
        unbefore seen --
    and against it
        hair grown white that had been dark . .

"So many of our People
    safe throughout so many season circles
        that it brought me great joy
    and in the sharing of this joy
        gave an inappropriate understanding
            to too many.

"Lost in contemplation of this clear image,
Aware that it implied my survival also past
    the probable length of life . .

"I failed to note
    the rapid behavior of many of the People,
        surer than I
            of the accuracy of this vision.

"And when I first noted how it was around me,
    it was because
        many cried out in pain at the effect
            that their application of my vision
                had upon their lives.

"YOU SEE HOW IT IS
    MY BROTHERS, MY SISTERS.
        IT IS THIS . .

"*No Person with Such Vision*
    wisely looses that Vision on his People
        without retaining continuing responsibility
          for its interpretation.

"FOR I TELL YOU NOW . .
  I see before me
    that exact image
      that entered my mind
        so long ago.

"Each individual Person I saw then,
  I see now.

"Each darkened head
  turned white with passing winters.

"New eyes regard me now
  as they appeared to regard me then.

"And that mountain
  at the base of which we now camp
    is in no way different
      from that mountain I saw then.

"ALL THIS IS TRUE.
  AND YET
    ANOTHER THING IS TRUE ALSO.

"The survival apparent in that vision
  obtained only
    for those retained within it.

"Not one of those we left behind
  had a place in this . . or that . . vision.

"*We gave ourselves too little time*
  to understand
    all possible meanings of that image
  and, in this manner,
    precipitated too many
      into that Great Silence.

"*Too many possible people*
  lay still then
  and lie still now against this Earth
    for want of patient waiting,
    for want of greater understanding,
    for want of a willingness
      to see possible inconvenience
      in that probable image.

"*Let us never again be a People*
so quick in action
based on probable vision
that we fail to spend our energies
in understanding the many possibilities
that may yet explain
each probable vision."

AND ALL SAW HOW IT WAS . .
HOW VISION IS ONE THING
AND APPLICATION ANOTHER.

AND FROM THAT DAY TO THIS,
The People have remembered
to walk
the double circle of possibility,
devising -- each in their own way --
various explanations for any Vision
so that they will fail
in precipitate action
and ensure thereby
perhaps some more tomorrows
than first understanding might enable.

LET US REMEMBER
THIS WISDOM.

LET US WALK
THE DOUBLE CIRCLE OF POSSIBILITIES,
CHOOSING ONLY THEN
SOME LOGICAL PATH.

REMEMBERING TO CHOOSE
SOME FEW OF THE PEOPLE
TO WALK
THE SOUTHERN DISAPPEARING PATH.

SO BE IT.

⋈⋈⋈

Fly Like Eagle:
The Telling Of One
Who Could Not Walk

NOW I HAVE TOLD YOU HOW IT WAS
   For one
      whose hair grew gradually white
         above thoughts
            that saw beyond present circumstance.

NOW I WILL TELL YOU HOW IT WAS
   That the People learned to see beyond as well,
      beyond their own perceptions,
      beyond their own understanding
         and in that way
            beyond present circumstance.

   FOR THIS
      Is the Telling
         of One Who Could Not Walk.

   THIS
      IS THE TELLING OF FLY LIKE EAGLE.

AND THIS WAS THE WAY OF IT . .

IT WAS LONG PAST THE TIME
   when any of those we have told you of
      still walked the Earth.

AND YET
   THE PEOPLE CONTINUED . .

   Continued walking on a general southerly path
      that was -- from time to time -- also East.

AND NOW
   There came to be among the People
   a woman
      whose compassion
         and natural concern for others
            caused them to give her the name
               She Is Mother.

And this was a quiet joy to her . .

Even this giving of so valued a name --
   for although she had a compassionate awareness
      of each of the People,
   although she was the one most sought
      for her wisdom by those with young,
   although she had from among the People
      a life-long friend
         who was aware of her value
         and who walked with her always,
   even so, had she no young of her own.

LIFE HAD NOT GIVEN HER
   THIS GREAT GIFT.

AND IT CAME TO BE
   That one and another saw how it was,
      in lacking young of her own,
         she turned more surely
            toward all short of leg . .

So that the People saw that each such
   had at least two mothers.

AND THEY SAW THIS WAS GOOD.

• • •

NOW
    As the Circle Dance of Seasons continued,
      this one and that
        doubled in size and became two persons,

And yet
    She Is Mother did not,
      despite the patient attention
        of her life-long Friend.

UNTIL AT LAST SHE SAW
    that life meant to withhold from her
      in some continuing way
        this great and coveted gift.

NOW IT WAS
    That circumstance bent and turned
      and became something other than it had been.

For her life-long Friend thought that --
    if he could not be father to one child --
      he would be father to the Whole People.

AND FOR THIS REASON
    He joined a small group of strong young men
      looking for a new way
        through confusing mountains.

And -- although he was no longer young --
    yet he kept pace with these abler legs,
      adding his greater gathered wisdom
        to their thoughts . .

So that these young men began to say
    that older legs carrying such wisdom
      were welcome to slow their younger pace.

AND IT CAME TO BE
    That this older one from among the People
      was always asked and often went
        to join these forward groups
          looking for a wiser path
            through Endless Mountains.

AND IT ALSO CAME TO BE
   That these separations from one another
      made the joinings of these life-long friends
         even more filled with joy,
   So that the nature of their days
      was enhanced thereby.

NOW, FOR A TIME,
   THIS WAS THE WAY OF IT . .
      occasional partings
         followed equally by rejoinings,
      so that their mutual life
         was woven together in a different way.

AND
   THIS WAS ALSO THE WAY OF IT.

   Perhaps in these changing patterns
      some different mutual accommodation
         was reached,
      some different sharing of energy . .

   So that it came to be
      that this wise and compassionate woman
         saw within herself
            the possibilities of Tomorrow
            and learned to understand its promise.

            • • •

NOW DURING THIS TIME --
   While life was evident and yet awaited --

IT CAME TO BE
   That this life-long Friend
      of a wise and compassionate woman
         agreed to lead a small gathering of young men
            who sought some greater understanding
            of the nature of land to the East

AND IT CAME TO BE ALSO
>That this small gathering of valued persons
>>was never again seen by the People,
>>>so that all came to regard their parting
>>as also the last image any would know
>>>of these young and vigorous men
>>>>and their wise and purposeful friend.

AND NOW
>All sorrowed and many sorrowed greatly
>>at this loss.

AND
>Although she who was a life-long friend
>>sorrowed also,
>Yet she undertook
>>some tranquil approach to this great sorrow
>>>out of concern for the double life
>>>>she shared with one not yet known.

>"Later"
>>-- she said --

>"I will shed my bitter tears.

>"Now"
>>-- she went on --

>"I am aware of a purpose
>>greater than my own sorrow."

AND SO IT WAS
>That this wise woman
>>continued in her usual great and kind concern
>>>for all the People,
>>losing for awhile
>>>in the complexities of her thought
>>any great sorrow for the companion lost to her,
>>>aware instead of the future companion
>>>>who apparently planned to join the People
>>>>>on some near day.

NOW, AS SUCH THINGS ARE,
    Even did This One
        whom the People called She Is Mother
            become a mother at last . .
        for her expectations
            were no greater than the actuality.

    Her future companion
        joined the People at last.

BUT, AS SUCH THINGS ARE,
    This new companion,
    This great Gift of Life,
    This small person came to be
        not only short of leg
        but also was that leg twisted and bent
            so that only the side of one foot
                could be walked on.

NOW, AT THAT TIME,
    This People was indeed a Walking People
        and it was their full purpose to remain such.

FOR THIS REASON
    IT HAD BECOME THEIR CUSTOM
        to invite the very young --
            for whom walking
                would prove a great difficulty --
        to go with some few and elder persons who would,
            with love and compassion,
                invite this young, never-walk person
                    toward that Great Sleep
                      in which we become at last
                        one with Earth.

    IT HAD BECOME THEIR CUSTOM ALSO
        to begin this sleep
            as quickly as this inability was seen,
        so as to save the mother
            from the sorrow of a fully developed fondness
                for this never-walking person.

AND IN THIS MANNER
DID THE WHOLE PEOPLE
 take upon themselves
  the full responsibility
   for such decision,
 it being considered too great a sorrow
  for one who was newly mother
   to bear this responsibility herself.

AND YET I TELL YOU
 None among the People was anxious
  for this new and saddest responsibility.

One who held no further promise
 of tomorrow's child,
One whose life-long companion
 had walked in some way too far from the People,
One who was mother at some time
 to nearly each and all of the People . .

Even this one
 now sat with a beautiful child
  whose foot twisted under him,
   holding no promise at all of tomorrow.

NOW
 The eldest from among the People,
  understanding as he did this circumstance,
  came forward to speak.

"You see how it is, my daughter"
 -- he began --

"Here is a never-walk child,
 and you well understand the way of it.

"Yet I, who am old"
 -- he went on --
"find no joy in such a task.

"Even so"
 -- he concluded --

"It is I
 who will take this young one
  on his longest walk.

"For it is I
    who will remember to love him
        as he proceeds on his journey."

AND
    The sadness of those eyes
        caught at the heart
            of this wise and compassionate woman,
        for it seemed to her his sorrow
            was somehow greater than her own . .

So that she learned
    an understanding of those from among the People
        who take upon themselves
            these greatly unloved tasks
                so that the People may prosper.

And her eyes grew dim sooner for him
    than for herself.

"Let me save us both, my Father"
    -- she replied --
    "from this wandering sadness.

"Let me take upon myself
    all responsibility
        for this never-walk child.
Let me keep him and tend him.

"IN THAT WAY
    let me stretch out the life
        of my own greatly loved companion,
            he whose older legs learned a faster pace.
    Let these legs of mine learn to carry.

"NOW
    since it is our necessity
        to be a Walking People
    and since one at least among us
        must take responsibility
            for those who cannot walk,
                let me be that one.

"For although I love this child
and will love him more over time,
even so, on that day
I can no longer carry him --
even on that day --
I myself
will walk with him into the forest
and will return alone."

AND MANY SPOKE AGAINST THIS,
As they valued this woman beyond any other
for her daily behavior
And were concerned lest she find herself
unable to leave her only Life Gift
sleeping in the forest,
depriving therefore all the People
of her valued concern.

AND YET AGAIN SHE SPOKE,
Promising again
this certain commitment,
this certain purpose and her certain return.

AND WHAT WITH THIS AND THAT,
none among the People were anxious
to deprive this gentle and purposeful woman
of her Life Gift.

Neither was any among them anxious
to take responsibility
for this one more Great Sleep.

AND SO IT WAS
That She Is Mother was mother at last
and, bereft of her life-long companion,
took a new companion to her heart,
carrying him gladly.

AND IT CAME TO BE
That over many Season Circles
the People grew used to seeing
this purposeful woman grow smaller
under the growing weight she carried,
gladly aware of the person
whose bright eyes and happy smile
her willing weariness enabled.

NOW
    As this young one learned and grew,
      he came to understand how it was
        that walking, for him,
          was a task not easily accomplished . .
        so that this mother to his person
        and to his Spirit
          walked for him.

AND HE SAW HOW IT WAS
    That all the People
      shared some task or other
        in addition to walking . .

So that it became his thought
    to learn some task
      the unlikely-footed might undertake
    and to share in that way
      his double mother's general concern
        for the Whole People.

SO IT WAS
    That as the People settled to Earth
      weary with their great walk . .

This One
    would begin his four-legged dance,
      searching out possible sustenance.

And also This One
    perceiving the nature of forward progress,
      would cause himself
        to be as far as possible
          along that probable path,
    finding some rock or other
    and climbing ponderously thereon
      so as to ease the necessity
        of lifting such a growing weight.

AND IT CAME TO BE
   That This One and his double mother
      learned each such an interactive dance . .

   That all the People saw and learned
      and came to understand
         how great cooperation might become
            between two purposeful people
         and how such cooperation
            might enable the apparently impossible.

   So that This One
      grew to become nearly a man,
   And yet
      was he carried from this place to that
         by a mother so constant in her purpose
            that she bent nearly double
               under this growing weight.

          • • •

NOW IT CAME TO BE THAT ONE DAY
   This One found his way to a distant rock
      along the probable path of the People . .

   And -- sitting thereon -- allowed himself
      to consider the bent-double condition
         of this purposeful woman . .
      for circumstance was such
         that she no longer
            fully rose from this position
         even when disencumbered from his weight.

   And, seeing before him another Bending Woman,
      his nature rebelled at the thought.

   Hot and bitter tears
      found their way from angry eyes
         and spattered their individual pattern
            on the gray surface of crumbling rock.

AND THAT MOTHER,
As she approached through the forest,
heard his mumbled words
and came to understand
that the pain she had taken
from the oldest among them
lay now on her son's heart . .

And she came to understand
how the Gift of Life
is always
sometimes a burden . .
the greatest burden of all
to those who feel themselves
a great weight on bending shoulders.

AND SO IT WAS
That this compassionate woman
learned a new and better compassion . .

And saw how it was
that she must give her son
a greater gift than Life Itself.

She saw how she must give him
the gift of a personal purpose greater
than bending two shoulders
and gladdening the heart between.

AND SO
She sat where she was and thought.

Following possibilities down many separate paths,
she looked for some task
which the slow four-legged might essay
and which might be a gift for others
beyond apparent burden.

AND THEN AT LAST
SHE SAW HOW IT WAS
THAT THE GREATEST GIFT OF ALL
MUST BE GIVEN BY THE GIVER.

And she remembered
that an inability to walk
did not predict an inability to think.

AND SO
  She went to her son and asked . .

  "Wherefore these bitter tears
    for one so gifted with love and laughter?

  "For surely among the People
    none are so gifted
      either with a gladsome nature
      or with a gift for the pattern of words."

  "It is not enough, my mother"
    -- he answered.

  "I sorrow for bent shoulders
    and for others seeking sustenance
      that I might eat."

  "You are right to concern yourself, my son"
    -- she replied in apparent inability
      to understand his focus --

  "For who will carry you one day
    when I am gone?"

  "That is no concern of mine"
    -- he answered in some amazement --

  "For where you lie
    there will I also stay,
      sustaining myself as best I may,
        and join you at last
          in that Great Sleep."

NOW
  In some seeming anger,
    this True Mother spoke . .

  "It was not my thought
    that either the nature
      of the life-long companion lost to me,
    or my nature either,
      should be lost to the People
        for lack of my mere presence.

"I see in you, my son, echoes of both
    and would not have those echoes lost
        in some disconsolate mourning
            against a sorrowing Earth.

"So be advised
    that I assign you now a task
        that is yours and yours alone.

"Those who cannot walk
    through no carelessness of their own
        may yet fly like Eagle.

"When you understand what I say,
    even at that time
        will you free yourself and your People
            from a great burden."

AND
    No amount of subsequent cajoling
        would coax from his True Mother
            any further word . .

So that it became a great puzzle in his mind
    what wisdom might be contained
        in such apparent foolishness.

AND IT CAME TO BE
    That -- when the People reached
        another seasonal place where they might stay
            and gain both rest and energy --

This four-legged young man,
    he whose eyes
        increasingly followed Eagle's path . .
This one left the People with such quiet
    that at first none knew he had gone . .

And -- when they discovered his unfilled place --
    his mother answered them . .

    *"I believe he has gone
        to find some purpose to his life."*

AND ALL KNEW
　　How easy it was
　　　to allow the mere round of days --
　　　　the gathering, eating, sleeping, singing,
　　　　walking, and wondering at various ways . .

ALL KNEW
　　How easy it was
　　　to lose oneself in this regularity
　　　to forget how from here to there
　　　　is part of some greater purpose.

　AND
　　None then wondered
　　　at the disappearance
　　　　of one who could not walk . .
　　Wondering only
　　　at the whether-ness of his return.

　　　　　• • •

NOW MANY DAYS AND A CHANGING MOON
　　Came, turned, and left again
　　　over the mountain . .
　　And the People still wondered
　　　whether the slow four-legged
　　　　might ever return.

AND THEN ONE MORNING,
　　Sun nearly visible over the eastern mountains,
　　　this increasing light brought wonder with it . .

　FOR,
　　　sitting atop his usual rock
　　　　so that eye-to-eye with those who stand
　　　　　is no great difficulty --
　　　sitting there
　　　　was their four-legged friend,
　　　　　the only son of a True Mother.

　AND,
　　　clutched in his hand,
　　　　were three great Eagle feathers --
　　　　　greater and longer than any had yet seen.

AND,
    when all asked the nature
        of disappearance of person
        and appearance of feather,
    he replied
        that he had gone
            to answer his Mother's question.

And all were so pleased to see
    those bright eyes and gladsome smile --
        even atop legs that did not function --
            that they gave over too many questions
        and allowed themselves
            a slower, quieter learning.

AND THIS WAS THE WAY OF IT -- he said --

He had wondered after Eagle's path
    and thought to find it
        while the People gathered strength.

Following that purposeful ascent with slower step,
    he had nonetheless worked his way
        up that distant mountain to the East --
    the one now called Dawn Woman's Mountain --
        and had more slowly found
            this great gathered-stick nest
        that was home to Eagle and his and her young.

NOW
    COMING TO UNDERSTAND
        the daily-ness of Eagle's purpose,
            their feeding of their young,
            their in and out soaring,
                looking always
                    for new food for growing young . .

HE CAME TO UNDERSTAND
    the nature of their search
        and to understand
            that somehow this was a search he must join.

AND YET
    HE DID NOT UNDERSTAND
        THE ANSWER TO HIS MOTHER'S QUESTION.

SO
    He continued in this manner,
        watching Eagle,
        gathering sometimes some of the food
            carefully brought by Eagle
            and carelessly dropped by their young.

HE CAME TO UNDERSTAND
    how the nature of the food changed
        as the young grew

AND HE SAW AT LAST
    how it might be
        that a People grow and age
    even as these Eagle chicks
        grew in size and length of days.

AND IT SEEMED TO HIM
    that the nature of food
        for a growing People
            in a changing circumstance
                might also change.

AND SO HE UNDERSTOOD HOW IT WAS
HOW ONE WHO COULD NOT WALK
MIGHT YET FLY LIKE EAGLE

AND ONE FROM AMONG THE PEOPLE
WHO WAS CARRIED
MIGHT YET CARRY THAT PEOPLE
TO A NEW AND BETTER CIRCUMSTANCE.

AND
    THIS IS WHAT HE OFFERED THEM.

"I have seen"
    -- he said --

"How True Mother
    has bent beneath my growing weight.

"And I know"
    -- he went on --

"How she rescued my life
    from the Great Sleep
        when I was yet young.

"I have no wish"
   -- he concluded --

"To extend my life
   as a burden to hers."

AND
   Those who wondered whether True Mother
     would allow the probable implications
      of these words
        were startled to see her quiet smile.

They had forgotten, you see, as she had not,
   those three great Eagle feathers
     clutched so purposefully
      in hands that also walked.

"This is my offer to you"
   -- he spoke to the Whole People --

"If two or more of you
   will from time to time relieve True Mother
     of this great burden
      which is my personal self,
  I will in return
     search out all new possible sustenance,
      testing its safety
        on this unwalking person.

"AND"
   -- he added --

"When that gift of possible sustenance
   is inadequate to encourage such carrying,
     then will I and True Mother
      stay in that place
        till Earth rises up to meet her."

AND ALL SAW HOW IT WAS,
   How all valued the presence
     of True Mother and of her True Son
      so greatly
     that, for this gift alone, many were happy
      to join in such carrying.

And two young men brought forth a pole
    on which True Son
        might be carried between them
            and said . .

"When this great and growing weight
    grows too much,
        let others take our places
    so that all
        may at last share with True Mother
            as she has shared with us."

AND THOSE WHO NOTICE SUCH THINGS
    saw the quiet and joy-filled smile
        that lightened her face.

AND,
    As for this Mother to the People herself,
        she saw at one instant
            how it would be . .

How her only son
    would so learn a great skill with new things
        that his wisdom
            would be increasingly valued,

How by mere smell or slight taste
    he would teach himself to understand
        the nature of all new sustenance,

How none would be still against the Earth
    while he was there
        to guide them in his unwalking way
            past berries better left uneaten,

How four from among the People
    would come to build a many-poles litter

And how the People would argue
    for a place at the end of one such pole
        rather than against it.

AND IT WAS SO.

> *A People*
> > *ready to recognize*
> > > *the wise compassion of True Mother . .*
> > *Were a People*
> > > *ready to recognize*
> > > > *the growing Wisdom*
> > > > > *of one who could not walk.*

><><><

NOW
> THIS MIGHT BE THE ENDING OF THIS TELLING . .

> *FOR YOU AND I NOW RECOGNIZE*
> > *HOW THE PEOPLE DECIDED*
> > > *never again*
> > > > *to cause any Great Sleep*
> > > *for the mere lack of an ease with walking.*

> *THEY HAD BECOME A PEOPLE*
> > *-- even as we --*

> *UNWILLING*
> > *to lose the wonder*
> > > *of such possible wisdom*
> > > > *in exchange for mere ease of transit.*

THIS IS A GREAT LEARNING
> *AND IT IS ENOUGH . .*

YET THERE WAS MORE.

FOR
  ON THAT DAY
    OF WHICH I SPOKE . .

  ON THAT DAY
    when True Son made his first offer . .

  ON THAT SAME DAY
    when the People accepted it . .

  TRUE SON
    lowered himself from his sitting rock
      and -- walking in his usual way --
    crossed to his True and Double Mother
      and laid three great Eagle feathers
        in her lap.

AND FROM THAT DAY TO THIS
  THERE HAS BEEN AMONG THE PEOPLE
    NO GREATER REWARD FOR WISDOM

  THAN THE GIFT
    FROM ONE TO ANOTHER
      OF THREE FEATHERS OF EAGLE . .

  EAGLE
    whose Wisdom
      sees beyond present circumstance,

  EAGLE
    whose great, feathered wings
      carry him, carry her, so high
    that Vision
      extends into Tomorrow and into Tomorrow,
        seeing possibilities
          long before they arrive.

AND THIS ALSO . .
    Many Season Circles
        passed in quiet learning and greater ease.

AT LAST
    this one more Bending Woman
        bent close enough to Earth
            to join at last
                with that Great Mother to us all . .

AND A WHOLE PEOPLE
    joined her only Son
        in keening their loss,
        singing songs also
            for the joy in their learning.

AND TRUE SON
    In his usual manner
        carried his mother slowly
            to an elevated place

AND -- laying her there --
    covered her slowly
        with rocks small and then great,
            building a seeming mountain.

"So that"
    -- he said --

"The other four-leggeds
    will leave her undisturbed
        to join with her True Mother."

AND
   Even this seeming mountain
      was not enough
         for a True Son
           of such a True Mother.

   Even did he make his slow way to near mountains,
      finding thereon, as he knew how to do,
         each Eagle nest.

   Asking feathers from each,
      he brought them slowly back . . .
         and wove them, one by one,
           through this small mountain
            of gathered rocks.

   "FOR WISDOM"
    -- he said --

   "FOR VISION . .

   "FOR COMPASSION . .

   "FOR LOVE . .

   "FOR CARING
     FOR A WHOLE PEOPLE . .

   "FOR CARING
     ESPECIALLY
       FOR THIS ONE . .

     "A GIFT OF EAGLE FEATHERS
     TO MARK THE NATURE
     OF THIS PERSON.

   "I HAVE SPOKEN."

Sheltered Valley

YOU HAVE HEARD
   HOW OUR PEOPLE LEARNED
      ALONG THEIR SOUTH-THROUGH-MOUNTAIN PATH.

NOW HEAR
   HOW IT WAS
      DURING A LONGER LENGTH OF DAYS . .

FOR
   The People came to a large and open valley,
      set about by many mountains . .

   And this valley was nearly as wide
      across the stretch of Sun
         as it was from North to South . .

   And through that valley ran three streams
      which joined one another
         in their southward trek.

      "Even as we join one another
         on our southward path"
           -- someone said.

AND
   It occurred to the People
      that for some Walks of Days
         there had been no space
      in which the People had settled
         long enough to live and grow and prosper.
   Indeed,
      since leaving the Water Walking People
         there had been no settled time . .

   AND IT SEEMED TO MANY
      that the People
         were beginning to lose their Way of Life
         as Place Keepers.

AND FOR THAT VERY REASON,
Some of those
who had walked to this new and gentle valley
returned to suggest a Telling Camp . .
Such as the People
had come to have from time to time,
so that the Old Songs could be remembered
and perhaps new ones devised.

AND DURING THESE TIMES
Some from among the People
took special responsibility
that these songs
found a continuing home in some memory,
While others of the People
chose only to be responsible
for the Learnings contained therein.

NOW
Those who saw in this valley
some promise of continuance
began by suggesting
that it might be a long time indeed
before this People
greeted the Eastern Ocean,
especially if they chose
to continue their southern path . .

AND ALL SAW
BOTH THE LAUGHTER
AND THE WISDOM
IN THIS.

NOW
Those who sought this continuance
began to ask for the Oldest Songs . .
those that talked
of a Great Center Place,
those that talked
of encouraged seeds and a usual home.

And in this way a Whole People
was encouraged to consider some respite
in their eventual search for Ocean.

"Perhaps"
-- someone said --

"Our Ocean
　　will be the sky overhead
　　　　and its reflected image
　　　　　　in these streams that join."

AND
　　ALL SAW HOW IT MIGHT BE SO.

AND
　　Gradually the People spoke with one another,
　　　　choosing this place and that
　　　　　　to build rounded houses,
　　　　searching for other possibilities of shelter . .

And some of their nature
　　chose to live near one or another stream . .
While others, aware of the possibilities
　　of sky water falling
　　　　and melting snows running down,
　　chose some elevation or another
　　　　not too far from stream . .

Until someone suggested . .

　　"Perhaps we need to choose two places --
　　　　one close to stream for that convenience,
　　　　one higher and away
　　　　　　when that proves inappropriate."

AND SO THE PEOPLE
　　Chose to choose two locations
　　　　for each center place.

AND YET
　　The nature of this sheltered valley
　　　　encouraged groups none too large
　　　　　　to look for and to find
　　　　　　　　various possibilities
　　　　so that the Center Place
　　　　　　became rapidly many such center places.

NOW FROM THIS TELLING
  WE LEARN CERTAIN THINGS
    AND FAIL TO LEARN OTHERS.

WE LEARN . .

  That the People
    continued in their walking ways
      over some few Walks of Days.

  That the People
    maintained a path greatly more South
      than East.

  That some from among them
    carefully kept all Ancient Songs
      stored in their memory.

  That the People
    remembered their settled ways
      and chose to return to them.

AND WE FAIL TO LEARN . .

  How long a walk it may have been
    from the Second Dry Place
      to this Sheltered Valley.

  How many children's children's children
    may have come and gone during this walk.

  Why our People,
    who mainly purposed to find a path
      to the Eastern Ocean,
    walked so continuously South
      through the mountains . .
    though perhaps the nature
      of those mountains themselves
        predicted this.

FOR
  Although this walk
    is lit here -- and also there --
      by Two Great Learnings . .
    the daily regularity of this long walk
      has been lost.

Perhaps for those who walked it,
each day was so like another
that none sought to record it.

Perhaps the constant movement
discouraged the long discussions
necessary to an ingathering of thought.

Perhaps for this very reason
those keeping all Ancient Songs
now sought some singing
by each of the People.

WE KNOW THIS . .

THAT FROM TIME TO TIME
THOSE WHO REMEMBER SUCH THINGS
BECOME TOO FEW.

WE KNOW
that Ancient Wisdom grew from a child
too curious to be discouraged.

WE KNOW
that another child listened to her,
preserving much.

AND YET
WE ALSO KNOW
that no one at all
thought to record this regular walk South,
or at least too few
thought to remember it.

AND YET
WE ALSO KNOW
HOW MUCH HAS BEEN RECORDED.

FOR HAVE I NOT SUNG TO YOU,
day after day,
the gathered thoughts of many, many people
over countless Walks of Days?

HAVE I NOT SUNG TO YOU
   of beginnings so ancient and learnings so great
      that nothing at all --
         or at least very little --
      in present circumstance
         would cause us to suppose such things?

LET THIS BE ANOTHER OF OUR LEARNINGS.

LET US REMEMBER
   THAT TODAY'S USUAL PATH
      MAY BE TOMORROW'S DIVERSITY.

LET US REMEMBER
   TO SING OF EACH PATH,
      HOWEVER USUAL IT MAY SEEM . .

   So that children
      born to no Ocean
         yet remember the taste of salt.

   So that children
      born to no mountain
         remember its height

   So that children
      born to no continuing walk
         yet hear the footfalls.

      SO BE IT.

NOW I HAVE TOLD YOU HOW IT WAS.
How a People
after long South Walking
settled from place to place
in this sheltered valley.

NOW HEAR HOW IT WAS
That those who concern themselves
with Ancient Ways and a growing People
grew concerned
at the manner of that growth.

For a People
who had woven themselves together
through many disparate circumstances
Now became a People
who sought various ways through ease.

And those who kept the Ancient Songs
sat with one another
considering how it might be
that an easeful People
might lose their forward purpose.

"You see how it is, my Brothers, my Sisters,"
-- someone said --

"We who were concerned
that too many Ancient Songs
might lie scattered and forgot
along so continuous a path
now are concerned
that these same songs
may lie scattered
on this easeful Earth so long
that the very nature of sky waters
will carry away all traces
of what we presently value."

AND ALL SAW IT WAS SO,
THAT ONE WAY AND THE OTHER . .
ALL THIS ANCIENT WISDOM
MIGHT YET BE LOST
TO SUBSEQUENT OTHERS.

AND SO
   This very same gathering
      of those who kept the Ancient Songs . .
   Devised an agreement
      by which each harvest
         of the fruit of encouraged seeds,
      each ingathering of winter provender,
         might be followed by a general celebration.

AND AS THEY REMEMBERED
   the gifts of the earth,
      both in thanksgiving
         and in some resident feasting . .

SO ALSO WOULD THEY REMEMBER
   the gifts of those who went before,
      and many Ancient Songs were sung again.

AND THIS WAS THE WAY OF IT.
   A People grown satisfied
      with the plenty of this place
   Became a People unwilling
      to change this new and easeful way
         for the mere thought
            that some previous circumstance
         had disenabled in some sudden manner
            a different and previous easeful way.

AND SO
   THOSE WHO REMEMBER SUCH THINGS . .

Those who remember
   that Not for a Long Time
      and Never are not the same understandings . .

These ones devised among themselves
   a way to keep all Ancient Wisdom
      over many Walks of Days . .

FOR SURELY
   These ones understood that,
      as light and dark follow one another
        again and again,
      change will surely come . .
        sheltering mountains
          will turn to a sudden battering rain,
        quiet streams fill and overfill,
        cold become warm and warm become cold.

AND
   Those who fail to remember Ancient Wisdom
      will greet such change
        with startled, unaccepting eyes . .

Eyes dazzled therefore by this change
      as if it were a sudden and brilliant light . .

Eyes so dazzled will fail to perceive
      either the true nature of that change
        or the many possibilities
          through which a People
            may weave a rope of continuance.

AND SO
   THOSE WHO UNDERSTAND SUCH THINGS
      LEARNED
        TO REMEMBER ANCIENT WISDOM
        AND TO SING THE SONGS FROM TIME TO TIME . .

SO THAT THE CHILDREN'S CHILDREN
   THOSE WHO KNEW ONLY THIS SHELTERED VALLEY . .
      YET REMEMBERED
        HOW IT HAD BEEN BEFORE . .

REMEMBERED
    the salt taste of Ocean,
    the avalanche roar of a pounding Sea,
    how it is
      to ride a shaking Earth and a moving Ocean,
    how it is
      to learn and grow and change.

AND THIS WAS ALSO THE WAY OF IT . .
THOUGH NO GREAT CHANGE
RAPIDLY ARRIVED,

YET FROM TIME TO TIME
the streams did fill and overfill,
snows came in greater or lesser quantities,
an Earth which shook in no great way
yet shook a little from time to time
so that someone would say,
"Earth is reminding us
of what may one day be."

AND SO
A People turned now to a quiet way --
become, perhaps,
too used to a changeless way --
began to think again of change . .

AND . . . AFTER AWHILE
It was generally agreed
to call a general gathering
of all the Valley People
so that they might speak with one another.

AND THIS WAS THE QUESTION THAT WAS ASKED . .

"If it is our purpose
to remain in this valley
to which our grandfathers,
our grandmothers came,

"WHAT IS OUR PURPOSE HERE?"

AND
ALL SAW HOW IT WAS.

HOW WE WERE STILL A PEOPLE
FOR WHOM MERE CONTINUANCE
WAS NOT ENOUGH.

AND -- AS THEY SPOKE TO ONE ANOTHER --
This purposeful People thought together
    until they were agreed on certain things.

AND THESE WERE . .

Let the Ancient Songs
    be close kept by some and heard by all.

Let us know
    which ones from among us
        will carry this purpose
    so that we know
        where we may find
            this Ancient, valued keeping.

Let us in this easeful circumstance
    remember
        that what is may not be
            on some subsequent morning.

Let us then remember
    to look for change and its many patterns.

LET US,
    WHO HAVE COME TO BE A PURPOSEFUL PEOPLE
    ESTABLISH A PURPOSE FOR THIS PLACE.

Let us find a way
    to live with streams
        that sometimes overfill.

Let us find a way
    to live with varying snows.

Let us find a way
    of building for ourselves
        houses greater
            than the rounded dwellings we know now
        houses
            that may yet learn
                to include a broader group
            as do some of the deep dark places
                of the Earth.

AND
    Let us find some way
        of giving in this present, easeful place
           some of the gifts
               given the People in other places.

We do not seek to find some proximate Ocean,
    yet we remember it.

Let us find some way
    to remember its salt tang
        so that the children's children
           may yet remember our Eastern purpose.

FOR TOMORROW
    MAY YET MAKE THIS THE WISEST CHOICE.

We do not seek to leave
    this Sheltered Valley . .

Yet let us from time to time
    encourage some from among the People
        to walk out from here in many directions,
           returning to explain
               such distant possibilities.

Though this Valley,
    filled with all manner of sustenance
        and containing an Earth
           that takes joy in encouraged seeds,
              provides well for our People,
    yet no where
        do we find those warm pools
           which give ease from many discomforts
           and which are now contained
              only in these Tellings.

Let us find some way
    to bring easeful warmth
        to those who seek this healing,
    whether too many years
        or too great cold
        or too great effort
           engender original pain.

AND SO IT WAS AGREED.
  This or that one accepted each task
    and those with a common task
      were drawn from disparate groups
    so that other learnings
      might engender other thoughts.

AND
  Why and when
    and in exactly what manner
      has been lost,

  Yet the manner they devised
    has not.

AND THESE
  WERE THEIR NEW UNDERSTANDINGS . .

NO HOUSE
    WAS ANY LONGER BUILT IN ANY PLACE
    EASILY OVERRUN
      BY A RAPIDLY GROWING STREAM.

The People developed a way
  of more carefully studying
    the nature of land near any stream
  so that they could predict its overswelling

When those too loathe to walk to water
  were -- time and again --
    suddenly hip deep in what they sought.

AND, AFTER A TIME,
    the People developed an understanding
      of how close is too close
      and how far is far enough --
    so that such sudden water-standing
      became only a memory.

AS TO SUDDEN SNOWS,
   THIS VALLEY LAY BEREFT
     OF ANY EASY SHELTER
       OTHER THAN THAT BUILT BY THE PEOPLE . .

And years of deeper snow
   were difficult indeed,
     as all the rounded dwellings
      lay easily buried
     and few and hardly enough
       were any deep dark places
        which might otherwise
         have offered shelter.

NOW IT SEEMS
  That someone suggested the wisdom
   of building one house upon the other.

No one is any longer sure
  how exactly it was devised . .

But the image of a house upon a house,
  and also the image
    of a great cave's depth,
  and also the image still retold
    of the heavy log houses
      built by the Water Walking People
  and how it was that one such
    joined the fire at its center
      all too quickly,
    preventing six within from finding their way
      through the only door . .

ALL THESE THINGS AND MORE
  combined
    to encourage what we see now . .

A BUILDING
  high enough to exceed the snow,
  long enough to include many of the People
    and a variable distribution of fire,

A HOUSE
  with two doors, not only one,
    so that -- let fire be what it may --
  all the People
    might find some outside way.

AND WHETHER AT THAT TIME
OR WHETHER SINCE . .

HOUSES OF THE DESIGN
   WE KNOW NOW AND UNDERSTAND
     BEGAN
       THEIR PATTERNED DANCE ON THE EARTH.

Long and also high,
   as if house rested on house,
     many living within,
   an even row of fires
     rather than one centered within the circle,
   and ease of construction
   and security in any storm
     enhanced again and again . .

SO THIS GIFT
   WE GIVE OUR CHILDREN TODAY
     BEGAN, AT LEAST, IN THAT FAR TIME.

AND AS FOR THE WARM POOLS,
   NONE WERE EVER FOUND
     IN THAT PLACE.

BUT THE WAY OF IT WAS THIS . .

No purpose
   was any longer found
     for the rounded dwellings
   and they became special places
     for learning,
   so that the regularities of the larger house
     need not be disturbed.

And whether it was the image
   of some bubbling liquid over a small fire,
Or whether it was the general learning
   of the greater heat in the smaller dwelling
     is not known.

WHAT IS KNOWN
   IS THAT IT WAS AT THIS TIME
      that the People first brought
        the warmth of mountain pools
          inside the small rounded dwelling
      so that hot stones and water
        might encourage one another
          into a general condition
            beneficial to many circumstances.

     . . .

NOW
   I HAVE TOLD YOU
     how a cohesive People
     scattered themselves
       over a Sheltered Valley.

   I HAVE TOLD YOU
     how they began to remember
     the value of common purpose.

   I HAVE TOLD YOU
     how they devised a way
       to live with nearby stream,
       to build large and commodious houses
         proof against certain mishaps,
     how they learned a way to bathe in air
     as they had bathed in warm pools.

NOW
   HEAR OF THE NATURE OF CHANGE . .

For there began to appear in this valley
   a People who were not Bear
   and who were yet more different
     than any two-legged yet recorded
       by any previous People.

They traveled in individual ways,
   appearing now and then in small groups
     no greater than two or three.

Now these ones were very tall,
   many as tall as, many taller than,
     the largest of our own People.

FOR SOME TIME
   These ones were rarely seen and quickly left.

AND AT THIS TIME
   It was in no way clear to us
      whether they wore furred skins --
         even as we --
      or whether this was their own apparent nature.

   AND
      remembering the misunderstanding of him
         who first learned the way of softened skins,
     we had no wish to assume
        any such inappropriate understanding.

AND YET AT LAST
   It came to be understood
      that this furred condition
        was natural to them.

IT WAS AT THIS TIME
   That many chose to regard them
     as some new one
        from among our Bear cousins.

AND YET
   None were ever seen
      resting all four feet on any earth at all --
        and from time to time --
    one or another
       were seen to be carrying this or that . .
    so that the discussion among the People
      was as great
        as it was unresolved.

NOW ANOTHER THING
    BEGAN TO OCCUR.

FROM TIME TO TIME
    Some of these new cousins
        would appear too close to some one house
            for any within to feel at ease.

AND AT LAST
    Some of the women noted
        that such sightings
            occurred especially at times
        when many of the women
            were proving to themselves
                they expected no young . .

So that the men from among them
    grew even more concerned
        at these beings who approached
            and yet did not approach at all . .

And many began discussing the need
    for houses built closer together
        and circles of defense
            as some other Peoples found useful.

                • • •

NOW
    IT WAS ALSO UNDERSTOOD AT THIS TIME
        THAT ANOTHER CHANGE OCCURRED . .

AND THIS WAS
    that succeeding season circles grew colder,
        one than the other,
    so that it was the thought of many
        that this increasing cold
            brought this strange People
                either South from farther North
                or down from higher mountains.

AND NOW
　　DISCUSSION WAS GREAT.

It would seem our Sheltered Valley
　　grew less sheltered with each Winter Count,
　　less sheltered from cold,
　　less sheltered from disparate others.

SO THAT ALL SAW NECESSITY
*　　FOR SOME GREAT CHANGE.*

Either houses would be built together
　　for mutual protection . .

Or each individual house
　　　　must devise some defense . .

Or some way
　　of meeting and coming to understand
　　　　this extraordinary People
　　　　　　must be discovered . .

And also some way
　　of building and rebuilding houses
　　　　on top of newly fallen snow
　　　　　　must be devised.

SO IT WAS
　　That during this continuing and great discussion,
　　　　the tenth Winter of Great Cold
　　　　　　was counted.

AND ALL THE PEOPLE
　　SAW HOW IT WAS

　　　　THAT WINTER BECAME MORE
　　　　-- YEAR AFTER YEAR --
　　　　AS THE TIME OF WARMTH AND GROWING
　　　　　　BECAME LESS.

AND THE PEOPLE
  Were at a loss
    to decide which was the greater difficulty.

BUT THIS THEY KNEW . .
  Great Cold for Ten Winters may cease
    and warmth return -- or not.

  The stretch of increasing cold
    might well reach
      beyond the children's children's children.

AND SO
  WHAT WITH ONE THING AND ANOTHER,
  A PEOPLE
    SATISFIED WITH WHERE THEY WERE
    RAPIDLY BECAME
      A PEOPLE UNWILLING TO STAY.

AND -- WITH NO REGRET --
  Even this People, every one,
    rolled all they intended to carry with them
      into any appropriate skin

AND -- AS EARTH GREW WARMER --
ROSE AS ONE BODY
  and found the clearest passage East
    through mountains,
      leaving all behind
        they had created,
      carrying with them
        each and every Learning.

NOW, LET US LEARN
  TO BE A PEOPLE
    WHO REMEMBER THE PROBABILITY OF CHANGE.

  A PEOPLE WHO REMEMBER
    HOW IT IS

    That when you stand and walk
      through a changing circumstance
        both something of sustenance
        and something of shelter
          may go with you . .

AND YET
  THIS, AND THIS ALONE,
    GOES ALWAYS WITH YOU . .

  WHENEVER YOU STAND AND WALK,
    WHEREVER A NEW PATH TAKES YOU . .

  THIS, AND NO OTHER,
    GOES WITH YOU . .

    ALL OF IT,
    EACH OF IT,

        CONTAINED WITHIN EACH,
        CONTAINED WITHIN ALL . .

For out of that Sheltered Valley
  the People walked,
    carrying wherewith
      to sustain life, for awhile,
    and carrying wherewith
      to begin life anew.

AND YET
  WHATEVER MIGHT BE LEFT BEHIND
  WHAT THEY HAD LEARNED
    WENT WITH THEM.

  AND WITH THEM THEY CARRIED,
    SOME OF THEM . .

  AND SOMEWHAT THEY CARRIED,
    ALL OF THEM . .

  ALL THE GATHERED LEARNING
    OF A WISE AND CONTINUOUS PEOPLE.

    MAY WE BE AS WISE.

    MAY WE ALSO LEARN TO REMEMBER.

Grass Ocean

Dark Ocean

Squash Sister

Squash Blossom

Two Ways

Small Fruit

Ocean Coming Like a Great Wall

Squash Blossom's Children

Ocean Crossing

Grass Ocean

NOW
I HAVE TOLD YOU
HOW IT WAS
FOR OUR PEOPLE ..

How it was
they walked out
from under a thunderous rain.

How they traced a path
through Ocean.

How another path
was woven
through Endless Mountains.

How they found
and also left
a Sheltered Valley.

NOW
HEAR HOW IT WAS FOR THEM
WHERE THEY NEXT CAME TO BE.

FOR
As they marked out a path
through these great mountains
with many individual footfalls,
So did they also come at last
to the eastern slopes of those same mountains ..

AND SOMEONE AT LAST
returned from a forward walk
to speak of descending mountains
and of farther vision
across a more even land.

THEN ALL THE PEOPLE
Came to a place
from which this vision of distance
was enabled
by some space between mountains ..
and all were amazed.

NONE AMONG THE PEOPLE
    Had ever lived during a time
        when Earth
            did not rise in sharp and jagged ways.

Looking out
    over this gently rising circumstance,
        one also that held some apparent motion,
    none found within any explanation.

UNTIL AT LAST
    Someone suggested . .

"Perhaps it is Ocean.
 Perhaps here at last
    we have reached the eastern edge
        of this Great Island on which we stand."

AND ALL SAW HOW IT MIGHT BE SO . .

How what lay beyond
    held only a gentle rise and fall
        with some apparent movement
            in every direction . .

AND ALL REMEMBERED
    how this was, indeed,
        a part of the description
            of the nature of Ocean.

AND YET SOME REMEMBERED
    the thunderous nature of Ocean's edge
        and wondered why no such sound was heard
    so that above every two feet
        was a person eager to learn the nature
            of this broad expanse of movement.

NOW
    It was in the mind of all the People
        to reach the edge
            of these sharp jagged mountains
        and to touch with closer hand
            the true nature of what lay beyond.

BUT
    Purpose is one thing and arrival another
        so that two days passed
            before the People walked their way
                to the edge of this new Ocean.

AND
    Remembering how it had been long ago
        when the People reached the Western Ocean,
           the People kept pace with one another
        so that all might walk as one
           until they stood hip deep in a Salt Ocean.

AND THE PEOPLE DID ARRIVE,
    stretch out each hand
        and touch the nature of this New Ocean,
    wade hip-deep in its nature to find --
    no salt at all,
        nor even anything truly damp.

FOR
    This was a different Ocean,
        one also tossed by wind,
           but beyond that
                more stable than the always-moving Ocean.

This Ocean was -- of its nature --
    green in many various ways.

Moving always,
    yet it hardly moved at all.
Hip-deep therein,
    no foot at all was damp.

For this ceaseless tossing Ocean --
    vast as the eye might see --
        was filled
           all with the tossing, seeded heads
             of so much standing grass.

These seeded heads,
    tossing in the wind,
        seemed an apparent Ocean

AND OCEAN IT INDEED WAS.

In its own way
as vast,
as difficult to cross . .

So that the People
named this place our Grass Ocean,
and found a place among the hills
where much water
ran out upon the level land.

*AND THIS PLACE
WAS A NEW CENTER PLACE
FOR A LEARNING PEOPLE,
AS YET SEEKING AN EASTERN OCEAN
FOR MANY WALKS OF DAYS.*

Dark Ocean

NOW
   IN THIS PLACE
     MANY THINGS CAME TO BE.

   Every seed now carried
     was encouraged
       into some yielding part of Earth
        close enough to water
         to benefit therefrom,
       far enough away
         to prevent rapid drowning.

THE PEOPLE . .
   Who had come out from standing forests
     onto this Grass Ocean
       began again
        to build their rounded dwellings . .

   There being none among them
     who either preferred to return to forest
     or to bring that forest close to hand.

AND SO IT WAS, FOR A TIME,
   That a way newly become ancient
   was contained
     only in the memories of the People.

   Some returning -- from time to time --
     to the now distant and forested mountains,
   Reminding themselves
     of the accuracy
       of this memory at least,
     so that it became a usual thing
       among the People -- from time to time --
       that one or another
        would make this walk.

AND ANOTHER THING OCCURRED.

A careful study of this place
in every direction was made
so that all knew
that the path to mountains
was some few days.

North and South
presented a limitless edge of mountains
washed
by an even more limitless Grass Ocean.

And to the East,
no one at all
returned to speak of anything more
than a continuous Ocean.

NOW
This Ocean was different
than the one before.

No Water Walking People were anywhere found
on its grass surface . .

AND YET
ANOTHER PEOPLE
TRAVELED THE SURFACE
OF THIS VAST OCEAN.

They did not arrive
on some silent wooden surface . .

Rather, they thundered from place to place
in such a tumult
that the People gave them the name
Thunder on the Earth.

And these, also,
were a shaggy four-footed People,
dark in hue and of various sizes.

NOW
    This would seem to be
        a very nearly limitless source of sustenance,
            these four-footeds,
        but I tell you now
            it was not so.

    For this People
        traveled in such numbers
            that their very movement
                brought terror to anyone near.

    Even the strongest from among our own community,
        brave though they were,
            had no wish to find themselves
                beneath so many sharpened hooves . .

    For this other People moved in such ways
        that they were a kind of Ocean
        unto themselves,
            washing here and there
                with no apparent purpose,
            drawing all before them,
            leaving this vast Grass Ocean
                both trampled and consumed . .

    So that where they had been was easier walking,
        save for the awareness
            that this same dark and washing Ocean
            might return
                to wash over any hapless wanderer
                    in a most unforgettable manner.

SO THAT MANY WINTERS
    Passed in study of this new Ocean
        before the larger Ocean of Grass
            at last knew the feet of Go and See,
                looking -- finally --
                    for the Eastern Ocean,
            or at least
                for the Eastern edge
                    of so much Grass.

Squash Sister

NOW AT THIS TIME
  The People chose
      to keep their place among the hills
          at the edge of great mountains.

  They chose also
      to learn to understand this place
          and all it might contain,
      so that the pounded seeds of much grass
          were also used among the People
              as sustenance.

  Yet the People continued
      in their manner
          of encouraged seeds of all kinds.

  It was not their thought
      to come one day to argue
          with that darker Ocean
              over who might make better use
                  of so much grass.

AND
  As the People found this and that of value
      for sustenance . .

  So were the seeds of that rooted brother
      encouraged toward earth,
  So that the People might learn
      which seeds are best carried
          by a People who one day purpose
              to reach the Eastern Ocean.

AND IT WAS AT THIS TIME
  THAT EARTH GAVE US A NEW GIFT.

WHEREAS WE WERE A PEOPLE
Who greatly valued the podded seeds
which might be easily eaten
or kept and dried
and later simmered in water
so that even a greater softness than before
was achieved . .

WHEREAS WE WERE SUCH A PEOPLE . .

NOW
some from among us
began to encourage toward Earth
a smaller seed in a larger pod.

For this pod
was so large
as to be eaten for itself,
the seed in this rooted brother
being greatly lesser than wherein it was.

And this pod
also grew to such a size
that one might feed a number of people.

And these pods
grew here and there
in various sizes and shapes
so that the People began a great search
through these hills
for the varying kinds.

NOW
This rooted brother
grew also in vines,
Yet these were vines
that hardly climbed at all,
the pods being of so great a size
as to disallow it.

AND SO -- between one thing and another --
The People began to devise different ways
in which these two rooted brothers
of such differing natures
might live together --
with the People --
in some mutual continuance . .

So that appropriate ceremonies
began to be devised also,
in which these rooted brothers
and their fruit
became one with the People
and traveled always with us . .

SO THAT NONE OF THE PEOPLE
ANY LONGER
WENT OUT FROM OUR CENTER PLACE
WITHOUT THESE SEED SISTERS.

Squash Blossom

NOW
There came to be among the People
one who was newly arrived
in the usual manner,
one who -- as she grew --
showed increasing understanding
of all that grew

So that many said . .

"You see how it is,
she is the True Granddaughter
of Growing Woman.

"Where she walks . .
the People will soon find sustenance."

And all laughed at the image
of vining plants
growing from each footstep.

YET IT WAS NEARLY SO,
For This One
somehow understood
the nature of Earth
and of her relation to any seed at all,
so that each seed she encouraged
grew to a greater size than any other.

AND SO IT WAS
That the People chose for her
an appropriate and an honoring name.

"Where she is,
there sustenance for the People
soon follows.

"So we give her the name
of something we value,
something of great beauty,
something
whose mere existence predicts plenty.

"WE CALL THIS WOMAN
SQUASH BLOSSOM."

AND IT WAS SO.

A STRONG NAME,
NEVER BEFORE GIVEN,
WAS GIVEN NOW
TO THIS TRUE DAUGHTER
TO GROWING WOMAN.

AND THE PEOPLE SAW HOW IT WAS
THAT MANY GIFTS
CAME TO THEM THROUGH HER HANDS
AND GAVE HER IN RETURN
THE GIFT OF THEIR RESPECT.

Two Ways

NOW DURING THIS TIME
   The People had begun
      to find disparate others among the hills.

   These ones lived from the nature of the land itself
      and from the great herds,
         taking what might be left behind,
            even the very old
               or those who -- for one or another reason --
                  lost pace with the whole herd.

   Neither did any such People
      encourage seeds toward Earth
         as had been our repeated way
            since time beyond time.

   Yet much might be learned from these ones
      about the searching out of sustenance
         above and below Earth.

   And some of these ones also
      were given to cliff edges
         where one or another from this dark and tossing Ocean
            might walk too far out
               over a rapidly changing circumstance
                  to be suddenly met with Earth
                     well below that same cliff edge.

AND,
   Even as our People
      had learned how to encourage seeds toward Earth,
   So did this People
      learn to encourage a dark Ocean toward cliff edge
         so that an occasional mischance
            became a regular occurrence.

AND AS BETWEEN THESE TWO WAYS,
   The thought of the People was this --

   • That any seed so encouraged --
      even if the People forgot where it was --
         might make its own way in life,
            enhancing the whole.

• That even should so many such seeds
    sprout and also grow
        that their progeny greatly exceed probable need --
    Even so might such seeds be left to their own way,
        or dried against a changing circumstance.

• That in times
    when too few seeds might sprout or grow
        then other ways on the Earth
          might still sustain the People.

NOW THE THOUGHT OF THE PEOPLE WAS ALSO THIS.

• That much of the Dark Ocean now found its way
    from time to time over some proximate cliff.

• That only some small part of this Dark Ocean
    spilt over cliff
        was useful to this other People.

• The rest settled against Earth
    as if there were no hunger
        nor any further need.

• Some few of the other four-leggeds
    might find easeful living for awhile,
        also those that flew
          and found such ready food appropriate.

But it was the thought of our People
    that life was enhanced in no way
        by this clotted pool from the Dark Ocean
And --
    unless it was our purpose to assure sustenance
        to all the small and six-legged
          for many generations --
    the doing seemed excessive of the desired end.

AND
    Even as the People understood
        that the greatest gathering of sprouted seeds
          might yet be outlasted
            by the hunger of those who come after,

So did they understand
  that even this Dark Ocean might yet run dry.
And so it was in their mind
  to seek self-sustaining ways upon the Earth
    so that a limitless number of subsequent others
      might celebrate this Wisdom.

AND YET, IN NO WAY
  could they make this understood
    to any other People.

These Ones looked out at the dark and tossing Ocean,
  seeing how wide it was from one edge to the other,
    and did not see how even the greatest pool
      may dry under an unyielding sun,
        interspersed with too little rain.

NOW IT CAME TO BE
  That the People began to be discontent in this place.

None of those around them
  encouraged seeds toward Earth
    nor thought to learn it.

Whereas the great herds
  and those who follow after
    from time to time were gone,
    so did they also return
      and -- respecting no encouraged seed --
    one or the other might consume
      or trample all possibility of tomorrow.

Even in this way
  were some seed sisters lost beyond retrieval,
    while yet others remained.

And although the People were glad of the continuance,
  so were they also sad at the loss --
    for it is known that at this time
      whole seed families were lost.

AND IT CAME TO BE
  THAT THE PEOPLE
    BEGAN TO THINK
      OF THIS MOST RECENT CENTER PLACE
        AS A PLACE OF GREAT LOSS.

Small Fruit

NOW
  Another thing occurred
    which gave the People even greater concern.
  For this neighboring People
    would from time to time hold a great celebration.
      Nor was it any we yet recognized.

  For the very nature of the People
    changed at this time
      so that they became other than we knew.
  Nor did we seek any proximate place at these times --
    for there was much blind staring into air,
      and yet much leaping and dancing,
        every manner of behavior
          in no predictable way occurred
  so that we found all greatly disquieting.

                    • • •

NOW SINCE IT WAS KNOWN
  That some small parts of the spined plant
    were eaten at this time,
  It gave the People thought of the many berries
    too quickly consumed in that time long ago . .
  And how it came to be
    that too many with too great a hunger
      came to be still against the Earth.

AND ALL OF THIS
  Gave the People great thought
    that that which is too quickly joined with the People
      may be parted only with great pain.

AND ALL OF THIS
  Gave increasing disquiet to the People.

Yet from among them
   there was one of changeable nature.
And This One
   found a wandering way more pleasing,
     yet had no wish to leave his familiar People.

And so -- from time to time
   he sat with one
     and then the other People.
And This One
   attended such a celebration
    -- watching without joining --
      so that he was as eyes and ears to the whole.

Back with him then
   came some of this special fruit
    with which these others celebrated,
      saying it had been known among them
       for some time
        and caused them no harm.

YET IT SEEMED TO US
   THEIR VERY BEHAVIOR WAS HARM ENOUGH.

AND YET
   This one of our own People sat among us,
    showing us this strange small fruit,
   And before any agreed,
    took of his own decision one such at least.

Now none could change what was --
   and so we only sought
    to care for one possibly afflicted.
Yet soon This One
   fought like some one cornered
    by the sharp and hungry teeth
     of some Great One who eats little grass --

Many of the People
   tried to restrain him.
    His great thrashings about
     did great damage to many.

Then something occurred
    which had never before happened.
No memory among the People
    speaks of any such.
Nor did any of the People on that day
    have any way
        to prepare themselves for such a thing.

FOR
    When the strongest from among the People
        stepped forward,
            intending to save this precipitate person
                from some self-damage,
            seeking to bind him in place with two strong arms
                while others brought ropes --

Even then did this flailing person
    take up a skinning knife and slash and cut
        this strong and purposeful man
So many times and in so many ways
        that later they counted
            no fewer than seventeen penetrations
                of his personal self by this unwanted knife.

Through it all,
    this strong and purposeful man
        bound with his own arms
            this greatly foolish person,
        placing in this manner his protecting self
            between his People and this sudden damage.

And some
    were able to pound from his hand
        this offending knife --

And others
    were able to bind legs and then arms with ropes,
        so as to truss this offending man
            like some clawed and angry destroyer --
        and, bound in this manner,
            he struggled with ropes
                instead of with the People.

And those who loved him
   watched carefully
      to assure little harm to his bound nature.

Yet those who cared for the strong man
   found little joy in the watching.
For his life
   poured out from each unexpected opening.

And at last
   he lay still against the Earth,
      asking only after any other damage
         that may have escaped his watchful care.
And the People greatly mourned his loss.

And yet
   before any caught the first gleams of another day
      there was another loss to mourn --

For That One
   whom the People had bound to restrain him,
That One who thought to try only a little
   of the strange food,
That One who raged
   and cut the Life from his strong brother,

That One now lay --
   breathing no more --
   tongue swollen -- face dark --
   choked it would seem
      from only a very little
         very small fruit.

NOW
>The People were greatly distressed.
>>No ancient memory spoke of such things.
>>No word gave promise of resolution.

>And yet
>>here were ways none of the People at all
>>>wished to follow,
>>ways which -- nonetheless --
>>>suddenly sat at our Fire.

>And it seemed to them
>>that -- as we desire some distance
>>>between a Dark Ocean and encouraged seeds --
>>so did we desire some distance
>>>between this Small Fruit Way
>>>>and the children's children.

>And yet, merely lifted eyes
>>brought an instant image of another Ocean
>>>so vast that few had any real wish to cross it.

>And this Grass Ocean was in turn
>>washed from time to time
>>>by a darker and more dangerous Ocean.

>In the midst of that Grass Sea,
>>what survival could there be for a People
>>>washed under pounding hooves?

AND SO, FOR A TIME,
>The People remained where they were,
>>keening their loss, fearful for tomorrow.

>But This One and Another began storage,
>>keepings so that no other seed family
>>>might be lost beyond retrieval under pounding hooves.

>And some began the storage that predicts travel,
>>though no resolution had yet been agreed.

AND SO IT WAS, FOR A TIME,
>That all thought of the necessity of decision,
>>many discussed this and that,

AND YET
>all hesitated
>>to other than continue their present path.

XXXX

Ocean Coming Like A Great Wall

THEN
   IT CAME AT LAST,
      as unpredictable
         as any storming Ocean,
      as purposeful
         as any Great Water Wall . .

   THE DARK OCEAN RETURNED . .
      and washed across
         the Way of the People,
      stormed across
         their Purpose,
      slashed to ribbons
         every rounded dwelling,
      stamped into purposeless gruel
         every sprouted seed.

AND YET
   NONE OF THE PEOPLE
      WERE LOST . .

   NONE
      pounded under a restless, dark surf . .

   NONE
      crushed under flailing hooves.

   FOR,
      unlike rounded dwellings,
         the People have ears.

   AND,
      unlike our rooted brothers,
         the People can run --
      and run they did that day
         to any elevation at all.

ONCE
    The Earth Thunder was heard . .

ONCE
    This Ocean's direction
        was ascertained . .

    Each and every of these two-footed persons ran . .
        ran carrying those yet too young,
        ran carrying those whose as-yet-short legs
            were no match for a Dark Ocean,
        ran carrying any sustenance at all . .

    So that all dwellings were lost --
        and yet some skins retained.

    All sprouted seeds were lost --
        and yet some sustenance retained.

    ALL ELSE
        LAY CRUSHED
            UNDER SHARP,
                UNCOMPREHENDING HOOVES.

NOW
    The People celebrated
        the wisdom of quick feet and ready bundles.

NOW
    They celebrated
        the wisdom of knowing which to carry.

NOW
    They celebrated
        the wisdom of seeds
            stored out of reach of pounding hooves,
                assuring Tomorrow.

AND
    As the Dark Ocean washed away after a time,
        the People returned,
            gathering what they could
                from a fragmented scattering
                    of What Had Been.

AND NOW
   The People
     sat to talk with one another.

   For Today was gone,
     washed away by a dark and pounding surf . .

   And Tomorrow remained to be built,
     and whether such building was wise
       on such a chance-filled shore
     or whether it was not
       remained to be decided.

AND
   Some spoke with no joy at all
     of a return to mountain . .

AND
   Some spoke of a Grass Ocean
     that might be crossed
       by quick feet ready to climb . .

   And others mentioned how it was
     that some said the other edge
       of this Grass Ocean
         lost itself in forest . .

   But none at all described the North.

   For North was the direction
     of this Other People
     and of Greater Cold also.

NOW
   When all had spoken save one,
      this was the way of it.

   Many described
      a careful path East,
      a quick path across a Grass Ocean
         with little rest for a moving People,
      one which stopped only during the truly dark
         at the top of some hill lit by torches,
      where both the hill and the unwanted light
         might deter a Dark Ocean . .

   One crossed
      with the sustenance at hand
         and whatever might be found along the way . .

   One quick enough
      to find tomorrow's place for encouraged seeds
         before the shorter days
            and colder wind of another Winter
               crossed their path.

AND ALL SAW THE WISDOM IN THESE WORDS . .

AND YET
   MANY SAW ALSO HOW IT WAS
      that one from among them
         had not yet spoken,
      one whose wisdom they valued.

AND SO, AT LAST,
   All turned
      and invited some word
         of encouraged seeds and Earth wisdom . .

And Squash Blossom spoke,
   and these were her words . .

"I see how it is for you,
   my Brothers, my Sisters.

"You are seeking still
   some Eastern Ocean
     beyond the forest we expect to find
       at the other edge of this Grass Ocean.

"BUT MY WAY IS THE GROWING WAY
   AND THESE ARE MY THOUGHTS.

"That from here to there
   is too far for this year's planting.

"That only a forest
   marks the edge of both Oceans
     and which tree
       will give way to encouraged seeds?

"That one way not discussed
   is South.

"That South is warmer
   and also some say
     provides sharp elevations
       as deterrence to sharp hooves.

"Perhaps in some more southerly place
   such elevations
     may be warm enough for encouraged seeds
     and sudden enough
       that no Dark Ocean
         may wash that high.

"*I, FOR ONE,*
   WILL SEEK SUCH A PLACE,
   WILL TURN MY STEPS SOUTH
     AND LET THOSE WHO WILL
       WALK WITH ME."

NOW
 A sudden, gusty storm of many thoughts
  broke over the People.

SOME SAW HOW IT WAS
 THAT SINCE TIME BEFORE TIME
  NONE OF THE PEOPLE
   HAD WALKED AWAY FROM ANY OTHER.

OTHERS SAW HOW IT WAS
 the eldest among them and some still-carried
  walked South
   rather than climb an Ocean of Mountains.

THEY SAW ALSO
 how more decided for the South
  than for the North
   at that greater parting
    in a very Dry Place.

THEY SPOKE
 FOR THE RIGHT
  TO SUCH DECISIONS.

THEN
 One rose
  to remind the People
   of something they had forgot.

"Who"
 -- he asked --

"Will carry with them
 the gathered seeds
  of a Whole People?"

AND ALL SAW HOW IT WAS
 That little enough had been saved
  for a Whole People
   to carry with them.

Even if no seed
 was eaten for sustenance . .

Even so, little enough
 was assured for Tomorrow.

"YOU SEE HOW IT IS"
-- some one said --

"How the Whole People
and this Promise of Tomorrow
may not be wisely parted,
one from another."

AND ALL SAW HOW IT WAS,
    And spoke for unified purpose,
        most speaking for the East,
    but some few
        speaking for the probability of South
            which Squash Blossom described.

AND
    THIS WAS THE WAY OF IT.

    Through much discussion
        no unified way was found . .

    Two in three
        describing an eastern path,

    One in three
        singing a southward song.

    YET ALL AGREED
        the seed family was not wisely divided.

THEN,
    When it became clear
        that no general agreement --
            either South or East --
                was reached . .

    Squash Blossom rose again,
        patiently looking into the growing silence
            around her,
        until the Circle of the People
            had one purpose only . .
                and that purpose was to hear her words.

"FOR A LONG TIME"
  -- she began --

"I HAVE UNDERSTOOD
  THAT THIS DAY
    WOULD RISE UP TO MEET US.

"Neither had I any wish
  to remain after this day
    in any proximate place.

"For this reason"
  -- she continued --

"I have set aside
  all the More Than Enough
    our rooted brothers gave us,
  set it aside
    in such a way as to assure survival
      over many, many Winters.

"NOW"
  -- she concluded --

"I SAY THIS.

"I say
  that when I rise
    and turn my footsteps South
  not one from among the stored seeds
    of the general People
      walks with me.

"RATHER
  those seeds walk with me
    that I have kept
      for just such purpose."

AND ALL REMEMBERED
 The many additional gardens
  planted here and there
   by this Growing Woman.

ALL SAW HOW IT WAS
 They thought she taught herself
  new ways of encouraging growth.

ALL SAW NOW
 HOW SHE TAUGHT HERSELF ALSO
  WISE THOUGHTS OF TOMORROW.

Squash Blossom's Children

NOW
   THIS WAS THE WAY OF IT.

TWO IN THREE OF THE PEOPLE
   CHOSE THE EASTWARD PATH . .

   Chose to carry the gathered seeds
     of a general People
       across a restless Ocean,
       past its dark storms,
       toward an edge of forest
         more protective -- perhaps --
           of their chosen circumstance.

AND ONE IN THREE
   CHOSE THE SOUTHWARD PATH . .

   Walked with Squash Blossom
     and her gathered seeds . .

   Walked with her growing wisdom,
     toward a circumstance -- perhaps --
       devoid
         of sudden dark and pounding storms . .

   Walked toward the assurance
     of a warmer, dryer way.

   And with them went,
     the People learned,
       even some from among the seed families
        thought lost.

FOR
   When Squash Blossom
     offered to share these small stores,
       the People answered her . .

   "Let the fruit of your wisdom
     walk with you
       as the fruit of our wisdom
        walks with us.

"Let us each
  benefit therefrom.

"Let us each
  learn from a changing circumstance."

AND SO IT WAS.

  Squash Blossom
    and those who walked with her
      turned their footsteps South . .

AND
  FROM THAT DAY TO THIS
    WE HAVE REMEMBERED
      THIS GROWING WOMAN
      AND HER CHILDREN.

OUR PEOPLE . .
  TURNED THEIR FOOTSTEPS EAST,
    MARKING OUT A DIFFERENT PATH.

AND . .
  AS EACH PATH
    IS MARKED WITH ITS SPECIAL WISDOM . .

  LET US BE WISE ENOUGH TO REMEMBER
    THAT OF ONE WAY AND THE OTHER,
      BOTH HAVE WISDOM.

Ocean Crossing

NOW FOR OUR PEOPLE,
  THIS WAS THE WAY OF IT.

  FOR EASTWARD
    washed a changing Ocean of Grass . .

    GRASS SO TALL
      the tallest man
        might easily disappear therein.

    GRASS SO TALL
      no vision at all
        beyond an outstretched hand
          might be obtained.

  Nor was it anyone's wish
    to follow a wandering stream path.

  Rather
    they chose a straight path East,
      greeting Dawn Woman each morning
        with a cry of recognition.

AND SO
  Vision was obtained in two ways.

FROM TIME TO TIME
  One lighter person
    ascended to some tall shoulders,
  So that one -- with the other --
    exceeded the reach of Grass.

  And at such times many called out,
    asking where was Bear,
      remembering in that way
        an ancient circumstance,
      remembering in that way
        how many and what variable circumstances
          may be survived.

AND THE OTHER WAY WAS THIS . .

When some high hill was approached
    at some time of day
        that grew rapidly dark . .

Then all the people together
    would begin a new spiral dance.

Pounding their feet against Earth,
    lowering in that way
        the reach of Grass . .

A triple row of the People
    followed by another -- and yet another --
        stomped out
            their general Will to See . .
        spiraled patiently, slowly,
            from bottom to top of that Hill
        so that no blade of grass of any height
            was left standing.

THEN,
    From the top of that pounded hill,
        the nature of East and West
            was ascertained
    and tomorrow's general direction
        carefully chosen.

AT LAST,
    Having eaten what that day offered,
        no future seed yet touched,
            all but a few lay down to sleep.

And these few carried torches . .
    that this small possibility of daylight
        might continue,
    that any from among our four-footed Brothers
        might be discouraged from joining us,
    that a Dark Ocean
        might not forget its general purpose
            and lose this People underfoot.

AND SO THEY CROSSED,
  THIS PURPOSEFUL PEOPLE . .

AND SO THEY CROSSED,
  DAY BY DAY . .

AND SO THEY CROSSED
  THIS GREAT AND GRASSY OCEAN . .

  Step by patient step,
    some from among them
      sleeping rarely and only in snatches.

AND
    Not among this People
      was spoken any word of rest
        or of ease or of Enough!

  For all understood
    their mutual purpose.

  All understood
    that the only Enough
      was shaded by forest trees.

  And only words
    of mutual encouragement
      sprung from any heart.

AND
    After some most high and difficult pounded hill,
      some one would say . .

    "There is some value
      in No Mountains at All . .

    "For who would hope
      to beat flat the grass
        of such mountains as all remember?"

  And the general laughter
    carried the People through another night
      and toward another day.

Some thought
    was yet given
        to Squash Blossom and her Children . .
so that a fortuitous stream was praised
        for its liquid bounty
and that dryer place chosen by one in three
        stood in dismal contrast
            to this present circumstance.

A WALK OF MANY DAYS
    Became a walk of changing moons,
        so that much was made of bright moonlight
            and the continuous walking it enabled.

Much also was made of a darkened moon,
    and the sleep that enabled as well . .

So that Moon and No Moon became a double gift,
    each useful in its own way.

How many Moons
    came and turned and left
        no one any longer counted --
            or spoke not of it --
    remembering how it was
        that Two Strong Brothers forgot to count
            the cost of the gift
                they sought for the People.

"We seek a gift
    for the children's children"
        -- they told one another,
            and to the youngest they said . .

"You may yet live
    to see a sheltered forest"
        -- bringing general laughter.

AND YET I TELL YOU NOW
  HOW IT WAS FOR THEM . .

  How purpose and sure direction
    unbroken by any convenient wandering . .

  How a willingness to walk
    when light was enough
      and a willingness to sleep
        when it was not . .

  How the quicker footed
    sought out water and sustenance . .

  While the slower footed,
    those encumbered by age,
      by the very young,
      by too much to carry,
        kept some pace
          with their faster Brothers . .

  How all met
    toward a pounded grass-flattened hill . .

  How all slept
    in the sure awareness of the watchers . .

  ALL OF THESE REALITIES
    MARKED THE DAYS . . AND NIGHTS
      OF A PURPOSEFUL, MOVING PEOPLE.

UNTIL AT LAST
  One Brother sitting on another
    for a double height
      sang out of a darkened horizon.

  All listened . .
    and heard no moving feet
      of a Dark Ocean.

  And all continued
    in their eastward purpose,
      each vision of horizon
        darker than before.

UNTIL AT LAST
   One of double height sang out
      how it was,
      how a darkened horizon
         rapidly became
            the individuality of trees.

AND A GREAT SHOUT WENT UP . .
   and many purposes
      followed by subsequent arrival
         were sung.

SO THAT THE WHOLE PEOPLE . .
   EACH AND ALL
      WITH A GLADDENED HEART
      KEPT SLOW PACE
         WITH ONE ANOTHER . .

AND
   WALKED AT LAST

   WALKED AS ONE . .

   Paced out the fulfillment
      of this most recent purpose,
         leaving footprints in the dust
            under many spreading trees . .

   Found a place at last
      at the edge of a Great Forest
      as great -- perhaps --
         as the Ocean just crossed --
      the other edge of which
         might yet be
            a Salt Ocean to the East.

LET US CELEBRATE
   THEIR PURPOSE

LET US HONOR
   THEIR WISDOM

LET US REMEMBER
   THEIR PATIENT BEATEN PATH . .

SO BE IT.

First People's Child

Many Paths to Learning

Many Paths To Learning

NOW
    I HAVE TOLD YOU HOW IT WAS
       FOR OUR PEOPLE . .

          Traced their path
             across that vast and other Island . .

          Threaded their way
             across rocks washed by Ocean . .

          Followed their many and various footsteps
          South,
             and East at last
                across another Ocean.

NOW
    HEAR HOW IT WAS
       IN THE FOREST.

FOR I TELL YOU NOW,
    Those who spoke of Many Trees beyond Grass
       held in their thoughts
          an accurate image of circumstance.

The forest here was indeed
    one composed of many trees.

So many, that some one pointed out . .

    "It cannot be so different to Eagle,
       this Ocean and the other.

    "We who do not fly
       saw that Great Grass Ocean
          from Mountains Beyond.

    "This Ocean of Trees
       may be seen only by the wingeds . .
          or by the very tall!"

And all laughed at this understanding,
    seeing it was so.

NOW
    Trees give a fortuitous circumstance.

    No dark and rolling Ocean here!
        Only from time to time
            a slight trickle along some widened stream,

        SO THAT THE PEOPLE SAW THAT THIS WAS GOOD.

    Nor did there grow here
        any of the spined plants
            that carry small fruit.

        AND THE PEOPLE SAW HOW THIS WAS GOOD ALSO.

AND YET
    THEY SAW ANOTHER THING.

    They saw how it was
        that the same trees
            that discouraged a Dark Ocean
            also discouraged any encouraged seed,
        so that it became a great preoccupation
            to find places -- here and there --
        too removed from the edge of the Grass Ocean
            to allow the full strength of the Dark Ocean,
        yet devoid enough of those same trees
            to allow the warmth and light of Sun.

HERE
    The People encouraged seeds toward Earth.

HERE
    THEY LEARNED
        YET ANOTHER NEW WAY.

                    xxxxx

NOW IT WAS
  DURING THIS TIME,

  DURING THESE NEW LEARNINGS,
    THAT THE PEOPLE
      CAME TO UNDERSTAND
        HOW IT WAS
          THAT ANCIENT SONGS
            HELD MUCH ACCURACY.

For -- from time to time --
  the People had heard of distant others,
    those who had crossed Walk by Waters
      before it disappeared under a growing Ocean,
        only to appear again.

These Ones, it was said,
  were Followers After,
    trailing the Great Herds
      for the plenty they imply.

These Ones also were said
  to have great skill and bravery beyond their size
    in trapping against some cliff
      the largest of all those Great Tusked Beings.

In that manner, it was also said,
  one of their number would leap down from cliff top,
    bringing a large rock in descending arc
      to crash unimpeded at base of skull.

And the Great Tusked One,
  busy engaging the many spear points
    which had driven him, driven her,
      against that cliff,
        felt the sudden, crushing blow,
          knelt down, and rolled at last
            into Silence.

NOW
  These tellings were well known
    and often heard.

  Well known also was direction of others
    gained by him who leapt from cliff.

FOR,
    As it was thought
        the most difficult, most dangerous,
           most beneficial of tasks among that People . .
    So was the completion thereof
        the beginning of a certain agreed direction.

    That is, Skull Crusher --
        it was he and he alone
           who often decided this and that
               among his People.

IT WAS NOT OUR THOUGHT EVER
  TO GIFT ANY ONE OF THE PEOPLE
    WITH SUCH WILLING COMPLIANCE
      WITH ONE SOLITARY PERCEPTION.

AND YET ANOTHER THING WAS SO . .

    Although such tales
        were well known among us . .
    Although we heard them
        from time to time from disparate others . .

    We have never been a People
        to believe or disbelieve anything at all
           merely because we prefer it.

AND SO . .
    Although we heard such tales . .

    Although such ones
        were usually called First People
           as they were first
               to come to this Great Island . .

    Even so,
        never had any of our People
           seen such ones.

IT WAS SAID
    They were difficult to see,
        being exceeding fearful of others.

But it seemed to us
    that such ones
        unafraid of the greatest
            from among the Great Herds,
                had little reason
                    to fear those only somewhat taller.

AND YET
    Someone pointed out
        that one Great Creature
            that a People may surround
        may indeed be less fearsome
            than a People double your height
                and numerous enough to surround you.

AND
    WE SAW
        HOW IT COULD BE SO.

We saw
    how a People become brave from necessity
        might find little necessity
            in friendship.

AND YET
    We thought of all our constant curiosity
        had enabled us to learn . .
    And had no desire to become brave
        in relation to Great Beings
            at such a cost.

NOW IT CONTINUED TO BE SO
    That -- as the People searched here and there
        for open places among many trees
            which might enable encouraged seeds --
So did they also search for this First People.

For some said
    they had left the Grass Ocean
        to disappear among trees.

And we could see how that might be --
    as the tall grass and the Dark Ocean
        were difficult enough for those
        with legs the length of ours.

But
    though we searched,
        none were found . .
    though from time to time
        remains of a small fire were found
    so that we began to conclude more accuracy
        in these ancient and recent Tellings.

AND THEN
    ANOTHER THING OCCURRED
        FOR WHICH WE WERE IN NO WAY PREPARED.

Walking between close standing trees one day,
    some of our People nearly stumbled
        across the folded remnants of a gathering.

And these folded remnants . .
    were a People,
        bent double in apparent pain,
        prostrate on the Earth.

None yet breathed
    so that we saw no way to assist them.

Some of these were still warm,
    so that we saw
        this great damage was indeed recent.

AND YET,
   None any longer drew breath,
      all had severed their Earth connection.

   In walking here and there,
      we saw how it was.

     These were a small People,
        barely able -- the tallest of them --
          to look over any shoulder
            from among our own People.
     And we thought again
        of the Great and Tusked . .
        and of the nature of bravery.

THEN SOMETHING ELSE OCCURRED
   THAT NONE
      FROM AMONG OUR OWN PEOPLE EXPECTED.

   IN THE MIDST
      OF ALL THAT DISAPPEARING LIFE,
        AN APPEARING LIFE WAS FOUND.

   For a sharp wail
      from a hungering small one
        marked his presence
        and caused all to witness
          how life sustains itself
          even in such circumstance.

FOR
   Although this entire People
      lay still against the Earth,
        here was one from among them
          unwilling to do so.

   And we carried him
      to one of our recent mothers
        so that he might be fed
         in the usual manner.

AND,
   Although there was much fussing and kicking
     by this small one
       at a clearly changeful circumstance . .

   Yet did he learn
     the eventual value of sustenance
       which fills one hunger.

   Yet, as he grew,
     it remained always clear
       that our People
         were never other than strange to him,
       even she who nourished his Earth self
        during those much-growing years.

NOW THIS WAS THE WAY OF IT.

THIS YOUNG ONE,
    Brought among us
        by a circumstance disastrous to this People,
            never learned
                in any of the ways
                    usual among our People.

AND YET HE LEARNED!

His speech was never the equal of ours,
    his words slurring and indistinct
So that we greatly wondered
    whether this were a condition
        peculiar to his People
           or specific to him.

Some
    found him unable to learn through speech,
While others
    remembered that ancient Ocean People
        who never seemed to speak at all
           and yet understood one another.

FROM TIME TO TIME
    This one or that
        would reach clear communication,
           one with the other.

Yet none
    found this condition sustainable.

Neither did anyone find a way to ascertain
    whether this difficulty was individual
        or specific to his People.

AND THROUGH ALL THIS,
    This growing Person grew more restive
        and increasingly chafed
           as if some one
               rubbed him with an irritating burr.

And this condition
    increased and increased again.

THEN AT LAST,
   When few any longer held hope
   of an easeful communication with This One,
   Some one noticed
      that all those things which he regularly carried
        were no longer in place.
   Neither was it possible to find him.
   Neither did he return
      for any subsequent prepared food.

AND ALL CAME TO UNDERSTAND
   They might never see that face --
      angrier than it was sad --
      undaunted by any apparent failure.

   FOR,
      If he did not understand in our way,
        still he found his own way to understanding,
        so that he taught himself these things.

AND WE SAW HOW IT WAS
   THAT THIS IS ALWAYS THE WAY
      WITH THOSE
        WHOSE LEARNING NATURE WAS OTHER
        THAN THE PEOPLE AROUND THEM.

AND
   There was much talk of learning
      and of patience
      and of the many paths Life offers.

   For -- as a clearing may be reached
      from many and different directions --
      so may any understanding at all
        similarly be reached.

AND FROM THAT DAY TO THIS
   Our People have taught themselves
      a great patience
      with various ways of learning . .

   So that no other young and learning face
      need slowly darken under a changing moon
      of inconsistent willingness
        to allow any new Pattern of Learning.

AND FROM THAT DAY TO THIS
Our People have sung this song . .

As there are many ways
to any clearing
As "from here"
may be many different Paths . .

Let us respect
the many ways of learning
Let us understand
that the same tree is many sided
the bark thereof
varying according to perspective.

As the Earth
undergoes many and varying changes
dependent only on location
As Mountain
is high from the Plain
and Plain low from above . .

Let us remember
that all is part of the whole
Our varying perceptions
limit or enable
as we choose.

LET US CHOOSE . .

TO ENABLE . .

SO BE IT.

We Call the River Beautiful

The Telling of Red Squirrel and Grey

The Telling of Grey Squirrel

The Telling of Red Squirrel

The Sun People

Meeting

Their Way

Their Song

Further Learnings

The Great Earth Snake

And We Leave Them

We Call The River Beautiful

NOW IT CAME TO BE
 That the People
  lived at the edge of a river
   they called O-Hi-Yo
  and they valued this river greatly.

FOR THIS REASON
 They had chosen
  as their new Center Place . .

 A bend in the river so great
  that the river itself nearly surrounded them,
   washing the shores
    from East to South to West.

 And also to the North
  was land so wet as to be called swamp . .

 So that, living here gave no confusion
  with disparate others --
   they becoming distracted
    with our settled ways.

AND
 This river-washed land
  was great enough
   so that the People
    could learn and grow and prosper.

BY THIS TIME
 We had grown great enough
  so that we had divided ourselves
   into three communities --
    equally spaced on the land --
  and Beans and Squash
   established here and there between us.

DURING THIS TIME
    It was our custom
        to invite the small four-footeds into snares.

    Larger four-footeds were generally sought --
        and also found --
            on the other side of wet earth,
                as few now remained in our Circle of Earth.

SO IT WAS
    That some from our People who were men
        left our Earth Circle from time to time
            seeking larger skins
                and the sustenance they contained.

AND
    Since this going and finding was a lengthy task
        filled with both difficulty and danger,
            we taught ourselves ways
                in which to respect this effort
                    by putting to good use
                        all that was found . .
        so that much more than sustenance was used,
            although this also was cut and dried
                against an improvident tomorrow.

    All other parts
        of each of our Four-footed Brothers
            were carefully considered and as carefully used,
        so that antler and hoof and claw
            was as useful to the People
                as any warm winter robe.

AND AT THIS TIME
    It was said . . and said again . .

    "For all we find a purpose --
        bone and sinew, hide and hair --
            as yet we find no use for either eye.

    "Who then can devise such purpose?"

AND IN THIS WAY
Did the People remind one another
of the careful use
respect for the four-footed --
and respect for the two-footed also --
will require.

AND IT WAS AT THIS TIME ALSO
That the People spoke to one another
of the great value of such things . .

Even as no seed was loosely scattered,
but kept for Tomorrow . .

Even so should none of our four-footed Brothers
needlessly offer up his life, her life,
so that our children might search
through an unwanted pile of flesh.

FOR THE PEOPLE
Remembered the great and solitary Tree Eaters,
so coveted by us and others
that they slowly disappeared.

These ones were as tall
as one man sitting on another's shoulders
and -- although we sought them for food --
showed no concern at our approach . .
so that it was our thought either
that they meant to offer themselves
as food
or that it was difficult
for them to understand
that those so much smaller than they
held any relevance
to their life path.

These ones
were particularly coveted by our People
as they were so large
that the Whole People
might eat for many days
from their plenty,
so that it had become our custom --
after seeds were encouraged toward Earth --
to seek out one such
to sustain a hungry People.

And we greatly preferred this
    to the much plunging off of cliff
        favored by nearby others.

AND YET
    EVEN THIS CAREFUL REGARD
    FOR EARTH'S PLENTY
        WAS NOT ENOUGH.

For these ones slowly disappeared,
    even as Great Bear
        had become more and more unusual
            in the deep, dark places of the Earth,
    even as Sharp Tusk was sought for
        farther and farther from our People.

SO THAT WE SAW HOW IT WAS
THAT TODAY'S PLENTY
    MAY BE TOMORROW'S LACK . .
        EVEN WHEN CARE WAS GIVEN
        TO THE POSSIBILITY.

SO WHEREAS
    Great Bear and Sharp Tusk
        were not missed nearby,
            the effort to find them when needed
                became great.

As for the Great Tree Eaters,
    those much like beaver
        save for size and resting nature of tail,
    as for these ones -- the time came
        when none at all were found.

Nor -- from that day to this --
    has any of our People
        found such a being.

AND FOR THIS REASON . .
 AND FOR MANY OTHERS . .

The People learned a careful way
 of assuring Tomorrow . .
  by studying the nature
   of other Peoples --
    their various Four-footed Brothers . .
   so as to assure the continuance
    of their nature
     as well as our own.

AND IN THIS MANNER
 DID THEY LEARN . .
  AND CAREFULLY REMEMBER . .

The season, the place,
 and the patterns necessary --
  not only to gather sustenance --
  but also to assure continuance
   for our Four-footed Brothers.

The Telling Of Red Squirrel And Grey

NOW DURING THESE DAYS
 The People
  became satisfied with their life pattern . .

 So much so
  that no change at all seemed appropriate to them,
   for both sustenance and continuance
    were assured in a way
     that brought no intrusion from others.

AND YET,
  THOSE WHO NOTICE SUCH THINGS
  SAW HOW IT WAS . .

 That many
  may find satisfaction in a continuous way,
 Whereas some few
  never will.

 And it is these
  who bring with them
   the possibilities of change
  that allow a wise People
   continuance past calamity.

AND SO IT WAS
 That these careful markers
  of a variable path
   through a changeless time
 Devised among themselves some wise way
  to use the surging energy
   of those who do not naturally follow
    a changeless path
   to build increasing possibilities
    for Tomorrow.

AND
 First, it seemed to them,
  that some additional purpose
   needed to be found
    in the learning
     of so many Ancient Songs.

FOR I TELL YOU NOW
   Much of a life was already consumed
     in the patient learning
      of so much gathered wisdom.

   It seemed to those responsible for such things
     that a changeless time gives little reason
      for so much patient remembering,
     even as a rapidly changing time
      leaves little energy for such things.

AND IT WAS THEIR PURPOSE
TO DEVISE A BRIDGE
   ACROSS EACH SUCH CIRCUMSTANCE.

   Even as the absolute commitment
     to responsible memory
      is asked of some, but not all,
       in any generation . .

   Even as this may provide some bridge
     across changeful circumstance . .

   Even so did they search out
     some bridge across a changeless time
      when little reason
       for the careful keeping of a variable memory
       may be apparent.

AND SO IT WAS AT THIS TIME
   That those responsible
     set themselves the task of devising a way
      to mark the memory path
       with something
        beyond mere recitation,
       something beyond
        a present changeless circumstance,
       something beyond
        this time and this place.

NOW AT THIS TIME
    The People
        still retained some seeds of this and that.

    And among the seeds
        were the cones
            of the tall, straight pines
        from which the People had built their Long Houses
            in their Sheltered Valley
                in the Sharp, Jagged Mountains
                    to the West.

    In this place,
        none such were found,
            and the People built smaller houses here
                than before.

SO IT WAS
    That it occurred to some
        that a double and a continuing purpose
            might be achieved in this way . .

    Let some from among the Learners of this Ancient Way
        choose a long path West,
        choose a path
            past forest,
            past a green and waving Ocean,
            past even the Dark Tide
                that washed its shores . .

    Let some such Learners
        choose a path
            toward the Sharp, Jagged Mountains to the West.

NOW
    LET THEM WALK THAT PATH
        full of awareness
            of what was,
        full of awareness
            of the great difficulty of a Grass Sea crossing,
        full of awareness
            of the danger of a Dark Tide washing,
        full of awareness
            of the nature of protection from that Tide
                offered by Jagged Mountains,
        aware also
            of the nature of pine so tall and straight
                as to enable a Great House to be built.

NOW
  IN THIS WAY, IT WAS THOUGHT,
      there would be
          much learning,
          much learning
              of the footstep path
                  through such a circumstance,
          much learning also
              of the accuracy -- or lack thereof --
                  of many Ancient Learnings.

  IN THIS WAY
      some purposeful learners
          might teach themselves
              the accuracy at least
                  of some of the Ancient Learnings.

  FOR IT WAS THE THOUGHT
  OF THOSE RESPONSIBLE FOR SUCH THINGS . .

      That one who spends much of any waking life
          in such patient learning
              might wisely be encouraged
                  toward the additional learning
                      a two-foot walk may provide.

AND
  IT WAS THEIR THOUGHT ALSO . .

      That those whose nature is not fully contained
          within a changeless circumstance
              might be encouraged down this path also,
          so that their variable energy
              need not disturb the patient,
                  continuous way of the People,
              nor need it be restricted by them.

AND
  WHEREAS IT WAS WELL UNDERSTOOD

      That some from among such long-walk people
          might never find the other half
              of the Circle Path leading back to the People,

      It was their thought
          that the benefit
              of both learning and appropriate use of energy
                  was greater than the possibility of loss.

AND SO IT WAS
    That those among the People
      responsible for such things
        devised a regular way
          of inviting Those Who Had Learned
            to understand that Learning
            in a different way,
            to follow a two-foot path
              along an already ancient
                yet still-preserved way.

NOR
    Was any encouraged to feel shame in any way
      if Here and Now
        was enough for them.

RATHER,
    These were also honored
      as those who assured an Ancient Way
        through present circumstance.

These Ones were honored
    for Keeping an Ancient Way
      as were any who chose the two-foot path
        honored for the showing of it.

AND
    With ceremony and with purpose,
    each was honored,
    each described by the Whole People
    as Ones Newly Responsible.

AND THEN
    Those who kept the fire of this Learning
    close to the People
      were honored for their patient way . .
    As those who chose to walk the path
    were honored for their dancing way.

NOW AS SUCH THINGS OFTEN ARE,
   FROM TIME TO TIME,
      THERE CAME TO BE
         MORE OF ONE THAN THE OTHER.

So that it became a task for present Keepers
   to encourage in such a way
      that some, yet not all, of the New Learners
      chose the two-foot path.

For during some times
   nearly all chose to go,
      leaving none
         to study the path of deer or bear.

AND
   IT WAS NOTED AT SUCH TIMES . .

That although some from among the People
   who learned and were also female
      might choose to go,
   these were few and not many . .
Yet many and not few
   of those who learned and were also male
      might so choose.

AND FROM TIME TO TIME,
   It was the staying
      and not the going of such young men
         that preoccupied the Keepers.

AND YET AT OTHER TIMES
   Things were such
      that few chose the two-foot path.

AND AT SUCH TIMES
   It became a great preoccupation of the Keepers
      to assure at least one going out --
         accompanied also by a return --
      during the span of any one usual life-change
         from the disability of youth
            to the disability of age,
         from New Eyes Wisdom
            to Walk the World Wisdom,
         from none or little hair
            to long white braids.

"Let no such span ensue
with none at all
returned from the Two-Foot Path"
-- they said to one another.

AND SO,
SEEING VALUE IN THIS,
SUCH WALKING
BECAME A SACRED PATH.

FOR
That which is necessary
to the well-being of the People
is truly Sacred.

AND
Enhancing Ancient Wisdom
with New Learning
is surely necessary to a People
who -- time and again --
have rescued their Way
from too rapid change.

FOR SURELY
I TELL YOU NOW . .
THE CHANGELESS . . WILL CHANGE.

LET US UNDERSTAND THIS WISDOM.

><><><

NOW, I HAVE TOLD YOU HOW IT WAS
How over many ensuing generations
those responsible for such things
devised and redevised
the learning of memory,
as well as ceremonies
appropriate to such learning.

NOW
They devised also
the possibility of a Sacred Way to Understanding
filled with such purpose
that it came to be known as a Sacred Journey --
or perhaps a Sacred Mission --
through which any Learner of Memory
might see
with those eyes given to him, given to her,
the accuracy
of at least some of that memory.

NOW HEAR HOW IT WAS
For two Learners from among the People
whose learning names
were Red Squirrel and Grey . .

Squirrel
for the quickness of each motion
and for the wisdom
of gathering today's bounty
for tomorrow's banquet,

Red and Grey
for the nature of their Vision.

NOW IT WAS AT THIS TIME
That none from among the People
had gone out from among them
on any Sacred Journey
-- and returned --
for so long that only the eldest among them
remembered the going out
and none among them a return.

AND THOSE RESPONSIBLE FOR SUCH THINGS
Began a long discussion
of too little change
and too long with little new learning . .

Until they began to discuss among them
　　the wisdom of choosing any new Learner at all
　　　　to be encouraged toward such a purpose.

FOR SURELY I TELL YOU NOW,
　　None such among them
　　　　spontaneously arose . .

So that those responsible for such things
　　began to wonder whether this purposefulness
　　　　marked by unceasing curiosity
　　　　　　might have disappeared
　　　　　　　　from among the People.

NOW THERE WERE AT THIS TIME
　　Two young men
　　　　who were so different and so similar
　　　　　　that they were given the Learning Names
　　　　　　　　of Red Squirrel and Grey . .

For one
　　in his constant search for wisdom
　　　　seized and cherished each new acorn.

And the other
　　in his constant search for newness
　　　　buried each acorn quickly,
　　　　　　so as to move on to the next.

AND THOSE RESPONSIBLE FOR SUCH THINGS
　　Began to wonder what might be enabled
　　　　by two such quick and different minds.

AND THEY SAW HOW IT WAS --
　　How Red Squirrel gathered and cherished
　　　　each and every wisdom Ancient Learning enabled,
　　　　　　distributing all
　　　　　　　　in an effective pattern in his mind . .

And how Grey Squirrel ran quickly
　　from one Learning to another,
　　　　not always deciding
　　　　　　which to bury and which to eat.

So that those responsible for such things
    began to say . .

"Look
    at what the Red Squirrel Way enables . .

"Look
    at the wise pattern of the forest
        his many buried acorns predict."

    -- and --

"Look
    at what the Grey Squirrel Way enables . .
        he carries so many acorns in his cheeks
            he has become a Moon Face . .
        his forest is uneven and improvident --
            too few acorns committed to Earth."

    -- and --

"Let us find a way to test him,
    to enable him to learn the difference
        between quick travel and a Wise Path."

SO IT WAS
    That those responsible for such things
        began increasing talk of Sacred Journeys
            and the many learnings enabled thereby.

NOW
    It was Grey Squirrel
        who heard them.

    His wandering nature
        brought him visions of more new learnings
            than even he could carry in his cheeks.

    And he began to ask
        when he might be allowed
            the further learnings
                necessary for such a Journey.

FOR
    Though all that may be required
      from here
         to the Sharp Jagged Mountains to the West
           were two feet and a willing heart --
    yet some further learning
      about the nature of the land between
        was requisite for success
    and the last of the pine cones
      brought back from such a Journey
        from the tall and straight pines
          that grow there
      would be given only to one
        who had earned permission.

And Grey Squirrel knew
    that without such permission,
    without ceremony,
    without the Sacred Pine Cone Pouch --
      his Sacred Journey would become --
        only a very long walk.

NOW
    With Red Squirrel
      it was not so.

He held in his heart
    no great wish to leave his People.

Neither did he greatly covet New Learnings
    for their newness only.

It was in his heart
    that a lifetime
      might easily be spent in true understanding
        of only that Wisdom already gathered.

AND SO,
    He sought no permission
    and no Sacred Pouch.

RATHER,
    He sought to continuously join
      the Circle of Understanding
        where also sat
          those responsible
            for the Memory of the People.

NOW
   Summers came and went --
      followed each time by Winter . .
   Until all were agreed
      that the Learning Names
         of Red Squirrel and Grey
           had been fulfilled.

All saw the time had come
     for the ceremony
        which marked the next change.

AND SO
   Those responsible for such things
      began to walk through each community crying . .

   "Come and see, come and see.

   "There are yet more
      who may be listened to.

   "Yet more whose singing voice
      may be trusted with Ancient Learnings.

   "Come and see, come and see."

AND SO
   The families of Red Squirrel and Grey --
      and some few others
        who also sought learning . .
   Prepared a Great Sharing of Earth's Plenty
      in celebration of those from among them
        whose purposeful nature carried them
          through long days and nights
            of patient listening,
         long years
           of learning to understand . .
        until at last
          many from among the People
            might find some value
              in listening to the listeners.

AND ALL THE PEOPLE
   Brought their respect
      to a Ceremony of Recognition.

All understood
    that marked here was recognition
        for those of continuing responsibility . .
    as it was they
        who enabled and predicted the learning
            of these new others.

Recognition also
    for New Eyes Learning,
    for these New Eyes
        would soon grow old in wisdom,
            bringing one understanding --
            and the other --
                together in one person.

Many among the People
    also understood
        that this ceremony
            marked a day of no little importance --
        one on which Red Squirrel and Grey at least
            would be offered
                the Sacred Pouch and a New Mission.

AND IT WAS SO.

FOR THOSE
    With the responsibility
        for keeping such a Sacred Pouch
            from one generation to another
                offered it now to Grey Squirrel
        because, they said,
            his quick mind sought a greater Earth Dance
                than could be contained within the curve
                    of one great river.

And it will not surprise you to learn
    that Grey Squirrel
        took up this Sacred Pouch with eager hands,
    promising to return it
        full of fresh pine cones
            from the Sharp Jagged Mountains to the West.

"And when I return"
--- he intoned ---

"Then all will surely learn the accuracy
of these valued Keepings."

NOW THOSE RESPONSIBLE FOR SUCH THINGS
Turned to Red Squirrel
and asked his thinking,
suggesting he might choose
to go with his Grey Squirrel Brother,
sharing his individual wisdom
and bringing greater assurance
to the homeward path.

YET
Red Squirrel resisted this suggestion.

"I have no doubt"
--- he said ---

"That my Grey Squirrel Brother
will return,
bringing with him
much new learning of the Peoples
between here and there.

"Neither have I any wish"
--- he went on ---

"To leave my People.

"For surely I see how it is
a life may be easily spent in understanding
what has been already gathered.

"Yet I have heard you, my Fathers,
as you have described how long it has been
since anyone at all
has gone out and returned
with any great new learning,"
--- he concluded ---

"AND SO IT IS
that I ask a Sacred Journey also.

"Let my Brother Grey Squirrel
    walk West to those Great Mountains.

"Let me
    walk West and also South.

"He and I both
    may find those Mountains.

"Let him return
    with new learnings of new Peoples.

"Let me return
    with New Learnings of an Old People.

"Let me look for
    -- and find --
        Squash Blossom's Children."

AND ALL SAW THE WISDOM IN THIS.
    For who might know
        what greater learnings had been found
            by the children
                of such a purposeful and learning Woman.

AND
    THOSE RESPONSIBLE FOR SUCH THINGS
    ANSWERED . .

"YOUR WISDOM IS GREATER THAN OURS MY SON.

    "Let it be so.

    "Let Grey Squirrel seek
        -- and also find --
            the Western Path.

    "Let Red Squirrel seek
        -- and also find --
            the children
                of that ancient Growing Woman,
                the one we call Squash Blossom."

AND IT WAS SO.
    Each Journey was prepared for
      and in early spring
        each left along a path
          shared to the Grass Ocean
          and separate thereafter.

NOW YOU WILL KNOW
    That if neither Red Squirrel nor Grey
      had returned,
        then this Telling would here end.

BUT I TELL YOU NOW
    We know two Tellings,
      divided from each other
        as their paths divided.

WE KNOW
    THE TELLING OF RED SQUIRREL.

WE KNOW
    THE TELLING OF GREY.

>∞∞<

The Telling Of Grey Squirrel

NOW IT WAS
   That two young and learning men
     left the People that spring.

These two
   found a regular path through forest
    and -- as their greatest learning
      was thought to lie on the other side
       of the Grass Ocean --
     neither made they any effort
      to learn of Peoples close by.

  RATHER,
    they paced the breadth of the forest
    as quickly as they may,
      providing necessary sustenance
     as they went
        from the forest itself.

THEN AT LAST . .
  As both knew and each expected,
   the edge of the forest was reached . .

AND WHEREAS
   the forest was often dense,
    so dense that to step sideways
     was also to disappear,
       this Green Ocean was even more so.

For between trunk and trunk
  lies some little space,
    enough often so that you and I
     may walk between.

Yet between grass and grass
  lies so little space
    that the hand must be stretched out
     to part that grass
       merely to provide a view
        past either shoulder.

AND SEEING IT WAS SO,
　　Even as the Ancient Songs spoke of,
　　　　one said to the other . .

　　"Here you and I part from one another,
　　　　my Brother . .

　　"For surely
　　　　one step beyond this place
　　　　　　predicts that I shall never see you again.

　　"For even if we search most diligently,
　　　　never will we find one another in this Ocean.

　　"We are drowned . .
　　　　in a lack of vision."

AND IT WAS SO.

　　FOR AT THIS TIME
　　　　Appropriate parting words were spoken . .

　　And one Brother
　　　　stepped into a Grass Ocean
　　　　　　facing West,

　　While the other
　　　　faced West and also South.

　　And of Red Squirrel
　　　　we will hear more later.

NOW
  This is what has been preserved
    of all that Grey Squirrel learned
      on his Journey West -- and East again.

FOR I TELL YOU NOW
  That he did, indeed,
    reach Sharp Jagged Mountains . .

Did, indeed,
  find pine as tall and straight
    as Ancient Songs remembered . .

Did, indeed,
  fill his Sacred Pouch
    with as many cones as it might carry
      so that some might be retained
        by the People
          Past many such Journeys
          followed by no return at all.

AND IN THIS
  THERE WAS LEARNING . .

  FOR
    Grey Squirrel saw how it was
      that Ancient Songs held such accuracy
        that his path was wisely guided by them.

AND YET IN THIS
  THERE WAS NO NEW LEARNING . .

  For the mountains were what they were --
    and the trees also --

  Grey Squirrel saw little of the Dark Tide,
    for he sought to avoid it . .

  AND YET
    HE SAW ENOUGH
      TO UNDERSTAND THE ACCURACY
      OF THE SONG

AS DID THOSE WHO WENT BEFORE HIM,
   He crossed this vast ocean
      from hilltop to hilltop,
         sometimes stamping down the grass
            to give some view,
            some assurance of direction,
            some awareness of the possibility
               of approaching mountains
      and at night also,
         did he often sleep under a flaring torch
            embedded securely in the ground,
              for this seemed to him also
                 more visible from afar
                   than a three-stick fire.

   As his crossing from East to West
      was of this nature,
         also was his travel
            through these Western Mountains solitary,
               as he sought his first purpose.

YET,
   now that his Sacred Pouch was full,
   now that first purpose had been attained,
   now he turned his thoughts
      to second purpose . .

AND THIS
   WAS THE LEARNING
   OF OTHER WAYS.

SO NOW
   Grey Squirrel began a patterned search
      for disparate others.

   It was his thought
      to find some People at this Edge of Mountain
         before losing himself once more
            in a Grass Ocean.

   It was his thought
      that such a People
         might show him a clear path toward the East,
            leading now from one People to another,
        so that the simple learning
         of What Was Described
            might be enhanced
               with some new understanding.

AND SO IT WAS.

    For Grey Squirrel
        found just such a People,
        sat at the edge of their community circle
            with each sharp cutting edge laid before him . .

    UNTIL AT LAST
        he was cautiously invited
            to join for awhile this community.

AND HE LEARNED THESE THINGS.

    He learned
        that this People
            was generally smaller than his own,
        so that his size worried them greatly.

    He learned the wisdom
        of stooping as he walked and sitting often.

    He learned the wisdom
        of respect for the concerns of others.

AND HE LEARNED THIS ALSO.

    He learned
     this People
        often carried their houses with them,
            moving from this place to that
                as the possibility of sustenance indicated.

    And these houses
        were rounded shelters of a different kind,
            consisting of the kinds of skins
                that might be rolled and carried
            and of long poles
                that lent support thereto . .

    So that, whereas the work
        of carrying such rolled skins and such long poles
            was in no way small --
                neither was it beyond possibility.

FOR
>as our People had done long ago,
>>skins were placed on poles
>>>and dragged over even land
>>as they were carried over rough . .

So that this People
>understood a kind of traveling community
>>that danced a regular pattern
>>>over the Earth.

AND
GREY SQUIRREL SAW HOW IT WAS

That those who live in relation to Dark Tides
>and the possibility of finding this and that
>>in some regular place
>>>would find such a traveling community
>>>>of infinite worth.

AND YET
>A People who encouraged seeds toward Earth
>>in some regular way
>>>would not.

For a falling branch
>requires a sturdier house to withstand it

And a People
>who have learned to live together as many
>>need a larger space in which to dwell.

AND SO
>*ONE WAY -- AND THE OTHER --*
>>*HAD VALUE.*

AND GREY SQUIRREL
>*UNDERSTOOD IT WAS SO.*

NOW
It became apparent to Grey Squirrel
that his standing presence
still gave discomfort
to this smaller People.

And so
he began to inquire about the way East,
finding these ones all too eager
to indicate a way
by which he might soon leave.

AND HE LEARNED
That to the East lived several Peoples
who kept some usual community
during this and that season
at some regular place . .
so that the seeking out of such a place
as the Earth warmed
or the snows fell
would likely find some resident People.

AND SO,
As the Earth warmed
for a new Seasons Dance . .
He set out for the great meeting
of two great rivers,
traveling for the first time
down some river bed,
surer now
of his ability to avoid any Dark Tide.

AND
Those who dwelt at Mountain's Edge
celebrated his departure
so that he wondered
whether they celebrated
his presence among them more
or his leaving of it.

AND
HE REMEMBERED THESE THINGS.

NOW
    He stepped out along a river,
        growing in size toward the East,
        seeking the Great Joining,
        seeking this other People.

AND IN FINDING THEM,
    HE FOUND ALSO HIS GREATEST LEARNING.

NOW
THE BEGINNING AND THE END OF IT
WAS THIS . .

Grey Squirrel found the rivers joining
and waited there to build some shelter,
as he had no wish
for a People whose usual way
found a place at this joining
to find instead a community of one.

AND SO
He sat by his three-stick fire
from time to time . .
And moved out also seeking sustenance
until his community
was joined by those he sought.

AND IT WAS ON SUCH A DAY . .
Returning from a short march East
that he was met by insistent others.

These ones sought his purpose here
and found in him
some answer to their questions.
For they sought also explanation
of the individual fires
clearly set in this location.

And when they learned of his purpose . .
how he had learned from near-mountain dwellers
of a brave and strong People
who came from time to time
to this rivers joining --
they allowed him courteous greeting.

AND HE SAW HOW IT WAS.
How the words brave and strong
brought softening to many faces . .
So that he came to understand
the value of respect.

AND HE SAW HOW IT WAS.
    How this was a taller People,
        some few of whom matched his own height . .
    So that he came to understand
        the value of similarity.

AND
    Although he was accepted as a guest,
        he was in no way accepted as one of them.

    NONETHELESS,
        as his presence caused them little concern,
            he thought to spend the stretch
                of one more Seasons Dance with them
                    learning to understand their way,
        so that this wisdom
            also might find its way into his Sacred Pouch
        and so that Earth warming again
            might be the time of his going out
                across what remained
                    of the Grass Ocean to the East.

AND IT WAS AT THIS TIME
    That he learned
        to understand the movements of the Dark Tide
        across this Ocean,
            even as we understand them today.

AND IT SEEMED TO HIM
    THAT MUCH HAD CHANGED.

For he learned
    not of a Dark Tide,
        but of great herds here and there.

And he saw
    that a Dark Ocean
        had been divided into many little seas.

And he wondered
    whether this change
        related to the much plunging off of cliffs
            that so concerned his distant relatives . .
    or whether this change
        related to possibilities
            he knew not of.

AND IT SEEMED TO HIM
THAT SO GREAT A CHANGE
MUST BE RELATED
TO MANY POSSIBILITIES,

BUT HE SAW HOW IT WAS
That the Grass Ocean
held less peril than before . .

And came to understand
that the safety of his westward crossing
had more to do with this great change
than with his own wisdom.

AND HE SAW HOW IT WAS
THAT THIS LEARNING
WAS ONE
THAT HIS OVERWEANING
AND TOO RAPID NATURE
HAD GREAT NEED OF.

AND
As he sat in such contemplations,
he was joined from time to time
by one or more of this People
who sought to learn from him as well.

And he was generous in his answers . .

UNTIL HE SAW HOW IT WAS
that his People,
with their encouraged seeds
and their long memory,
seemed in a different way
too tall for easeful comfort
for this People
with their moveable houses
tracing the patterns
of many Dark Seas.

AND SO
These things he spoke lightly of,
as if they held slight meaning.

AND THIS, TOO,
   WAS A GREAT LEARNING
      FOR A GREY SQUIRREL PERSON
         WHO CARRIED TOO MANY LEARNINGS
         IN HIS CHEEKS.

FOR
   Understanding the uncomfortable awe
      much of these learnings engendered in others,
         he came at last
            to digest each acorn . .

HOLDING IT BEFORE HIM
   So that he might understand its value
      measured against a People
         who remembered
            their grandfathers' grandfathers --
            and little else before . .

   Measured against a People
      who understood their own way well,
         but saw little value
            in other ways . .

MEASURED IN EACH SUCH MANNER
   HE UNDERSTOOD AT LAST
      THE TRUE VALUE
         OF THE ANCIENT SONGS
            OUR PEOPLE HAVE PRESERVED
            SINCE TIME BEFORE TIME.

"They are dried meat
   in a cold winter"
      -- he told himself.

"They are the wisdom
   to keep one Winter robe
      through a warming summer"
         -- he also said.

"They are water
   for a desert crossing,
      carried by a People
         from a rain-soaked forest.

"THEY ARE YESTERDAY'S WISDOM . .
PRESERVED
TOWARD A VARIABLE TOMORROW."

AND HE SAW HOW IT WAS

That his People
might be quick to understand
a Dark Tide changed to many smaller seas --
or the dark and previous tide
implicit in them . .

Whereas another People
might be slow to understand any such thing,
their wisdom gathered only
from their grandfather's grandfathers.

AS THIS WAS A LEARNING
FOR GREY SQUIRREL . .

LET IT ALSO BE A LEARNING
FOR US.

NOW I WOULD TELL YOU, IF IT WERE SO,
    That this was the end of Grey Squirrel's learning . .

    That he returned peacefully to our People
        with a calmness of Spirit
            gained from such contemplation.

YET I TELL YOU NOW
    IT WAS NOT SO.

    For Grey Squirrel, being as he was --
        tall and pleasing to look at and able --
            had not escaped the notice
                of those among this People who were women.

    Neither, be it said,
        had they entirely escaped his notice.

AND SO IT WAS
    That one among them
        who came to look at him with longing eyes --
            found that gaze returned.

    And -- as such things will be --
        these two found every apparent reason
            for close proximity,
                and many other reasons apparent only to them.

    Until a general tone of disapproval
        began to follow each around the community.

NOW THIS WAS THE WAY OF IT.
    Grey Squirrel,
        for all that he had learned,
            had learned little
                of the way of such things among this People,
        so that -- from that day to this --
            we hold no understanding of what ensued.

    Yet two of their young men
        invited Grey Squirrel on a search for the great birds
            that find that land most pleasing and --
                after a day of many findings --
        they returned to the community
            to be met by many angry men . .

So that it was at once apparent
    that something had transpired . .

And was soon apparent
    that his welcome here had evaporated
        like water drops scattered on rock
            warmed by a blazing sun.

And those who had invited him
    in a friendly way that very morning,
        turned now against him
            and all shook spears in his direction,
                leaving no doubt as to purpose.

And he saw the sad eyes
    of She Who Found So Many Reasons
    and understood the way of it.

He saw in his mind
    that he was not prepared for travel
        and began to ask their patience
            toward that purpose.

But each word from him
    brought greater anger,
        until some began to run toward him.

AND HE SAW HOW IT WAS
    That too many women had spoken for him
    and, therefore, too many men against.

And he saw
    how his quick smile and his ready gaze
        had won him
            both too many friends and too few.

And now
    those who might help him
        would not for the very urgings of the others.

AND HE SAW HOW IT WAS
    That leaving was the only solution.

He had brought with him from the mountains
    not one Sacred Pouch
        stuffed full of cones from the tall straight pines,
        but two.

One of these he carried always with him.
    The other he had left behind.

Diving now into his small house,
    he was deterred by many hands and turned aside.

He cast away all thoughts of the second pouch
    and turned to leave as quickly as he may.

And this leaving
    was encouraged by fast steps and loud shouts,
        angry gestures and occasional thumps,

UNTIL
    Grey Squirrel was running --
        running at such a tumultuous pace
            from such an angry People
                that he gave thought only
                    to the finding of his own feet.

All that day he ran --
    and on across the darkened grass --
        until at last
            he fell to Earth,
        little able to continue,
            shouts grown only distant.

And it was then
    he discovered his loss.

FOR
    His tightly bound Sacred Pouch
        had some how been cut --
            cut as a purposeful offense perhaps --
            but cut in such a way
                that little by little --
                    all day running . .

Each and every cone
    from the tall straight Jagged Mountain pines
        had found its way out of the Sacred Pouch,
        out and onto the nature of the Grass Sea land,
        out and away from the reach of any of the People,
        out and beyond any purposeful retrieval.

And a man --
    full of hope and joy
        and accomplishment that morning,
            greeted the next early light devoid of each.

Carrying with him now
    only that which our People
        have come time and again to understand.

Whatever the circumstance . .

Whatever the event . .

When you stand and walk
    you take one thing --
        and one thing only -- with you.

You carry with you always and each day,
    every time you stand,
        all . . that you have learned.

AND GREY SQUIRREL STOOD NOW . .

CARRYING WITH HIM ALL OLD LEARNING . .

CARRYING WITH HIM MUCH NEW LEARNING . .

    STOOD
    AND TURNED HIS FOOTSTEPS HOME.

The Telling Of Red Squirrel

NOW
  I HAVE TOLD YOU HOW IT WAS . .

  How Red Squirrel and Grey
    began their Journeys together,
      separating their path one from the other
        at the Edge of the Great Grass Sea.

  I HAVE TOLD YOU ALSO
    How it was for Grey Squirrel.

  HEAR NOW
    HOW IT WAS FOR RED.

FOR
  Although Grey Squirrel and the Dark Tide
    never met one another,
      the southern path of Red Squirrel
        rapidly darkened.

  This One
    came on such multitudinous numbers
      of great and somewhat shaggy four-leggeds
        that his path changed and changed again . .
    until he began to lose his sense
      of how far South was South
        and how far West was West.

NOW
  Red Squirrel -- although a forest person --
    had spent some time
      in learning to know star patterns.

AND HE SAW HOW IT WAS
  These patterns
    changed in predictable ways
      from East to West
    and in unpredictable ways
      from North to South.

And he drew for himself
   many times on Earth
      and sometimes on the skin of this or that
         the generality of these changing patterns,
   so that he might surely recognize
      when North was far enough on the return.

AND HE FOUND ALSO
   That traveling at night was easier
      as the Dark Tide moved little at such times . .

So that the patterns of his days and nights
   reversed themselves for awhile.

It was his thought
   to trace a straight line
      from North and also East
         to South and also West.

Yet circumstance made no allowance
   for this possibility.

AND SO
   His footsteps traced a wandering way
      between pools in the Dark Tide,
         so that star patterns alone
            gave him any sense of the relation
               between here and there . .

AND
   HE CAME TO VALUE THEM GREATLY.

IT HAD BEEN HIS THOUGHT ALSO
   to trace a path
      to the Sharp Jagged Mountains
         South of Grey Squirrel's purpose,
         and yet North of the Great Dryness
         Old Songs spoke of.

SO IT WAS
   That when all before him stretched a land
      of little grass and much dryness --
         dotted here and there
            by no dark pools at all
               from that general tide . .

He turned his steps
   along the edge of almost-grass,
     following that path generally West
   until the mountains he addressed
     seemed sharp enough and jagged enough
      to parallel at least
        the ancient description.

       • • •

AND NOW
  BEGAN A PATIENT SEARCH.

For whereas Grey Squirrel's path
   required only
     any finding at all of such mountains,
     any finding at all of appropriate pines,
     and any finding at all of People there . .

Red Squirrel sought one thing
   and one thing only.

Where in this vast land
   of great dryness and occasional rivers,

Where in this nearly endless stretch
   of Where-to-Walk,

Where dwelt Squash Blossom's Children?

AND SO IT WAS
  That many Moon-Turnings
   passed before his eyes.

Here and there he found a People,
   and learned a little of them.

Here it was easier --
   and also more difficult --
     to find disparate others,
   as the great dryness predicted few,
     yet also predicted any settled place
       would be edged by some nearby stream.

AND SO
   Red Squirrel traced a patient path
      up and down each water,
         gaining some understanding
            of this land and of its scattered Peoples.

HE SAW HOW IT WAS
   That many chose sharply higher ground
      and a long walk to river.

AND HE WONDERED AT THIS.

Squash Blossom had said --

   "Away from the Dark Tide."

And yet
   no such tide at all washed this place.

AND HE WONDERED ALSO
   Whether what was now dry
      had earlier been less so,
         allowing some Dark Tide washing.

AND HE SAW
   THIS MIGHT HAVE BEEN.

YET
   Many other possible causes struck his mind.

Had not his own People chosen a place
   washed on three sides by river
      and on the fourth by standing water?
Some easeful separation from disparate others
   being their thought.

Perhaps these ones,
   lacking broad rivers,
      found some easeful separation
         in height.

AND YET,
   Where were those
      from whom they sought separation?

Each People seemed so distant from any other
   that no additional distance which is height
      seemed relevant.

AND SO
  Red Squirrel found many questions
    and few answers.

  He found Peoples also
    who called Squash Blossom sacred . .

  Yet he was unable to determine
    whether this held any previous relevance
      to Growing Woman,
    or whether this merely honored the nature
      of the plants they grew.

FOR THIS WAS HIS FIRST GREAT LEARNING . .

  That whereas his own People
    were the only ones
      to encourage seeds toward Earth . .

  All others
    studying the ready bounty of Earth . .

  Each of these living-high People
    encouraged seeds!

  They grew
    not only beans -- which he knew --
    and squash -- which he knew . .

  But grew also
    a tall-standing grass
      which yielded great swathed heads
        containing many large seeds.

  AND THESE HEADS
    THEY VALUED GREATLY,
      speaking of them in respectful tones,
      showing even greater respect
        than shown to either beans or squash.

  AND IT WAS BY THIS
    That Red Squirrel concluded
      that this tall-standing grass
        was a recent learning.

• • •

NOW
 Red Squirrel
  passed three Season Circles in this land,
   one at each of three high-living places . .

 And it was the third
  which caused him to think of Growing Woman.

FOR
 He had been encouraged toward this place
  by the sound of his own language,
   which some said
    held similar patterns to this third People.

 And when he heard them,
  he saw how it was this might be so,
   for their sounds held for his ear
    much similarity.

AND THIS PEOPLE
 Described themselves as different
  from all others there . .
 Held Squash Blossom
  as an even more sacred reality,
   and gave other signs of kinship.

AND SO IT WAS
 That Red Squirrel
  spoke to them,
  called them Close Brothers,
  and said he would sing for them
   the Ancient Song of Growing Woman.

AND
 Although they saw in this
  some similarity . .

 Although they recognized
  all similar spoken patterns . .

 Although they granted
  many other similarities . .

 Yet were they greatly offended at his words
  which turned Squash Blossom
   from a Sacred Being
    into a Walk the Earth person.

AND
   ALTHOUGH RED SQUIRREL EXPLAINED
     HOW IT WAS

That among his People
   That One was declared Sacred
     who became
       through some word or deed or general being
     essential
       to the well-being of the People . .

Still
   this People
     never lost their sense of offense.

AND
   at the end of the Season Circle,
     as Earth warmed once more,
       invited him to return to his own home.

AND SO IT WAS
   That though in his own mind
     Red Squirrel thought he had found
     Squash Blossom's Children . .

       THEY SAID
       IT WAS NOT SO.

NOW
   I HAVE TOLD YOU
      OF THE TALL-GROWING GRASS.

This possibility Red Squirrel
   learned to understand,
      brought with him
         many seeds,
      brought with him
         the calling name Mah-Ees,
      brought with him
         the ways of gathering and drying
           and wet and dry cooking.

YET THESE THINGS
   RED SQUIRREL ALSO LEARNED . .

That these Peoples
   generally spoke of wondrous others
      who had come down from northern mountains
         bringing gifts -- sometimes --
         asking food -- sometimes.

And these ones
   were not like other two-leggeds,
      though their legs were no more than two.

INSTEAD
   They had elaborate and brilliant heads and faces,
      so startling to each living-high People
         that they made images of them
           to remember,
         and celebrated their arrival --
           whether they came or no --
              with ceremony and with respect . .

So that these visits
   came to take a Center Place
      in the life of these Peoples.

And though Red Squirrel
   saw many such ceremonies . .

While he was there
   no strange people came,
      so that it was only the representation of them
         he was able to recall.

AND YET
  He showed us many and beautiful images,
    which he fashioned according to his memory,
      upon his return to us.

AND WE WONDERED GREATLY
AT SUCH BEINGS.

For never
  in the long reach
    of any Ancient Song
      was any such contained.

And we began to wonder
  whether these amazing beings . .
    had also been brought by Black Bird.

AND
  IT WAS GREATLY DISCUSSED
    AMONG US.

NOW
You will already understand . .

You who have grown next to the People . .

What great gifts returned to us
with Red Squirrel and Grey.

For among Red Squirrel's many treasures
were the colored seeds of corn.

AND
THE PEOPLE DID NOT HESITATE
TO ACCEPT
THIS THIRD SISTER.

AND FROM THAT DAY TO THIS,
The tall and stately form
of our Third Sister
marks the regular path
of every growing place.

For it was from this distant People . .
perhaps from the very nature
of Corn Herself
that we learned the pattern
of regularity
which marks our fields today.

For Squash and Beans
trace their variable and graceful patterns
around the stateliness of Corn . .

OUR THREE SACRED SISTERS HAVE . .
FROM THAT DAY TO THIS . .
BROUGHT JOY AND ABUNDANCE
TO THE PEOPLE,
HEALTH AND WELL-BEING,
AN ORDERED WAY OF DAILY LIFE.

AND THESE ALSO . .
ARE GREAT GIFTS INDEED.

NOW YOU MAY WONDER
  HOW IT WAS
    WHEN GREY SQUIRREL RETURNED . .

  HOW IT WAS
    WHEN RED SQUIRREL RETURNED . .

AND THIS WAS THE WAY OF IT.

  Each who rejoined his People
    was welcomed
    and listened to with patient ears.

  Grey Squirrel,
    full of his own lack
      in returning no cones at all from any pine,
        expected some harsh words . .
    yet none came.

  More than three Season Circles had passed
    before his face was seen again.

  Yet more than five passed
    before Red Squirrel also joined them,
      was welcomed
      and listened to with patient ears.

AND NOT UNTIL THEN
  WAS ANY JUDGEMENT MADE . .

  For those who had earned a seat
    at the Circle of Singers of Ancient Songs
      were loathe to evaluate either
        before evaluating both.

NOW
  They sat together for many days,
    now and again inviting Red Squirrel or Grey
      to sing once more
        some part of his Learning Song.

AND FINALLY
  This wise Circle of Men, Circle of Women,
    reached agreement,
    pronounced its findings,
    and called for a general celebration.

AND
    THIS WAS THE NATURE OF IT.

That
    before the Sharing of Earth's Bounty,
    before any further Telling was sung or danced,
    before any other celebration,
        both young men stood to accept judgement
           from those from whom they learned.

And one by one
    they intoned this judgement.

       • • •

"YOU SEE HOW IT IS . .

    "How both young men
        have earned a different name . .

    "How Grey Squirrel
        might now be called Woman Finder"

And after the general laughter --

    "How also Red Squirrel might now be called
        Offends Others With His Learning."

And this brought a sorrowful sound.

"YET I TELL YOU NOW
    That sometimes wisdom only comes
        after great foolishness.

    "And those of us
        who dare to walk a foolish path
           may yet both learn and show a wiser way.

"SO IT IS
    That Grey Squirrel
        returns to us with a Sacred Pouch
           full of none at all
               of the great straight pinetree cones.

"Yet that same Sacred Pouch
is full to the brim
with many Learnings.

"Our Brother has shown us a wiser way,
one full of awareness
of the value of our Ancient Songs . .
one full of awareness
of the value of sensitivity to others.

"Turn a listening ear,
My Brothers, My Sisters . .

"Turn a listening ear
to each new People.

"AND REMEMBER TO SEE THEIR FACE,
BEFORE YOU SEE YOUR OWN.

"This Younger Brother of ours
has learned this.
We have heard it in his words.

"AND THEREFORE
We give him a new name.
Not Woman Finder,
but Wisdom Finder we call him.

"FOR SURELY
Though he sought only
to prove his own worth,
and that of the Ancient Songs . .

"He has found instead
the Wisdom of Other Peoples,
and a wiser way toward learning."

AND WITH THAT
Grey Squirrel, Wisdom Finder,
was given many gifts --
and some responsibility as well
for the learnings
of those
who go out to speak for the People.

"NOW
    Our Younger Brother Red Squirrel
       returns with many gifts.

"He brings us
    the Tellings of disparate Peoples . .
      and we wonder much
        at their understanding.

"He brings us a greater gift.

"FOR SURELY
    This One is Woman Finder.

"He has found our Third Sister,
    and brought her to us
      to join the Circle of Beans and Squash.

"These Three we find Sacred,
    and understand great value
      in the living with us.

"LET US LEARN
    FROM OUR THREE SISTERS.

"LET US ASSURE THEM
    AN EASEFUL PLACE,
    AN HONORED PLACE AMONG US.

"LET US REMEMBER
    THAT THEIR WAY AND OUR WAY INTERTWINE,
    BRINGING BOUNTY TO BOTH.

"LET US MAKE FOR OURSELVES
    A NEW TASK,
    A GROWING WOMAN TASK,
      AND STUDY THE WAYS OF EACH,
        SO THAT WE MAY LIVE TOGETHER
        IN HARMONY.

"NOW
    YOUNGER BROTHER,
    TRUE WOMAN FINDER,
      WE GIVE YOU
        THE NAME OF MANY GIFTS."

AND
    As he gave them
      many gifts of learning,

SO NOW
    They gave him
      many gifts in return
      and responsibility also
        for the learning
          of those who go out
            to speak for the People.

AND
    FROM THAT DAY TO THIS,

    OUR PEOPLE
      HAVE ALWAYS REQUIRED
        OF THOSE WHO GO OUT TO SPEAK FOR US . .

      GREAT UNDERSTANDING

      AND LISTENING EARS . .

      SO BE IT.

                ×◇◇◇×

The Sun People

NOW
   The People were content in this place.

   No reason for any other choice
      occurred to them.

   This bend of River
      marked the edges of a circle
         within which the People grew and flourished.

   The gifts of Corn and Beans and Squash
      brought nourishment to many
         and assured continuance down many generations.

FOR I TELL YOU NOW,
   THE VALUE OF OUR SISTER, CORN,
      WAS GREAT, INDEED . .

   And the health and endurance of the People
      grew accordingly
         so that longer lives
            were noticed over time
         and the beginning of life
            was also improved,
         so that this brought great joy to the People
            as they noticed these changes.

   More Life
      looked out of the faces
         of both the very old and the very young.

   AND ALL THE PEOPLE
   SAW THAT THIS WAS GOOD.

NOW DURING THESE DAYS
   Those who concern themselves with such things
      saw that increasing health
         which smiles out from dancing eyes
      is wisely balanced with increasing health also
         of those things that continue
            past the existence
               of anyone from among the People.

AND SO IT WAS
    That they turned their attention
        to the nature and quality
            of that which might be learned . .

    So that enhancement of the Self
        that rises and walks from here to there
            might be balanced by enhancement
                of the Self that sits within.

    The nature of this enhancement
        was two-fold.

FIRST,

ALL
    That had been learned
        by a purposeful People
            was examined and honed again and again . .

    So that new and learning others
        might be greeted by many possibilities.

    It was in the mind of those considering such things
        to prepare a way to design viable paths
            for any feet at all . .
                those even of Fly Like Eagle,
                    those Never-Walk feet --
                those even of First People's Child,
                he who seldom speaks.

AND SO IT WAS
    That this wise Council
        began the work that must precede
            all efforts toward viable learning.

    First it is necessary, they saw,
        to understand the nature of the Learner.

AND SO IT WAS
    That they designed a way of enabling learning
        which listened more often
            than it spoke.

FOR THEY HAD COME TO UNDERSTAND
A GREAT TRUTH ..

To enable learning
  one must first apprehend
    the nature of the Learner.

AND THEY CAME TO UNDERSTAND
ANOTHER GREAT TRUTH ..

A path toward learning
  which enables any two feet at all
    to reach some destination
      must be designed for that pair of feet.

AND THEY CAME TO UNDERSTAND
ANOTHER GREAT TRUTH ..

The one most able to design such a path
  was the Learner himself,
  the Learner herself.

SO THAT THIS WISE COUNCIL,
  Understanding such things,
    designed a way
      to enable the learning of learning
        which our feet have followed
          from that day to this ..

Understanding always
  that, as we learn, we too
    join that wise Council,
    sit with the Old Ones,
    enable great understanding
      with our New Eyes,
    and bend the learning path once more
      in an even wiser direction.

FOR IF WE ONLY LISTEN
  TO ANCIENT WISDOM,
    FROM WHAT SOURCE
      WILL THE NEW LEARNING COME?

SECOND,

AS THE PEOPLE
   Had learned
      to listen for other possibilities . .
         for that which speaks without speaking,
         for that which sees beyond . .

   So wisdom's path
      showed them the value of designing
         a possible path toward such learning
            for those whose nature and curiosity
               carried them in this direction.

NOW IT WAS THOUGHT AT THAT TIME
   That not all the People
      were either naturally skilled in this way
         or yet found any interest in such learning,
   much as some
      become one with the nature of drumming
         and others do not.

AND IT WAS DECIDED AT THAT TIME
   That, as with any other skill,
      all are wisely invited down that path . .

   Yet none
      wisely encouraged past their own interest.

SO THAT, AT THAT TIME,
   A SEPARATE LEARNING PATH WAS CRAFTED . .

   AND FROM THAT DAY TO THIS,
      all are invited down the Strong Spirit Path . .

   AND YET
      none are encouraged
         past the edges of their own purpose.

AS THIS IS A PARTICULAR LEARNING,
  SO IT HAS A PARTICULAR DESIGN . .

AS SOME ELEMENTS
  ARE WOVEN THROUGH THESE ANCIENT SONGS,
    SO OTHERS ARE NOT . .

AND YET
  The path is open
    to those whose skill and interest
      carries them in that direction . .

  Even as every other path is open
    to each and all of the People.

FOR WE ARE A PEOPLE
  WHO LEARN -- AND LEARN AGAIN --
    TO LIVE TOGETHER AS ONE . .

  And that which divides us from one another
    must turn and join the Circle once more . .

  Even as the Learning Circles
    of North, of East, of South, of West,
      turn and rejoin the Circle of Community.

AS WE UNDERSTAND SUCH THINGS,

AS WE SHOW OURSELVES THIS WISDOM . .

  SO LET US SEE IN EVERY CIRCUMSTANCE
  IN ANY PATH AT ALL
    THE POSSIBILITY OF A RETURNING CIRCLE.

    SO BE IT.

NOW DURING THIS TIME,
   This Long Learning time,
      the People met two others
         they had not known before.

The natures of these meetings
    were different,
    and yet the same . .

FOR
    though the nature of these meetings --
    these brief joinings of two Peoples --
      were different in every other way,
        they were the same in this . .

EACH PEOPLE,
EACH DIFFERENT OTHERS,
   WERE OF A NATURE
     NEVER BEFORE
       APPREHENDED BY OUR PEOPLE . .

So that we came to rapidly understand
    the value of willing apprehension
      of That Which Is . .

For the mind
    that turns away from circumstance
      merely because it is unfamiliar . .
That mind
    truly ceases to learn.

AND SO I WILL TELL YOU NOW,
   FIRST OF ONE PEOPLE,
     AND THEN OF THE OTHER.

NOW THIS WAS THE WAY OF IT.
  Those who sat together
    to design the Learning Path
      of those of Strong Spirit
        sought also their own learning.

AND AT THIS TIME
  They sought to understand
    whether down this path also
      the Ancient Learning
        showed us any possibility . .

FOR THE ANCIENT LEARNING
    TELLS US
      THAT WHAT MAY BE DIFFICULT FOR ONE
        MAY BE EASILY ACCOMPLISHED BY MANY.

NOW IT WAS
  That they sought to understand
    whether the joining together
      of many Sees Beyond
        enhanced either focus or distance.

  And they sought also to understand
    whether the nature of the Ocean People --
    they who spoke without speaking --
      might also be enhanced by joining together.

AND SO IT WAS
  That many things came to be understood.
    and that these things also
      are part of a different Telling,
  And yet
    the meeting of Two Peoples is not.

FOR IF THERE IS WISDOM
  IN LEARNING,
    AND WE SAY THERE IS . .

PERHAPS THERE IS WISDOM
  IN REMEMBERING
    TO TURN HOME AGAIN AND AGAIN . .

So that the threads of connection
need not be stretched too far,
So that the nature of the land between
may be learned and understood.

FOR THIS WAS THE WAY OF IT . .

As this wise Council sat together,
joining their thoughts,
joining their will to learn,
They asked a great question . .

"DOES ANYONE AT ALL
EXPLORE WITH THEIR MINDS
THE NATURE
OF THE LAND BETWEEN HERE AND THERE?"

. . .

NOW
Much was learned during this time . .

AND YET
Nothing at all
that might be considered a response
was apprehended.

Of patient learning
there was much . .

AND YET
nothing was found
of an echoing resonance --
no implication
of any other pattern of thought.

NOW
As a child of the People
you will understand
how such things may be --
you will understand also
how such things may be exceeded
and New Learning
encountered all too quickly,
for a slow approach
always enables broader understanding.

AND YET ON THAT DAY
  No slow approach was possible . .

For that Council
    stumbled all too quickly
      onto sudden perception.

For the question was asked --

  "Do any here
    also explore
      the nature of the land between?"

AND AN ANSWER CAME.

No pale image of possible thought was here.

No echo of a distant perception.

AND YET DISTANT INDEED IT WAS . .

FOR
    beyond and beyond
      had been the nature of this exploration . .
    beyond this double circle of Earth and Ocean,
    beyond Earth's Moon Sister
      reflecting the light of Sun,
    beyond even the brilliance of Sun --
      that giver of regular light to those of us
        who dance a spinning Earth . .

  BEYOND AND BEYOND.

AND
    The nature of this response
      was dim in no way,
      tentative in no way either.

  The nature of this reponse
    was like a loud and strident voice
      in a quiet meeting.

NOT ONE
    AMONG THIS WISE COUNCIL
    FAILED TO HEAR IT.

NOT ONE
FAILED TO UNDERSTAND
ITS IMPLICATION.

For this answer
sought no interim measures --
no slow and patient exploration
of the land between.

THE ANSWER WAS THIS AND THIS ALONE --

"WE ARE COMING!"

AND YET
Who was coming,
by what means,
and with what purpose --
none of this could be learned.

Neither could any among the People
reassure themselves of the accuracy
of this perception in the usual way.

FOR
If they rose
to walk toward this possibility . .

If they chose in that way
to go and see . .

Who among them
could describe the two-foot Path?

AND SO
This Wise Council
sat to consider all possibilities --
counseled also with others in the community . .

Until it was decided
too little was known
of this too eager People.

No invitation at all
   had been implied . .

AND YET
   An invitation
     had quickly been accepted,
       and none of the nature of it
        was known or understood . .

So that all were agreed
   that so eager a People
     should be dissuaded from any such plan
       until more understanding was gained.

AND SO IT WAS
   That this Council
     sat once more,
     sat and joined mind and mind
     until all
       thought in the same direction,
     and the nature of their thought
     was this --

"WHOEVER YOU ARE,
   DO NOT COME . .

"Give us time
   to learn to understand one another.

"Give us time
   to learn to understand ourselves."

AND
   Although no answer was heard,
     neither was any greater proximity implied . .

So that after many days of such concentration
   it was decided
     to turn our thoughts elsewhere.

AND FROM THAT DAY TO THIS,
Those who learn such things
have been slow to join together
with too distant a focus,
the results of which
can scarcely be determined.

SO THAT THIS
BECAME A GREAT LEARNING ALSO . .

TOO GREAT A SUCCESS
MAY DISCOURAGE FURTHER EFFORT
AS EASILY
AS NO SUCCESS AT ALL

Meeting

FOR A LONG TIME THEREAFTER
   The People
      were content with their Way.

   Their focus was self-circumscribed
      and kept closer
         to the daily nature of their lives . .

   So that something was learned
      of those beyond the River Bend,
         but little of those at greater distance.

SO IT WAS
   That the nature of the next encounter
      was greatly surprising to the People . .

   Amazed as they were
      at the differing appearance
         of this New People . .

   Relief was also felt
      that they were so similar.

FOR
   THIS PEOPLE
      stood and walked in the ordinary manner,
      traveled the River on curving platforms
         as many do,
      carried spears
         that were recognizable as such.

   Having traveled in many directions
      and brought home the learnings,
         none were surprised
            that these ones
               dressed differently than we . .
               wore their hair in a different manner.

   One thing and one thing only
      was difficult to understand . .

Each of these ones
　　wore a disc of some shape or other
　　　　hung about his neck
　　　　　　which shone from time to time
　　　　　　like the sun itself . .

So that some from among our People
　　said --

"Look,
　　they carry the sun about their necks!"

AND FROM THIS
Comes the name we have given them . .

FOR EVER SINCE
　　WE HAVE CALLED THEM
　　THE SUN PEOPLE.

AND YET
　　It was understood
　　　　as quickly as it was said
　　　　　　that no sun at all hung about any neck . .
　　　　for the nature of sun is heat so great
　　　　　　that any close approach
　　　　　　　　must lead to quick disaster,
　　　　and so the sometimes nature
　　　　　　of this sporadic brilliance was considered.

AND IT WAS DECIDED
　　That for some reason
　　　　that we not yet understood . .

These shaped discs
　　caught and held the sun from time to time --
　　　　much as Moon in her steadier and gentler way
　　　　　　reflects the nature of Sun to us.

· · ·

NOW FOR THIS PEOPLE
   We held amazement of our own,
      for they walked our tended fields
         commenting much.

None seemed surprised
   at the nature of encouraged seeds,
      but at their presence in this place.

The growing of replenished seeds itself
   seemed familiar to them.

AND WE LEARNED
   THAT THIS WAS SO.

FOR
     as they came again and again --
     as we learned to talk with them --

     THIS WAS THE WAY OF IT.

In that place
   they had found none at all
     who encouraged seeds toward Earth
   and were greatly amazed to find any at all
   who did so.

They were further amazed
   to find we also kept corn --
     which was their own
       principal source of nourishment.

NOW
   There were among them -- they said --
     many whose principle concern
      was the building of things,
   and these ones needed help just now,
     as they began a major task
      of many years duration.

They needed help also
   in the growing of corn --
     for those who build must also eat.

AND SO
    This was their offer to us.

    That we come and dwell among them,
        growing their corn,
        carrying this and that for the builders . .

    And that in exchange for this
        they would see we had plenty to eat
            and much to wear.

NOW
    We petitioned separate council,
        as it was difficult for many
            to restrain laughter --
        therefore the value of mutual respect
            required some distance.

    "These Ones"
        -- some one said --

    "Offer
        sustenance to the well-fed,
        clothes to the well-clothed,
        protection to those
            who know how to protect themselves.

    "For our place here yields all we need
        and of its nature
            is well filled by our People,
                leaving room for few others."

    "And yet
        something else is here"
            -- some one also said.

    "Here
        there is room for learning.

    "Learning at least
        about a new People,
        a new building way
            that requires many years,
        and the nature of discs
            that catch Sun.

    "Perhaps also somewhat may be learned
        about the growing of our sister, Corn."

AND SO
　AFTER MUCH DISCUSSION,
　　THIS WAS THE NATURE OF OUR DECISION . .

THAT IT WAS OUR NATURE
　to prefer to keep our River Bend Place --
　　our near island.

AND SO
　two in three of the present communities
　　would stay
　　　and continue in the usual manner.

THAT IT WAS ALSO OUR NATURE
　to seek to understand
　　new ways and disparate others.

AND SO
　one in three of the present communities
　　would go to live among this Sun People,
　　　gaining what might be learned
　　　　to share with this
　　　　　and subsequent generations.

AND
　in exchange for this learning
　　this group would agree to grow corn
　　and to carry this and that.

THAT IT WAS OUR FURTHER NATURE
　to share all things in equal measure.

AND FOR THIS REASON
　would each community
　　go in subsequent increments
　　　of three years each.

　Enough
　　to learn a new way.
　Too little
　　to forget the old.

AND SO IT WAS AGREED . .
   This Sun People
      preferred one willing community
         to three unwilling ones.

   AND
      on the following turn of the season cycle,
         when Earth is opened once more
            to receive the willing seed
               of our Three Sisters,
         the southernmost of our three communities
            went to learn and grow.

          . . .

NOW THIS WAS THE WAY OF IT.

   For too many years as we see things now
      our People danced the Third Year Dance . .
         return to a land
            and a way they preferred
         also sent the next community hence.

AND YET
   Much was learned
      in the growing of corn
         and in the manner of construction.

   Little was learned
      of the nature and purpose
         of this great piling up of things.

FOR
   The planting of corn
      we understood.

   We kept to ourselves
      the growing of other things,
         for this Sun People
            had little interest in our diversity.

AND WE SAW
   HOW IT WAS
   HOW THE LEARNING
     WAS NOT MUTUAL.

For this Sun People --
   we came to understand --
     held us in little value
       as other than those who dug
       and those who carried.

"You see how it is"
   -- some one suggested.

"How these ones think
   it is only the wearing
     of shining discs about the neck
       that enables thought."

And we laughed,
   remembering disparate others
     who held a similar view.

FOR IT IS OFTEN SO,
   AMONG THIS PEOPLE AND THAT,
     WE FIND A FAILURE
       TO RECOGNIZE ANY WISDOM
         DISSIMILAR FROM THEIR OWN.

LET US BE A WISER PEOPLE.

LET US REMEMBER
   TO RESPECT
     MANY WAYS OF LEARNING
     AND HOW MANY PATHS
     TOWARD WISDOM
       THERE MAY YET BE.

   SO BE IT.

Their Way

NOW, AS I HAVE SAID.
    Too many Season Circles came and went
        while we continued in this manner.

    For a time came
        when it was clear to all
            that we had learned from the Sun People
                all they were willing to let us see --
            and some few things else.

    Our time with them
        came to be an endless round
            of dig and carry . .
        so that no one at all
            saw any longer any value here.

    Corn enough for ourselves
        we could easily grow --
            Squash and Beans also --
        and no extra corn nor any carried Earth
            was necessary in our Home Place.

FOR THE WAY OF IT WAS THIS . .

    Some of the People all of the time
        and all of the People some of the time
            grew no Corn at all.

RATHER,
    They began their day by choosing a basket --
        one which would be their constant companion
            till day's end.

        For lift and carry
        and fill and carry
        and overturn and carry
        and begin again
            was all that filled their waking moments.

    Each of the People so assigned
        began the day with some little sustenance.

    They were free to select a basket,
        but never free not to choose.

They were free also
　　to select a path back and forth.

For down to the river
　　which curved around their building place
　　　　was steep and short in one direction
　　　　and gradual and long in the other.

"We have a third choice"
　　-- some one said.

"We can choose to disappear!"

AND SO IT WAS
　　That each Person considered strong enough
　　　　lifted a basket to one shoulder,
　　　　found the stream by one route or the other,
　　　　filled that basket with Earth,
　　　　　　with water, with crushed rock,
　　　　and returned by either route
　　　　　　to the top of the hill
　　　　　　to spread out this Earth provender
　　　　　　　　as the builders directed.

Who were the builders then?
　　Those who directed? . .
　　or those who carried?

WE CONSIDERED THIS MUCH.

. . .

NOW
　　You might say to yourself --
　　　if you are still awake --
　　　　that at least we could learn
　　　　　the nature of what was built.

YET I TELL YOU NOW,
　　IT WAS NOT SO.

FOR
    Only those who directed the building
        were allowed
            to see both beginning and end.

    Great screens of woven reeds
        were erected
            against the possibility of meaningful vision,
            the probability of understanding . .

    So that even those from among their own People
        who worked at our side -- and these were many --
            were allowed no opportunity at all
                to understand the nature of the construction.

    So that when we asked them
        "What is here?"

    They answered us only
        "What is necessary."

AND WE CAME TO UNDERSTAND
    That only a few
        would ever be permitted
            to understand either nature or purpose.

    For surely no house was built here,
        unless it was a place for mole or rabbit.

    For no opening was ever constructed,
        no cave or tunnel of any kind.

    Merely a solid Earth
        was woven back and forth
            in some pattern we not yet understood,
                compacted against a yielding Earth.

AND OUR PEOPLE
    Grew disquiet in this circumstance.

    "What learning
        is any longer here,"
            -- they began to ask one another --

    "That lends relevance
        to dig and carry?"

AND NO ONE AT ALL
FOUND AN ANSWER.

SO IT CAME TO BE
    That the People grew discontent
    and sought some way
        to end our agreement.

    But to every such petition
        the answer came --

    "We will come and find you."

AND
    Since the People
        had no wish to yield up
            their River Circled Home,
        nor either any wish
            to resist this Sun People
                by any strident means . .

    They decided among themselves --
        and said as much --

    "It is our decision
        to help you
            until this work is finished.

    "It is our decision
        to help you
            no more after that."

AND SO IT WAS AGREED.
    An unwilling People
        continued the Dance of Dig and Carry,
        valuing the six years
            in nine for learning,
        valuing the three years in nine
            hardly at all.

AND THEN
   ANOTHER THING WAS DECIDED.

   "Have we not seen -- time and again --
      how much may be learned of a People
         too sure of their own wisdom,
         too sure we have none?

   "Have we not learned also
      how much may be heard
         by ears too young to seem a danger
            to a guarded way?

   "Let us choose, then, one from among us
      too young to be noticed by a People
         who notice only themselves.

   "Let us choose one from among us
      who already shows great retentiveness of mind
         and willingness to learn."

NOR WAS THIS A DIFFICULT TASK
   For during all this time
      and countless Season Circles
         the People had never ceased
            in their chosen task
               of learning how to learn.

   So that the ablest from among them
      who had not yet achieved the Fifth Winter Count
         was chosen --
         and chose also this task --

   So that he began to spend his days
      following this one or that
         from among the Sun People,
      learning in that way
         which would tolerate his presence.

   He began also -- sometimes --
      to teach the very young from among the Sun People
         some few of our learning games
      so that these ones
         might grow in greater respect for our way.

NOW
    This young and growing task
        gave the People
           some reason
              for their dig and carry,
           some hope also
              of a more agreeable tomorrow.

AND SO IT WAS
    That this arrangement
        continued for a full cycle of time --
           nine Season Circles.

For this young and growing one
    chose to stay with the Sun People
        when his community left --
    which brought much laughter to them,
        thinking the greater wisdom of their way
           had been learned by one, at least.

AND SO IT WAS,
    When the second community left,
        he chose again to stay.

AND AGAIN IT WAS AGREED
    For by this time
        he counted twelve winters only
           and had not achieved his full height.

AND -- as he was careful
    never to ask too many questions in any one day,
    never to show apparent curiosity --
        so was he accepted by this Sun People
           as a young and learning person
              less able than they.

NOW
   AT THIS TIME IT CAME TO BE

That one among the Sun People
   became his special friend.

And as our chosen one
   hastened to carry anything at all
      for his Sun Brother,
   so did no one at all
      understand the true nature of his learning.

   BUT HIS SUN BROTHER
   UNDERSTOOD IT.

For though no one else
   found a way to string this answer and that
      on a common thread
         and consider what it might become,
         SUN BROTHER DID.

AND
   As it became apparent to him
      how much his Corn Growing Brother
         had learned --
      neither did he resist it,
      but encouraged it instead,
         speaking to him before others
            as if he were not quite able of mind
               and therefore
                  lacked any capacity for learning.

Nor was it apparent
   why he did such things.

Yet his need
   for this growing friendship was apparent --

AND OUR PEOPLE
   CONSIDERED IT A GIFT.

NOW DURING THIS TIME
 Our young and learning friend
  indeed learned many things.

 So that our People
  came to value their patience even more.

FOR
 Although his friend
  would speak no word
  nor answer any question put to him,
   he took our young learner with him,
   stopped up his ears in no way,
    neither forbade he any questions
     put to another source.

 So that -- what with one thing and another --
  our young and learning friend
   learned indeed the nature of this Sun People --
    where they had come from and why,
    how they had lived in that place,
    and how they came to it.

 So that we began to consider
  that this People kept their own Tellings
  as carefully as we kept ours . .

 And we became anxious
  to add their learning path to our own.

 So that as our young and learning friend
  brought home each treasured thought,
   others from among the People
   sorted and culled
    as you might sort and cull
     fresh seeds for keeping.

Over many, many turnings of the Moon

Over many Season Circles . .

Although
   they grew no closer in understanding
    of what they patiently built . .

THEY PLANTED THESE SEEDS OF THOUGHT
   AND FROM THEM
     GREW THE WHOLE LEARNING PATH
    OF THE SUN PEOPLE.

AND
   THIS WAS THE NATURE OF THAT PATH.

Their Song

NOW
    We come from the beginning of things --
        from our first island.

    And there
        our distant elders set up a way of life
          that was greatly pleasing to us.

    They found
        that living together on one so-small island
          engendered more similarity
            than an active life requires.

AND SO
    They took the natural division of the island --
        split as it was by mountains
          into five separate lowlands
            with access to Ocean . .

    And devised a division of our People
        into five separate clans,
          each priding itself
            on the nature of its distinction
            from all others.

OVER TIME
    The interactive nature of these groups
        brought great benefit,
          for each would try to exceed all others
            in some respect or other.

AND FROM THIS
    MUCH WAS LEARNED
        OF THE NATURE OF MANY POSSIBILITIES.

AND AMONG THESE
    Were the construction
    of great and wonderful buildings,
        greatly surpassing any you see here
    and lasting beyond any wearing away
        of rain or storm
    as they were constructed
        of the hard parts of Earth
          and carefully crafted.

AMONG THESE ALSO
　　Was the ability
　　　　to let wind work for you
　　　　　　as you travel across great waters.

AND OUR WORLD
　　Became an expanding one,
　　　　with much learning about this or that people,
　　　　　　islands one could sail around
　　　　　　　　and broader lands we could not . .

　　Until we came to understand our world
　　　　as islands,
　　　　　　wrapped with Ocean,
　　　　　　　　and greater lands beyond.

　　　　　　　　• • •

NOW
　　DURING ALL THIS TIME
　　WE HAD DISCOVERED MANY THINGS.

　　Our People
　　　　set foot on other islands
　　　　　　and made them our home.

　　But the nature of our way was such
　　　　that the reach of any island
　　　　　　was enough for us,
　　　　and the great expanse of the broader lands
　　　　　　made us always wonder
　　　　　　　　what might lay beyond.

　　So that we greatly resisted any home
　　　　on the broader lands.

NOW
　　DURING ALL THIS TIME

　　WE PROSPERED AND GREW . .
　　　　FOUND OUR OWN PATH TO LEARNING,

　　　　UNTIL WE WERE GREATLY CONTENT
　　　　WITH THE WHOLE.

OUR WISDOM WAS SUCH
   That many did little else
      but learn . .

AND
     we established great buildings for this,
     studied the stars
       and the nature of all found lands,
     gathered these learnings
       into our great buildings
     and heeded the Council
       of those whose learning was so deep
         that they encompassed all we knew.

FOR
     few were any longer capable
      of learning the whole,
     and the much sailing about --
      exchanging this and that --
       required such great concentration
        that we valued their wisdom even more.

NOW
   After the passage of so many years
     they must remain uncounted . .

Our expanding way of life
     took on a regular nature,
       such that constant change
        was part of the regularity . .
     and yet on our home islands
       continuity was also a part.

THEN ALL THINGS CHANGED.

For on the next celebration
     of the change of seasons . .

Those among us
     whose white robes covered great learning
       spoke of new and terrifying events.

The sky, they told us,
   would soon turn black.

Black rain would fall,
   covering all the land.

The ground would shake and toss
   like a great bull throwing off its assailant.

Bits of our island
   would begin to disappear . .

AND -- AT LAST --
   our First Island
     would sink in its entirety
       into the Ocean from which it came.

NOW
   This was a wondrous thing to contemplate,
     seeing how it was
       nothing we had ever learned
         spoke of a time
           when our island had not been
             the Center of our World.

And these learned ones
   devised some gradual acceptance
   of the wisdom of their words.

"You see how it is"
   -- they told us --

"How this understanding tells us
   we must prepare
     to leave the Center of our World,
   and yet we understand
     the difficulty of this choice.
   and so this is our suggestion.

"Let each clan confer within itself
   and decide whether or no
     it is willing to leave
       on our word alone.

"We have identified five destinations
    to which a whole clan may make its way.

"That clan which first selects to go
    will have first choice
        and may make their way to that location
            assured of arrival.

"That clan which makes second choice to go
    will have second choice
        and may make their way
            as soon as provisions are enough again
                for such a voyage.

"Those clans which do not choose to go
    will see the beginning of the black rain.
        And that vision
            may encourage them hence.

"As soon as provisions are again enough
    the third clan so choosing may embark.
        They will be asked to find their way
            across the great and unknown Ocean
                that lies beyond our own.

"The fourth and fifth clans
    will proceed accordingly . .

"For they will come to understand
    their hesitance to heed our Council
        as a great lack . .

"For the Earth will shake beneath their feet
    and the grass barely grow
        through the black rain
            which will continue over time.

"AND SOME OF US
    WILL NEVER LEAVE AT ALL . .
        BUT SINK BENEATH THE OCEAN
        TOGETHER WITH THE ISLAND
        THAT HAS BEEN OUR HOME."

NOW
    You may imagine the consternation.

    No one had any wish
        to leave an island so much a home to us . .

AND YET
    NONE HAD ANY WISH
        FOR THEIR LIFE
            TO DISAPPEAR
                BENEATH AN OCEAN.

AND SO IT WAS
    That the northernmost clan,
    That one whose land was most buffeted by storms
        chose first to go
        and chose the closest site --
            one known for an evenness of climate . .
                which was West,
                    but mainly South of our island,
                which land was washed by a great river
                    whose origin was unknown to us.

AND SO
    The work was begun.

    The ships built.

    Provender for so short a voyage provided.

    AND THE PEOPLE LEFT.

NOW
    The clan which chose next to leave
        was the eastern clan.

    And the reason for their choosing
        is unknown to us.

AND YET IT MAY HAVE BEEN
    Their respect for the findings of those
        who spent their life in learning,
            for many of them
                were from this eastern clan.

AND
> They chose the next closest location,
>> traveling West and then North
>>> so as to pass the outreaching tip
>>>> of the great peninsula to our West
>>> and so as to proceed along its coast
>>>> in a northerly manner
>>> and so as to select
>>>> a site along its edge to their liking.

> And no great amount of provender
>> was necessary for this voyage
>>> and yet many ships were necessary.

AND OF THEM WE HEARD NOT AGAIN.

NOW
> There remained three clans . .

> And to assure survival
>> of some part of the People,
>>> each such clan
>>>> was asked to cross the Western Ocean.

> For it was not clear
>> to those
>>> who spent their life in learning
>> just what damage might be created
>>> by a great island's sudden descent,
>> nor how far
>>> that damage might extend.

> And so great distance was asked
>> as a benefit to probable survival.

AND
> As the distance was great,
>> so was it necessary
>>> to gather much provender.

AND IN THAT MANNER ALSO
> Were more ships required,
>> so that much time passed
>>> before the third clan was prepared.

AND THIS WAS OUR CLAN.

We are they
who went West and West.

We are they
who sailed toward an unknown sea
under a darkening sky
for the black rain
had begun to fall.

NOW FROM A SUBSEQUENT TIME,
We have learned that our First Island
did, indeed, begin to shake,
bits breaking loose
and dropping into the sea.

SO THIS AT LEAST
We know came in fulfillment
of the findings of those
who covered their life long learnings
with the white robes of their office.

OUR WAY
Lay across the great ocean.
and many ships were lost along the way.

But as they broke in this or that storm,
the disappearance of what was provided
into many mouths
already so lightened the load
that those on a foundering ship
might safely transfer to one more water tight.

AND
as the storms came and went,
as the moon turned in its course
three full times and began again . .

None had yet seen any land at all
so that we began to think
that -- unlike our own home Ocean --
this one had no land at all at its edge.

AND THEN AT LAST
    Some land was sighted.

    Moving with caution
        so that we might understand
            the nature of this place
            and whether there were any living there
                who might disagree with our arrival,
        we sailed round this island,
            discovering its limits,
            and seeing none
                to whom our arrival might be displeasing.

NOW AT THIS TIME
    There was discussion
        among the ships still left together
            as to whether this island
                should be our destination
                or some more western land be sought.

    For if this was the first island we found,
        surely it would not be the last,
            and some broader land beyond that
                might be expected.

    We had no reason to assume
        that the remaining ships might long survive
            nor easily be replaced.

    And we understood
        how a brief visitation
            might easily become
                an unchangeable decision.

AND SO
    Since many storms
        left us with at least more than enough water,
            we decided on a western course.

AND YET
    as our leaving of our First Island
        was decided for us by circumstance
            beyond our ability to change it,
    so was our arrival on this New Island
        also decided.

For as we turned to the West,
    two of our remaining ships
        foundered,
        took on water,
        and began to sink so rapidly
            that nothing at all could change it.

So that those in either ship gave thanks
    for their ability
        to make their way through water unaided
        and swam to shore.

AND SO IT WAS DECIDED.

Two ships sunk
    off the western coast of this island
        left us with three remaining
            out of all the many.

Not one in four of our people
    were any longer gathered here,
        and yet among us we were many.

So that we built a new way
    on this New Island
        and sailed our remaining ships West
            from time to time,
        discovering a broad land, indeed,
            and many we did not recognize
                already living there.

So that we turned our attention
    to this New Island
        and the rebuilding of our ships.

AND AT THE END OF EACH CYCLE
FROM THEN UNTIL NOW . .

We cause ourselves to remember that day . .
    build a ship
       in the old way,
    sail it into that same sea
       with many young and strong,
    founder it
       in a purposeful way,
    and celebrate
       our arrival at the first Western land
         with the energy
           of so much swimming ashore.

Further Learnings

NOW
  YOU WILL UNDERSTAND
    HOW IT WAS FOR OUR PEOPLE.

YOU WHO LISTEN TO ME NOW.

HERE
  WAS A DIFFERENT PEOPLE,
  A SAIL-THE-WATER-PEOPLE . .

COME, IT WOULD SEEM,
  AS FAR AS WE
    FOR A SIMILAR REASON
      IN A DIFFERENT WAY.

FOR THEY CROSSED THEIR OCEAN
AND WE WALKED ROUND OURS.

AND FROM THIS WE LEARNED
  That more than we
    fled from a shaking circumstance
      to a quieter land.

AND FROM THIS WE LEARNED
  That our Ocean to the West
    was indeed matched
      by an Ocean to the East . .

For was it not
  just such a Three Moon Ocean
    these ones had crossed
      in a westerly direction?

AND SO
  There came to be
    much discussion
      of alternate paths.

For this learning was so great,
  that any additional such
    that might be culled
      from an unsharing People
        was greatly wished.

AND YET
   This new understanding
      of the accuracy of our expectation
         of an Ocean at the eastern edge
            of this Great Island
      also gave us good reason
         to rethink the value
            of our River Circle home
               so beset by this Sun People.

AND SO
   TWO SIMULTANEOUS PATHS
   WERE DECIDED UPON . .

  The first path
     carried our young and growing Learner
        back to his familiar task,
           newly aware of its value.

  The second
     found several of our People so suddenly ill
        that only a quick return
           to our River Circle home might heal them.

AND IN THAT MANNER
  An exchange was enabled
     so that those too ill to dig and carry
        found themselves suddenly healed --
     that healing
        requiring only the setting of either foot
           to the Earth of our River Circle home --
     this act
        causing them also to develop a sudden ability
           to speak and share all that we had learned.

  And their first words
     enabled the other half of the circle.

  For -- at their request --
     those best able
        to learn and retain with accuracy
           found themselves willing to return
              to the land of Dig and Carry
     so that they might hear for themselves
        the voice of our Young and Learning Person.

AND IN THAT MANNER
  Was all learning
    rapidly shared with all of the People . .

  So that whatever circumstance might come to be,
    all would greet such change with knowing eyes.

AND FROM THAT DAY TO THIS
WE HAVE COME TO VALUE
THE NATURE OF THIS SHARING.

  So that those who gather such understanding
    cull it carefully
      from many bits of individual circumstance,
    gather until this new learning
      takes on a certain coherence,
        representing at least
          the short form of a Whole Telling.

AND AT THAT TIME,
  Those who gathered such things
    found a way to rapidly share
      this new understanding
        with the Whole People.

AND IN THAT WAY
  Is the rapt attention of the Whole People
    caught in the net of New Understanding,
      and not spent on daily small details.

AND YET
  Each New Understanding
    is rapidly spread to each and all
      so that Great Change
        may be equally met by general understanding.

AND AS YOU WILL SEE,
  This approach to Wisdom,
    engendered at first
      by the distance of one community
        from those remaining in the River Circle,
    came to have great benefit then
      as it has great benefit now.

  For all cannot,
    but some can,
      carefully attend each small detail.

AND YET
    The gathered wisdom of the Whole People
    requires that all be rapidly aware
    of each New Understanding.

LET US REMEMBER
THE VALUE OF THIS WAY

   • • •

NOW IT CAME TO BE
    That the next focus
        of our Young and Learning Person
            was the manner of arrival
                for this Sun People
            from the island they had earlier reached.

AND
    It was quickly learned
        that this was greatly South
            beyond the farthest end of this great river
                and across the open water.

    Knowing as he did
        the full nature of Ocean to the West,
            as he listened
                to their Song of the Great Water,
                    he showed no surprise.

    And for this
        they judged him uncomprehending.

    And for this
        they judged him even safer than before.

AND YET
    HE LEARNED.

    Heard their Telling
        of slow exploration and new settlements,
            great cities and monstrous constructions.

For their cities
    had become gatherings of many communities
        with constructions for dwelling places
           and for ceremonies only,
      great buildings
          from which to continue their study
            of the changingness of star patterns.

AND IT SEEMED TO US
    That perhaps this explained
      their much building up of Earth.

For in this place
    were no easy accesses
        to the hard parts of Earth
          they spoke of for construction.

And in this place
    they accustomed themselves
        to the use of Earth
          and water and crushed stone.

                      ◊ ◊ ◊

NOW AT LAST
    Our Young and Learning Person
    chanced one question --

"If there is a great water beyond this river,
    it must be very difficult to cross
        and I not understand what reason
           would bring you from that place to this,
           seeing how it is
              you found it so pleasing."

NOW
    FROM THESE WORDS
      TWO FLOWERS GREW.

    One opened
      and showed us
        much of what we sought to learn.

The other opened
and showed us
the end of our learning.

AND THIS WAS THE WAY OF IT.

. . .

The one from among the Sun People most garrulous
heard this seemingly chance remark
as he was meant to do
and sat to answer it.

"We lived very well in those places.

"Our more than grandfathers
built great places of solid stone
which exceeded these earth moldings
as a mountain exceeds an ant hill.

"They kept among these buildings
sheltered places that were held sacred
and in which we carefully tended
our Sacred Corn.

"Now this was a great keeping, sacred,
and known only
to those with authority for the task.

"FOR IN THAT PLACE
OCCURRED THE MOST SACRED TASK OF ALL,
THE BLENDING OF CORN."

NOW
Our young and growing Person
sought greater understanding of this ceremony.

And it was his judgement
that pride further loosens a garrulous tongue
where insistence will not.

And so he said --

"Ah, I understand.

"We do that as well.
   For we often take the kernels
      from many ears of corn and mix them."

"No, you do not understand at all"
   -- was the reply.

"The much mixing of corn kernels
   does nothing at all save begin a stew.

"No -- our grandfathers
   were both wiser
      and more skillful than this.

"It is not the kernels
   that must be mixed,
      but the soft down
         that covers corn tassels --
            one with the other."

AND
   What with one thing and the other,
      evidencing always
         a seeming misapprehension . .

Our Young and Learning Person
   culled from this man's pride . .

Many understandings of how it was
   their responsible persons carried carefully
      from one corn tassel this golden dust . .
         joining in that way
            the nature of one corn plant
            and the other . .

Much as we might ask our women
   of greater size or strength or ability to learn
      that she bring forth at least one child
         for the People
            fathered by one of our men
               of similar stature or ability.

And this had been of great benefit to our People,
   increasing strength and height also --
      wisdom perhaps . .

So that our Young and Learning Person
    understood easily
        the nature of this Dance of Golden Dust.

AND YET
    He appeared otherwise,
        laughing quietly at the idea dust had value --
    planting in this way
        the seeds of further conversation.

. . .

NOW
    This was the last such conversation.

    This same garrulous man -- much time later --
        found our Young and Learning Person
            under a tree, apparently asleep.

    Stopping to gaze at this so still form,
        he asked the general air
            whether there lingered under that sleeping brow
                some greater understanding
                    of what had been shared.

    Unable to resist his own curiosity,
        he placed one toe under the sleeping form
            and jostled him awake.

NOW
    Our Young and Learning Person
        slept in no way at all.

    Rather, he lay in apparent slumber
        directly along the path
            this garrulous man
                might be expected to take unescorted.

AND SO IT WAS.

For slowly opened eyes
   revealed only one person --
     and his curiosity.

"Tell me"
   -- this one asked --

"Whether you have pondered
   what I said some time ago
    and whether you now
      have any understanding of it."

For it was clear
   This One was troubled by his too free words.

Scratching his head and looking dubious,
   our friend answered --

"I think you talk
   only to hear your own words!

"What you say is too improbable.

"It does not seem to me
   so great a People
     would trouble themselves with corn dust.
   I see no such now.

"It does not seem to me probable
   that anything at all
     can be built with great, moved stone.

"I see you building now
    with mud and pebbles only.

"It does not seem probable
   that a People
     living in so great content
       would bother to cross a Great Open Water
      for the mere pleasure
       of a more difficult life.

"And so finally
   I say a simple thing.
     One which I do understand.

"I do not believe you --
   and think you merely mean to amuse yourself
      with my credulity."

And with that
   he rolled over
      and apparently went back to sleep.

• • •

NOW
   Nothing is as distressful
     to those whose pride is great
      as unwilling ears.

What could in no other way
   be coaxed or compelled from them,
     tumbles easily into an unattentive void.

AND SO IT WAS.

For this proud and garrulous man told again
   of great buildings of moved stone,
     cloisters sacred in nature
       for the exchanging of the golden dust of corn,
   great celebrations and ceremonies
     marking each change in star patterns,
   great images carved from stone
     so that anyone at all might think
       some one from among the People
        stood transfixed
       and even greater faces
         peering out from an even denser forest.

"It all sounds so wondrous"
   -- our Young and Learning Person replied --

"That I especially do not believe you.

"For what People
   would ever be so foolish
     as to leave so wondrous a place?"

AND THIS AT LAST
    Broke the final restraints
        on an overly garrulous tongue.

    For from thence
        ensued the Telling
            of how it was his People,
                who were few,
            dealt with the many
                already living on this broad land.

    How
        they dazzled them with wind-driven ships,
        overwhelmed them with this and that manner
            of accomplishing the seemingly impossible,
        won their loyalty
            with promises of greater and greater bounty.

UNTIL AT LAST
    All this numerous People labored daily
        in fields established by the few,
        on buildings designed by only several,
            in pursuance of ceremonies
                they poorly understood,

    All directed,
        as our Earth construction was directed,
            by the few among many
                who understood the purpose thereof.

    And our Young and Learning Person
        saw how it was
            that a People living in such a manner
                might come to consider all others
                    dull of understanding.

    He wondered further
        whether any understanding was dull at all,
        or whether it was the unwillingness
            to share understanding
                which engendered disinterest.

    And he wondered further
        whether an inability to understand
            might be more than met
                by an inability to explain.

All these things occurred to him
and yet no unguarded
light of apprehension
shown from either eye,
so that such light in no way
brought halt to the exclamations
of an unrecognized and prideful man.

AND SO IT WAS
That he continued in his Telling
of how his People essayed the difficult work
of design and ceremony
and the generation of great bounty,
while this larger
and increasingly unappreciative People
were asked only
to dig and carry and cut stone.

UNTIL ONE DAY,
After a new increase
in that which would be necessary
for the next major ceremonial
had been announced,
his People awoke to a silent city.

For during the night,
all of this toiling, unapprehending People
had left.
So that the city was silent, indeed.

. . .

NOW THIS WAS THE WAY OF IT.

FOR A LONG TIME
Individual toilers
had disappeared into the forest
and were not seen again.

And yet the families stayed,
so that each city --
for now there were many --
had a secure number
of toilers in the field and cutters of stone.

NOW
As the number of the disappearing ones
had increased,
so also increased
the caution of those who directed.

For no increase in what was asked
was announced
until an equal increase
in the bounty of grain
was predicted.

So that this directing People
saw no reason
for such a sudden disappearance.

BUT
Our Young and Learning Person saw it
and wondered not at all
it had occurred,
seeing in his mind his own People --
his Three Community People --
disappearing into a less dense forest,
trading gladly increasing bounty
for a lack of labor
which none at all understood.

AND AT THAT MOMENT
A great determination arose within him
to learn at least
the nature of this present construction
of Earth and water and crushed rock.

. . .

AND YET
His ears in no way closed
to the continuations of this prideful man
who spoke now of many emissaries
sent out into their dense forest
to petition a return of the toilers,
speaking of greater bounty
and less construction.

He listened also
　　to the sadness in this man's voice
　　　　as he told how it was
　　　　　　that not one such emissary --
　　　　　　not one sent singly --
　　　　　　not several sent together --
　　　　　　　　ever returned.

So his People grew greatly alarmed
　　and sent out a large and heavily armed party
　　　　to the greatest neighboring city,
　　　　　　asking some relief.

Nor did even one
　　from among that delegation return.

SO THAT THIS WAS THE WAY OF IT . .

The so dense forest
　　consumed more and more
　　　　of the strongest and bravest of his People
　　　　　　and spit none of them back.

Time came and went to replant corn
　　and their stores grew lower and lower.

No ceremonies at all were held --
　　save those
　　　　which petitioned some greater understanding.

"Those who retain all learning
　　once told us"
　　　　-- he said --

"How it was our island
　　would sink beneath a yielding ocean.

"Yet none at all could tell us
　　how our great city could slowly sink
　　　　beneath an encroaching forest."

BUT
    Our Young and Growing Person understood,
        that an Island People
            divided into Five Sharing Clans
                is not the same at all
                    as a Broad Land People
                who seek to hide this and that
                    from those who dig and lift and carry . .

For when you hold things close
    so that others may not see . .

You put to different use
    that same hand
        that might reach out
            and touch some new understanding.

IN THAT MANNER
    Might the close keeping of an old way
        prevent apprehension of a new.

*AND OUR YOUNG AND GROWING PERSON
SAW HOW IT WAS
    THIS WAS A WISDOM WORTH SHARING.*

AND
    Each and every inconvenience
        of his Learning Path --
            and they were many --
                disappeared in the bright, shining light
                    of new apprehension.

                    ● ● ●

AND YET
    This garrulous man --
        beads of shining moisture edging either eye --
            went on to say
                how his more than grandfathers
                    had come to a great decision.

Unable to reach any others of their own People
through the so dense forest,
they crowded persons and provender
onto every ship --
set forth across the Great Water
to the Great River they knew to be there,
greatly North of where they were,
where perhaps they might find some place
to build again
and level fields
and cultivate their valued corn --
some place where a more willing People
might more easily cooperate.

AND
OUR YOUNG AND LEARNING FRIEND
SAW HOW IT WAS . .

That this lack of cooperating others
had engendered a division within this People
as between those who directed
and those who only dug and carried.

AND
IT BECAME A GREAT PURPOSE
WITHIN HIM

TO ENCOURAGE SUCH LEARNING
AMONG HIS OWN PEOPLE
SO THAT NO SUCH DIVISION
SHOULD EVER OCCUR.

AND FROM THAT DAY TO THIS
WE HAVE ALWAYS BEEN A PEOPLE
WHO CHOSE
NO SUCH DIVISION,
BUT CHOSE INSTEAD
THE WILLING APPREHENSION
OF ALL THE PEOPLE.

AND HE SAW ANOTHER THING AS WELL.

HOW IT WAS
His People had become a People
who only dig and carry --
if only for three years in nine --
those three years were spent
in doing only what was directed.

The further reality --
that much happened after dark,
much learning
was gathered and shared
and stored for a different future --
in no way changed
the directedness of their days.

AND HE CAME TO SEE
HOW IT WAS

That -- though he had no word for this --
his People had nearly become
an Only-As-Directed People.

AND
HE SAW GREAT VALUE
IN IMMEDIATE CHANGE.

The Great Earth Snake

NOW
 One thing remained
  that he wished to learn,
   and about this
    he had greatly thought.

 He wished to learn
  the nature of the shielded construction
   on which his People spent their days.

NOW
 He awaited only an appropriate time.

 And soon it came --
  for a dark night
   devoid of any light at all from moon,
   devoid of any light at all from stars
    as all the sky was filled with mist,

JUST SUCH A NIGHT CAME.

AND
 Our Young and Learning Person
  stepped forth carefully --
  dug his way
   under a near-forest edge
    of the great woven screens
  and carefully walked
   from one end to the other
    the entirety of this construction,
     seeing in this darkest night,
      with no eyes at all.

 Finding his careful way with feet and hands,
  he traced and retraced
   a regular, quiet pattern over the whole . .

 Until he could walk with no hesitation at all
  from one end to the other
   the general pattern.

"It is a snake"
  -- he said to himself --

"A Great Earth Snake.

"Our leg-less brother
  who curves and bends his way over the Earth
    curves and bends his way here --
      of Earth entire.

"My People
  have labored
    for three triple circles and more,
    hauling dripping stone-laden baskets
    up some precipitous slope
      for the final purpose
        of leaving a Great Pattern of Snake
        on the Earth!

"IN THIS I SEE NO VALUE."

• • •

NOW THIS WAS THE WAY OF IT
  FOR THREE THINGS HAPPENED
  NEARLY AT ONCE.

First,
  Our Young and Learning Friend
    shared all he learned from the garrulous man --
    shared as well his new understanding
      of what his People had become . .

For though he had no word for it,
  he saw he wanted none . .

And he was successful
  in transmitting his understanding
    to a People with a long memory
      who thought much on the nature
        of this directed change.

AND
    WHAT WITH ONE THING AND ANOTHER . .

What with the increasing difficulty of their toil,
    going farther and farther
        for the things they carried . .

What with their growing reluctance
    to spend their lives in this manner,
        whatever the learning . .

What with this new understanding
    of unceasing demands . .

What with this further reassurance
    of Ocean to the East . .

Every mind was now bent on a new way . .

And runners were sent through the night
    to two remaining communities
        for consultation on all new Learnings.

SO THAT ALL WERE AGREED
    THAT THEIR RIVER CIRCLE HOME
        MUST BE LEFT
            TO THE KINDNESS OF EARTH.

Nor was this decision in any way
    dampened by a recent flood
        which washed across one whole community . .

So that even the most hesitant
    were now convinced
        that a changing People
            had need of further change.

NOW
    The second thing that occurred
        grew from the garrulous man,
            who found great dissatisfaction
                in the uncomprehending nature
                    of our Young and Learning Friend
                    and spoke much of it . .
            until his words were heard by those
                who harbored less belief in the dullness
                of that young one's mind.

AND THEREFORE
    A GREAT COUNCIL WAS CALLED
    AND MANY BROUGHT TO WITNESS.

And the Sun Brother of our Young Friend,
    when directly asked,
        said he had no reason
            to think his friend dull --
            merely uncurious,
                as he had never at all asked any questions.

BUT THEN
    Others spoke out
        saying there had -- on rare occasions --
            been some question or other.

And some
    even remembered his presence
        during this or that discussion . .

Though most
    still forgot to remember he was there.

Until it became clear
    that much
        might have been learned.

AND AT LAST
    They asked our Young and Learning Friend
        whether at least he had heard these words,
        and whether especially
            he had learned anything from them.

NOW
It will not amaze you to learn
that our Young Friend had thought much
on the possibility of such a question
and wondered much
what his answer might be.

He thought
not only of his own People,
but of this People also,
and of those
who on some tomorrow
might be encouraged
to take up the task of dig and carry.

HE SAW HOW IT WAS
that this People
made more limited demands,
designing buildings in Earth only
and none at all in stone . .
for all their constructions
were more easily built
than those described
by the garrulous man.

AND HE SAW HOW IT MIGHT BE
that this was the result of wiser choice,
or how it might also be the result
of a loss in understanding how.

BUT
He sought to encourage
some greater learning,
some greater wisdom
in this designing People.

IT WAS HIS GIFT
TO SUN BROTHER'S CHILDREN.

AND SO
He had formulated his words carefully,
and these were they --

"I have heard this and that,
some of what this man said also,

"And yet
I find it hard to believe.

"I find it hard to believe
that such a Wise People
could learn so little
from a changing circumstance."

AND WITH THAT
HE CEASED
AND THE TUMULT BEGAN.

For this People could not decide
whether he truly understood or no,
whether they were pleased to be called wise
or displeased to be called slow of learning.

So on that day,
nothing at all was decided.

And on the next night
it was very dark, indeed.

And We Leave Them

NOW
> Since all had been prepared . .

> Since the Two Remaining Communities
>> had gathered summer's bounty
>>> into wherewith to carry . .

> Since the dig and carry community
>> were in every way
>>> prepared to stand and go . .

> Only learning the nature of what they built
>> kept them where they were.

> So that no understanding
>> of the possibility of flight
>>> might reach this Directing People,
>>>> only a few among those here
>>>>> knew how near they were
>>>>>> to stand and walk away.

NOW
> This Young Learner came to them
> with his gained understanding
> of the Great Earth Snake.

AND NOW
TWO THINGS OCCURRED.

> First,
>> they gave a new name
>>> to one who sees with his feet.

> They called him
>> Sees at Night . .

> *AND FROM THAT DAY TO THIS*
>> *THAT NAME*
>>> *HAS BEEN SACRED AMONG US.*

Second,
    prepared as they were to go,
        word was rapidly spread among all the People
           that the time had come
             to stand and walk,
           that all was prepared
             at their River Bend Home
             for an entire People
                to disappear into a less dense forest,
           that a happy greeting
             to an Eastern Ocean home
                may yet await them.

AND
    All was done so quickly and so quickly agreed,
        that their purpose
           to stand and walk on the very next night
             was impeded in no way,
        leaving one day only
           for the People to protect themselves
             from the inquiring eyes
               of the Directing People,
                who never at all ceased to question.

AND ON THAT SAME DAY
    Was our Young and Learning One --
        he whom we now called Sacred,
           and called also Sees at Night --
             recalled to the Great Council.

AND THEY SPOKE TO HIM
    The greatest punishment they could imagine --
        for they banished him
           from their presence,
        ordered him
           on the very next day to leave,
        and forbade him
           even to find any place
             among the Three Communities on the River Bend.

AND
    He raised his eyes to them . .

    Looked straight
        at those principal in the Council
           and said --

    "This I promise you.

    "From tomorrow's dawn
        you will not again see my face.

    "Nor will I set foot again
        on our Circle Island,
           but will travel to some so distant place
               that you and I shall never again meet."

AND
    They saw from the sadness in his eyes
        when he turned to his Sun Brother
           that his punishment was great.

    For he stretched out his hand
        to his life-long friend
           and spoke --

    "I have valued knowing you"
    -- he said --

    "And in leaving
        I wish you and your People
        some greater Wisdom."

AND HE SAW HOW IT WAS
    His friend understood
    more than was spoken.

AND IT WAS HIS HOPE THEN,
  AS IT IS OUR HOPE NOW,
    THAT THIS SUN PEOPLE
      DID INDEED FIND SOME GREATER WISDOM.

NOW
   As it was dark,
      all the People quietly arose
         and disappeared in small groups
            in different directions
         so that no general leaving would be noticed.

Traveling in these same small bands
      along differing and agreed paths,
         they left no great swath of a passing folk
            for a Directing People to follow.

Returning in these groups
      in the shortest time possible . .

Never stopping for rest,
      this Dig and Carry People
         spent their strength in constant motion,
            carrying their will to learn
               beyond the reach
                  of an unsharing People.

Gathered together at the River Bend
      they found the People of two minds.

One preferring an East and also South direction
      for the easier winters.

One preferring an East and also North direction
      as they valued the deep snows of winter
         which drew the People together
            to learn and understand.

AND SO
   OUR PEOPLE WERE ONCE MORE DIVIDED . .

With one in three --
      those we call the Gentle People --
         going East but also South . .

And two in three --
      those we call our continuing ancestors --
         going East and also North.

Walking quickly away --
      both of them --

Leaving a double trail
   for a Directing People to follow . .

Moving too quickly
   for a People unprepared for such travel . .

LEAVING FOREVER
   THEIR RIVER BEND HOME
     LIT BY TOO MANY SHINING DISCS.

LEAVING THIS VALUED PLACE
   as they had left
     their Edge of Mountain Home,
   as they had left
     their Sheltered Valley,
   as they had left
     the Western Ocean
       and the Great Island before it.

Moving once more
   across a changing Earth,
     they sought yet another Ocean.

Taking with them
   all the Gathered Wisdom
     to cull and sort
       during many long Winters.

Taking with them
   the expanding thoughts
     of Sees at Night,
   his many Tellings,
     and the calling names of a distant land
       and its great cities.

TAKING ALL THIS WITH THEM,
   THEY ROSE
     AND ESSAYED A FOREST DENSE ENOUGH,

     FINDING AT LAST
       THAT DISTANT OCEAN.

BUT THAT . . .

IS ANOTHER TELLING.

The Eastern Ocean

The Stone Hill People

The Western Way

Understanding

We Search

The Eastern Ocean

NOW YOU HAVE HEARD
HOW IT WAS FOR OUR PEOPLE

How they left their land
under a thunder of falling rock.

How they walked
a difficult and water-washed path.

How they found varying paths
through Endless Mountains
carrying with them
all Ancient Songs.

How they traced new paths
through new mountains
and across a Grass Ocean.

How they met new Peoples
and learned from them.

How they rose
and walked East one night,
carrying with them what they could,
leaving behind all else.

NOW
HEAR OF THEIR ARRIVAL.

Hear how a People
continued purposefully East
until the sharpest ears
heard a distant sound
and the smell of salt met them.

Hear how they continued
in this slow and steady manner
until anyone at all from among them
might stand hip-deep
in a new salt Ocean.

AND YET
    This Ocean
        was different from the last.

    Here a bright, shining path
        was laid down across the water
            early in each day
        as it had been before and beyond
            in our last Great Island home.

NOW
    The People kept to this shore
        celebrating the many wisdoms
        of understanding
            such Great Waters
                down many walks of days.

AND
    One stood forth
        who sang this for them.

"You see how it is"
    -- he sang --

"How the early morning sun
    walks toward us
        above a Bright Shining Path?"

"You see how it was"
    -- he went on --

"How the last Ocean we knew
    traced that path from West to East
    as this is East to West."

"You see how it was
    before even that"
        -- he concluded --

"How the last such path from East to West
    led to our Edge of Ocean home,
        our Great Center Place
            which we have never replicated.

"NOW
    PERHAPS ON THIS SHORE
    THERE CAN BE SUCH AGAIN."

AND YET IT WAS NOT SO.

For no mountains
    looked suddenly down
        over this Ocean in this place.

Rather it was a gradual land,
    giving easy access to Ocean
        and merely arrival
            at this third remembered Ocean
                was greatly celebrated.

So that someone stood
    and sang another song --

"You see how it is
    My Brothers, My Sisters.

"You see how much purposeful walking
    has carried a determined People
        over a vast Island.

"You see how it is
    the children's children --
        and all who follow after . .

"YOU SEE HOW IT IS
    WE HAVE WALKED
        FROM SEA TO SHINING SEA.

"LET US BE A PEOPLE
    WHO REMEMBER.

"Let no great difficulty
    so concern us
        that no one at all remembers
            the Ancient Songs.

"Let us create a life here
    that is pleasing to us.

"AND
   NEITHER IN THIS PLEASURE
    LET US FORGET
     THE MANY SINGLE FOOTSTEPS
    THAT MARKED OUR CONTINUING PATH.

"SO BE IT."

AND
   THESE WORDS WERE REMEMBERED
    AS A GREAT GIFT.

. . .

FOR SOON
   The People discovered
    that past this walk of Endless Forest
     even at its edge
      where washed the Eastern, Shining Sea,
    even there already dwelt . .
     not one People . .
      but yet two.

AND SO
   They soon discovered --
    for just to the South of the broad bay
     where they began to construct small dwellings . .
   They soon discovered a different People.

   One who lived
    by searching the land around
     for what they preferred
    and by encouraging some seeds
     in a disorderly manner.

AND
   These were a People
    who seemed neither to fear us
     nor to have any great curiosity.

   They explained how it was --
    what with one thing and another --
     that they saw too little land
      between them and the next People
     to allow a People
      of such numbers and such vigor
       to live between.

AND YET,
    Since they seemed not anxious
        that we go . .

    And disinclined to insist
        that we leave at any near time . .

    WE BEGAN TO LEARN HOW IT WAS.

    To the North of this People
        lived a small group of energetic People
            with extraordinary ways!

WE BEGAN TO SEE HOW IT WAS.

    The People to our South
        were not adverse
            to having us between one People . .
            and the other.

AND SO
    We lived this way for awhile,
        neither intruding greatly on the other . .
    Until this People to the South
        came to us saying --

    "YOU SEE HOW IT IS . .

    "How those things
        we are used to finding
            among trees and over grass
                are less often there.

    "AND SO IT IS
        that we must ask you to leave --
            though we would rather have you living near
            than those others to the North --
        we are surer you will move
            than they."

            . . .

NOW
    The possibility of a plan occurred to us.

Although this Southern People
    might be surer
        of our compliance
            with their forest needs
        than of the compliance
            of those to the North . .

We were a People
    who remembered many ways
    and who had managed survival
        through a greatly varying circumstance.

WHAT WITH THIS THING AND THAT . .
    What with all the Peoples
    we had known
        and tried to understand . .

Perhaps some alternative
    might yet be found . .

This People encouraged farther North
    or our People
        tracing a northward path beyond them.

AND WE CAME TO UNDERSTAND
    How it was
        the Southern People
            thought they would not move.

How it was
    they saw little value
        in even voicing such a request.

FOR THIS WAS A PEOPLE
    WHO BUILT THEIR CENTER PLACE
    WITH GREAT DIFFICULTY.

THIS WAS A STONE LIFTING PEOPLE..
 A People
  who raised with great difficulty
   some solid piece of Earth herself..
  cut it to suit some preference
  or purpose of their own,
  and laid it in place
   -- one after another --
    until some extraordinary assemblage
    was arranged.

NOW YOU SEE HOW IT WAS..
 How the People to our South
  were a People greatly amazed by such things..
   so that they seemed to them
    incomprehensible..

And any People behaving thus
 beyond the reach of ordinary words.

AND YOU SEE HOW IT ALSO WAS..
 How we were a People who remembered,
  and who sought through that memory
   to learn.

How we were a People
 who came to understand Water Walking
  and the pattern, if not the purpose,
   of a Great Earth Snake.

We were a dig and carry People..

A People
 who understood how much might change
  from the mere moving of a little Earth
   continued over many, many Season Circles.

It did not seem to us so extraordinary --
this cutting and moving of sizable stone . .

AS WE KNEW THAT . .
THAT WHICH IS IMPOSSIBLE FOR ONE,
MAY BE POSSIBLE FOR MANY.

AND WE KNEW ALSO
how much may be accomplished
by a slow and steady purpose --
even the crossing of a Whole People
from Sea to Shining Sea.

WE SAW
THAT THIS, TOO,
WAS NO SMALL THING.

The Stone Hill People

AND FOR THIS,
   AND FOR MANY OTHER REASONS,
    WE STUDIED
     HOW THIS PEOPLE LIVED.

For they kept closer than we
   to their home place,
    which had Great Walks carefully placed --
     in some ways similar to the Sun People
      the eldest among us still remembered.

And one of these Great Walks
   led from South to North
    toward the center of their Stone Hill.

AND WE SAW HOW IT WAS
   That sporadic individuals
    might come and go in any way at all --
     and yet groups of any size
      always approached
       along this Northward Walk.

WE SAW HOW IT WAS ALSO
   That these great stone pieces
    were not placed simply here and there
     in any convenient place,
      but seemed to follow
       some careful pattern of their own.

WE SAW HOW IT WAS ALSO
   That these stone places
    were nearly dwellings.

Not the near-mountains the Sun People described,
   but places
    that might be entered --
     even as our houses might be entered.

And we wondered
   whether this might not be true also
    of the Sun People's great gathering places.

IT SEEMED TO US
    That this was a People
        who purposed to build in stone --
           and that this purpose
                would be so great among them
           that they would ill consider any
                who did not follow their craft.

IT SEEMED TO US
    That -- like the Sun People --
        they would find no wisdom in our way . .

And discussing this,
    someone at last said --

    "Let us send them
        to live with the Sun People."

AND SUDDENLY
    What was said in near jest --
        became a continuing purpose . .

Until all discussed
    how this and that might be tried,
        encouraging the Stone Hill People
        toward the West.

          • • •

NOW IT IS SOMETIMES SO
    That no matter
        what careful thoughts are added together --
        nothing of value ensues.

AND YET,
    This was not such a time.

This time was such
    that -- as we discovered --
        the Stone Hill People
           were no longer content with their place.

As carefully crafted as it was,
    carving here and there --
        especially on many wooden posts --
        they had, perhaps,
           outlasted their purpose here . .

So that leaving their Stone Hill
   and all its careful crafting
      seemed not so much to them.

But this
   was a thing we learned later.

NOW
   We stood
      with that distant image
         of great and difficult work before us --
   and wondered
      how the People and it might be parted,
         one from the other.

AND THIS WAS THE WAY OF IT.

IT SEEMED TO US
   That this People were not numerous,
      though they had been resident here
         for some time.

Our People were more numerous,
   even after the long trek just ended.

So that it seemed to us
   so few People
      in such a carefully crafted circumstance
         indicated they were less now
            than they once had been.

AND,
   If their memory was long enough
      to remember this --
         then perhaps
            they felt the lack of others
               like themselves.

NOW IT IS SO
    That they built with stone.

IT IS ALSO SO
    That the Sun People spoke of such places.

IT IS FURTHER SO
    That this Stone Hill People,
        though they wore no shining discs
            about their necks,
        had other implements and rings
            about their person
                of similar stuff.

YET IT WAS SO
    That this People were of paler hue
        than the Sun People.

AND SO IT WAS DECIDED
    That they might --
        or might not --
            be from a similar place.

    Perhaps we would one day learn
        that long living to the South
            had given the Sun People their darker hue.

    But it was our purpose now
        to assume kinship . .

    For it was this very presumed kinship
        we hoped would carry a Stone Hill People
            West toward Earth Mountains.

NOW
    THIS WAS THE WAY OF IT.

From among us
    we selected a delegation . .

And instructed them
    to approach in a respectful manner,
        using those words which are gladly heard
            by those who value their own wisdom
                more than the wisdom of others --

"WE HAVE COME TO LEARN."

FOR
    As we learned --
        and approached disparate others --
            this had seemed to us the wisest path.

Even those
    who have scarcely learned from their own living
        how to lean three sticks together,
            understand that this is no small thing,
                this leaning of sticks,
        and may keep it close as a wondrous thing,
            sharing it only rarely.

AND SO IT SEEMED TO US
    That this People,
        who had learned from their own living
            how to lean three great cut pieces of stone
                together . .

Such as these
*   are likely to treasure their own wisdom.*

AND SO IT WAS
    That our delegation
        approached from South to North . .

    All five carefully chosen
        for a sharp mind and a willing heart.

    All five showing great respect
        and, in the language of the People to the South,
            we said, and said again --

        "WE HAVE COME TO LEARN."
        -- and --
        "THESE CONSTRUCTIONS ARE WONDROUS."

AND SO IT WAS
    That our New and Learning ones
        were shown with no great reticence
            into the center for sitting.

AND
    So as to fail to disturb the nature of this meeting,
        we watched all from as far away
            as our sharpest eyes would allow.

AND THIS
    WAS THE NATURE OF THAT MEETING.

    It was rapidly apparent
        that these Stone Hill People
            were as slow to share their wisdom
                as the Sun People had been.

AND SO IT WAS
    That -- rather than alarm those who found danger
        in the sharing of understanding --
        we shared our own.

    Little at all was said
        about Ocean to the West
        or about a Water Walking People
        or about any at all of our Ancient Songs.

    We had no wish
        that they find us too interesting.

Rather we spoke
 of our recent journey,
 of how it had not taken us as long
  as had seemed probable to us.

AND
 We spoke even more of a People
  who wore shining discs about their necks,
  who bent till backs would hardly straighten
   over their drawn plans,
  who built constructions many years in the making
   the purposes of which we scarcely understood.

We spoke of great mountains
 built by countless willing hands.

AND
 We spoke at last of a People,
  driven from their Island Home
   by a changing Earth . .

And how it had come to be
 that they crossed a Great Ocean
  from East to West
   in search of -- they knew not what --
   in search of a place, we thought,
    for the children's children.

AND ALTHOUGH
 It seemed they thought much
  of what we said . .

It seemed also
 they had no will to show it.

UNTIL AT LAST
 They said that we should go,
  seeking no further learning from them,
   for they had much to discuss among them.

NOW IT SEEMED TO US
 They showed -- all unwilling --
  great consternation.

SO THAT IT SEEMED TO US
 That what we said
  may well have had great effect . .

Perhaps even the effect we sought.

AND SO
   We left this Stone Hill,
      walking in a ceremonial way toward the South,
      and gave them time to consider.

. . .

NOW THREE TIMES
   The moon came and turned and left.

   Nothing at all
      was heard of the Stone Hill People.

UNTIL ONE DAY --
   As it began to grow dark --
      seven of their men came to us,
         asking great questions
            of direction and rivers,
               forests and mountains,
               ways that were easy
               and ways that were hard.

AND IN ALL THIS
   We answered as fully as we could.

   We saw our words had indeed some great effect.

   It seemed to us likely
      that these seven would essay the journey,
         bringing back word of possibility.

AND SO
   We sent some quiet word -- even as we talked --
      to the People to the South
         that this and that might yet occur.

LONG INTO THE NIGHT
   WE TALKED . .

   Nor stinted we in any way in our answers,
      responding in all
         as if we ourselves
            would make the journey.

   For the great success of these seven
      might yet find us a place on this Great Island
         next to the Eastern and Shining Sea.

AND SO
   We sat patient with them,
      drawing patterns on the Earth
         which they copied in their own way,
      talking much
         of rivers and of mountains
         of sustenance and safety . .

FOR IT WAS OUR WISH
THAT THEY SUCCEED.

AND WITH THIS THOUGHT IN MIND,
   We spoke also
      of the Grass Ocean that lay beyond . .

So that this People would come to understand
   how our memory exceeded this recent Telling.

We spoke
   of the Great River
      that carried the Sun People toward us
   and of how this Great River
      met a Great Water to the South.

AND ALL THIS
   Seemed to hold such wonder in their eyes
      that it seemed to us certain
         that our wish for ourselves would --
            in this manner --
               enable their wish for themselves also.

For we saw how it was
   they thought the Sun People near-Brothers --
      and we saw that it was likely so.

NOW ALL OF THIS
   Was as close as we might wish
      to what we sought.

AND YET
   ONE MORE THING OCCURRED.

Before they left us
   that same night,
      drawings of this and that
         carefully kept between them,

Before they left
    these were their words.

"If one day you arise
    and see no one at all
        on our Stone Hill . .

"Be aware
    that it is yet ours
        and to it we may yet return.

"Be aware also
    that there are those you cannot see
        and yet who guard our Sacred Places.

"Be aware --
    and choose some other place
        for your living."

AND IT SEEMED TO US
*   THESE WORDS*
*   HELD GREAT WISDOM.*

For we are not a People
*   who build with stone . .*

And any roof at all
*   might shake itself and fall*
*   without our understanding*
*   the nature of such things*
*   and moving away in time . .*

Even as the day of Rocks Like Rain
*   caused some, long before,*
*   to walk away to another place*
*   and others to stay*
*   and become one with Earth or Ocean*
*   for lack of foresight.*

And to these seven
*   we said we held their Stone Hill*
*   as Sacred to their People --*
*   and among us*
*   it would be inviolate.*

AND SO THEY LEFT
    Apparently filled with satisfaction,
        and we heard no more from them.

It was apparent to us
    these Seven would soon begin a journey,
        and we wished them well on it.

WE UNDERSTOOD HOW IT WAS.
    Our next task
        would be many discussions
            with the People to the South,
        asking of them due patience
            while many, many moons turned and left . .

So that these Seven might go and return again,
        asking of them due patience
            until they and we
                might learn the success of their journey.

AND THEN
    Runners came
        from this Southern People arriving from the North.

"They have gone
    as you said they might"
        -- they announced at once --

"And we show you many, many grateful hearts --
    for these ones
        were a strange and worrisome People."

And we answered them
    that we asked patience,
        for after these Seven
            a Whole People might yet follow.

"You do not understand"
    -- they answered us.

"We have been there and returned --
    to their Stone Hill as you call it.

"We saw no one leave.
    No one at all."

And they laughed --
    and laughed again at our amazement.

"We show you many, many grateful hearts"
    -- they went on.

"We have been there and back
    to learn what might be so . .

"And although we saw no one at all leave,
    surely many did just so.

"FOR THEY HAVE ALL LEFT,
    THERE IS NO ONE THERE AT ALL."

AND THIS WAS THE WAY OF IT.

This People to our South
indeed showed us many grateful hearts.

For our Tellings of a Sun People
and Earth Mountains to the West
had clearly encouraged
the Stone Hill People
to rise and walk away.

And this Southern People
had found the circumstance
lacking in comfort
which also contained
so disparate a People.

For this Stone Moving People
lacked respect for any way
dissimilar to their own.

AND FOR THIS REASON
Were we slow in choosing any location
for Corn or Beans or Squash . .

For we had no wish
to seem too dissimilar from this People
who now welcomed us.

AND THIS WAS ALSO THE WAY OF IT.

The Seven from the Stone Hill People
had asked
that we respect their constructions . .

AND SO WE DID,
seeing they were sacred to them
and understanding also
that many among our People
found little comfort in a stone roof,
as we remembered a distant place
where such places collapsed,
crushing all within.

And we were a People
　who preferred houses
　　that lacked the capacity to crush life
　　　at such times.

AND ALSO,
　There were those among our People
　　who found this or that place
　　　greatly disturbing in nature now and then . .

　So that no one at all had any desire
　　even to live in those out-lying houses
　　　constructed from no stone at all.

　We chose instead
　　to build houses in our own manner
　　　in communities of our own design
　　　in several locations
　　　　that were pleasing to us . .

　For no River Bend
　　limited the spread of our living now
　　　and a great area
　　　　lay unwalked by any two feet,
　　　　　so that of land
　　　　　　there was greatly enough.

AND
　We lived as close brothers
　to the People to the South.

　They in their turn
　remembered their own grateful hearts.

AND
　From them we learned much,
　sharing that which we found appropriate.

AND THIS
　WAS THE NATURE
　OF THEIR SONG.

The Western Way

OUR BEGINNING
LAY FAR BEYOND THIS PLACE
TO THE WEST
AND TO THE WEST
AND TO THE WEST.

IT CAME TO BE
That there was great discontent
among our People.

Many who lived at the edge
of Great Mountains That Touch the Sky
began to think
that some change in the manner of our living
might be appropriate.

AND YET
Others heard
only the old way and the old songs
and would give us no space on the Earth
to sing our changing songs.

FOR THAT REASON --
AND FOR OTHERS --
IT WAS DECIDED
THAT WE WOULD STAND
AND WALK AWAY
FROM THEIR CLOUDED ANGER.

For surely
clouds gathered against the Sky Touch Mountains . .

And surely
angry lightnings began to dance between them.

AND SO
We rose and we walked,
turning our faces mainly South
along the Edge of Mountains.

AND
    After the dance of too many days
        to begin to count them . .

    We found ourselves
        seated on the side of mountains
            looking out over a land
                drier than we had ever seen before,
                    and we beheld a wondrous sight.

FOR
    Below us and across a way
        lived a mountain different from any other.

    It was as if some Great Sky Hand
        reached down and carved it smooth --
        much as the very young
            may form this and that of mud,
            making a smoothness
                out of any rough surface at all.

NOW
    This mountain
        was not smooth where the land raised up,
        but was so nearly even on top
            as to perhaps give no sense
            of variation in level
                to any walking feet at all.

    This alone
        was a great amazement to us.

    Greater still
        was our amazement at the apparent life
            across this even surface . .

    For houses were there --
        and two-leggeds also.

    So that we knew
        that some access there must be
            to this even surface,
        or this was a People
            who never left its narrow confines.

NOW
    We are a cautious People.

    We approached slowly
       and were greeted
          with sticks and angry chatter for our pains.

    We fled then
       and found some refuge far away from them.

    We found a broad and open valley
       which was as if some rainbow
          touched to Earth
             and poured out its many colors
                onto the yielding sands.

FOR THIS PLACE, ALSO,
   WAS A GREAT WONDER.

    Our People --
       hardly believing their eyes --
          filled many carry skins
             with these wondrous colors --
    as it was their thought
       to return to a place
          we had chosen for ourselves
             high in the mountains --
    and those who waited there
       might wish to see
          these many wondrous colors
             touched to Earth.

NOW
    As sometimes happens with such things,
       this new wonder
          became a central focus in our lives.

    For the People
       stood so amazed at these Earth colors
          that they became central to our existence
       and much thought was given
          to the manner in which
             such a wonder might indeed
                become a part of our lives.

AND SO
>   The People chose
>> from among the various possibilities --
>> tried this and that --
>   until it was learned
>> that some things responded to these colors
>>> and others did not.

. . .

NOW
>   There was a second concern
>> on which the People lavished much thought.
>   It was our wish
>> to make some arrangement
>>> with this Flat Mountain People
>> so we might exchange with them
>>> the gifts of the mountain
>>>> for the gifts of the rooted ones
>>>>> they so carefully tended.
>> for nuts and deer and berries seemed to us
>>> a most equitable exchange
>>> for the seeded fruit of their labors.

AND YET
>   We were able in no way
>> to show to this Flat Mountain People
>>> the wisdom of our thought.
>   For whomever we approached --
>> they chased us away with great sticks,
>>> thinking, we supposed,
>>>> that we meant to take from them
>>>>> their carefully tended seeds.

AND
>   In no way
>> could we persuade them
>>> to listen to our thoughts
>   So that
>> we became greatly discouraged
>>> and thought to walk beyond this place
>>>> to one which contained fewer people
>>>> or people at least with listening ears.

AND YET
    Before us lay great discouragement --
        for South and East were greatly dry,
        and West was drier still,
        and North was from whence we came
            and to which we could in no way return.

    So that we sat within ourselves
        and pondered this predicament.

    We could become --
        we understood --
            a Mountain People,
                one which lives on mountain fruit alone.

AND YET
    We had a will to understand
        more than the limits of this mountain
    and none
        to constantly confront a stick-waving People.

AND SO
    We sat within our own thoughts --
        looking for a way for our People
            which contained great benefit
                over many long lives.

    For were we not a People
        who sought to craft new faces on the Old Ways?

    New faces
        through which to look out
            toward a changing Tomorrow?

WE WONDERED MUCH
    AND NOTHING WAS DECIDED.

    • • •

NOW DURING THIS TIME
>This and that use was found
>>for the many colored Earths.

Until at last
>someone turned from marking a basket
>>to marking his own skin.

Hands and arms were first --
>feet following after,
>>until someone reached out
>>>and colored face and shoulders as well.

AND
>There was much laughter saying --

"Is this
>one of the New Life changes we sought?

"Now perhaps we will become
>truly a Rainbow People."

NOW AS IS OFTEN SO
>For awhile
>>no one at all saw any use for this
>>>save mere amusement.

AND THEN
>He Who Had Painted
>>covered -- one day --
>>>his whole body with such stuff,
>>>turning over on his head a decorated basket
>>>and asking --

"Who is a human being now?"

AT FIRST
>we saw only laughter in this.

THEN AT LAST
>We saw how it might be
>>that such decoration
>>>might cause anyone at all
>>>>to forget the possibility underneath
>>>>>for wonder at the appearance itself.

AND SO IT WAS
    We slowly evolved a plan.

Watching and waiting,
    we came to better understand
        this Flat Mountain People.

We saw how it was
    they planted seed and carried water.

We came to understand
    the value of water to them.

AND SO IT WAS
    We developed between us
        many ways of coloring the body
        and many kinds of baskets --
            as well as other coverings --
                for the head.

AND SO IT WAS
    That we began --
        from time to time --
            to send three from among our People
                down to the edge of their fields.

Until we were clearly seen --
    and leaving deer in our place --
        we returned to our mountains.

NOW IT CAME TO BE
    That we would return
        to the place where deer was left --
            and find corn in his place.

AND WE SAW HOW IT WAS
    We had achieved our purpose,
        if only in a small way.

AND SO
    We left deer and nuts and berries
        and returned to find much corn.

IN THIS MANNER
   We acquired part of what we sought

   And -- over time --
      were able to modify the balance
         by leaving --
            if we were pleased
               with the amount of corn last given --
                  extra baskets of nuts and berries
            and -- if we were not pleased --
               less of each and even a smaller deer.

   So that we saw how it was
      a sort of communication was established
         in which each People
            might speak through those gifts they gave --
            and gave in return.

AND SO IT WAS
AND SO IT CONTINUED.

• • •

NOW IT CAME TO BE
   That in some years
      rain was so little
         that corn was little also --
            little in size,
            little in number.

   And in those years also
      might berries and nuts be less
         and deer more seldom seen --
      so that the giving of gifts was less.

AND WE THOUGHT MUCH ON THIS.

In some years,
 clouds would gather over the mountains
  and yet no rain fall.

So that we came to wonder
 whether this Flat Mountain People understood
  whether clouds brought rain or no --
   and what this implied for corn.

THEN,
 Following after three Season Circles
  with little rain at all,
   corn growing smaller and smaller,
  there came great clouds
   even before the usual time,
  and these clouds spat forth moisture
   as had not recently been seen.

AND SO IT SEEMED TO US
 That this season
  would follow the old pattern.

And for this reason
 we painted ourselves,
  put on our various assumed natures
  and went down to the Flat Mountain People
   carrying what berries, nuts,
    and deer could be given --
   dancing the nature of coming rain.

AND
 We were met with apparent understanding
  and joined in celebration
   so that one People and the Other
    were of one thought in this.

And the exchange of gifts
 exceeded wise care for tomorrow,
  but not the nature of the celebration.

AND --
 As the season dance came and went --
  corn in the fields was much improved,
   as were berries and nuts in the mountains,
    with deer following soon after.

AND SO IT WAS
    That -- for a time --
        some from among our People
            went down in every good rain season
                for an exchange of gifts.

UNTIL AT LAST
    Our way changed again,
        some of our People
            beginning a southward trek
                toward some different mountains
                    greatly beyond our present circumstance.

AND
    As the nature of sky
        showed little and less rain
            over many, many seasons,
    we came away from that place --
        walking mainly East
        and finding at last
            our present circumstance.

Understanding

NOW YOU SEE HOW IT WAS
    FOR OUR PEOPLE.

Having a long memory as we did,
    we were more used to meeting those
        who possessed little such memory
            than those like the Sun People
        who perhaps possessed even more than we.

YET IN ALL THIS LEARNING
    AND IN ALL THAT HAD BEEN GAINED,
        we had never before
            learned a thing long gone
        which was so similar to some element
            in our own Tellings.

Yet here were our brothers to the South
    singing an ancient song of their own keeping
        of a land so distant
            perhaps a full Life might now be spent
                in walking from here to there --
            even more distant counted in generations.

AND YET
    THIS TELLING
        AND THE TELLING OF RED SQUIRREL
            PAINTED SIMILAR PICTURES.

Of Peoples living on Flat Mountains
    with carefully tended corn here and there.
    and water doubly valued
        as it always is
            in the Great Dry Places of the Earth,
    and those of strange and different shape
        coming to announce the near arrival of rain.

AND WE SAW HOW IT WAS
    THAT ONE TELLING -- AND THE OTHER --
        CAME TOGETHER
            TO MAKE OUR UNDERSTANDING
            EVEN MORE SURE.

AND WE SAW HOW IT WAS
THAT ONE TELLING
MIGHT EXPLAIN THE OTHER
IN CERTAIN WAYS --
OR PERHAPS NOT.

And we wondered whether this People
who waited for those who announce the rain
might find value in this Telling --
or might not.

For the Water Walking People
were surely the cousins
of those who arrived over the Water --
and yet they knew it not.

One thing and another fit here together
so as to make a whole Telling --
or perhaps not.

One day perhaps
one of the children's children
will return to that twice visited place
and look and consider and learn
whether these Tellings --
that of our neighbor People to the South
and that of Red Squirrel
relate to one another . .
and in what way.

But of Flat Mountains --
there must at least be some.

NOW OVER MUCH TIME
   We lived
      to the North of our Southern Brothers,
        and they and we were equally satisfied
         with this arrangement.

IN ALL THIS TIME
   The Stone Hill People never returned
      and yet we left their place inviolate --
        out of respect
        and out of limited understanding.

   Stones only were left
      as most of the carved poles
        seemed to have disappeared --
         carried, evidently, with them.

       . . .

NOW
   Though we were content
      we did not spread out fields
        of Corn and Beans and Squash.

   Rather,
      we limited ourselves to the forest provender
      and encouraged seeds only
        in natural clearings here and there.

YET
   No one at all
      was content to live in this way
        past the third grandchildren growing time.

AND SO
   We slowly encouraged those groups
      living more to the North
        to evidence an evolving growing way . .

   So that these apparent changes might move slowly South
      giving our Southern Brothers time
        to come to understand them --
      and giving us hope
        that our Three Sacred Sisters
         would -- at some near day --
          have their old preeminence among us.

AND
> We were careful
>> to measure the views of our Southern Brothers
>>> so as to offend them in no way.

> Neither had we any wish
>> that they begin to think of us
>>> as they had thought of the Stone Hill People,
>>>> desiring therefore *our* further migration.

AND ALTHOUGH FROM TIME TO TIME
> Some question was raised about strange ways,
>> we reminded them of their own Telling
>>> of the need for change among the People --
>> and learned not to remind them of it.

FOR
> They now saw themselves
>> as Those Who Remain.

> Aware of this shift in their perception,
>> we began to explore -- from time to time --
>>> the nature of things in every direction.

> For perhaps
>> it would soon seem to them
>>> that *ours* was a changing way --
>> though as yet
>>> we sought merely
>>>> to return to our old ways.

. . .

AND YET
> THIS DID NOT OCCUR.

FROM TIME TO TIME
> They came to us --
>> asking about this or that apparent change.

> And yet
>> they never seemed to find these changes too great.

> So did we also
>> maintain our communities closer to them
>>> in a manner they more easily recognized.

Those among the People
   who preferred this or that
      arranging themselves accordingly.

"LOOK"
   -- someone said --

"We are arranging ourselves
   into five distinct clans
      on our Earth Island --
   though surely no mountains divide us."

And all laughed
   at this purported similarity
      to another People recently left.

       . . .

NOW
   We continued in this manner
      beyond the stretch to grandchildren
         and to grandchildren beyond.

Nor were any of our People
   dissatisfied with this circumstance.

The mountains were lower
   than any great mountains we remembered.
Surely
   these were no Touch the Sky Mountains.

AND YET
   THERE WAS VALUE HERE AS WELL.

For Ocean was near at hand
   as was a yielding forest.

Clearings were scattered here and there,
   with many encouraged beyond.

Berries abounded.

And of deer there was no lack --
   for those who went North and West
      to encourage needed clearings
         found also adequate deer.

AND IN THAT MANNER
WAS OUR LIFE
GREATLY SATISFYING TO US.

YET
It came to be not so
for our Brothers to the South.

For they spread out
upon no encouraged fields at all,
and for that reason --
and for few encouraged seeds --
deer enough for us
was too little for them.

AND SO
They called a Great Council of the Two Peoples
and said to us with a sad heart --

"This little land
grows even less under so many feet --
and deer disappears too quickly
and berries are picked too fast --
so that one People and the Other
can no longer live in this small space.

"We urge you --
our Recent Brothers --
you who are so clever at such things --

"WE URGE YOU
TO FIND A WIDER SPACE
AND TO SETTLE THERE."

AND WE SAW HOW IT WAS
Our wisdom now
brought with it a greater responsibility
for our Brother People
were saying to us --

"You who know how to change and grow --
and to keep the memories
of various circumstances . .

"YOU ARE THE ONES
MOST SKILLFUL AT CHANGE.

"SO, AS WE PERCEIVE CHANGE
 IS NECESSARY,
  WE ASK YOU
   TO UNDERTAKE THE TASK."

AND WE WONDERED MUCH
 AT THE WISDOM OF SHARING WHAT WE KNEW
  WHICH SOMETIMES GAVE BENEFIT,
   BUT MORE OFTEN DID NOT.

AND YET IT SEEMED
 That any two-legged at all
  might one day learn from Memory
   which exceeds both themselves
    and their own People.

AND THEN
 Someone pointed out --

 "It is like First People's Child.

 "If each person learns in a different way
  and at a different point --
   perhaps each People learns this way also.

 "Quick on some things,
  slow on others
   and greatly valuing
    those things they quickly learn
     as more important
      than those things they learn more slowly."

AND WE SAW
 HOW IT WAS THIS WAS SO
  AND HAVE REMEMBERED HER WISDOM
   FROM THAT DAY TO THIS.

 For we were not a stone building People
  and saw little value
   in the piling up of stone.

AND YET,
 we had come to know others
  who found it not so.

IT SEEMED TO US
  That this much piling up of stone
    had slowly destroyed the Stone Hill People,
      leaving little time
        for understanding where they were.

AND YET,
  The Sun People also found great value in this
    and did not see the toilers
      disappearing in the forest.

So perhaps
  there was value in many stone houses.

BUT WE AS A PEOPLE
  DID NOT SEE IT.

MIGHT WE NOT, WE SAID TO ONE ANOTHER,
  BE AS PATIENT
    WITH THOSE
      WHO DID NOT UNDERSTAND
        OUR WAY?

We Search

NOW
    WE SEARCHED FARTHER THAN EVER BEFORE,
        LOOKING
            FOR A SPACE ON THE EARTH
                FOR THE CHILDREN'S CHILDREN.

To the North
    lived others in round houses.

And we had no wish
    to argue over this part or that of the forest.

But to the North and also West
    lay a land of many long lakes --
        with no one at all living there
            from among the two-legged.

AND SO WE CHOSE TO MOVE --
    Some of us --
        and to slowly learn
            the nature of the land around.

AND,
    As we slowly learned in this manner,
        we came to find a lake to the North
            that was greater than all the rest.

Not a mere pouring of waters
    between two mountains was this,
        but a vast water --
            stretching North beyond sight --
                East and West also along the shore.

NOW I WILL TELL YOU A THING
    THAT WILL BE A GREAT WONDER TO YOU.

FOR IN ALL THIS TIME
    The People
        had come to perceive the nature of many lakes,
            none of which
                held any salt taste in their waters.

    They had come to find at last --
        after much searching --
            three Great Oceans
                filled with the taste of salt.

NOW
    They stood at the edge of this Great Water --
        untouched by any taste of salt --
            and wondered much.

    For this water was so great and so vast
        that no distance runner
            would reach its end in a day.

    So vast also
        that many of the aspects of Ocean were here.

    For at the edge of this Great and Wonderful Water,
        the waters tumbled themselves into waves --
            even as at Ocean's Edge.

    So that we knew
        either limit of this water
            must be far, indeed.

AND WE STOOD IN WONDER,
GAZING AT THE BEAUTY AROUND US ..

    Until some one spoke and said --

    "In all our travels
        we have seen nothing like this,
            this vast lake
                with its tumbling waters.

"NOWHERE
　　IN THE MEMORY OF THE PEOPLE
　　　　IS SUCH A THING CONTAINED.

"In all our travels
　　we have looked for a home at an Ocean's Edge --
　　　　and yet no one here can tell us
　　　　　　how to cross
　　　　　　　　the Great and Shining Sea to our East.

"If we cannot find such a place,
　　though we have searched and found two Oceans,"
　　　　-- he went on --

"Let us now decide
　　for this lake
　　　　so vast as to be nearly an Ocean.

"Let us decide
　　for these Great and Tumbling Waters.

"Let us give a name to this place"
　　-- he concluded.

"Let us name it
　　for the beauty we see all around us.

"As we have called none such before --
　　let us now
　　　　call this Great Lake -- Beautiful.

"FROM THIS DAY FORWARD
　　LET US CALL IT BEAUTIFUL LAKE.

"AND LET IT BE
　　A NEW CENTER PLACE
　　　　FOR THE CHILDREN'S CHILDREN."

AND
    ALL SAW THE WISDOM IN HIS WORDS.

    They heard it --
        and their eyes grew damp --
            for nowhere here
                were any of the two-legged.

    No Stone Hill People
        yielding to our explanations.

    No Brothers to the South
        seeking some greater space.

    Here
        lay only Beauty
            and an open way.

AND
    WE SENT FOR THE REST OF OUR PEOPLE . .

    SO THAT THE CHILDREN'S CHILDREN
        COULD BEGIN
            TO KNOW THEIR NEW HOME.

Beautiful Lake

Many Learnings

A Different Way

Beautiful Lake

NOW
  AS WE HAD LEARNED
    AT THE EDGE OF THE EASTERN OCEAN

IT IS ONE THING
  TO FIND A PLACE ON THE EARTH
    THAT IS PLEASING TO YOU
AND QUITE ANOTHER
  TO BE ALLOWED TO STAY.

Although there were
  none but isolated traces indicating
    other than Bear and Deer
      followed regular patterns here --
So it had been
  at the edge of the Eastern Ocean.

And yet that swath of forest and clearing
  was too well edged
    with People to the South
      and People to the North.

"At least we can be sure"
  -- some one said --

"There is no one at all to the North,
  save those who swim."

And all laughed
  at this relevant understanding.

"To the East and West then"
  -- some one else said.

And some were asked to follow the southern edge
  of this fresh water inland Ocean
    to East and to West.

And after many days they returned --
  reporting again no sign of residence.

AND SO THIS IS HOW IT SEEMED TO US --
Nowhere along the southern edge
of this Great and Beautiful Lake
was there any sign of others
who preferred this place.

REASSURED IN THIS MANNER --
We sent for those we had left behind,
divided ourselves
into appropriate communities,
chose places
along the southern edge
of this Great and Beautiful Lake,
and arranged ourselves
in such a manner
as to predict a long future.

. . .

BUT IT WAS NOT TO BE SO --

FOR DURING THE THIRD SPRING . .

During that time
of swelling buds and early flowers . .

Even then --
we arose one morning
to find a delegation
of new and different People,
standing at the edge of this Great Water.

WE WELCOMED THEM
AND ASKED TO UNDERSTAND THEIR PURPOSE . .

What with signs and other things
they made known to us
that we were to go away.

This was greatly puzzling to us,
as we saw no other folk
who sought to live here.

And our puzzling remained
until a more expanded understanding
of the manner of their speech
was sorted out by those essaying this task.

WHEN THIS WAS AT LAST ACCOMPLISHED . .

When we had at least three among our People
who began to understand in some detail
the patterns of their speech,
we began to understand them.

This was, they said, a part of the forest
for future settlement of their People.

Nor had they any intention
of yielding up
the southern edge of a Great Lake
which they called the center of their world
to mere wandering others.

We explained to them, as best we could,
that wandering was not our way --
that we had carefully come
from the Edge of the Shining Ocean
to our East
to this place we had chosen --
both for the Great Water
and for the clear lack of any residence.

We suggested to them
that it might please them as much
to have us here
as it pleased our Brothers to the South
past the grandchildren's grandchildren.

BUT THIS SEEMED A PEOPLE
ILL PREPARED
TO UNDERSTAND SUCH THINGS.

And we noted they made no attempt
to learn the patterns of our speech
nor to understand our purpose.

AND WE SAW HOW IT WAS OFTEN SO
That a People
so values the patterns of their own speech
as such a gift
that any other patterns seem to them
mere cacophonous noise.

So, often do they also value
any understanding but their own
irrelevant to any sensible purpose.

They see neither learning, nor wisdom,
nor anything of value
in any way but their own.

WE HAVE NEVER BEEN
SUCH A PEOPLE

. . LET IT BE SO.

• • •

NOW YOU SEE HOW IT WAS.

How these others had no ears for listening,
but only a great wish
that we had never arrived.

Neither would they listen
to our suggestions of possibilities
which might be as beneficial to their People
as to our own.

INSTEAD,
Finally one of them stood --
and pounded his spear on the Earth
until all was silent
and these were his words --

"You still do not understand"
-- he began.

"WE ARE A PEOPLE
WHO KNOW OUR OWN MIND
AND WHO KNOW
HOW TO ACCOMPLISH OUR PURPOSE.

"OUR PURPOSE IS THIS . .

"That one day, as we continue to expand,
 our People will live to both South and North
  of the Great Water.

"Our purpose
 is to have no others here until then.

"Our purpose
 is that you leave at once
  to compensate us
   for ever having arrived at all.

"AND WE SAY THIS --
 we will return when the leaves fall.

"Not one of us, not five, not seven,
 nor yet ten tens of us will come.

"Instead a number of us
 so vast you cannot comprehend it
  will come --
 and with spears and with arrows and with clubs
  we will drive you out,
   offending many in every way possible.

"KNOW THIS AND SPEAK NO MORE . .

"If you are not gone with the falling leaves
 we will assure it
  and many among you
   will be sadder for the loss."

AND
    All these words were measured
        by the pounding of his spear on Earth --

    So that we came at last to understand
        that here were a People
            who did not limit
                the use of spear and arrow
            to the necessity of gathering wherewith to eat.

    Not only deer and elk
        felt the sharp sting of a flying arrow,
            but those among the two-legged
                who did not please them
                    felt its sharp sting also.

    We wondered
        if such also found their way
            into the cooking pot.

    For surely a People
        who would raise their hand
            against a Brother People
                would not stop at mere destruction.

AND YET
    We saw
        how great was our lack of understanding.

    We saw also
        how much more willing our People were
            to learn to understand the ways
                of this angry People . .
            than they were to understand ours.

AND SO
   THIS WAS OUR DECISION.

   As the leaves fell --
      so would we also leave this place --
         taking with us
            everything we had grown and gathered --
         all manner of seeds and nuts --
            berries and pounded berry cake --
         our Three Sacred Sisters
            would flourish here also
               and would go with us when we left.

   Everything we had built would be taken down
      and carried with us or burned
         as a token of our determination to leave.

   WE HAD NO WISH
      TO GIVE THIS ANGRY PEOPLE
         TO UNDERSTAND OUR PURPOSE TO RETURN . .
      THOUGH THIS WAS INDEED OUR PURPOSE.

AND
   This moving of houses began at once
      so that winter
         would find us in secure place.

   Now the place we chose . . was chosen
      as it was clear
         no one would want to live there.

   It was a place of bogs and marshes
      that pleased no one at all for living.

IN THIS MANNER
   We thought to forestall
      any further promise
         of violence against our persons.

NOR WAS THIS THE END OF ALL WE DECIDED.

FOR WE DECIDED ALSO
    to learn to understand this Angry People,
    to learn their ways and their habits,
      their manner of use
        of spear and arrow and club
          against those of four and two-legs --
    the daily pattern of the life
      they chose for themselves . .

So that, as we moved back to the southern shore
    of our Beautiful Lake --
      we would do so
        filled with understanding
        and able to maintain our Place.

FOR THIS PURPOSE,
    We asked
      some of the strongest and sharpest of eye
        of our young men
          to spend this same summer
            watching the nearest of this folk.

AND THIS THEY DID . .
    While all those
      remaining to the South of this Great Water
        toiled as never before
        gathering all they could
          deer and berries,
          bear and nuts,
          all the seeds of our Three Sisters
            who were always with us.

And others
    carried logs and support poles and woven mats,
      so as to prepare our next place
        for an early winter arrival.

AND THOUGH FROM TIME TO TIME
    ALL SEEMED IMPROBABLE OF ACCOMPLISHMENT . .

YET AS LEAVES FELL FROM EVERY TREE --
    SO WERE THE PEOPLE
      PREPARED TO LEAVE THIS PLACE,
      PROMISING TO RETURN.

NOW
    After our arrival at this new and marshy home,
        some from our Watchers returned home,
            speaking of many things learned . .
            speaking also
                of more things yet unlearned.

So that we came to understand
    that this was a People
        greatly adept at understanding the ways
            of elk and beaver and bear,
        sure also of their way through the forest,
        surer still of their way across the waters.

FOR THIS WAS A PEOPLE
    Who built the lightest water craft
        we had ever seen --
            surely the easiest to carry . .
And who were adept at causing these narrow craft
    to go precisely where they chose --
        interacting with the water
            in such a way as to assure it.

NOW
    Over quiet waters
        this may be no amazement
    But over tumbling waters
        of forceful streams . .
    Over the tumbling waters
        at the edge of the Great and Beautiful Lake --

Even in these places
    were hand and eye and paddle so used
        as to assure the purposed arrival.

AND WE SAW HOW IT WAS
    WE HAD INDEED
        MUCH TO LEARN.

Many Learnings

NOW
 THOSE WHO HAD BECOME OUR EYES AND EARS
  near the southernmost community of this People
   suggested several things . .

That others be asked to take their place
 carefully watching this southernmost community
  at the Eastern Edge of the Great Lake,
 avoiding as carefully any contact with --
 or even the awareness of --
  this watched People.

That some from among those who had watched
 return to our center place in the marshes --
  so that all might learn to understand
   what had been gained so far.

That others from among those who had watched
 go down among this People
  and offer to perform for them
   any task they might wish
 in exchange for a Great Learning --
 in exchange
  for a slow and growing understanding
   of the manner
    of their forest-path walking
   and the manner
    of their water travel.

AND WE SAW HOW IT WAS
 That this was a People
  who valued their own way greatly,
   and were incurious about others . .
 So that we thought,
  carefully approached,
   such a purpose might yield great benefit.

AND SO IT WAS AGREED AMONG US
 That part of our purpose
  over several season circles
   would be a slow learning
    from this Angry People.

NOW THIS WAS THE WAY OF IT.

Some from among our young men were asked --
and also agreed --
to go down to this People
and offer their effort in any way at all
in exchange for food.

A People
valuing their forest ways above ours
would find this a likely request.

As the Angry People
grew used to our presence among them
and began to value
the results of our efforts on their behalf,
then perhaps more careful watching
or even occasional questions
would be allowed.

BUT THIS WAS OUR DECISION
ON THE ORDER OF PURPOSE
For these Learning Ones.

FIRST . .

Learn a great fluency
in their patterned speech.

Essay no question at all
until an absolute understanding of the answer
could be assured.

There seemed no value
either in wasted questions
or in earning their respect
as thinking persons
too quickly.

SECOND . .

> Agree to any task at all
> > whatever its nature
> > > and agree unflinchingly.

> It was our estimation
> > that this
> > > would generate much laughter among them
> > > and less concern for our presence
> > as they had among them an exact determination
> > > as to what tasks were given
> > > > to those among them who were women
> > > > and those among them who were men.

> It was much less so among us
> > so that that which would cause them
> > > great consternation,
> > held little value in our eyes.

THIRD . .

> Watch slowly.

> Gaze at nothing with apparent eyes.

> Rather,
> > let a general awareness of your circumstance
> > > be wherefrom you learn.
> > as they become more used to your presence,
> > > arrange your tasks
> > > > such that casual and wandering eyes
> > > > > may instruct you further.

> Do not ask to learn.

> Rather,
> > wait until they ask for your help.

> Then -- apparently all unwilling --
> > say how it is you do not understand the task,
> > > until they insist on explanations.

> Show a willing hand,
> > but an unwilling mind.

> *LET THEM CONVINCE YOU TO LEARN.*

IN THAT MANNER
   May we proceed with greater wisdom
      than we did with the Sun People to the West
         for too much curiosity
            often begets worrisome fear
         but too little curiosity never does.

AND IN THIS REMAIN CONSTANT.

   While with this People
      be celibate complete.

   You are not there to argue over women
      as Grey Squirrel was once known to do

   Neither are you there to beget children
      which are neither ours nor theirs.

   In such circumstance
      you will be quickly asked to leave.

Set your minds to this --
   while you are among this People
      you are neither male nor female --

   YOU ARE THERE TO LEARN.

AND WITH THIS AND WITH OTHER STRONG WORDS
SO IT WAS AGREED AMONG THE PEOPLE
AND SO IT WAS DONE.

NOW OVER MANY SEASON CIRCLES
  THIS WAS THE WAY OF IT.

    Some of our young men went out to learn,
      some to watch,
        and others to return.
    And we worked out agreements as to this
      among us.

    So that no regular pattern
      might become apparent,
        we chose this one or that one
          to go or to return in no regular way.

    Neither was the number
      of our young men among them always the same --
      but constantly varied --
    so that no general purpose
      might be ascertained therefrom.

NOW FIRST,
  Three of our young men went down --
    and were accepted.

    These were rapidly joined by fifteen more,
      who arrived from their watch-place in the hills
        in an apparently random manner.

    As we gained skill in their patterned speech,
      we learned much,
        for they were greatly pleased
          with the manner of our careful leaving --
        pleased also at our final act
          of burning what we could not carry.

    And -- as we expected they might --
      for this reason
        they allowed our marsh-bound place
    and for this reason
        they allowed some few among our young men
          to toil among them.

    And they did -- as we expected --
      assign these young men
        the worst of their women's work.

IN THIS WAY
    did the willing compliance of our young men
        assure them further we were a People
            deserving little regard.

AND WE SAW NO REASON WHY
    THIS UNDERSTANDING OF US
    AND WHO WE ACTUALLY WERE --
    NEED NECESSARILY MATCH.

Indeed we saw much reason
    why we had little reason
        to encourage any accurate understanding.

AND IN THIS AND IN OTHER WAYS
    Did they indeed proceed as we had predicted,
        showing us we had learned much in little time.

For they quickly regarded our young men
    as inconsequential
        and our whole People
            as unworthy of consideration.

Even did their frequent habit
    of striding past their womenfolk
        as if they were not there
            work to our advantage --
    for they quickly strode past our young men
    and almost as quickly
        began to forget they were there.

And especially since
    even the women among them
        came to have little regard
            for those who toiled for them
                and showed no other interest --
    even they
        began to speak for more such willing help
            and less concern.

So that we sent more of our watchers
    down from the hill . .

Until we were thirty-five
    among a much more numerous People
        nor did we allow the number to be more.

AND IN THAT MANNER
    was great familiarity and little concern
        encouraged.

NOW AGAIN AS WE PREDICTED,
    More and more tasks
        were assigned to these willing hands
            until the beginnings of learning
                were there.

    For the women began to show
        the crafting of this and that
            until our young men
                had taken up many tasks on their behalf.

AND AT LAST
    Some of the men among them
        began to see how their work, too,
            might be made easier,
        so that they began to speak in favor
            of the showing of some of these tasks
                to our young men.

    And these same young men
        encouraged these thoughts --
            not by strident words or actions . .

BUT FROM TIME TO TIME
    One of our young men would take his sewing
        and -- seeking some better light
            and cooler air --
        carry it to some stream edge
            where one from among their men
                Bent and shaped the wood
                    for one of their light watercraft.

AND FINALLY,
    seeing him sitting there
        with needle and sinew,
            he spoke in angry disgust --

 "Why are you not helping me?
    why do strong hands like yours
        merely ply a needle
    when you could help me bend this framework
        as it should be?"

And our young man looked up in great surprise.

"I could not possibly help you"
   -- he replied --

"For I have no notion of what you do!"

"But you could learn"
   -- insisted he who bent wood
     for this light craft.

"I am not sure"
   -- he answered in some hesitation.

"Perhaps I could . . . "

      • • •

AND THAT WAS THE BEGINNING --
AND THIS WAS THE END.

Slowly one and another
   began to convince the others
     of the wisdom of using such willing hands
      to some better purpose.

AND WE LEARNED.

WE LEARNED --
   to craft canoes
     from birch bark only
   to craft better paddles
     than ever before
   to craft better arrows with truer flight
     than ever before seen
   to craft clubs
     whose only purpose
      seemed to be
       the breaking of a Brother's head.

WE ALSO LEARNED
   BETTER FOREST CRAFT.

For this People
   who encouraged no seeds nor sought any
     had therefore devised many and better
      ways through the forest
       than any we had seen--

And it was for this
    the men valued themselves so well.

And there was some cause --
    though an awareness
        of how much yet there may still be to learn
           has some value also . .

BUT OUR YOUNG MEN
    LEARNED AND LEARNED AGAIN
        and returned to our home place in the marshes
        -- some of them --
           so that more might learn
        and others were sent in their place . .

UNTIL ALL OUR PEOPLE
    UNDERSTOOD ALL THESE SKILLS
    AND IN SOME THEY EXCELLED . .

So that the People from whom we learned
    sometimes now said --

    "You have learned so well
        what we have sought to teach you
           that in some things you now outdo us."

AND SO
    They invited some of our young men
        to join their groups that sometimes went
           to argue with a neighboring People.

AND
    THIS RAISED MUCH CONSTERNATION AMONG US . .

    FOR NEVER
        had any of our People raised a hand
           against any two-legged Brother --
             save only once --
        and in that Telling
           the People found little joy.

SO IT WAS WITH GREAT SADNESS OF MIND
    That the People contemplated
        this most recent offer
           of Learning.

AND FROM AMONG THE YOUNG MEN
   SOME SPOKE FOR IT . .

SAYING WE COULD MAKE NO WISE DECISION
   ABOUT A RETURN
      TO THE EDGE OF OUR BEAUTIFUL LAKE . .

UNTIL WE TRULY UNDERSTOOD
   THIS WILLINGNESS
      TO RAISE ONE'S HAND
         AGAINST A NEIGHBOR BROTHER.

AND WE SAW HOW THIS WAS SO.

WE SAW ANOTHER THING AS WELL.

WE SAW
   How living in this marsh-bound land
      did little enough
         for the health of our People.

For those who were ill
   had greatly increased.

These marshes were,
   in some way we not yet understood,
      different from the standing water
         that edged our River Bend Home.

And some from among the People
   had even rendered up their lives
      due only to this illness.

AND SO IT WAS
   THAT THE WHOLE PEOPLE
      GAVE RELUCTANT ASSENT
         TO THIS NEW LEARNING.

AND TO THOSE YOUNG MEN
   Who took up this task they said --

"WE ARE A LEARNING PEOPLE.

"We are not a People
   who lightly value any life --
      not Wolf, nor Bear,
      nor any among the Two-legged.

"You go out from here
  to learn new and harmful ways --
    and to bring back to the People
      this new understanding.

"But as we are a People
  who would do no unnecessary harm . .

"So are we a People
  who do not send you forth
    lightly regarding your life or learning.

"AND SO WE SAY THIS --
  whatever you do --
  whatever this new Path
    to a new Learning requires --
      do that thing with a whole heart --
      nor stint in any way
        merely because their way and ours
          follow such different paths.

"As we are not a Water Walking People
  and yet you learn the nature
    of birch bark water craft --
  so let it be with this also.

"Whatever it is they do
  in the nature of their arguments
    with neighbor Peoples . .

"SO LEARN THAT WAY,
  that all our People
    may surely learn from you
      an understanding
        that will meet and even exceed
          our need for understanding.

"FOR YOU NOW STRETCH OUT YOUR HAND
TO CATCH THE WISDOM WE WILL NEED
TO DECIDE OUR FUTURE PATH."

AND AS THEY CLEARLY UNDERSTOOD --
SO WAS IT DONE.

Ten and then twenty of our young men
  joined these out-going groups
    who went to argue with neighboring People.

AND AS THEIR LEARNING WAS GREAT --
SO DID OUR WISDOM BECOME GREATER.

AND ALL THE PEOPLE
LEARNED TO UNDERSTAND
A NEW WAY.

. . .

NOW
THIS NEW WAY
WAS IN NO WAY PLEASING TO US.

IT INVOLVED A WILLING HURTFULNESS
UNKNOWN TO US
BEFORE THIS TIME.

AND YET, WE SAW HOW IT WAS.
How a return to the shore of Beautiful Lake
would be rapidly followed
by many such arguing visits.

Many among our People,
many among theirs,
might therefore lie still upon the Earth,
rising to greet no further Dawn.

AND SO WE SAW HOW IT WAS
That any return to Beautiful Lake
would require a willingness
to become a People
adept at such hurtful ways --
or at apparent invisibility.

NOW
THE CIRCLE OF THE PEOPLE GATHERED

AND NOW
Each brought the gift of individual vision
to add to the understanding
of the Whole People.

THE COUNCIL CIRCLE WAS DRAWN --
AND THE MANY GIFTS OF LEARNING
LAID WITHIN --
AND YET IT WAS NOT ENOUGH.

ALL SAW HOW IT WAS
our preferred place required of us
willing hurtfulness.

ALL SAW HOW IT WAS
this marshy land caused much illness.

ALL SAW HOW IT WAS
our Brothers to the South
might prefer even greater distance
between them and such a Learning People.

NOWHERE
WAS THERE RESOLUTION.

. . .

Many spoke for our present place
despite its varying health.

Many spoke for the shore of Beautiful Lake
despite the change in nature it required.

Some spoke for an agreed return
to our Edge of Ocean home --
some further agreement
with our Brothers to the South.

AND AT LAST
A delegation was sent
asking for Return to Ocean,
explaining the difficult People here,
and promising many and regular gifts
of corn and deer and berries
in exchange for some agreed space
on the Earth
near Ocean.

Yet this brother People
    stopped their ears against our cries,
        hearing their own concerns
           instead of our words.

AND SO
    This delegation returned
        with no hint of agreement
        with only the same constant purpose
           of space for their own People
           to be who they were.

               . . .

NOW YOU CAN SEE, PERHAPS,
THE NATURE OF OUR CIRCUMSTANCE . .

HOW IT WAS
    That neither North nor South
        nor East nor West
           was any longer possible to us --

AND AS WE WERE --
    WHERE WE WERE --

WE WERE A PURPOSEFUL PEOPLE
WHO WERE SLOWLY DYING.

AND SO IT WAS
    That more and more among our People
        spoke once again for change --
        a change none desired
        yet a change continuance seemed to require.

FOR TO THE WEST
    lay a People
        we had no wish to see again.

AND TO THE EAST
    lay a Great and Shining Water.

AND TO THE SOUTH
    lay a Brother People
        we would rather keep as friends.

AND TO THE NORTH
   lay an arguing People,
   yet a People
      who thought to keep some part of Earth
       for tomorrow's children.

AND WE SAW HOW IT WAS
   That we would rather
      learn to argue with such a People --
       even in harmful ways --
         rather than return West
   or argue in this New Way
      with our Southern Brothers.

YET
  NOT ALL THE PEOPLE
    WERE WILLING FOR SUCH CHANGE.

AND SO,
   OVER MANY LONG DAYS OF MUCH SAID,
   WE DIVIDED FROM ONE ANOTHER . .

ONE IN TWO OF THE PEOPLE
   choosing to remain who they were,
   choosing no harm against any Brother Person,
   choosing this wet and marshy place instead.

AND ONE IN TWO OF THE PEOPLE
   chose a new way,
   a life sustaining way,
   a way of willing defense
     against the willing harm
       of arguments
         laid out by heavy wooden clubs.

AND THESE ONES
  Returned to Beautiful Lake,
    well prepared for this new life,
      rebuilt the houses burned before,
      placed a forest of trees
        around each gathering of Long Houses,
    and formed in this way three communities
    near the shore of this Beautiful Lake
      we chose to call home to us all.

AND
  When all houses were securely built,
    each gathering protected
      by a line of our Forest Brothers
        brought here in preparation
          for such a defense . .

  Then did we call
    all our young and learning men back,
      asking that they return to our new place.

  Then also did we send
    a delegation of our wisest Persons.

  And with them did we also send
    ten of those
      who had best learned the nature
        of these purposeful arguments
        and willing harm to others.

  As our Wise Delegation
    approached the nearest community
      of this People . .

  Those whose hair
    was sprinkled with the white of many winters
      stepped forward
  while those who had best learned the nature
    of purposeful harm to others
      formed a standing wall behind them.

WE HAD COME AT A GATHERING TIME
  JUST BEFORE THE BEGINNING OF WINTER.

Gathered in this place --
  as we knew --
    were therefore three communities
      of this Arguing People.

It was these we addressed.

"WE HAVE COME"

  -- we began --

    "TO EXPLAIN OUR NEW PURPOSE.

"MANY WINTERS AGO
  three of your People
    came to us at our new home
      on the Southern shore
        of this Beautiful Lake
    and explained how it was
      you purposed that place
        for your children's children.

"As you requested,
  we went away,
    even destroying
      the very houses we had built.

"NOW MANY WINTERS HAVE PASSED.

"The children's children begin to arrive,
  and yet
    we see no increase in your numbers.

"FOR THIS REASON --
  and for the ill-health also
    our place among the marshes engenders --
  we have come to live for a time
    on the South shore of this Beautiful Lake.

"Since we have learned so much from you
  we offer to show you our best skills as well.

"Let those who would learn
  to partake of the bounty
    of corn and her sisters . .

"Let those who would learn
  to build secure and stable houses . .

"LET THOSE WHO WOULD LEARN FROM US
  COME TO US THIS NEXT SPRING
  AND WE SHALL BE AS GENEROUS
  IN OUR EXPLANATIONS
    AS YOU HAVE BEEN IN YOURS."

. . .

NOW
  Since it never at all
    was the intent of this Arguing People
      to explain anything to us,
    their amazement was great.

They saw with sudden eyes
  the ten standing behind . .

Remembered
  that all our young and learning men
    had left their communities . .

And began to add together
  all those things taught to them.

Whereas they had thought they trained
  only this one or that . .

THEY BEGAN TO SEE
THEY HAD TAUGHT A WHOLE PEOPLE.

AND THEN
  One of the largest and strongest
    of the women among us stepped forward,
      offering gifts
        of corn and squash and beaded strips
      she, too, thanked them
        for all she had learned from them.

And many eyes caught the arc-shaped swing
   of the club tied at her waist --
      so that it became rapidly apparent
         how much had been learned and by whom.

Now those from among our delegation
   who also carried such gifts
      bent to set them forward on the ground --
   and from each belt also swung a similar club
      carried in clear purpose.

And the ten standing behind
   held heavier clubs in their hands.

And some from among this Arguing People
   had seen these very clubs
      swung to some purpose --
   so that with one thing and another
      our intent became clear.

"Let those who would learn from us
   as we have learned from you
      come to us in the Spring.

"LET THESE BE NO MORE THAN THIRTY-FIVE."

This chant was begun by he who spoke first,
   continued by she who spoke second,
   and echoed by each who was there
      as each turned and left --

Last of all was it chanted by the ten
   who now formed a standing wall
      between one People and the other,
         an image of purposefulness.

AND WE LEFT.

   LEFT THIS PEOPLE
      TO TALK AMONG THEMSELVES.

Left them too close to winter
   for any of their purposed arguments.

Left them a Winter for discussion
   and many images to remember.

Left them with corn and squash --
    strips beaded in our own manner,
    strips beaded in theirs,
       all reminders
          of how much had been learned
          and how much might be offered.

Left them to remember
    that none of their women carried clubs --
      yet all of our women
         attached them to their belt
            like some small needle case.

Left them to remember
    what this might imply.

AND OUR WINTER WAS CALM AND SECURE.

Houses carefully built in the summer
    were proof against any Winter Wind.

And the wall of trees
    devoid of roots or branches
       planted in a row in this rootless way
          was complete around each community
      so that the direction of any argument
       against our choice of living place
          might be known and watched.

Corn, Beans, and Squash
    had been gathered from many harvests
    and equally shared
       between those who chose the old way
         and a marshy home
       and those who chose a new way
         and a Lake Edge place.

Those from among our forest Brethren
 whom we seek
  for warm robes and Winter nourishment
   had been sung to
   and invited to help us in our new home.

Much had been gathered for a long Winter . .
 and for the difficult Spring
  that might yet follow.

For none knew how much time might remain
 between arguments with this Northern People
  to encourage any seed at all . .

AND
 All purposed a continuing home
  at the Southern edge
   of our Beautiful Lake.

AND THE WINTER CAME --
AND THE PEOPLE WERE CONTENT.

MANY FEASTS WERE HELD
AND ALL THE OLD SONGS SUNG . .

 To remind us
  who we were . .

 To remind us
  of the value of the many things
   that we had learned . .

 To remind us
  of the many difficulties
   met and resolved . .

TO REMIND US
 OF THE VALUE OF CONTINUANCE
  FOR SUCH A PEOPLE.

AND THEN
 THE SPRING BEGAN.

NOW
    THIS WAS THE WAY OF IT.

Three communities strongly built . .
    each Long House
        proof against any storm,
    each community
        surrounded by its standing wall,
    each community
        provided with a sure supply
            of both nourishment and water
                for many months
            should there be little time
                for such things.

The community
    closest to the neighboring People
        contained within its group
    the strongest of both male and female --
        three out of every five such persons.

One out of every five
    joined the second and third communities.

All was ordered in such a way
    that the first and easternmost community
        would be the first
            to withstand any purposed argument.

YET,
    IF THAT COMMUNITY DID NOT SURVIVE,
        there was strength in the second
            and even in the third commmunity
                to survive subsequent arguments
                should they occur.

ALL WAS IN READINESS FOR SUCH ARGUMENT.

Clubs carved for each individual,
    bows and arrows also, as well as spears,
        so that no tool for such an argument,
            should it occur,
                would be lacking.

All was in readiness, also,
to greet as many as thirty-five learners
and to instruct them in the ways
of Corn and Beans and Squash --
as well as any other thing
they might seek to understand.

As soon as spring arrived
watchers were sent out
to mark the arrival
of either such group.

At the same time
the young went out to encourage seeds,
here and there,
in secluded places in the forest.

At the second and third communities,
regular fields were planted also.

• • •

AND THE VISITORS ARRIVED.

More than thirty-five came
and none showed any interest in learning.

RATHER,
They threw themselves against our forest wall
and sought out high places
from which to send arrow after arrow
into our midst.

They tracked every path also,
seeking those who might wander away
from our secure walls.

BUT WE WERE PREPARED,
SECURE AGAINST THEIR USUAL ATTACK,
RESERVING OUR OWN STRENGTH
FOR A LONG FUTURE,
FOR SURELY,
WE PURPOSED NO FURTHER MOVES.

At the first sight of these visiting others
    word had been sent
        to our second and third communities.

Their task
    was to be unapparent,
        to grow corn and beans and squash,
        and to prepare for all possible tomorrows.

AND SO IT WAS
    THAT SPRING AND SUMMER AND AUTUMN PASSED.

Our first community was constantly watched
    and frequently harassed
        and many shouts predicting starvation
            echoed through the surrounding trees.

THEN,
    AS THE SNOWS BEGAN,
    ALL BUT A FEW WATCHERS . .
        LEFT.

These we captured one by one
    inviting them in for a feast,
    and sending them home
        with a full stomach and a wondering head,
        each accompanied by three of our own People
            carrying gifts of corn and turkeys.

Nor could they in any way
    deduce the origin of either.

At the same time,
    many from the other communities arrived
        with heavy packs of everything good,
    the two communities
        providing a full year's provender
            for the third.

                    • • •

AND ONCE MORE
We spoke the same invitation.

"Your watchers seemed so curious"
-- we began --

"That we invited them in
to partake of our continuing bounty --
some of which we bring to share with you."

"We know"
-- someone went on --
"How to bring forth bounty out of little at all.
and again we invite
perhaps as many as thirty-five --
and as few as one --
to join us for at least three Winters
so that you may also learn
these bountiful ways."

NOW
THERE FOLLOWED SEVERAL TURNINGS
OF WINTER TO SUMMER TO WINTER ONCE MORE.

AND IN EACH
VARIOUS THINGS OCCURRED.

FROM TIME TO TIME
Some individual from this northern People
would come to ask to learn --
only to turn away from those tasks
he considered women's work
and refuse, therefore, to learn.

FROM TIME TO TIME
Some group -- large or small --
would come to harass our First Community,
guarding this entrance from any exit --
thinking thereby
to at last engender starvation.

As each such group left --
we called out to them,
offering them gifts
of corn or beans, deer or turkeys,
in exchange for their great efforts
in coming to visit us.

THEN
A group came and howled for someone at last
to come out and fight . .

We called back
that five from among us who knew this skill
would come out to fight five of their People
so trained --
since this was so greatly their wish,
we would oblige them in this way.

AND AT LAST ALL WAS AGREED --
All but five of their group
retiring to the forest --
These five calling out for their opponents.

AND THEY CAME.

Five of our People
suitably trained,
provided also with club and lance,
the tallest of their kind --

Five such People
came out from our wall of cut trees --
came out
and offered their willingness for combat --
stood with club and lance in either hand --
and viewed the amazed faces
of this Northern Five . .

FOR
each and every one from among us
coming out from behind our cut tree wall --
each and every one -- was woman.

• • •

NOW
   The howling grew greater.

   Our Formidable Women strode forward --
      offering combat --
      complaining greatly
         when the Northern Five refused to fight.

   For surely
      it was as we understood it.

   The division of tasks
      between those among this Northern People
        who were men
      those among this Northern People
        who were women
            was exact and invariable --
              as it was not with us.

FURTHER --
   This concept of willing harm to others
      was as new to our men
        as to our women --
            neither finding it a natural human event.

AND --
   As it was among our People --
      to engender some understanding
        of the tasks of others --
      such tasks were often shared
        across usual divisions.

   So might a man learn the many skills
      usually left to women.

   So might a woman learn the many skills
      usually left to men.

   These cross-over People
      built bridges of understanding,
      wove threads of further connection
        back and forth throughout our People
      so that neither those who were old
        nor those who were young
      persons who were male
        nor persons who were female
          need ever lack understanding
            of another's circumstance.

AS IT HAS BEEN SO AMONG OUR PEOPLE
SINCE TIME BEYOND TIME,
SO IT WAS NOW.

And this alone
    so disconcerted our Northern neighbors
      that they hardly knew
        which foot to pick up
        and which to put down.

      . . .

NOW
    Our Five Formidable Women
      charged the Northern Five.

Again and again they charged,
    shouting angry words in this manner --

"You keep us from our sewing."

"We have meals to cook
    and must come out and oblige you."

"How can we tend our homes
    if we stay here arguing with you?"

AND YET
    These Northern Men had as yet no answer,
      for their amazement was great.

THEN
    Our Five Valiant Women
      began running at them saying --

"Go home and leave us in Peace."

And when the Northern Five
    began calling for Warriors . .

These Five answered --

"We are here.
   Only beyond us
      will any of our men be found --
         as they are busy elsewhere."

And when at last in anger
   these Northern Five struck out calling --

"FOOLISH WOMEN"

Our foolish women
   defended themselves effectively
   and easily defeated
      these Five confused warriors --
calling out
      that the matter was settled --
         it was time to go home --
   and that these Five Men
      might stay to learn from our women
         as our men had learned from theirs.

• • •

NOW
   A strange thing occurred.

One -- and then another --
   of these Five
      professed such amazement
         at the skill of our women
           with club and lance
      that they offered to agree to stay to learn
         from women such as these.

And these two
   were our first Learning Others.

NOW I WOULD TELL YOU,
 IF IT WERE SO,
  THAT THIS WAS THE END
   OF OUR VIGOROUS DISCUSSIONS
    WITH OUR NORTHERN NEIGHBORS
    AS TO WHERE WE MIGHT LIVE.

BUT IT WAS NOT SO.

FROM TIME TO TIME
  This one or that agreed to learn from us,
    and we willingly showed them many things.

  They worked with the women for our Three Sisters --
    Corn and Beans and Squash.

  It was our thought
    that if this Northern People
      learned to dance
        with our Sacred Sisters
    their need for forest space would be less
      and our argument equally less.

  But of those who came to learn from us --
    most stayed,
      increasing our strength and our numbers
        as they came to prefer our way.

BUT THE REST
  STILL RESISTED IT.

  Came to harass us from time to time.

  And perhaps never did learn to understand
    the magic of our endless corn
      and always turkeys.

FOR
> During these long days
> and even longer nights
> of ceaseless discussion
> when one in two of the People
> chose this way,
> as one in two did not,
> so did we also discuss
> the many possibilities
> of our relocation.

AND FROM THIS
WE EVOLVED AGREEMENT

> That would assure
> to the best of our gathered wisdom
> the continuance
> of the children's children
> to the South of Beautiful Lake.

AND OUR AGREEMENTS WERE THESE . .

That we would build and secure a Community
five days journey
from this Northern People.

That we would then build and secure a community
three to four days journey
west of that.

That we would then build and secure a community
three to four days journey
west of that.

As soon as the first two communities
were complete,
That next early Winter
would we announce our new place
in the manner you have been told.

That we would offer gifts
of provender,
crafted goods,
and learning.

That we would prepare for war.

That we would use every device
   we could discover
      to prevent harm
      and discourage continuing hostilities.

THAT IF WE FAILED IN THIS,
   WE WOULD MAINTAIN OUR NEW PLACE
      WHATEVER THAT MIGHT REQUIRE.

• • •

FOR ALL THESE REASONS,
   Those who refused to follow such a path
      decided to maintain their marshy home.

AND WE HONORED THEM FOR THIS.

   "Do you"
     -- we told them --

   "Keep the old and gentle ways,
     while we essay the new.

   "Then -- when we have secured a place
     for the children's children
       along that Southern shore --
   we will return
     and ask you to join us there.

   "YOU WILL REMIND US OF THE OLD WAYS . .

   "WE WILL SHOW YOU THE NEW . .

   "AND PERHAPS THE CHILDREN'S CHILDLREN
     MAY LEARN BOTH
       SO THAT BOTH MAY BE KEPT."

SO WE SAID,
   AND SO IT WAS INTENDED.

YET
   Twenty Winters and more disappeared
      in the back and forth
         of this strange argument.

AND A NEW GENERATION STEPPED FORWARD.

AT LAST IT WAS AGREED
   After many Winters of varying argument
      that our place was assured,
         if often challenged.

   And a delegation was specified
      and sent at last
         to invite our Brothers, our Sisters
            to join us in this Lake-Side Place.

AND THE DELEGATION WENT SOUTH,
   Paced out the many days travel
      to that marshy place
         and found it at last . .
         found the marshes
         found the dwellings
         found this and that implement
         found even some preserved food

BUT FOUND NO PEOPLE AT ALL.

NO WHERE . .
   no matter how careful the search . .
      was any living being found,
         but evidence of sickness and death
            were found.

AND FROM THAT DAY TO THIS
  NO ONE AT ALL
    HAS EVER LEARNED
      OF OUR BROTHERS, OUR SISTERS.

WE LOST OUR GENTLE PEOPLE.

WE LOST OUR KEEPERS OF THE PEACEFUL WAY.

      • • •

NOW
  When the delegation returned
    their disconsolate pace
      spoke from a distance.

And when all were sure
  of what this slow-paced group had learned --
    then the sorrowing was great.

"YOU SEE HOW IT IS"
  -- someone said --

"How the continuation
  of an ancient and wise way
    requires the continuation
      of at least some of the People.

"We have accepted responsibility for a new way"
  -- she went on --

"And left responsibility for the old way
  with our Brothers, our Sisters
    who have disappeared.

"Now we hold in either hand,"
  --she concluded --

"Responsibility for one way --
  and the other."

AND ALL SAW HOW IT WAS . .

   How, if the old way were to continue,
    filled with gentleness and peace,
      some from among the People must be found
       to be responsible for it.

FOR SURELY
   THE STRIDENCE OF DEFENSE
     OFTEN OVERRIDES THE SOFTER SOUNDS
     OF A GENTLER WAY.

AND YET . .
   NONE SAW ANY VALUE AT ALL
   IN LOSING AWARENESS
     OF EITHER POSSIBILITY.

      • • •

AND SO IT WAS
   That this one and that stood forward,
    explaining their stronger feeling
     for the gentler way --
    and accepting responsibility for it.

AND THESE ONES WERE RESPECTED --
AND HONORED
   FOR THEIR WILLINGNESS
    TO MARK A DIFFERING PATH.

"Let us remember the wisdom of each"
   -- someone said.

"For surely
   the Ancient Way merits patient attention.

"And yet
   continuance has some value also"
    -- he went on.

"So that those who defend the People
and find that vigorous stridence
possible for them --
THESE ONES MERIT RESPECT ALSO.

"For surely
they equally enable
the keeping of an Ancient Way.

"Let us have the Wisdom"
-- he concluded --

"To respect Both Ways . .

"To value them,
and to remember -- from time to time --
to consider
which may be the appropriate Path --

TODAY."

LET US BE SO WISE.

LET US RESPECT EACH PATH.

LET US CHOOSE THE BALANCE BETWEEN THEM --

WITH A CAREFUL EYE.

SO BE IT.

NOW
   THIS WAS THE WAY OF IT.

FOR COUNTLESS WINTERS,
   Those who were skilled in war
     learned more effective ways of combat.
   Those who were skilled in peace
     learned more effective ways also . .

So that
   the changes in patterns of harm to others
     were not only more effective harm,
     but also ways where disagreements
      might be more gently settled.

And the changes were many . .
   and varied from time to time.

So that
   not only more careful designs for war clubs
     were devised,
   but ways also they might be used
     to do less harm.

And speaking of this from time to time
   encouraged both Peoples to value
     the strength of arm and quickness of eye
      which enabled a clear victory,
       yet no death at all.

AND FROM TIME TO TIME
   THIS WAS THE NATURE OF ANY BATTLE.

YET AGAIN
   WOULD CIRCUMSTANCE CHANGE . .

So that anger was greater,
   and therefore offense also.

So that many and not few
   lay still against the Earth
     after any battle.

AND YET
   NEITHER WAS WAR CONSTANT.

Those who spoke for Peace among us
   were often effective . .

And would from time to time
   go out to learn other ways
      and other patterns of speech,
   so that their words of Peace
      might be more easily understood.

AND IT CAME TO BE
   That these Keepers of the Peaceful Way
      also went out to speak to other Peoples
        in such clear tones

   THAT THESE SAME OTHERS UNDERSTOOD THEM
   AS A WISE AND JUST PEOPLE.

AND SO IT WAS
   That they were often asked to come
      and bring their special understanding
        to some dispute or other.

AND --
   IN INCREASING WAYS OVER TIME --

So were they also asked to mediate
   between one People and another . .

These Peoples
   coming to understand their judgement
      as both equitable
        and free of any constraints
           imposed by personal concern.

AND
   THESE WISE AND PEACEFUL PERSONS
   MADE THESE THINGS
      AN INVARIABLE AND INHERENT PART
      OF ALL THEY DID . .

Let no self interest
  enter into any judgement.

Neither let any interest
  of your own People
    cloud your eyes.

Weigh with even hands
  the benefit to all parties.

SEEK THE PEACEFUL WAY.

AND BEYOND THIS
  THEY LEARNED MANY SKILLS . .

Not only the patterns of speech
  acceptable to each . .

But ways of delaying decision past residual anger
  perhaps arriving later than expected
    with many tales of dire delays
      which turned anger to interest
      and allowed some greater distance
        between grievance and aggrieved . .

So that their final recommendation
  might be more easily accepted.

THEY LEARNED ALSO
  many ways of describing a similar circumstance
  and what resulted . .

So that all parties were attracted
  along the descriptive path,
    walking unawares
      beside a mind image designed
        to lend some greater understanding.

THEY SANG THESE SONGS SO WELL
    that all who listened
        gained greater understanding
        and sometimes agreed among themselves
          before even these Wise Ones
            heard their Tellings.

THIS THEY LEARNED TO DO SO WELL
    that often they began any such judgement
        with a time for singing general songs,
        some few of which were chosen
          for the specific learning
            needed in this circumstance.

AND NOW
    They began a way
        of sending the story tellers first,
            with Those Who Adjudicated
                following after . .

SO THAT WHEN THEY SPOKE,
    THEY SPOKE TO EARS
        THAT HAD LEARNED TO LISTEN.

FOR
    When still some contest was desired
        they would recommend
            some game or other usually played
            or some specific measure
                of the completion of some task
                    of extraordinary difficulty . .

So that some gentle judgement was found
    for those who succeeded that day --
        remembering always
            the next day might see a different success.

AND
    BEYOND THESE GAMES OF MEASURED POSSIBILITY
    LAY STILL ANOTHER CHOICE.

AND ALSO,
    Some test beyond the Peoples assembled
        would be made of Peace or War . .

    Whether doves
        suddenly produced
            from apparent nothingness
        and released in the Council Circle
            flew up toward Peace
            or down toward conflagration.

    And their predilection . .
        was to beat the air
            with strident wings
                climbing . . TOWARD PEACE.

All these skills and more were developed
   by the Keepers of the Peaceful Way . .

So that even were there war
   their voice was heard
      in the nature of the limits
         to the vigor of the hostilities
      or on the number involved.

AND YET
   IT WAS NOT ENOUGH.

For war still came and went
   among a People
      determined to keep their place on the land
   and a People
      determined to prevent it.

So that the Keepers of the Peaceful Way
   began to speak among those
      who knew the Ways of War
   how it was their judgement
      these harmful ways would wisely cease.

FOR IT WAS NOT ONLY HARM IN WAR
   THE PEOPLE LEARNED
      BUT HARM AT WAR'S END.

. . .

THIS WAS THE WAY OF IT.

This neighboring People
   had a way after war
      of treating those captured
         in a way they thought respectful.

As strength and fearlessness in war
   were valued . .
So were strength and fearlessness at war's end.

For these captives were called on
   in various ways
      to show both strength and fearlessness
         as their bodies were slowly destroyed.

NOW
FOR A PEOPLE
WHO VALUE THE WARRING WAY
THIS MAY HAVE MERIT.

BUT FOR A PEOPLE
WHO VALUE ALSO THE WAY OF PEACE
THIS IS A GREAT CONFUSION.

AND
THE PEOPLE WERE NOT RESOLVED.

There were those
who saw strength
in resisting such behavior.

There were those
who saw none.

. . .

NOW FROM TIME TO TIME
EITHER WAY WAS TRIED . .

Until it was learned
that showing only kindness to captives
earned no respect at all.

Rather,
greater harm to our own People
was the result.

Without such a test of bravery
this other People saw their men
as treated without respect . .

AND THIS ANGER
POURED FORTH ON OUR OWN PEOPLE
WHEN THEIR FATE WAS DECIDED.

So that, bit by bit,
the People were discouraged
from kindness in this way
and encouraged
toward tests of bravery
which gave great harm.

NO HEART WAS CONTENT WITH THIS . .

YET -- OVER TIME --
FEW INDEED ARGUED . .

UNTIL AT LAST
IT CAME TO BE
OUR REGULAR WAY.

NOW
There was one other manner
we learned from this other People --
their custom of marking the skin
with sharp points and dark dye.

IT CAME TO BE
THAT MANY OF OUR PEOPLE ALSO
MARKED THEIR SKIN IN THIS MANNER.

• • •

THOSE WHO KEPT THE PEACEFUL WAY
KEPT ALSO THE LONGEST MEMORY.

As it was less likely
their lives might be shortened by war . .

So was it considered wise
that they keep all Ancient Tellings.

IN THIS MANNER
Was some new separation engendered
between the People
and their own memories.

As the People
began to forget the Ancient Ways . .
So did they also
begin to forget a time
when no one at all
purposed any harm to any Brother.

So that this reality
began to seem a distant and improbable Past.

AND SO IT IS
for those who do not keep their own memories.

BUT
    The Keepers of the Peaceful Way
        kept also these memories --
            and knew them well.

    For them -- as for us now --
        both what was and what is
            were equally clear . .

    So that they saw both the peaceful
        and the afflicted circumstance
            as if with either eye.

    Neither did this vision
        engender any Joy.

    FOR THEY SAW WHAT WAS.
    AND THEY SAW WHAT COULD BE.
    AND THEY WONDERED MUCH.

    . . .

NOW AT THIS TIME
ANOTHER THING BEGAN TO OCCUR.

    For the People
        had flourished in this circumstance.

    New communities
        formed increasingly westward . .

    Until one place or another
        the People lived along the southern shore
            of Beautiful Lake.

AND
    From these three first parent communities,
        both children and grandchildren were born . .

    SO THAT EACH
    BECAME ITS OWN NATION
    WITH ITS OWN WAYS.

    AND THIS WAS SEEN AS GOOD.

They lived
  to the East and West and Center.

That Nation which was Easternmost
  was called the Keeper of the Eastern Door.

That Nation which was Westernmost
  was called Keeper of the Western Door.

That Nation which dwelt between
  was called the Center Keeper.

NOW
  The Keepers of the Western Door
    had learned ways
      to talk to their neighboring People
        who lived to the North and also West.

AND IT CAME TO BE
  That these two Peoples over time
    began to speak regularly to one another.

AND IT CAME TO BE ALSO
  That these two Peoples
    often exchanged Learning Ones,
      some staying to settle
        within either Nation . .

So that one People and the other
  began to call each other cousin.

NOW
  It was the custom
    of all Peoples to the North
      of this Beautiful Lake
    from its Eastern to its Westernmost shore
      to meet in general consultation
        every third Summer.

In this manner
  were the Arguing People we first met
    who lived to the North of the Eastern edge of this Lake
  joined in Council with Our New Cousins
    who lived to the North of its Western Shore.

And their place for this meeting
    was an island in the Great Lake
      to the West beyond our own
        kept free
            from any habitation --
    so that hunting there
      was good at such times.

AND THIS WAS THE WAY OF IT.

Every third year
    groups and whole communities would arrive
      representing their place
        and its other communities.

Even from the Northern Shore
    of Beautiful Lake
      did they come.

And those to arrive first
    had first choice of location
      and easiest hunting.

Those to arrive last
    had last choice
      and perhaps no hunting at all.

In years when many came in representation,
    some of necessity formed their group
      along the shore of the lake
    and came by water craft each day to council.

NOW
    This struck the Keepers of the Western Door
      as a great step toward Peace.

Especially did they wonder
    how it was a People so often at war
      could at such times
        behave in such peaceful
          and cooperative ways.

So that they asked their New and Increasing Cousins,
    how this was.

And they answered
    that the proclivity to War
        varied among the Peoples
           with those most close-kept
                by some circumstance or other
                    finding war as a way easier.

BUT AT THIS TIME
  IT WAS NOT SO
    AS BETWEEN THIS NEW COUSIN PEOPLE
    AND THE KEEPERS OF THE WESTERN DOOR . .

    FOR THEY LIVED TOGETHER IN PEACE
    AND IN INCREASING HARMONY.

        . . .

NOW
  It seemed to our New Cousin People
    that those of us they called their cousins
      these -- at least --
        should wisely be invited
          to one such summer meeting.

AND YET
  When they spoke for this,
    their Brother People
      North of the Eastern end of Beautiful Lake
        spoke against it.

  They spoke against our People
    whom they called usurpers . .

  They spoke against our varying ways,
    and against our presence
      in any summer meeting
        of these Brother Peoples.

AND YET
  OUR COUSINS SPOKE AGAIN.

THEY TOLD
  OF MUCH LEARNING . .

  of corn that grows
    when deer sometimes wander,
  of Peaceful Ways
    within a Great Long House,
  of children and of grandchildren
    who might live to a Wise Old Age
      if Peace would only come.

They spoke with such eloquence and candor
  that all heard them.

Yet this inclusion
  of a differing People
    seemed strange to many.

None remembered
  when such had been done.

AND SO IT WAS
  THAT NONE BUT THIS COUSIN PEOPLE
    SPOKE FOR THIS
      AND NO AGREEMENT WAS REACHED.

NOW
    Those among our People
        who were Keepers of the Peaceful Way
            had also spoken to these, Our New Cousins.

AND THEY HAD BEEN HEARD.

SO IT WAS
    That this Cousin People also began sending out
        some few of their People
            to speak with neighboring Nations.

    Gifts of corn and squash grown in their own fields
        went with them
            as did pots crafted in the manner
                of the People of the Western Door.

    So that some few others now saw some value
        in agreement rather than war.

AND THIS WAS THE WAY OF IT.

    Our Cousin People spoke again
        asking invitation of Three Nations
            to this summer gathering.

And all was changed.

    For now
        several other communities
            also spoke in this manner.

AND YET
    The Easternmost Peoples of this Council
        were not pleased --
        and grew angry at this insistence
            from their Western Brothers . .

    UNTIL ALL WAS NOISE
        AND NO WHERE
            WAS ANY AGREEMENT TO BE FOUND . .

And this summer meeting
   ended in consternation,
      as the Eastern Peoples declared
        that any such invitation
          would find them absent.

NOW
   Our New Cousin People were greatly concerned.

It was their wish to expand their circle
   to include those of our People
      they called their Increasing Cousins.

AND YET
   It was not their wish to lose in that way
      their Eastern Brothers.

AND SO IT WAS
   These two Cousin Peoples sat in council together . .

So that our New Cousins learned
   there was less than agreement also
      among the Three Nations.

Much was discussed . .

UNTIL AT LAST
   Someone rose and said . .

"If your Brother
   will not grant you a basket of corn,
      might he not grant you a handful?

"Let us use this lack of agreement . .
   to gain agreement.

"Do you, Our Cousins,
   at the next summer meeting
      tell your Eastern Brothers
        that our Eastern Brothers
          are no more eager to confer than they.

"Tell them you would nonetheless
　　see with some pleasure
　　　　some representation
　　　　　　from our Westernmost Nation.

"In that way
　　might they slowly grant
　　　　what they will not quickly allow."

AND SO IT WAS.
　　For at the next Summer meeting
　　　　this Cousin People rose and said how it was
　　　　　　the Eastern Nations
　　　　　　　　were no more willing to come
　　　　　　than their Eastern Brothers
　　　　　　　　were willing to have them.

AND YET, THEY SAID,
　　Some representation from the Three Nations
　　　　would assure greater prosperity
　　　　　　for Our New Cousin People.

And so they said how it was
　　that both this New Cousin People
　　　　and their Brothers to the East
　　　　　　might be assured of their preference.

"Let the Westernmost of the Three Nations
　　be invited"
　　　　-- they said --

"But not the Easternmost
　　nor even the Center Nation."

AND SO IT WAS.

> More than a handful of corn
>> was gained . .

> For the Keepers of the Western Door
>> were invited and sat comfortably
>>> next to their Cousin People.

> *As they were treated with respect,*
>> *so did they also treat others with respect.*

> Until the delegation from the Western Door,
>> though different in appearance and demeanor,
>>> became a usual element
>>>> in these Every Third Year Meetings.

NOW, OVER TIME,
OTHER THINGS BECAME POSSIBLE.

> For this securing of the Western Door
>> allowed to the Nation on each side of that Door
>>> a prosperity which rapidly became marked.

> Neither Eastern Nation could match them now
>> in ease of living or contentment.

> *AND THIS BECAME A THING TO LEARN FROM.*

> *Each such meeting*
>> *showed improvement in Our Cousins' way,*
>>> *until many saw how it was*
>>>> *a Learning People prospered.*

AND AGAIN THINGS CHANGED.

    For the next three years were years of drought
        followed by long cold Winters . .

    So that deer became less,
        as did all other forest creatures.

    So that difficulty for those
        who sought only forest provender
          was greater --
        and thin legs and slow walk
          followed soon after.

NOW
    When this third year came
        and none at all
          from the Eastern Peoples arrived
        all began to understand the difficulty --
          yet none at all saw any solution.

YET
    THOSE WHO KEPT THE WESTERN DOOR SAW IT.

    They returned to their Brother Nations
        and called for a Conference.

    "WE CAN CHOOSE"
        -- they said --

    "To let this Northern People die.

    "This will earn us
        the hatred and jealousy
          of all those who survive --
            as some surely will.

    "WE CAN CHOOSE"
        --they went on --

    "To destroy this Northern People
        in their weakness,
          so that no one at all seeks access
            through the Eastern Door.

"Yet by doing so
    we will surely earn the hatred
        of all other Northern Peoples,
            beginning, perhaps, some clatter
                at the Western Door.

"OR WE CAN CHOOSE"
    -- they concluded --

"To aid this Northern People
    in their adversity . .

"So that they may come at last to understand
    our preference for Peace
        and the value of our way."

FOR THIS WAS THE WAY OF IT.

Throughout the drought
    willing hands carried water gourds
        to any thirsty plant.

Understanding how it was
    that little water long enough
        would affect both deer and berry . .
    each of the Three Nations
        had hunted through that second summer --
           adding dried meat
               to much corn in storage
           and leaving fewer of our forest Brothers
                to starve for lack of Winter food.

IN THIS WAY ALSO
    WAS THE FUTURE OF THE PEOPLE
    ASSURED.

SO IT WAS
  That three difficult years for many
    were three easeful years
      of much water carrying
        and appropriate hunting for the People.

  For in the third year
    little hunting at all was undertaken --
      and in that way
        were our forest Brothers
          encouraged to increase.

SO IT WAS --
  WHAT WITH THIS AND THAT --
    DEARTH FOR MANY
      WAS PLENTY
        FOR EACH OF THE THREE NATIONS.

AND SO IT WAS
  With this understanding
    all met the choices proposed
      by the Keepers of the Western Door.

  One from among the Keepers of the Peaceful Way
    arose to speak --
    and all listened,
      anticipating his words.

  These were they --

  "From among these three possibilities . .
    no one at all will have any difficulty
      predicting the one we will choose."

  And he sat down.

Those listening laughed --
expecting a long explanation
of the value of Peace,
settling themselves for its long endurance,
they found themselves suddenly
on the other side of all that was said,
and celebrated its brevity --
completing the full text
with their own thoughts.

LET US REMEMBER THIS WISDOM.

• • •

AND SO IT WAS
That each of the Three Nations
gave from full storage
corn and beans and the dried flesh of deer.

AND SO IT WAS
That women and children
and some few Keepers of the Peaceful Way --
both women and men --
carried provender
to the three nearest communities
of their Northern neighbors,
promising more to come.

Moon Woman turned and left three times
before these purposeful delegations
ceased their weary walk.

Many Northern Peoples
spent a gladder Winter
than they had anticipated.

Many returned
to Winter with the Three Nations
so that no weary feet need
walk the path on their behalf.

AND
  It will not surprise you to learn
    that animosity slowly turned
      to willing and mutual acceptance.

  For this Northern People saw how it was
    they whom they had hoped to drive out
      now saved their People

AND THEY SAW HOW IT WAS
  SUCH NEIGHBORS
    MIGHT BE WORTH THE KEEPING.

                    • • •

NOW
  I would tell you if it were so,
      that the simple transportation of some food
        in a lean year
            turned enemies into Brothers,
            giving them recognition of one another.

YET IT WAS NOT SO.

  Grandchildren had come and gone
      while Our Cousin People
        and the Keepers of the Western Door
            walked the Path of Peace together,
      yet their Eastern Brothers
        were not so inclined.

  Generations
      of Those Who Keep the Peaceful Way
        had spoken themselves hoarse
            in protestation of too much war.

YET IT CONTINUED.

NOW AT LAST
  Some circumstance occurred
    that showed one and the other
      their value as Brothers.

YET ALL WAS NOT RESOLVED.

FOR THE BEGINNING
  IS NOT YET THE END --

AND LEARNING AND HABIT
  MAY FOLLOW EACH OTHER . .
    ONLY SLOWLY.

SO IT WAS
  That Our Cousin People rose once more
    at the next Third Summer Meeting
      and said how it was
    that the Eastern Door of the Three Nations
      had swung wide with generosity.

"Will we be"
  -- they asked now --

"Less generous with them?

"Can we still find no place at our Council
  for each of the Three Nations?"

SO IT WAS
  That invitation was at last given
    and accepted.

At the next Third Summer Meeting
  a small delegation
    from the Keepers of the Eastern Door
      arrived.

And with dignity and with respect
  these Eastern Peoples
    met one another.

AND YET ALL WAS NOT RESOLVED.

For there was no great wish on either part
   to sit at the same Council.

And the Eastern People said how it was
   that perhaps
      more Western than Eastern Door Keepers
        had carried them gifts of survival.

But Our Cousin People rose
   and asked if it really mattered
      which feet walked forward
        under such generous burdens.

Did not each such foot
   walk through the Eastern Door
      unimpeded?

AND THOSE WHO KEPT THE EASTERN DOOR
AROSE AT LAST.

"We have no wish"
  -- they said --

"To cause uncomfort among Brothers.

"For that reason do we say --
  we do not seek
    to sit around this Council.

"Rather,
  let our Brothers who keep the Western Door
    represent us here.

"Take home with you
  awareness of our respect.

"For you are the People
  who know the forest ways.

"You are the People
  with the lightest water craft
    of unequaled strength.

"And so we name you
  Those Who Know Such Things.

"SO DO WE GIVE YOU
THE GIFT OF LIFE --
AND GIVE TO OURSELVES
THAT SAME GIFT ALSO."

AND
With these words,
that delegation rose and left.

Little further was then discussed,
yet many set themselves the task
of resolving any incipient conflict.

AND FROM THAT DAY
FOR A LONG TIME . .

PEACE
WAS THE WAY OF THE EASTERN DOOR

AS PEACE
WAS THE WAY OF THE WEST.

A Different Way

NOW CAME THE TIME
    When the Keepers of the Peaceful Way
      were listened to with great intent.

FOR
    AS THEY HAD LEARNED THE WAYS OF WAR..

    SO THE PEOPLE NOW PURPOSED
      TO LEARN THE WAYS OF PEACE.

AND DURING THIS TIME
    MUCH LEARNING WAS ACQUIRED.

    Stripped of the necessity of War,
      much energy and purposefulness
        was available for other tasks,
          and one of these was learning.

    Coherent delegations
      went out to more and more distant Peoples,
        so that their nature
          and general way might be learned.

. . .

FOR A LONG TIME IT PROCEEDED THUS.
    But what has been done
      may yet be undone.

OVER TIME
    The People decided on the value
      of Keeping various Ways.

AND IT WAS DURING THIS TIME
    That two new Peoples were established..

    So that the Three Nations were now Five --
      spread along the southern shore
        of Beautiful Lake
      and around those narrow lakes
        which extend South from that larger lake
          like so many fingers.

Each of these Five Nations
   kept a separate way . .

And yet all were similar,
   so that they understood themselves
      as Brother Peoples.

AND YET OVER TIME
   THINGS CHANGED AGAIN.

For this and that reason concern arose
   that the People
      might lose their capacity for defense,
   an occasional altercation
      implying the possibility of war.

SO IT WAS
   That the People gradually
      began a kind of mock combat . .

Thus assuring themselves
   the possibility of survival.

And even the Keepers of the Peaceful Way
*   saw some value here.*

FOR SURELY
   They understood the possibility of War Again . .

And thought, through these mock combats,
   to establish some general understanding
      of the value of limits on any hostilities
      and of the value of all men as Brothers.

YET
   WHAT IS BEGUN TO GOOD PURPOSE
   MAY NOT PROCEED SO.

For these games became more than games,
   great and serious purpose
      increasingly attached thereto . .

So that efficacy in these games
   was increasingly valued
      and a kind of pride in Nation became more
      than respect for accomplishment.

NOW DURING ALL THIS TIME
    The adjudication of disputes
        was also emphasized.

    So that --
        as these disputes sometimes
            became worse --
        so did the possibility of resolving them
            increase.

    And groups of Three Persons
        of wise and disparate views
            were often chosen to resolve conflicts.

    Such groups became well known --
        a neighboring community
            often sending for such a group
                valuing the impartiality
                    they would bring.

    This became such a common practice
        that often even disputes
            of the most burdensome nature
            could be resolved
                without the anger of open hostilities.

AND YET
    These games
        began to take on increasing meaning . .

    Until the People
        began to forget their nature
            as Brother Peoples
        and to think only of their willingness
            to excel in these games.

    Such games
        ranged from community to community
            and those between Nations
                began to take on an ominous focus . .

UNTIL ONE DAY
THE GAME BEGAN
BUT DID NOT END . .

AND THE PATTERN
EXCEEDED THE NATURE OF GAME . .

AND ALL KNEW
HOSTILITIES
HAD AGAIN BEGUN.

. . .

NOW YOU SEE HOW IT WAS
FOR OUR DIVERSE PEOPLES --

How they began to forget
Five Nations had been one.

How they began to value
efficacy in what had become conflict
over their nature as Brothers.

How hostilities
averted with a Northern People
had become hostilities
among Brother Nations.

THIS OR THAT ISSUE AROSE --
And was increasingly resolved
by open conflict.

Brother and Brother now
increasingly fought with one another
over any real offense . .

So that only smaller and smaller things
were any longer resolved
by groups of three Wise Men.

AND
   WHAT BEGAN AS CONFLICT
   CONTINUED AS WAR.

Those who still kept the Peaceful Way
   were less and less listened to.

Those who sought these vengeful wars
   answered every plea for Peace
     in this manner --

"You who never fight . .

"You who keep only Peace on the land,
   have no understanding of the Way of War.

"What you say
   leads to weakness only . .

"So that should we accept your suggestions
   the People would rest defenseless
     in a world
       where defenses are often necessary.

"SPEAK TO US AGAIN
   WHEN YOU HAVE SOME EXPERIENCE
   WITH THE NATURE OF OUR WAY."

NOW
  THOSE WHO KEPT THE PEACEFUL WAY
  SAW HOW IT WAS . .

They saw
  the People
    become increasingly argumentative.

They saw
  increasing altercations
    resolved by strength of arm
      and fewer by wisdom of thought.

They saw
  a long and dark path ahead
    for all the People.

THEY THOUGHT MUCH ON THIS,
  held consultation one with the other,
  understood the unlistening ears
    of those who walked the Way of War.

UNTIL ONE DAY
  Someone suggested a different course --

"Let us"
  -- he began --

"Choose not only those among the young
  who have a natural proclivity
    for the Peaceful Way.

"Let us"
  -- he went on --

"Choose some from among the young
  who show possibilities for the Way of War,
    yet show also
      an ability to learn the value of Peace.

"Let us"
  -- he concluded --

"Offer such as these . .
  the education in thought and understanding
  and the Tellings of the long march of the People
    which we offer now to those
      who choose to walk the Peaceful Way.

"Then,
 as they reach the years
  when War is learned . .

"Let them go out
 to learn this way as well . .

"So that they can hold each Way
 in either hand
  and see how they may be balanced."

AND

 SEEING THE WISDOM OF THIS THOUGHT,
 ALL AGREED.

 AND IT WAS SO.

NO LONGER
 Did the Keepers of the Peaceful Way
  look only for those among the young
   whose natural penchant
    for a calm approach
     to the variabilities of life
    argued well
     for their potential
      to resolve disputes . .

They looked also
 for a quick eye and a strong hand,
  an easy stance and a firm grip.

These things also began to have value
 for the Keepers of the Peaceful Way.

SO IT WAS
 That the nature of such Keepers
 began to change.

Sturdiness had always been valued
 but now it was combined
  with some other skills --
 similar to and yet unlike
  the games played
   by those who walk the Way of War.

"Let us also"
-- some one said --

"Have games of eye and hand and strength.

"And yet
let us remember
how easily this may lead to war."

AND IT WAS AS SHE SUGGESTED.

Strength and endurance were tested now
as was care of thought.

So that the Keepers of the Peaceful Way
were as strong and as straight
as those bent on War.

Increasingly young men --
quietly and early trained
in care of thought
and awareness of brotherhood --
came to walk the Way of War
and to win the respect
of all who knew them.

Nor were these ones discouraged
by the Keepers of the Peaceful Way.

"Go and learn for us"
-- they were told --

"The Ways of War and its reasons.

"Perhaps with this understanding
we can seek some better path
toward Peace and Unity."

AND IT WAS SO.

    Young men over many generations
      studied the nature of War.

    Some came to choose
      the Peaceful Way

    Others came to prefer
      the Way of War.

AND YET
THE NATURE OF THINGS HAD CHANGED.

    The thought of each such group
      was expanded.

AND SO
  THIS WAS THE WAY OF IT
    FOR A CONTINUING PEOPLE . .

A long march over a Broad Island
  had led to this place.

Great distances and great difficulties
  had been both overcome and survived.

MUCH HAD BEEN LEARNED.

MUCH HAD BEEN KEPT.

The careful gathering
  of the Learnings of the People --
    begun so long ago --
  had continued
    until the Way of War was learned.

The divisive nature of this path
  separated also
    the Keepers of the Peaceful Way
      from those who walked toward War.

INCREASINGLY,
  It was the Keepers only
    who kept the long and continuous
      Learning of the People.

No great councils were any longer held,
  gathering the thoughts
    of all the People together
      with which to craft
        this gift to all future children.

INSTEAD,
  Smaller groups of patient People --
    from among the men,
    from among the women --
      learned to remember the ancient ways,
      learned to understand their value.

AND
    These groups also --
    These gathered Council Circles --
       sought ways in which to turn
          the thoughts of the People
             away from all-consuming War
             and toward
                the Brotherhood, the Sisterhood of Peace.

Sometimes
    they worked in small ways --
       resolving some minor dispute
         in a new and creative way,
       passing this new understanding
         from one to another . .

    So that more effective approaches
       to such difficulties
         might be evolved.

Sometimes
    they spoke to the People
       of other days and gentler ways . .

    So that they might remember
       other possibilities.

Many and various ways of asking the People
    to think once more
       of the nature of their path
         were developed.

Complex interweavings
    of the possibilities of thought
       twined through all their speech,
         every history told.

Reminding the People in this way,
    they prepared the seed bed
       for a different harvest . .

FOR AS SURELY
    AS THE PEOPLE
       WALKED FROM THERE TO HERE . .

JUST AS SURELY
    DID THESE ONES
       PURPOSE EVENTUAL PEACE.

AND YET
PURPOSE -- AND ACHIEVEMENT --
MAY BE TWO DIFFERENT THINGS.

For the continuing purpose
of a small group
may only with great difficulty
become the purpose
of a Whole People.

SO IT WAS
That continuing attention
to the manner of thought of the People
was paid
by the Keepers of the Peaceful Way.

Careful consideration
of the changes in patterns of speech
was also given . .

So that the People were assured in this way
of an ability
to express the possibilities of Peace.

Ways also to express gradations
in the nature of War
by these patient Keepers
of enhanced possibility . .

So that no one at all
any longer asked
merely whether War was or was not,
but asked now also
the nature and degree of that War.

AND ALL THIS WAS SEEN
  AS THE CAREFUL TENDING OF THE FIELDS
    WHERE FUTURE POSSIBILITIES MIGHT GROW.

THESE FIELDS
  WERE KEPT BY THE MEN.

THESE FIELDS
  WERE KEPT BY THE WOMEN.

TOGETHER
  these patient seekers after tomorrow
    laid out increasing possibilities
      like some sumptuous harvest feast . .

  So that the People
    increasingly began to understand
      its nature and variability.

TOGETHER
  these patient Keepers of an Ancient Way
    carried with them
      all previous learning --
    as a gift to the one-day listening ears
      of a newly comprehending People.

EVEN AS I SING THESE SONGS TO YOU NOW,
SO WERE THESE SONGS SUNG THEN
TO ANYONE AT ALL
WHO WOULD LISTEN.

AND WISDOM
AND PURPOSE
BEGAN TO SIT SIDE BY SIDE.

BUT
Whether These Ones
achieved their continuing purpose
of a Whole Peace
for a Whole People . .

Whether understanding and wisdom
took hands once more --
one with the other . .

What gifts
this Five Nations People
chose to give to their children
and -- after them --

TO ALL SUCCEEDING GENERATIONS . .

THAT -- MY PATIENT LISTENER --
IS ANOTHER SONG
FOR ANOTHER DAY.

Addenda

Annotations

Evolution of Conceptualization

Evolution of Process: Governance

Notes

Annotations

Part of the task of learning this extensive Oral History from my father was to study with painstaking care the changes in thought contained in these thousands of years of human experience. Thus, in the section of "Beginning Song", "Ocean to the West", my father encouraged me to notice that the first concept of the "sand" that the People found at the edge of the Great Water was as "dry, grainy earth" -- indicating that they had as yet no way of expressing "sand".

As I learned the body of the Oral History itself, I was also encouraged to ask questions. In response to these questions my father would sometimes answer with further information which -- although not specifically in the body of the oral text -- was also transmitted down the generations and is just as accurate as the text -- which in my opinion is very accurate indeed.

In a subsequent book, to be titled *A Tribe of Two,* I will explain all these learnings -- and the manner of the learning -- in detail. Here, it is my purpose to try to highlight all major differences with the general culture around us in the general comments below. The additional information which was also clearly transmitted down the generations I will include as notes on a page by page basis to this first writing down of the *The Walking People*. Though -- in order to break the flow of the text in no way -- no note reference number shows on the page of the text itself, the number of the page referenced will show at the beginning of the note in that section. Developments like the evolution of a word for "sand" I mainly leave to your personal wisdom, as my father left it to mine. General comments follow:

Time, Imaging and Understanding

The concept of time was very different from our present linear concept. To begin with, we use a number of misleading terms in English, terms that reflect an earlier explanation of the nature of the world which has since been disproven. In general, throughout the period during which this Oral History was gathered, there were no such terms -- no terms such as "sunrise", when the sun does not rise; "sunset", when the sun does not set. Rather, the earliest references are very direct statements such as "I see the sun", "it is light", "it is dark", "I see only Moon and Stars" -- with no specific words for day or night. (I learned to consider "day" and "night" as representing decisions about how the world worked, not the reality of moving light itself.) There was a different phrase for "it is dark" caused by, for instance, entering a cave, "it is dark *here*". Things were spoken of very directly and as doing rather than as naming; i.e., many more verbs than nouns.

From the earliest days, cycles were counted in terms of moon changes and in terms of sun variations. "Moon came and turned and left" is a poetic image in use at the time, not a daily phrase, and should not be presumed to mean anyone thought the moon really "left". You can so often see the pale reflection of Earth shine on the moon when it is otherwise "dark" that it is really illogical to assume anyone would conclude it was gone. It was assumed the relative location sometimes put Moon beyond direct vision, much like someone disappearing behind a mountain, as Moon often does.

As to Moon and other such cycles, it is important here to remember how the sky would look away from skyscrapers and city lights that dim the night sky. There is nearly no place on Earth where we can experience this now. Then, it was the only way things were. Only a central fire dimmed the night sky -- and several steps away from that fire cured the condition.

At that time, Moon was considered to "turn" in relation to the Sun. It was assumed that Moon reflected light from Sun. And, since it was clear that Earth also reflects sunlight (try looking from a tall mountain, from a dark cave, holding a rock in your hand off which the Earth light may shine!), that this might account for the paler light Moon sometimes shows us. You can also replicate this easily around a central fire.

Although terms like Moon Woman and Dawn Woman were sometimes used in my learning, I was always encouraged to find my own understanding of what this meant. As Earth is our Mother -- but one does not find eye, ear, nose, throat -- so is Moon also Woman (sometimes Grandmother), so does Dawn Woman bring the new hope of a new day, new enlightenment to our darkened eyes, if we will only see it. Thus, daily occurrences are used to help us understand . . . the nature of understanding.

What I learned from my father was that when we lose sight of the nature of imagery in language (mind images, we called them), the imagery itself limits, rather than expands, our understanding. Working your way through this is a little like the childhood puzzles where we are asked to "find the man's face in the tree". My father always encouraged me to "find the meaning behind the symbol, the mind image". Understand what "Dawn Woman" means, not who she is . . . So it has been for a long time, a long time.

Most of what we presently consider to be "time" was considered a matter of relationships. How do Earth and Sun and Moon relate to each other just now? Is the Earth or the Sun moving when Sun seems farther north? All things were considered to be moving. Perhaps this was the result of awareness of the "moving Earth" mentioned below. And "Now" describes the point you have reached along the Path. It means more nearly "here" (location) than "now" (time), but "now" works better in English.

The other aspect of "time" -- past, present, future -- was considered "change", not time. Change was a natural, an inevitable result of the cycles. Nothing remains the same. Everything changes all the time. Yet everything is circular -- not that it returns to being the same thing, not that the cycle is repeated, but everything comes back to the same place . . and the dance continues. ➢

Dance

All perceivable (and unperceivable) movement was considered to be a patterned dance that participated in these cycles, much as the People danced their circle dances. Many things were referred to as patterned dances, Earth dancing, Sky dancing, the Great Dance of the Universe. Though there was no specific word for "Universe", the usual term -- All Things -- can be effectively stated in English only as Universe. Nothing else has the same sense of total inclusion.

Earth

Earth is considered to be constantly moving. I remember how hard it was for me to understand the idea of "Terra Firma", after growing up this way. I was stunned to learn that no other child in my first grade class understood Earth was moving. Instead of understanding earthquakes as some sort of movement of Earth herself, they seemed to understand them as a terrible disaster, unnatural, a sickness. They were clearly thinking that "Terra" was really "Firma" and that any change from this was a violation of their trust. I, on the other hand, understood Earth as a moving, tossing ocean, with waves and ripples and currents just like the sea -- only slower!

Not only does Earth herself move -- as in "Rocks Like Rain" -- but she moves in relation to Moon and Sun. Everything is moving -- all the time, two-leggeds, four-leggeds, Earth, Sky, everything -- some slower than others, some faster. Earth is also considered to be a living entity. Everything is alive; rocks, clams -- both meat and shell -- everything contains energy and is therefore alive. Standing Bear, as he came to be called, expresses this concept in "Rocks Like Rain" when he listens to his Mother, Earth. "Listening" in this case I understand as sensitivity, not vocal transmission.

Although these basic concepts clarify as The Walking People progress, I cannot find a place previous to which the People did not think this way. Notice, I said a place, not a time. That is the manner of thinking of the People, also, as where you are says much about your relationship to other things, equally as does where they are. Your relationship is the relationship between these two locations and your resident energies, each and both of you have relations to other realities at other locations. Movement is the process of changing spacial relationships.

Distance

Distance was measured by Walks of Days. Thus descriptions of how to get from one place to another would contain how many days walk (Walk of Days) it would be, often with additional information in length of days at which time of year was meant.

This same concept carried over into individual life. Life, for each individual, was considered a journey -- a natural concept for a Walking People. Your "Walk of Days" meant almost exactly your lifetime. A number of Walks of Days meant almost exactly a number of consecutive lifetimes or generations.

Death

The present Western concept of "death" as the "end" of life was never a concept adopted by the People. Rather, from the earliest references to that process (in "Rocks Like Rain") "death" is described as "lying still upon the Earth", "Spirit running out". The idea is that Spirit is the continuing reality, your Earth Self is the temporary one. Spirit is considered a continuing kind of livingness that transcends many cycles.

One aspect of this idea is expressed at an earlier time in "How We Came to Value Age" as "walking North". Again, you continue to live, just away from the People -- and who knows where you leave your Earth Self behind? This ancient idea -- which was ancient at that time -- of the aged "walking North" is probably one reason why the People accept Snow on Top's decision at Walk by Waters with such relative equanimity.

Naming

As the nature of your place among the People changes, so does your name. Thus, Mother of Girl of Eight Winters eventually becomes Wisdom's Daughter. At first her clearest contribution to the People was this Learning Daughter. Later, her helping hands became Learning Ears and took in more and more of Snow on Top's wisdom. Thus she finally became Daughter of Wisdom. Snow on Top, of course, became Ancient Wisdom not when she became wise, but when the People learned to perceive her Wisdom. At that point her relationship to them changed, because their perception of her changed. Girl of Eight Winters becomes She of Eight Winters because the nature of her contribution to the People never changes, is always constant, and is recognized. Perhaps during this time there were also Teasing Names, as was later surely the custom. But I do not know that was so, as no Teasing Name is specifically mentioned.

Evolution of Language

In the Oral History the evolution of both language and thought is apparent . . and meant to be so. Thus, one tries assiduously *not* to state the original concepts in more complex word structures just because they are available now. (Human Beings is one exception, see below.) E.g., there is a difference between *sustenance* and *food*. Food I use rarely and for a particular reason. Usually it connotes some definite human processing from the original form.

Brothers and Sisters

The distinction between man and woman so ubiquitous in English was not so in the context of the culture of the Walking People. The earliest language for the distinction was "will be mother"/"will not be". Later, when personhood is a clearer concept, the basic word used for each individual could be stated very well in English as "Person". If it was important to know whether the individual were male or female, an ending was added connoting sex. This can be stated in English as person-female, person-male, but this is clumsy.

➤

Sister and Brother were the same word. It really meant First Relateds, including both male and female. (There were ten orders or degrees of relatedness in each of several contexts -- such as the circle of our small community, the broader circle of human beings, the circle of Earth's children including Wolf and Beetle and Rock, the circle of Universe.) The same was true of Grandfather, Grandmother. It was the same word -- but Grandparent or Sibling sounds too cold in English -- neither contains the warmth of belonging. So I have chosen to say -- for instance -- "Brother, Sister", using both terms in English.

Relatedness

This was shared with me as the Beginning of All Things. This explains that in the Beginning there was only One . . and this One was Thought Woman, She who contained the Essence of All Things. There was no other until Spider Woman came and saw the potential in the essence. She pulled out threads of Thought from this Essence, with which she spun all individuation in the Universe, simultaneously spinning the Threads of Connection which still provide the connectedness between each and every individuation and each and every other individuation.

Universe is like a three dimensional spiderweb, with each point where two threads cross, each focus, connected to every other. Touch any part of the Great Web of Life and you cannot fail to affect every other. Only great distance will dim the effect.

You see how it is? How each and every being is connected -- and therefore related -- to each and every other being? You see how it is that anything at all which affects the smallest part, affects also each element in the whole? Are we not, all of us, Brothers and Sisters in the Universe?

Of course, I was invited to understand who/what Thought Woman represented, "Perceive the Reality beyond the Image," my father suggested. Each of us, he said, has that responsibility.

My father said this Thought Image was our most ancient teaching -- and given my understanding of the Oral History -- that must be very ancient indeed.

This was never taught me as a "thing to learn" or as a "telling that explained the world". Rather, my father would suggest something like, "Some people say that everything is connected and some people say that it's not. I wonder how you see it?"

Months later I might actually have an answer for him, after much discussion and many learning experiences designed by him specifically for my small but learning mind. Eventually, I learned to see my own connections and explained it to him.

Then, and only then, would he describe to me how others had seen it. Then, and only then, did I learn about Thought Woman and her Sister.

Conceptual Training

I cannot know how old these Learning Structures are, but from my earliest years I was invited to experience conceptual training which was "very ancient, indeed". This training enables you to think in different contexts. Like Wolf, like Bear, like Fish. You learn to "think in" toward things that are very small and to "think out" toward that which is large. This has "practical" applications, such as being able to hold the image of a mountain in your mind as you decide on a path around it, and more "esoteric" applications, such as apprehending the nature of Universe from that perspective.

Along with this you learn to "think back" to how it was for the People at that time -- and to "think forward" to how it yet may be.

Evolution of Conceptualization

There are a number of continuing threads of evolving thought which weave through *The Walking People*. These my father encouraged me to perceive for myself. Then he added information also transmitted down the generations. Here are some of those threads.

Wisdom

Wisdom is consistently understood as other than the mere knowing of things. It is knowing how to use knowledge/understanding in a way that is harmonious with, that is interrelated with Universe (All Things). However, two particular aspects of wisdom do evolve as continuing threads through *The Walking People*.

New Eyes Wisdom: The value of learning from the very young is a repeated theme. New Eyes Wisdom sees with clear, new vision -- devoid of the cultural assumptions which will be later learned. Often, the very young -- those with New Eyes -- hear without being seen, as does Snow On Top during her childhood years. Girl of Eight Winters figures prominently in the recapturing of nearly-lost wisdom and understanding and again when the People gather to hear Ancient Songs. The young are sent to listen to Snow On Top when their elders fall into dispute. Including the young at council seems so easy for the Walking People that this may indicate continuation of a custom rather than a new idea. However, this is not clear, At least by the time referred to just before Walk by Waters, old and young are included at council.

Although New Eyes Wisdom is considered the special gift of the young, one may remember and acquire this gift at any age -- as in the "clear eyed vision" described in "Sad Partings."

My father helped me to see that the needless and harmful decision made at "Sad Partings" -- about 70 years after "Rocks Like Rain" measured by the age of She of Eight Winters -- led to a profound decision on the part of the Walking People. Never again were the young to be excluded from any decision, especially not from a decision which had such profound impact on their personal selves. This was, he explained, the bedrock of the inalienable rights of the young (children) to speak their own wisdom into ordered council. "Let us choose to be People whose youngest ears are welcome around any fire."

"For who," he asked me "will live with each decision longer?"

There was one other element which was related to but not the same as New Eyes Wisdom. The Water Walking People are so concerned about sharing their learnings that only the very young are sent. They bring with them their New Eyes Wisdom, which may enable them to understand the other way, the other culture better, but they also bring with them what my father called "a lack of height". That is, they may not be perceived as threatening.

This works very well with the Water Walking People and is, therefore, used again with the Sun People with extreme purposefulness.

Long Life Wisdom: Long Life Wisdom was also valued. This Wisdom is filled with an understanding of who the People have decided to be and why they reached that decision. "Merely reaching an advanced age," my father said, "in no way predicts Long Life Wisdom. If one is asleep along the way, does one know the path? And yet, some patient attention to circumstance may well lead to accumulated wisdom. Listen well and with great patience, then, to those of advanced years. Learn . . whether they were asleep or awake!"

Learning

The People consistently put such a value on learning, that lives are often risked in its acquisition. Go and See are referred to long before "The Day of Rocks Like Rain." This is how they know that Walk by Waters is North and also East.

It seems clear from the context that there is already an established tradition of using excess energy, of using restlessness toward the gathering of new understanding. In other words, my own understanding of part of this is that in easeful times, some individuals have more energy than is necessary for mere survival. These individuals seem to need of their own nature some great task. My father helped me see a number of times when this is clearly understood by the People and relevant tasks are assigned -- as with the Two Strong Brothers, who are given a monumental task by the Whole People, and again as in "We Call the River Beautiful" the ones the People choose as teachers give impressive tasks to Red Squirrel and Gray.

The theme of learning from other cultures is stressed again and again, from "Those Who Live in Round Houses" to "The Water Walking People" to "Red Squirrel and Gray" to "The Sun People" and beyond. Such learning is often sought at great individual and community costs. And still, no learning is enough.

The early Go and See "bring their Learnings back to the Center Place for Wisdom". Once cataclysm reduces the number of the People, these Learnings are brought back to the Central Fire of the People, their movable Central Place. The emphasis over and over is that "no learning is ever enough", even though they have learned to learn from one another.

If Learning is never enough, decisions must nonetheless be made. One aspect of this is learned quite early in Many Wisdoms where "There are many ways of decision, but quickly is often the best."

Memory In An Oral Tradition

Mnemonic storage has much greater value in an oral tradition than it does in a literate one. The ability to remember is the only access to "stored" information. Even with mnemonic devices such as a marked stick or wampum belts, memory is still the key. We should not assume, however, that this means only advanced years give such memory. Training in this tradition can begin in infancy and may continue nonstop throughout life. Total oral and visual recall is the goal, so that you develop the ability to "re-hear" a speech as if you were playing an audio tape in your head or "re-see" an event as if you were screening a movie of what you just saw. You are tested again and again for capability in these areas.

This capacity has often been shown by Native American orators where an entire speech would be recited back to the original speaker and then the reply added to the end.

"In the old days," my father said, "instead of radio we sang our songs -- and our songs were songs of remembering." Thus, the People walking from here to there or working together sang songs that incorporated their collective history, as well as recent events. More like the "Chanson de Rolande" than like "Greensleeves."

"And such memory," my father said, "is our gift to the children's children's children." "Let those who come after/receive this gift".

This gift was considered so valuable that extreme shock, sustained by all the People, was the result of nearly loosing it. "Not again would the People trust memory to only a few." A great deal of community effort was applied to these Keepings "to keep the memory of a Whole People from one generation to the next."

Listening

Such gifts can be transmitted only to the extent that someone has the patience to learn to listen. This art of listening -- "With a whole heart and an empty head anxious to be filled with new Understanding!" my father said -- is one of the primary trainings. In "The Walking People" it is a repeated theme. As is listening to one another, gathering wisdom for future generations.

Many Generations

From the earliest times treated in "The Walking People", the People understand that they are making irreversible decisions for all succeeding generations. If Walk by Waters was disappearing so quickly, who might return thereby? This sense of the impact on all future grandchildren is consistently understood and considered. When a decision to move the basic location South or East was made, the idea was -- "We also move the unborn seed of all Those Who Will Yet Be."

Appropriateness and Balance

These are two major cultural themes that I learned to understand through a study of the Oral History with my father:

Appropriateness: Rather than understanding action as either right or wrong, my father encouraged me to "look for appropriate action." And also for the appropriate time. "What is appropriate here," was his frequent question. Thus, what has been learned may be of little help in understanding present circumstance. As in "Sad Partings," what has been learned may be irrelevant to present circumstance. "Let us learn from this. Wisdom is wisdom, the source cannot matter." It is in this light that my father encouraged me to understand *The Walking People.*

That thing, that behavior, that choice, is appropriate which tends to lead toward health and well-being.

Balance: The second major theme that goes with Appropriateness is Balance. "That neither one way -- nor the other, But a balance between . . . ."

Real balance as among all elements engenders a circle. An unbalanced circle becomes an oval. The effect of this ovalness through trying to work with a Hoop which is bent to an oval shape is a great lesson. Balance also between specific differences is requisite to the whole Circle of the People. These specific differences include young/old, female/male, those who gather the four-legged/those who plant seeds and gather their fruit, etc. These may not be bilateral differences only, but quadrilateral, multipartite, etc. Balance is always requisite to continuance, at least in the long run.

Evolution of Process: Governance

Ordered Council

Bereft of their leadership overnight, forced into unaccustomed decision-making, the Walking People learn by doing. In so learning, they come to value greatly -- if they did not before -- the inclusion of each and every scrap of wisdom, each and every individual perception, in the context of an ordered council. For only in an ordered council can each voice be clearly heard. "They sat in Council over all they had learned, a circle of silent listening."

There is some indication this may have been true before, in that a decision is "agreed among the People" long before "The Day of Rocks Like Rain" when the small remaining group proceeds on its way. And yet their "first decision without the First Among Us" is also a great learning. The true nature of Leader as Teacher is shown in "How we Came to Value Age". This may imply group decisions or simply the efficacy of broad understanding within the group.

I find Leader as "Boss" nowhere in the gathered wisdom of *The Walking People*.

Decision-Making and Consensus

The theme my father encouraged me to recognize here is that information gathering must vastly precede relevant decisions -- no last minute frantic search for data, please! "Where would the People be today," he asked, "if no Go and See had found the path to Walk by Waters?" "Still on that other Great Island," is the logical reply.

The slow process of consensus follows the same path, carefully gathering all wisdom, perceptions, understandings from each and every person so that "many people together for wisdom" is a good description of a council session.

The rest of the process of consensus is to identify the decision or decisions with which everyone can live. That is, to identify the circle within which all the People stand. It is understood that each one of the People will walk often outside that circle, thus leaving room for individuality, but the Circle of the People is one within which they can all stand, their general agreement on how to live together. This is acted out in "Circles on the Earth" an approach to understanding of self and of one's relationship to one's community which is still celebrated as a continuing and new learning.

The timing of a decision is often critical. As the People learn to store sustenance against the time of great snow, so they learn to store information against a time when decision is needed, recognizing that no amount of information is ever enough. In "Rocks Like Rain" they decide to walk West as a way of deferring a decision for either South or North. That decision must finally be made based on all gathered understanding. Deciding to cross Walk by Waters is clearly understood by all the People as quite possibly irrevocable, a casting of the robe of the whole People to that other Great Island. They time their transit to begin as soon as a storm ends, to maximize the probable time without storm.

They already recognize that they are deciding for future generations -- and owe some quiet thought to that reality.

Unity Toward Purpose

This includes unity of thought and unity of action. "Many might do what few alone could not, even though the many have less strength." "What is impossible for one, is possible for many." This theme is repeated over and over in different ways.

The particular lesson my father encouraged me to understand was the process of weaving the rope "which bound a whole People" during Walk by Waters. He worked with me patiently until I understood that the idea itself could never have been devised by an individual in an isolated context. "Only the presence of many hands could assure such a purpose," he pointed out. This rope then was woven by the Whole People longer than any might imagine possible and in a shorter time. Used during Walk by Waters in such a way that each individual was effective and also joined with the whole to protect all other individuals, it was so great a learning that my father said, "The People have never been the same from that day to this. Purpose . . became our Great Rope, binding us across any changing circumstance."

Out of this also grows the concept that in consensus, there is more energy flowing from any group than can be accounted for by adding the sum total of all of its members. In other words, the quality of becoming an effective group of its nature generates energy. The current term for this is "group synergy". I have no clear answer as to whether this represents an evolved understanding or simply a continuance of what was understood from the earliest times.

Notes

Rather than break the text with footnotes, or even with footnote numbers, explanations of concepts that I also learned from my father as generational transmissions follow, shown by the page number on which the text is found. There were also a number of tentative conclusions my father and I reached after much study of the oral text. However, for the sake of *absolute accuracy* these tentative conclusions are specifically cited as such in each instance. Notes follow.

The First Principal Telling

Page 5: "Sharp Tusk" -- Here is the first tentative conclusion my father and I reached. In studying the nature of four-leggeds, we *guessed* that Sharp Tusk must now be called "wild boar". In thinking of the other tusked animals we know, it is not logical to assume that anyone at all would attempt to jump up above an elephant or mastodon. When I learned about earlier, now-extinct species, we considered sabre toothed tigers. But the usual behavior of Tiger is such that he would not be likely to cooperate with such a hunting procedure. So wild boar is our best guess. But then, what is *yours?*

Page 5: "Herds" -- this is a generational transmission and involves no guesswork on our part. There was no such concept as herding. I therefore hesitate to use the term "herds" because of the additional meaning of the term in English. Yet the best and most accurate statement in English I can think of -- Coherent Gatherings of Great Beasts -- sounds ponderous and stuffy. It is nonetheless a more accurate way of stating the concept. My decision is to explain the distinction here and to nonetheless use the term "herd" in the text.

On the other hand, later on Page 321, when the Walking People discover the Ocean People "herding" their women, this is the accurate word in English, but was a concept they themselves did not have and therefore found very difficult to understand or even describe -- much as anthropologists or specialists in international affairs today often struggle to understand and to describe the behaviors and assumptions of other peoples. Where I use the term "herding" here, it came down to me more nearly as "keeping them together against their will".

Page 6: "Food gatherers" -- Note that what we would now describe in English as "hunting" is here referred to as food gathering. Women usually gathered our Rooted Brothers. Men usually gathered the Four-Leggeds. It was all considered gathering.

Just as Sharp Tusk was encouraged to come to the Back Breaker, so was "hunting" -- at the time -- a process of encouraging other beings to come to you. This is still true today among many Native American groups. You "track" animals -- our Four-Footed Brothers -- only to find their usual paths. Then you wait beside the path and "invite" Deer or Elk to come to you. The idea is they make the voluntary sacrifice -- or gift -- and you are thankful to them. It is not clear at this point in *The Walking People* that this concept of volunteering was the concept at the time. It *is* clear that Sharp Tusk and other Four-Footeds were gathered, rather than hunted down -- *and* it is soon clear that the People express gratitude toward the Great Shaggies (in the Second Principal Telling).

Page 11: "Bear-Standing-Quiet" -- In learning this it was my task to explain this to my Father, rather than vice versa. But as it is my task "to ensure accurate understanding", I tell you now that "Bear-Standing-Quiet" represents the first painted image on the wall -- and the first time the People understood that this image might be used for learning.

Page 14: "First Among Us" -- From the text it is clear that the initial idea of selecting a few individuals as First Among Us evolved by the time of Rocks Like Rain into a clan or perhaps a caste system, where your place at either beach or mountain was initially determined by your birth. Clearly this could change depending on the nature of your person, skills, and contribution to the People.

Page 21: "Rocks still thundered" -- Although the beach is described as safe, it seems clear that some stones or boulders rolled down from the mountains onto the beach. It is just that none *rained* down upon it.

Page 25: "Without the First Among Us" -- My father pointed out that losing the First Among Us in one sudden day through calamity was one of the many continuing reasons why our People came to dislike anything at all like a priesthood and to value absolutely the willingness to share understanding among all those willing to apprehend it.

Page 27: "About this place we know three things" -- Here the only three remaining First Among Us say they know little -- and give only three small pieces of information. How little they know! And yet it is essential! In my learning with my Father he used this over and over to emphasize the value of keeping even information which is apparently irrelevant in the context of current circumstance. This early became one of the founding reasons for keeping the Oral History -- and for keeping it in such detail.

Page 68: "Gives Light" -- Here are two learnings: that there was no way of expressing different kinds of devices that "give light" and that the People did not keep a description of the kind of "gives light" used. Over and over in the Oral History my Father pointed out how simple, everyday things were not described -- and were therefore lost! "Let us Remember," he would add.

Page 75: "Decide and Do" -- I have found no way of giving this concept in English the emphasis it deserves. "Decide and Do our early morning song" means that the *moment* you open your eyes you begin your decisions for the day. Even opening your eyes is a decision -- and an important one. Thinking this way, my Father said, puts you in touch -- conscious touch -- with more of your mind and allows you to truly be the "captain of your ship", a phrase current during my grandfather's time.

"When you fail to understand the nature of decisions," my Father said, "you limit your acuity and allow happenstance to guide your path." I found this concept, deeply rooted in *The Walking People*, very different from what I saw and heard around me in the Western world, though it is now a very current focus of much organizational, decision-making training.

Decide and Do . . Our Early Morning Song!

• **Where were they?** -- My grandfather, during his time, remembered the day-count description of "how to get from here to there". Since my Father was not good at numbers (see reference to "dusty fingers") he did not learn this aspect of the history. To prevent it from being lost in one generation, my grandfather used to pore over atlases trying to figure out where the People were at that time. His basic, if tentative, conclusions have been borne out both by my subsequent research and by the subsequent findings of Western science (geology, anthropology, et al).

He concluded that the Great Center Place described in this section was either to the north or to the south of the point where the Korean peninsula joins the Asian mainland.

One geologist pointed out that north is more likely, given the description of "warm pools", earthquakes, etc. Around the World described in this section then becomes the Siberian mainland and the Kuriles. This strikes me as probable.

My grandfather also concluded that the People crossed when Ocean was lower from about Siberia to about Alaska. I later learned about the Bering Strait concept. My father and I spent a lot of time looking at the Aleutian Islands, wondering if that were the connecting way. Since then, I have acquired not only the gathered wisdom of Western science on this issue, but excellent undersea topographical maps of the Alaskan coast over tens of thousands of years. I would very much like to have similar maps of Siberia and East Asia!

In any event, my grandfather, my father, and I agree that Walk by Waters is likely to be an earlier name for the Bering Strait.

The Second Principal Telling
Page 97: "So that it formed a suspended curve" -- Here is another concept that is almost impossible to state in English. Language is a manifestation of the general philosophical consensus of a given culture. In English there is a sharp difference between animate and

inanimate. In many other languages, this is not so! The approach to Life I grew up with says that "all things contain energy, that which contains energy is alive, therefore everything, everything is alive."

This is relevant to the nature of Rope. Here the People have braided a Rope longer than ever before envisioned, binding themselves together as one whole. In English the rope is inanimate, is passive, is a tool. This People did not consider it so. Rather, Rope is woven, is braided from *Livingness*, from reeds, from sinew. This Livingness is retained even after uprooted, even after cut from Bone. Rope, then, is not a passive instrument of the People, but the result of an interaction between the energy of the Livingness of the substance from which it is braided and the energy of the Livingness of the People. It is the energy of the beings from which the sinew is cut which provides the substance. It is the energy of the People who cut and braid which provides the form. Thus, one People and Another, working together, engender Rope -- a manifestation of their cooperation which then binds the People together, becoming a symbol and a manifestation of their common purpose.

Which is a long way to explain why the usual English won't do. It implies a passive tool. In this passage, Rope is firmly fastened to a rock outcropping which is twenty feet or slightly more above sea level, threads its way through air to below sea level to where the rock shelf is washed by Ocean, then threads its way to Cliff Top beyond. The form of that Rope in air would be described in English as a suspended curve, but that sounds too passive. So do swinging, hanging, pendulous. "Arching" indicates an *upward* curve, rather than the reverse. However, it also contains in English an element of action, of activity, of energy which matches the *spirit* of what is intended here. However, it sounds so strange in English that I have opted for "suspended."

This Rope binds the People together, preserving them from adversity; this does not mean that it leaps up, Laocoon-like, and takes hold of the People. It does mean that all Life, all Livingness is perceived as in cooperation, in harmony, working together -- when we are wise.

Page 122: "More is achieved by a Purposeful People / Than by those who see only today." -- They may see today, but they won't recognize its fuller potential because they haven't identified their Purpose and its requisites.

Page 122: "Those who only Count Stones" -- Counting stones has several meanings, which are inherent in the culture, but not clear here. Stone counters estimate reality and keep track of relationships. On the basis of this data it is possible to decide. But decision is the necessary step toward purpose, without which you have only a pile of stones. The only difference between stone counting and computers . . is volume!

Especially in that context, perhaps it is wise here to point out the methodology and some of the criteria for Stone Counting.

First, Stone Counting began by gathering the stones. That is, Go and See would be sent to measure something -- perhaps the number and location of different kinds of berry bushes. Any one such person might be assigned a certain area and would gather up stones in his, in her hand to represent different things. Similar stones represented similar identities. Different colors, shapes, or sizes of stones might represent different kinds of berries, different areas, etc. Sometimes different colors *and* shapes of stones were used to double index. That is, a count of different berry bushes in different valleys might be taken by red stones representing one kind of berry, grey another; etc. These stones might be simply held in either hand if they were few or transferred to pouches hung from your belt -- in which case each pouch might represent something specific, like a particular valley; etc.

These stones were then brought back to a central location and carefully transmitted to a Stone Counter. This individual *must* have the capacity of remember which stone represents what. If the representation of different colors or shapes of stone was not worked out carefully enough in advance -- for instance -- he, she would have to make up for this lack with his, with her memory! Stones might be recombined to give you different measurements. How many Great Shaggies within walking distance? How many in a given valley? What combination of Great Shaggies *and* berries in a given valley? Maybe both would be gathered at the same time making maximum use of the people assembled.

As these stones were brought in, they were laid out by the Stone Counter in rows. These rows began with five (one hand) and might go on to double five (two hands) if a great deal of information was gathered. Remembering carefully who brought what kind of stones, representing what, from which area, the Stone Counter could move, rearrange, and recombine the stones to give different sets of information. Otherwise the People might have to begin again!

Counts which needed to be kept for awhile could be etched on different shapes or colors of wood or bone, with categories indicated by the variations in shape or color. Sometimes these counts were kept by drilling pockets in a relatively porous (easily drilled) substance. Then these pockets could be filled, for instance, with different colors of clay. (Season counts -- the equivalent of calendars -- were often kept this way.) This indexing, then, must be retained in the memory or a symbol invented for the category and etched on the same wood or bone .. in which case the symbol must be retained in the memory. Better yet, both.

Stone Counter was a valued position.

Whether gathering Great Shaggies or berries, both occupations require careful planning. Before gathering Great Shaggies, for instance, drying racks must be built, skinning knives crafted, all the People ready to fall to, etc. Each kind of berry ripens at a certain time. This, too, must be factored in to the general outline of other tasks and hands available to gather and dry. Baskets must be ready, more drying racks, someone to discourage the hunger of birds, etc. So accurate accounting is requisite -- and particularly necessary both in difficult times and in changing times, where simple replication of previous years is no answer.

To become a Stone Counter you *must* have hands-on training. That is, you must have spent a great deal of time doing the actual field work -- both so you will understand what is represented and so that you will understand the difficulties of Stone Gathering. You must demonstrate a good memory. More than this, you need repeated field experience. No matter how good you are at Stone Counting, you must repeat field experience at viable intervals to keep freshly in your mind what all this entails.

"Those who only count stones" were people who didn't have the good sense to get this field experience and were therefore out of touch with hands-on reality. My Father made this point to me again when I was explaining to him what I was learning in my university course in statistics. "Just you remember, Honeygirl, who are the Stone Counters?"

Finally, you can see in this note now how much is implied by one brief phrase that does not -- without this kind of careful recounting -- make the transition from one culture to another!

Page 143: "Occasional mounds of succulent grass" -- This passage indicates that the People began a new way of gathering, leaving these occasional mounds of succulent grass both out of gratitude and out of practicality. If they *always* speared any Great Shaggy attracted to these mounds of grass, a wise Great Shaggy People would soon learn to avoid them.

Page 182: Whereas caves which regularly flood show the marks of that flooding, the increased warmth of a newly occupied cave may turn reliable ice into spring flood once an ice dam thaws.

Page 190: The "dance of Sun from North to South" -- implies the changed relationship of Earth and Sun which we perceive as a dance from North to South and back again, we who are standing on Earth herself.

Page 196: "Sun is North task" -- describes those tasks that are appropriate when we perceive the Sun as farther North, at which times Earth is warmer and snow no impediment.

• **Where are they now?** From Walk by Waters, which is probably the Bering Strait, the People travel mainly East. Until recently, no adequate topographical map of this mountainous area of what is now called Alaska and Canada was available. However, a look at the excellent maps available today makes it clear that an eastward path from the Bering Strait does, indeed, carry you East of what we now call the Rocky Mountains. This is now generally recognized to be the path of many early migrants. I believe it was the path followed by *The Walking People*.

The Southern Path

Page 231: "The turning of the year" -- Refers to the point at which "darker every day" begins to become "lighter every day". This was conceptualized as the point at which new energy strikes the Circle of the Seasons so as to continue the turning of the Season Circle.

I learned this through working with Hoop and Stick. That is, children are traditionally given a Hoop with which to experiment, to learn the nature of energy and continuance. As you ponder and gain understanding, you see that this represents the Great Hoop of Life, any Circle, any Cycle. Without energy, it just lies there on the ground. To apply energy, you use the Stick . . and quickly learn that too much energy sends the Hoop in crazy patterns, or breaks it completely. The balance of the Hoop -- and the carefully applied energy of the Stick -- provide a description of how Life functions when it is functioning well.

Balance and Appropriateness are the lessons here.

Page 231: "Year" -- I have hesitated to use the word "year" because of its calendrical implications. Circle Dance of Seasons is a closer concept. Yet, later on, this longer term is less used and something closer to "year", yet without its calendrical implications, is used. The year itself . . is still a Circle . . and always related to Earth.

Page 240: "Became at last twice seven upon the Earth" -- There was a great deal of joking and word or number play used at the time this history recounts which is nowhere in our present culture -- except in some residual form such as jokes about "not being able to count past ten without removing his shoes."

Fourteen here, for instance, implies a great deal of joking about "four legs under two people", moving back and forth between concepts of "what's counted". This was always a good source of laughter. Here a number of images are implied. Fourteen is twice seven, which goes with joking about the number of fingers and toes, or fourteen is ten plus four, quite a different concept with a clearer and more dignified approach to fingers and toes.

One form of counting was simply to imprint your finger tips in the dust in different patterns, thus counting by fives, by tens. This was used as much then as calculators are used today. A person who could "count in the dust" *without* using finger tips -- i.e., manipulate number concepts in his, in her head -- was highly valued. Those without this skill would refer to themselves as "dusty fingers". My father still used this phrase . . about himself.

Page 283: "Those who learn during their twelfth Winter" -- It is interesting to study here the difference in concepts as between a People who have been in one place for a long time and a People who "walk a continuing path". This sense of Path seems to enable conceptualization of something close to past/present/future, rather than a cycle contained within now-ness. And yet, the Walking People, seeing that they see things that others miss, also ask themselves now and again what they, themselves, may therefore miss.

Page 291: Calling names -- In learning the various histories -- of which this is the major one -- I learned a number of words as clues. That is, I learned certain sounds which had been transmitted down the generations as one way of checking "when you got there". There were even directions toward destinations that would include "when you hear this sound, you are near" and some sound in the language of that location would be included.

The one sound included in this Telling was Hah-Vah-Ee-<u>Kay,</u> with the accent on the last syllable. I have no certain way of knowing if the destination referred to by the Strangers was actually what we now call Hawaii, but this seems logical to me.

I especially remember my father coming to me in great excitement just before the beginning of World War II. "Honeygirl, listen to this," he urged -- and invited me to listen to a radio program at the time which was broadcast from some hotel on Waikiki Beach. "Listen to the song," he told me. And -- as I listened to the sound of waves on the shore (some of you may be old enough to remember this, too!) -- they sang, "Hah-Vah-'<u>Ee</u>, Hah-Vah-'<u>Ee</u>-'<u>Ee</u>". I was stunned. "Sound like anything you know?" my father asked. It certainly *didn't* sound like the usual American pronunciation, which at the time was more like Hah-wah-ya or Hah-wah-yee.

• **Where are they now?** The way South led -- my grandfather, my father, and I believe -- along the eastern edge of the Never Ending Mountains, later called the Sharp Jagged Mountains, and more recently called the Rocky Mountains. From there the path of the Two Strong Brothers led West across mountains and down a major river. This is likely to be either the Fraser or the Columbia River. My grandfather and my father travelled down the Columbia River when moving from Nebraska to California. They thought it was "probably the right one". My own journey down that river in 1961 was filled with startled recognition. However, what do *you* think?

Ancient Songs
Page 316: "High Place" -- This finding of a high place is a very strong thing. This is not clear in this text, yet I believe it is not appropriate to change the words here. Traditionally this was semi-acted out in earliest presentations -- in pantomime. So that "no language!" came across clearly, as did the stupefying importance of being able to conceptualize looking out from high places. ➤

Living in any dense forest *teaches you that you can't see far!* Learning how to "see far" on the open plain is a critical and spectacular accomplishment. The acting out portrays how most of the people are too busy gathering seeds to "look up". (Roots are thought to be such a logical extension of seed/plant that discovering their edibility is not considered a major accomplishment.) It is the curious one, the one who seems inattentive to the "business" of seeds, who discovers the value of "looking far for water". This is considered a great lesson and the *bedrock* of valuing *all* approaches to life, not just the apparently logical, which can never reach beyond its present data base.

This acting out also included an acting out of those unwilling to leave trees until, loose rooted from lack of water, the trees sway . . and finally topple, precipitating the occupant to join the northward march. It is also acted out that some fled into the deeper forest and you spend some time realizing that they will probably just have to do the whole learning all over again, as the forest continues to die. The focus here is critical decision making at the critical time and the ability to recognize when that time has arrived!

Page 328: "Great Swimmers" -- Here the Teller will at some subsequent time (if the listener does not) raise the issue of "can we learn to breathe from those who breathe only water?" Thus encouraging the listener to understand that these Great Swimmers were addicted to open air, even as we.

It is the same with talking. If the listener does not notice what this passage may imply, then some exploratory questions may be asked. But all of this section is very, very *implicit* -- and meant to be that way. You must work at understanding . . and therefore truly learn.

In part, this grows out of the cultural preference for self-learning. If I tell you what's "right", whatever that may be, you'll never figure it out for yourself. In part, it's a structure which allows you to go back and think more nearly as people thought then, rather than passing the images through the prism of present language and assumptions.

Page 329: "Remembering always to ask the question, 'How might we seem to them?'" -- This was taught to me as a lesson well learned by the People . . and this continuing question -- "How might we seem?" -- is something my father asked me to answer again and again. And not just with the human beings! The Great Swimmers here are likely to be dolphins, since they are air breathing. So, by thinking how we may seem to Those That Swim, perhaps we will learn to see ourselves through other eyes. In my daily life, my father chose to ask me to look through the eyes of our chickens, rabbits, ants-who-live-in-the-driveway, and parakeets. Not a very flattering image!

Page 330: "None of our People has ever again seen our Central Place" -- This was our *first* Central Place.

Page 331: This section was *not* called "Who are the Human Beings". Rather, you are encouraged to devise your own name for it -- an older term would be "Who are the First Relateds". In contemporary English, the best phrase probably would be "Who are the Human Beings".

This giving of new names is considered to be the best pedagogy for this kind of conceptualization, in that the concept will be translated into contemporary terms and, therefore, not limited to the understanding inherent in previous word-forms. This is considered to be a constant way of evolving the actual learnings into terms understandable in the context of present experience, instead of freezing them into word patterns representative of one point in their evolution. Understanding *will* move past old naming patterns and casting them in such a manner will cause our understanding of such "frozen keepings" to warp, the threads of connection with the learning will tangle, and much will be lost.

Page 336: "First Among Us" -- See note for page 14.

Page 344: "Southern Mountains" -- My grandfather spent a great deal of time studying encyclopedias and atlases. It was his (always tentative) conclusion that this "place of wisdom" was probably what is now called Tibet and that the Walking People were living for awhile on the plains North of the Tibetan plateau.

• **Where are they now?** My grandfather traced the path of "Beginning Song". He thought their first Ocean was likely to be either the Mediterranean, or the Caspian Sea. The origin of the People, then would be south of the eastern shore of either of these bodies of salt water. He also concluded that, on leaving this Ocean, they travelled mainly East to a place which was North of the Himalayas. He saw many similarities between the Spirit Path handed down separately from the oral history and both Tibetan and Hindu thought. I have no reason to disagree with his tentative conclusions.

"Ocean Again" and "Growing Woman" are likely to take place in that same Great Center Place area he identified as either south or north of the Korean peninsula.

The Way East -- Sad Partings

Page 417: "Sad Partings" -- My father encouraged me to understand that respect for New Eyes Wisdom directly comes from the Sadness of Parting -- and as directly led to the rights of Children becoming an essential part of the thinking of the People. New

Eyes Wisdom, my father explained, helps you understand that the Emperor wears no clothes.

At this time, also, my father explained, the People became newly dedicated to a balance between those from among the People who were female and those from among the People who were male. This grows out of the Water Walking People having such difficulty respectfully recognizing our way.

Page 429: "Perhaps Bear was only waving greeting" -- This is a play on visual concepts. There was no exact way to "wave greeting". Rather, there was a hand symbol which represented "I see you" and which would then be followed by further information. When you met someone, then, you waited for the "I see you" sign and then waited to learn the direction of hand. The full "sentence" might be "I see you and go away", "I see you and come closer", "I see you and don't move until I have a chance to check you out", etc. This was part of the general acceptance of the necessity of slowly learning the new.

There was a general etiquette that said a single person approaching a group awaited the group's decision, a smaller group awaited the decision of a larger group (quick, get those fingers in the dust! -- see note for page 240), a travelling group awaited the decision of a resident group (this took precedence over group size), a person-male awaited the decision of a person-female, an approaching very-young awaited the decision of an is-older. This last was reversed if the very-young were in need. Then his, then her cry or other summons was considered absolute.

It is this whole complex structure that is implied here in "waving greeting". There must have been many comments about Bear lacking any reliable sense of etiquette. There is always much joking about how Bear can never decide whether he, whether she is two- or four-legged. A lack of this two-legged sense of etiquette indicates four legs, which implies its own etiquette.

• **Where are they now?** If our guess that the great river followed was the Columbia is accurate, then this Eastward march crosses the desert area in what is now called eastern Washington/Oregon and western Idaho and enters the Rocky Mountains somewhere in this area. Having heard so much about the "rainy northwest", I was stunned to discover that this area truly is as dry as a desert.

Three Mountain Tellings
• **Where are they now?** This chain of mountains, down which the People weave a mainly southerly path, logically is the chain now called the Rocky Mountains. My grandfather drove through some of this area and thought he had found the "Sheltered Valley". However, he couldn't find anyone to give him a name for it and could only say it was "somewhere West of Denver".

Grass Ocean

Page 502: "A Shaggy Four-footed People, dark in hue" -- This seems clearly to refer to the kind of buffalo we are familiar with. Whereas the "Great Shaggies" described in Forest of Mountains seem to me to be describing the larger species of buffalo (*bison latifrons*), which I have seen described as travelling more separately, as well as being larger. These last became extinct at some point.

Page 505: "Pods being of so great a size" -- These passages clearly refer to squash, which is described within the context of concepts current at that time.

Page 509: "Time beyond time" -- In the annotations I describe the difference in the concept of time. A more linguistically accurate "translation" might be "before and before" in the sense of Path. But "time beyond time" is not inaccurate and is more intelligible in English.

Page 509: "Over some cliff edge" -- This purposeful driving of a herd of buffalo over the edge of the cliff is borne out by bone piles found here and there.

Page 513: "This strange small fruit" -- It is logical to assume that this is what is now called peyote and that these passages describe a time when use of this plant was less guided by experience than it is now. Something like the contrast as between the use of alcohol by the early Greeks in bacchanalia and the current use of wine in the sacred ceremony of Communion.

Page 528: "Remembering Bear" -- You may recall this refers to the Great Bears in the Land of So Long No One Remembers How Long which were encouraged to leave the deep, dark places of the Earth by one man seated on another's shoulders, so as to "outgrow" Bear.

• **Where are they now?** The Grass Ocean clearly is an earlier term for the plains West of the Mississippi and East of the Rockies. Descriptions of this area from early Mountain Men talk of just such a shoulder-high ocean, now turned to grazed prairie or wheat land.

First People's Child

• **Where are they now?** The location of this isolated tale is difficult to pin down. It would simply be somewhere East of where the prairie became forest.

We Call the River Beautiful

Page 551: "Undistinct" -- There are many times in The Walking People where I have chosen to invent a word rather that use the standard English form. This is always specifically necessary, in my opinion, as it helps to prevent you from concluding that the exact meaning in English is the one described here. It is designed to encourage you to think about what the phrase might mean -- and to discourage you from assuming that you know.

Page 559: "The dancing way" -- My own family, in its five-generation West-migration, saw itself as following this Westward Two-Foot Path.

Page 563: "Red and Grey for their Vision" -- This is further explained on Page 564. I leave it to you to decide which was which through the following specific Telling.

- **Where are they now?** See below.

The Sun People

Page 620: "Brought by Black Bird" -- Came to be a respectful way of suggesting that there was more to be learned from a Telling than at first it might seem. See also *The Water Walking People*.

Page 636: "The Five Outgoings" -- These various locations are so clearly described that I am certain I know which settlements are referred to. As I learned about them in college or thereafter, I was truly amazed at how clear the connection seemed to be. But as an exercise, try placing this Home Island in different places and see which subsequent settlements this implies. This is the Path down which my father encouraged me.

Page 652: "The calling names of a distant land" -- Whenever possible, a few words or phrases were kept in their original pronunciation as a future reference and a check on probability. Three names related to this Telling have already surfaced. The great city from which help was petitioned was called Ush-mahl . . and beyond it lay Tee-kahl. The Great Center for Understanding was called Chee-chehn Eetzah.

- **Where are they now?** My grandfather's grandmother essayed her own Sacred Journey to find this area -- and was content that she did so. At least, she felt she had found the Great Earth Snake -- which no one had discovered at the time -- north of the Ohio River and West of a river flowing south into the Ohio. I have driven to this same Earth Mound -- and agree with her determination. It seems to me the two paths along which the People were allowed to choose to carry their burdens of earth and stone are still there today.

Their River Bend Home must have been reasonably near this location, perhaps along the river we call Ohio today. I remember the delight with which I learned in Junior High about the nature of oxbows and rivers! Even as described by this ancient People.

The Eastern Ocean

Page 681: "The eldest among us still remembered" -- Such clues to the passage of time recur here and there in *The Walking People*. From this I deduce that about 80 years had been spent in transit from the Great Earth Snake to the Eastern Ocean.

Page 694: "Close Brothers to the People to the South" -- With this Telling I learned another calling name. This People to the South called themselves Moh-ee-gahn.

Page 706: "Perhaps one of the children's children will return" -- My father made this journey and thought he had found both the "flat mountains" and the many-painted beings.

• **Where are they now?** After years of being told that "There are no stone constructions in New England", I learned about a place in what we now call New Hampshire which sounded like it might at least have been constructed by the same people as built Stone Hill. Since then, I have been to this location. Everything described in this oral history is visible there today, except, of course, those things that are described as having been taken away!

Discoveries like this have been for me a profound validation -- my own Sacred Journey, like the one my grandfather's grandmother took to Ohio all the way on foot from Illinois. My path was marked out by four wheels, but I was no less joyful on arrival.

Beautiful Lake

Page 733: "Until we were 35" -- Note that the People chose the same number as the number of adults (carry packs) who crossed Walk by Waters.

Page 743: "Placed a forest of trees" -- It seems probable that this was a new invention, the first stockade. Yet, though such things are usually made clear, it is not clearly stated here whether this device was learned or invented. No explanation was handed down.

Page 757: "Never did learn the magic of our Endless Corn and Always Turkeys." -- The interrelation of the three communities is clear in the text. However, there is an added learning not specified here. In addition to these agricultural arrangements, the easternmost community was built in such a way that under it ran a tunnel from forest to storage house. The forest door of this tunnel was carefully hidden and it was never approached by carriers from the second and third communities if any of this northern People were anywhere nearby. These "Northern Visitors" were always carefully watched by the Far Seers from these other communities, so that it was always known when they arrived and when they left. And -- if signs were given that provender was arriving through our Western Door, this easternmost community would create some vivid diversion designed to coax all Northern Watchers to the Easternmost Door. How much careful planning may precede the apparent accident of success?

Page 768: "Whether doves . . flew up or down" -- My father described how it was -- how capes were crafted with pockets within, wherein two doves nestled. These would "suddenly appear" in the hands of the cape wearer and would be asked the question of up (for peace) or down (for war). These council circles always had a Central Fire in the midst. And my father asked me, "How many doves you ever seen purposely fly down -- into a fire?" He often suggested we needed a device like this in the 20th century.

Page 773: "Who lived to the North and also West" -- The calling name of this People passed down was Hhhu-ron(g), with a long "h" sound and the final "n" having a nasal "ng" sound.

Page 791: "Three persons of wise and disparate view" -- We would say now, chosen to represent Left, Right, and Center. That is, a balance across the spectrum of opinion. Or these three might be chosen for their ability to see Forest (wholeness), Path (sequence), and a balance between. The purpose of the third person in the center was to eliminate the possibility of a tie or stalemate. The three of them worked together toward consensus.

• **Where are they now?**   The Beautiful Lake described here logically is the one now called Lake Ontario. As I learned it, the Great Spirit -- the Spirit of All Things -- rested His, rested Her Hand on the Earth. The heel of That Hand created the depression which filled with fresh water and which we now call Lake Ontario. The Fingers of That Hand settled on Earth and created those depressions which filled with fresh water and which we now call Finger Lakes.

In 1961 I first drove through this area and was stunned to learn how accurate the descriptions I had from my father were. As aware as I am of the painstaking learning involved in the handing-down of this history, as much as I therefore always expect total accuracy, each discovery is nonetheless a Great Learning for me -- a celebration of the continuing Wisdom of a People who never forgot . . to Remember.

Patient listener,

Kind thoughts come . . .

About A Tribe of Two Press

A Tribe of Two Press was established in 1983 as an act of cooperation between the Meredith Slobod Crist Memorial Fund and Paula Underwood. It's initial purpose was to publish *Who Speaks for Wolf: A Native American Learning Story* and to begin to gather support for and encourage awareness of this Oral History, *The Walking People*.

The name comes from the Third Winter Ceremony in which Paula's father gave her her Learning Name. As she tells it . .

> *In my tradition, a name is given to any child only when some person they are learning from has discovered enough about the way that child learns to give them a Learning Name. That name is given in a Third Winter Ceremony. At least three of the People should be present.*

> *The winter I was three years old, my father began coming home later every day. I had no idea why. Finally he came home one day and said,*

> *"Honeygirl, I've looked everywhere. I find Piute and I find Papago, but I find none of the People.*

> *"We are a Tribe . . of Two!"*

Hearing this story, Bob Helberg, designer of *Who Speaks for Wolf* and of the *Guide for Enablers of Learning*, suggested A Tribe of Two as the appropriate name for our Press.

The Press was reactivated by Paula Underwood, with Bob and Judy Helberg, in 1990 in order to assure that *Wolf* and *Guide* would be available for "Teachers and Other Human Beings". These two books are the basic texts for the increasingly recognized Past Is Prologue Educational Program (PIP), which was declared an Exemplary Educational Program by the U. S. Department of Education in 1986 and is listed in the catalogue of *Educational Programs That Work*.

Who Speaks for Wolf is the first of Three Learning Stories handed down in the same way as *The Walking People*. These Three Learning Stories were designed to work together to enable each person to teach themselves how to learn in each of the three critical ways — in terms of Body, in terms of Mind, and in terms of Spirit. All Three Learning Stories are now available on a cassette tape, *Three Strands in the Braid*.

Publication of *The Walking People* has been a primary goal for A Tribe of Two Press since its beginning. Publication of the other two Learning Stories is a remaining goal, with additional information to follow.

Information on these materials and on The Past Is Prologue Educational Program is available from:

Bob and Judy Helberg
A Tribe of Two Press
P. O. Box 913
Georgetown, TX 78627
(512) 863-5062

About the Institute of Noetic Sciences

Overview

The Institute of Noetic Sciences (IONS), founded in 1973, is a research foundation, an educational institution and a membership organization with 30,000 members worldwide.

The word *noetic* is derived from the Greek word nous, for mind, intelligence and transcendental knowing. The "noetic sciences" bring the full range of diverse modes of knowing to the interdisciplinary study of consciousness, the mind and human potential. Research topics at the Institute range from mind-body health and healing, meditation, and exceptional human abilities, to emerging paradigms in science, business, and society. The Institute does not conduct research internally, but provides seed grants for leading-edge scientific and scholarly research by others, organizes lectures, sponsors conferences and publishes books, a quarterly journal, research reports and monographs by leading scientists, philosophers and scholars.

It also publishes a quarterly newsletter and a periodic annotated catalog of books and tapes, and supports a variety of networking opportunities, member research projects and local member group activities.

The Central Role of Research

Research informs the Institute's work. As a foundation, the Institute makes seed grants which establish fruitful relationships with key researchers. Those relationships build and sustain connections to key organizations that are also doing work in the field of consciousness studies. A stimulating cross-fertilization of ideas results from all of these working partnerships, enlivening the entire organization not only with scientific rigor and scholarly integrity, but also with the creativity, vision, and hope that inevitably accompanies the exploration of new ideas. The research focus is threefold: emerging worldviews, applied research derived from an unfolding understanding of consciousness, and more fundamental research regarding the nature of consciousness.

Emerging Worldviews

It seems almost trite today to say that society is undergoing a profound transition. The Institute has been addressing this transformation for two decades, and today it continues to occupy a central place in research efforts. Unlike almost any other institution in our society, the Institute is addressing social change at the level of worldview, beliefs and values. It is inquiring into the process of transformation at the individual level, for organizations, and for key sectors of society (business and science). The Institute's work is based on a belief that this transformation is fundamentally about how science and spirit can be integrated, leading to worldviews that include integrative concepts such as "sustainable development" and "deep ecology." Since cultures and societies have been studying consciousness in many different ways and for some thousands of years, the Institute is also working to include the "Ancient Wisdom" of these earlier researchers.

Applied Research Areas

A second major focus is in selected applied research areas that are particularly relevant to emerging worldviews and an understanding of consciousness. Foremost among these has been work in health and healing. IONS has funded research in imagery, biofeedback, psychoneuroimmunology (the role of the mind, emotions, beliefs and personality in physical health), the role of spirit, the importance of "connection" (family, community, and, today, support groups), and a recognition of a broader conceptual understanding of health. Documenting and attempting to understand what are labeled "spontaneous remissions" has been an area of intense focus.

Altruism has been a research interest both because it appears to be a natural outcome of personal transformation and because research in healing suggests that altruism positively affects health. The role of consciousness in human performance of all kinds has been another subject of inquiry since the Institute's inception. These explorations have included peak performance in athletics and the work place, remote viewing, psychokinesis, and channeling.

The Institute also has maintained a long-standing research program into different states of consciousness. Consciousness has been altered by various means in nearly every culture known to us for purposes ranging from healing, gaining access to knowledge not available in a normal state, guidance in making life decisions in harmony with a source other than ego, to escape from our dominant reality. Meditation is one of the Institute's current research areas. A redefinition of health and healing also involves a redefinition of death; the role of spirit in our lives, and the question of survival of spirit after death of the physical body, are long standing and current research interests of IONS.

The Nature of Consciousness

The third focus of research is the field of consciousness itself. Work is focused in the detailed inquiries into consciousness of traditions such as the Tibetan, as well as recent Western scientific theories arising from quantum physics, biology and the neurosciences. The Causality Project, a current major program, involves leading Western scientists, including two Nobel laureates, in questioning the metaphysics of Western science based on challenges arising from the Western sciences themselves. Research into consciousness over twenty years points out the inadequacies of our Western scientific paradigm and strongly confirms the need to identify a suitable answer to the question: How is knowledge validated in subjective areas? The Institute believes that the time is opportune to forge alternative assumptions, indeed, a new epistemology that offers the tools currently lacking to strengthen inquiries into consciousness, mind, spirit and related areas. How has the science community in other, non-Western cultures validated their research into consciousness?

The Role of Research in Membership at the Institute

Past progress is proof that research helps legitimate promising new fields of inquiry. For members, it also provides validation and grounding, supporting them as they make vital connections between theories, exciting ideas, and the application of these in daily life. This grounding effect delivers an essential element of practicality for what would otherwise be an extremely esoteric endeavor. As a consequence, the Institute's efforts are tied to the most fundamental changes as they emerge both in research and in members' lives.

The advancement of consciousness is an individual matter; we know that our membership is comprised of individuals who are at the forefront of positive social change—committed to their own development and to societal transformation. In partnership with members, the Institute explores both the inner dimensions of human experience and the implications of consciousness research for personal and social change. Strategic partnerships with like-minded organizations and individuals expand educational opportunities, including the use of other communications media such as radio, television, videotape and film. The strategic plan for membership education encourages member participation in several ways, through local member groups, computer networking, a membership directory, regional meetings, annual international conferences, member field research, surveys and focus groups, and a travel-study program.

All members receive these publications as a benefit of membership:

- The *Noetic Sciences Review*, a 48-page quarterly journal that has become the leading periodical of its kind in the consciousness field, and definitely has become one of the leading resources for an informed public, a group at the forefront of societal change.

- The *Noetic Sciences Bulletin*, a 16-page quarterly newsletter for member-related communications, networking and education.

- *An Intelligent Guide to Books, Audiotapes and Videotapes*, an annotated, comprehensive mail-order catalog published three times per year.

The Institute of Noetic Sciences welcomes inquiries about any aspect of its activities:

Institute of Noetic Sciences
475 Gate Five Road, Suite 300
Sausalito, CA 94965
Telephone: 415-331-5650
Fax: 415-331-5673